OXFORD STUDENT ATLAS

Editorial Adviser
Dr Patrick Wiegand

OXFORD
UNIVERSITY PRESS

Great Clarendon Street, Oxford OX2 6DP

Oxford University Press is a department of the University of Oxford.
It furthers the University's objective of excellence in research, scholarship,
and education by publishing worldwide in

Oxford New York

Auckland Bangkok Buenos Aires Cape Town Chennai
Dar es Salaam Delhi Hong Kong Istanbul Karachi Kolkata
Kuala Lumpur Madrid Melbourne Mexico City Mumbai Nairobi
São Paulo Shanghai Taipei Tokyo Toronto

Oxford is a registered trade mark of Oxford University Press
in the UK and in certain other countries

ISBN 0 19 831877 4 (hardback)
ISBN 0 19 831878 2 (paperback)
Printed in Italy

2 Contents

page

Maps and satellite images _____ 4

Map projections and graphics _____ 5

British Isles Topographic maps

British Isles _____ 6
Orkney and Shetland Islands _____ 7
Scottish Highlands and Islands _____ 8–9
Northern Ireland Southern Scotland _____ 10–11
Northern England _____ 12–13
Wales West and East Midlands _____ 14–15
South East England _____ 16–17
South West England _____ 18–19
Ireland _____ 20–21

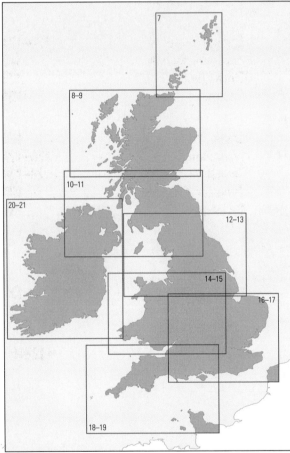
topographic maps of the British Isles

British Isles Thematic maps

Political	22–23	Employment	33
Physical	24	Population	34–35
Geology	25	Sport Tourism	36
Climate	26–27	Quality of life	37
Land use	28	Conservation	38
Farming	29	Pollution	39
Water Minerals	30	Transport	40
Energy	31	Trade	41
Manufacturing industry	32		

Europe Thematic maps

Physical _____ 42
Climate Ecosystems _____ 43
Political _____ 44
Population Wealth _____ 45
Economy _____ 46
Tourism _____ 47

Asia Thematic maps

Physical _____ 58
Political _____ 59
Climate Ecosystems _____ 60
Economy Population _____ 61

Asia Topographic maps

Northern Eurasia _____ 62–63
Middle East _____ 64–65
South Asia _____ 66–67
China _____ 68–69
Japan _____ 70
South East Asia _____ 71

Oceania Topographic map

Australia and
New Zealand _____ 72–73

Oceania Thematic maps

Climate Ecosystems
Population Economy _____ 74

Europe Topographic maps

Benelux and the Ruhr _____ 48
Scandinavia and Iceland _____ 49
France _____ 50
Spain and Portugal _____ 51
Middle Europe _____ 52–53
Italy and the Balkans _____ 54–55
East Europe and Turkey _____ 56–57

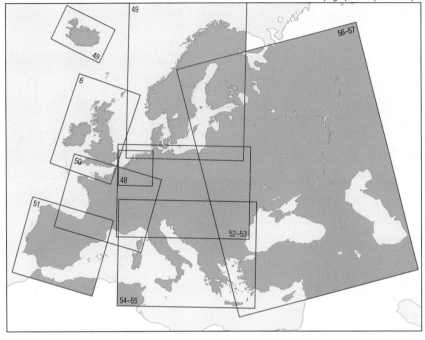
topographic maps of Europe

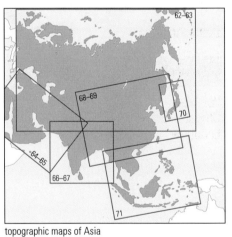
topographic maps of Asia

topographic map of Oceania

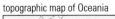

Contents 3

Africa Thematic maps

Physical Political _____ 75
Satellite images _____ 76
Climate Ecosystems _____ 77
Economy Population _____ 78
Tourism _____ 79

Africa Topographic maps

Northern Africa _____ 80–81
Southern Africa _____ 82
East Africa _____ 83

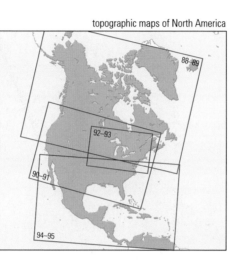
topographic maps of Africa

North America Thematic maps

Physical Political _____ 84
Climate Ecosystems _____ 85
Economy Population _____ 86
Tourism _____ 87

North America Topographic maps

Canada _____ 88–89
United States of America _____ 90–91
Great Lakes _____ 92–93
Mexico, Central America,
and the Caribbean _____ 94–95

topographic maps of North America

South America Topographic map

South America _____ 96–97

South America Thematic maps

Political _____ 97
Climate Ecosystems _____ 98
Economy Population _____ 99

topographic map of South America

World Thematic maps *page*

Political _____ 102–103
Physical _____ 104–105
Earthquakes and volcanoes _____ 106–107
Temperature and ocean currents _____ 108

Pressure, winds, and precipitation _____ 109
Climate regions _____ 110–111
Climate data _____ 112
Climate hazards _____ 113

Ecosystems _____ 114–115
Population _____ 116–117
Population trends _____ 118
Population migration _____ 119

Quality of life _____ 120–121
Economic activity _____ 122
Development _____ 123
Energy _____ 124

Trade Transport _____ 125
Environmental issues _____ 126–127
Tourism _____ 128–129
Time and distance _____ 130
Cyberspace _____ 131

Flags _____ 132–133
Datasets _____ 134–141

Index _____ 142–160

Oceans and Poles Topographic maps

Pacific Ocean _____ 100
Arctic Ocean Antarctica _____ 101

topographic map of the Poles

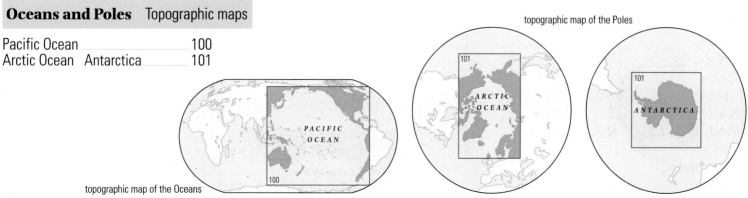

topographic map of the Oceans

© Oxford University Press

4 Maps and satellite images

Satellite scanners 'read' the Earth's radiation. The data can be organised by computer to form a visual image. In this image the colours are not real but have been arranged to show how the land is used.

Orange: rough pasture
Red: forest and woodland
Green: improved pasture
Dark blue: urban areas

Topographic maps show the main features of the physical landscape as well as settlements, communications, and boundaries. Background colours show the height of the land.

Greens: low land
Browns: high land

Thematic maps show information about special topics such as agriculture, industry, population, the environment, and quality of life. This map shows land use.

Dark green: forest and woodland
Purple: built-up area

Symbols on thematic maps

Point symbols

Dot map
Each black dot represents 100 000 sheep.
From p29

Economic map
Blue squares represent a main centre of the motor vehicle industry.
From p32

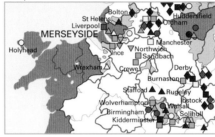

Proportional symbols
The size of the circles is proportional to the amount of greenhouse gas emission.
From p127

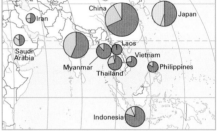

Line symbols

Isopleth map
Lines join places with equal amounts of sunshine.
From p27

Isotherm map
Some isopleths have special names. Isotherms join places with equal temperature.
From p26

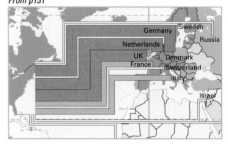

Flowline map
The thickness of the line is proportional to the amount of internet traffic.
From p131

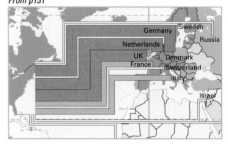

Area symbols

Choropleth map
Darker colours show areas with a higher percentage of land used for growing potatoes.
From p29

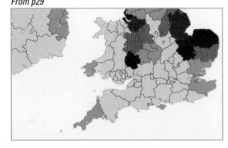

Environmental map
Each colour represents an ecosystem. Purple stands for mountains.
From p115

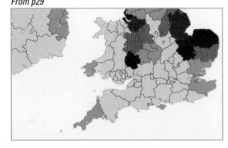

Political map
Colours have no meaning but are simply used to show where one country ends and another begins.
From p102

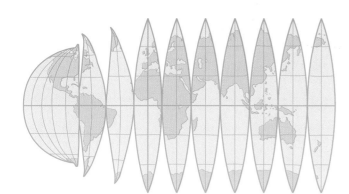

This map has been made by unpeeling strips from the Earth's surface. It would be difficult to use because gaps are left in the land and sea.

Parallels of latitude and meridians of longitude form a grid. Different grid patterns, called projections, can be used to turn the spherical surface of the Earth into a flat world map. It is impossible to make a world map in which both the sizes and shapes of the Earth's land masses are shown accurately. All world maps are distorted in some way.

There are many map projections. It is important that the projection used for a world map is suitable for the information shown on it.

Polar
Most world maps do not show Antarctica or the Arctic Ocean accurately. Polar projections give a better view of the poles.

Eckert IV
Equal area. The land masses are the correct size in relation to each other but there is some distortion in shape.

Mercator
Conformal. The shape of the land masses is correct but their size becomes larger further away from the equator.

Oblique Aitoff
Equal area. The arrangement of the land masses allows a good view of the northern hemisphere.

Graphical representation of data

Clustered column
Compares values across categories
See example p35

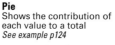

Line
Shows trend over time across categories
See example p33

Stacked column
Compares the contribution of each value to a total across categories
See example p32

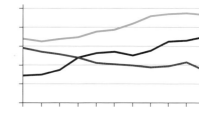

Pie
Shows the contribution of each value to a total
See example p124

Triangular
Compares trios of values
See example p123

Simple bar
Length of bar is proportional to each value
See example p128

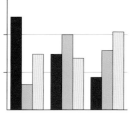

Scatter
Compares pairs of values
See example p61

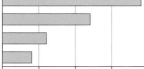

100% stacked bar
Compares the percentage each value contributes to a total across categories
See example p116

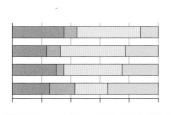

Line and whisker
Shows highest, average, and lowest values
See example p30

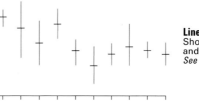

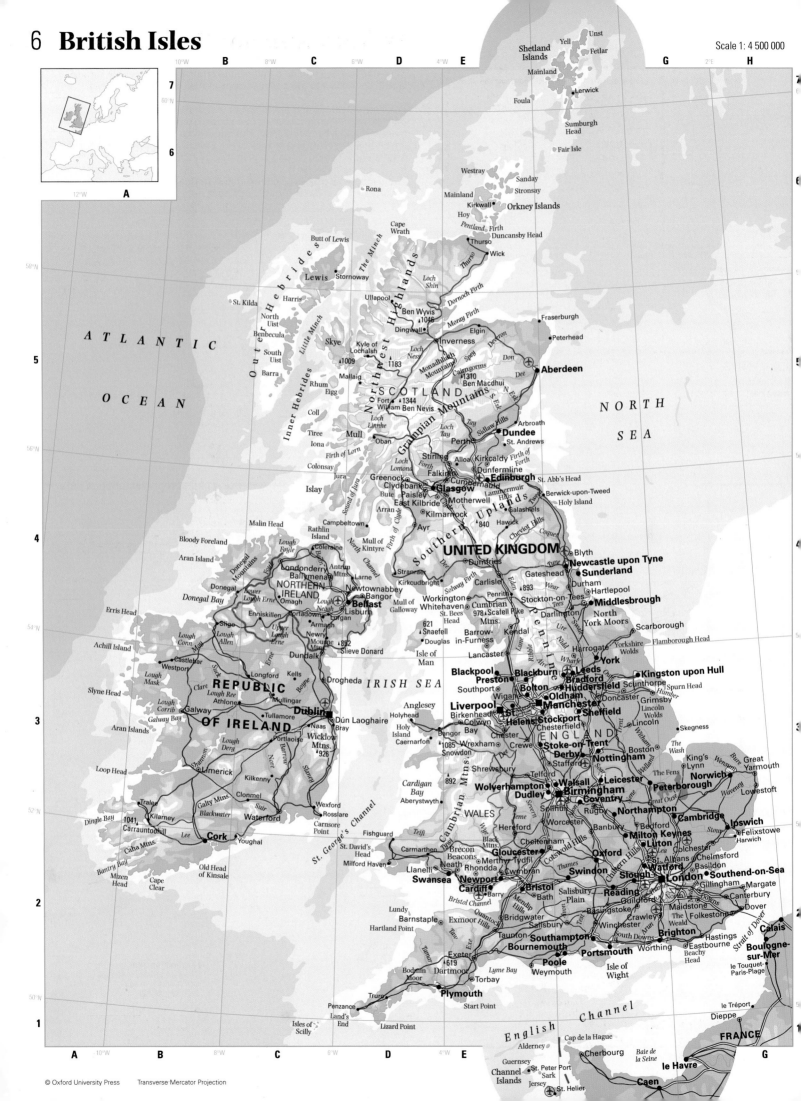

6 British Isles

Scale 1: 4 500 000

© Oxford University Press   Transverse Mercator Projection

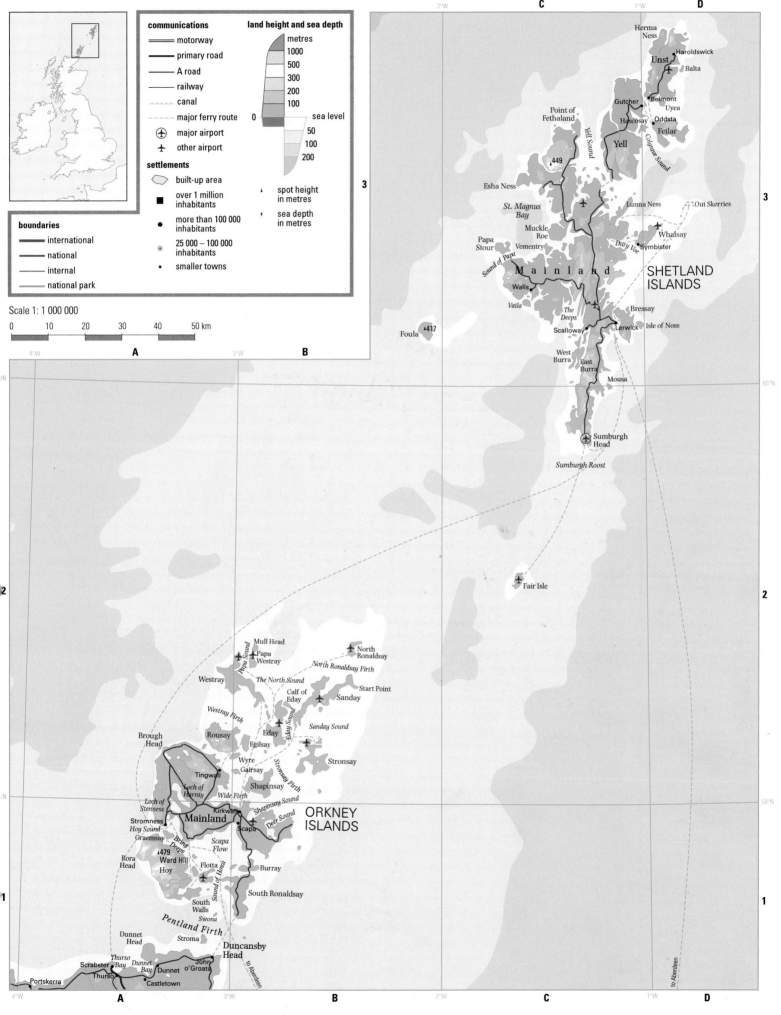

communications

motorway
primary road
A road
railway
canal
major ferry route
⊕ major airport
✈ other airport

settlements

built-up area
■ over 1 million inhabitants
● more than 100 000 inhabitants
⊙ 25 000 – 100 000 inhabitants
• smaller towns

land height and sea depth

metres
1000
500
300
200
100
0   sea level
50
100
200

▲ spot height in metres
▼ sea depth in metres

boundaries

international
national
internal
national park

Scale 1: 1 000 000

0   10   20   30   40   50 km

A   3°W   B

SHETLAND ISLANDS

Herma Ness
Haroldswick
Unst
Balta
Point of Fethaland
Gutcher Belmont
Uyea
Hascosay Oddsta
Fetlar
Yell Sound
Yell
Colgrave Sound
▲449
Esha Ness
Lunna Ness
Out Skerries
St. Magnus Bay
Muckle Roe
Whalsay
Papa Stour
Vementry
Dury Voe Symbister
Sound of Papa
Mainland
Vaila
Bressay
Walls
The Deeps
Isle of Noss
Scalloway
Lerwick
West Burra
East Burra
Mousa
Foula ▲417
Sumburgh Head
Sumburgh Roost

60°N

Fair Isle

2

ORKNEY ISLANDS

Mull Head
Papa Westray
North Ronaldsay
Papa Sound
Westray
North Ronaldsay Firth
The North Sound
Start Point
Westray Firth
Calf of Eday
Sanday
Brough Head
Rousay
Eday
Sanday Sound
Sound
Egilsay
Eday
Wyre Gairsay
Stronsay
Tingwall
Shapinsay
Stronsay Firth
Loch of Harray
Wide Firth
Loch of Stenness
Shapinsay Sound
Stromness
Kirkwall
Mainland
Deer Sound
Hoy Sound
Scapa
Graemsay
Bring Deeps
Scapa Flow
Burray
▲479
Ward Hill
Flotta
Hoy
Burray
Sound of Hoxa
South Ronaldsay
South Walls
Swona
1
Dunnet Head
Stroma
Pentland Firth
Duncansby Head
to Aberdeen
Thurso Bay
Dunnet Bay
Scrabster
Thurso
Dunnet
John o'Groats
Portskerra
Castletown

to Aberdeen

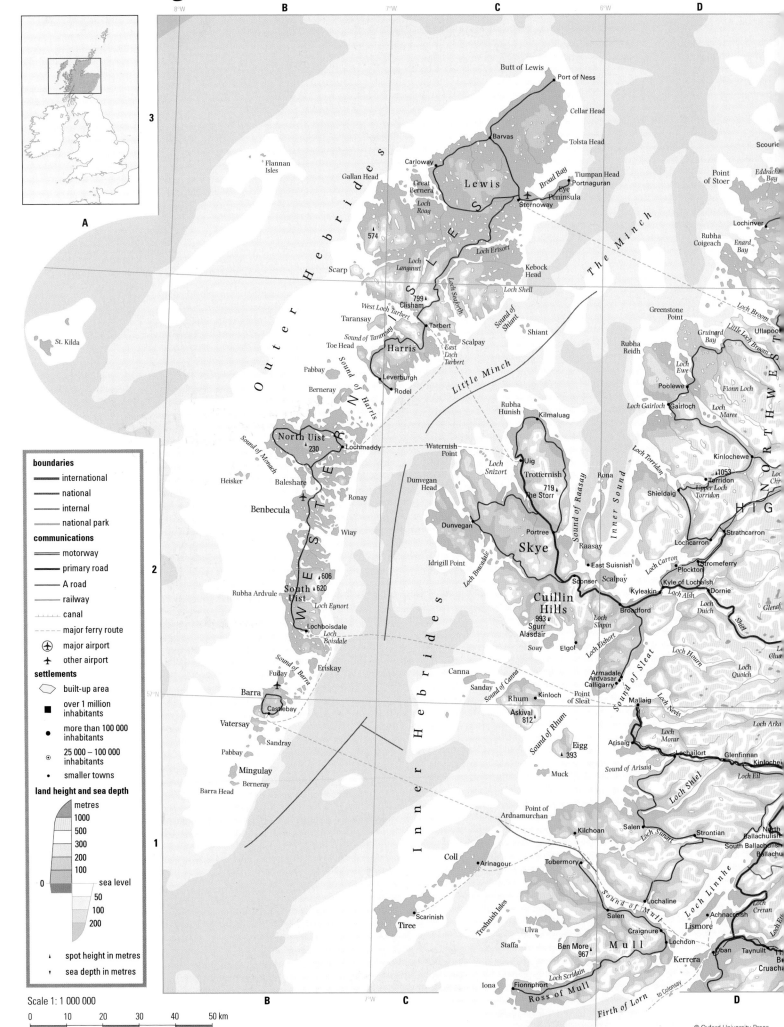

boundaries
— international
— national
— internal
— national park

communications
═══ motorway
━━ primary road
— A road
— railway
┼┼┼ canal
- - - major ferry route
✈ major airport
✈ other airport

settlements
▢ built-up area
■ over 1 million inhabitants
● more than 100 000 inhabitants
◉ 25 000 – 100 000 inhabitants
• smaller towns

land height and sea depth
metres
1000
500
300
200
100
0 sea level
50
100
200

▲ spot height in metres
▼ sea depth in metres

Scale 1: 1 000 000

0   10   20   30   40   50 km

© Oxford University Press

Pentland Firth

Cape Wrath

E   4°W   **G**   2°W   **H**

Dunnet Head   Stroma   Duncansby Head

Durness   Whiten Head   Strathy Point   Scrabster   Thurso Bay   Dunnet Bay   Dunnet   John o'Groats

to Stromness

Kyle of Durness   Loch Erriboll   Portskerra   Thurso   Castletown

Kyle of Tongue   Bettyhill   Strathy   Melvich   Halkirk   Loch Watten   Sinclair's Bay   Noss Head

oxford bridge   Loch Hope   Ben Loyal 764   Tongue   Loch Loyal   Naver   Mybster   Wick

Ben Hope 927   Loch Meadie   Loch nan Clàr   Dyke   Halladale   Strathy   Wick

3

Heay Forest   Loch More   Altnaharra   Thurso   Dunbeath Water   Lybster   Latheron

ostrome   Unapool   Ben Klibreck 961   Kinbrace   Berriedale Water   Morven 705   Dunbeath

Loch Assynt   Loch Shin   Helmsdale   Berriedale

Camsp 847   Ben More Assynt 998   Helmsdale

Ledmore   Lairg   Brora

58°N

Beinn Dearg 1081   Shin   Brora   Golspie

Evelix   Bonar Bridge   Dornoch   Tarbat Ness

Sgurr Mòr 1109   Ben Wyvis 1046   Loch Glass   Nigg Bay   Dornoch Firth   Tain   Portmahomack

Loch Fannich   Alness   Invergordon   Cromarty   Moray Firth   Lossiemouth   Findochty   Portknockie   Troup Head   Rosehearty   Kinnaird Head   Fraserburgh

Achnasheen   Loch Luichart   Garve   Evanton   Black Isle   Burghead Bay   Burghead   Buckie   Cullen   Portsoy   Whitehills   Gardenstown   Loch of Strathbeg

Bran   Meig   Loch Meig   Strathpeffer   Dingwall   Conon Bridge   Findhorn Bay   Findhorn   Elgin   Fochabers   Banff   Macduff   Rattray Head

AND   Loch Mionar   Muir of Ord   North Kessock   Kinloss   Forres   **MORAY**   Aberchirder   New Deer   Peterhead

2

ullardoch   Orrin Reservoir   Beauly   Fort George   Nairn   Keith   Turriff   Deveron   New Deer   Mintlaw   Buchan Ness

Farrar   Beauly Firth   **Inverness**   Rothes   Craigellachie   Huntly   Rhynie   Ugie   Boddam

Cannich   Glass   Beauly   Findhorn   Charlestown of Aberlour   Deveron   Oldmeldrum   Ellon   Hatton

arn Eige 183   Drumnadrochit   Dufftown   Bogie   Ythan   Pitmedden

Affric   Loch Affric   Loch Ness   Tomatin   Strathspey   Inverurie   Newmachar

Loch Mhòr   Grantown-on-Spey   518   Kintore   Dyce   Bridge of Don

Moriston   Invermoriston   Carrbridge   Don   Alford   Kemnay   **ABERDEENSHIRE**   Westhill   **Aberdeen**

Fort Augustus   Monadhliath Mountains   Spey   Aviemore   Tomintoul   **Cairngorms**   Cairn Gorm 1244   Don   ABERDEEN CITY   Nigg Bay

Invergarry   Loch Oich   Kingussie   Newtonmore   Ben Macdui 1310   Peterculter   Dee   Nigg   Cove Bay

935   Spey   Balmoral   Crathie   Ballater   Aboyne   Banchory   Portlethen

Loch Garry   Loch Lochy   Roy   1130   Braemar   Bridge of Dee   Lochnagar 1155   Water of Feugh   Cowie Water

Spean Bridge   **M O U N T A I N S**   Stonehaven

ort William   Ben Nevis 1344   Ben Alder 1148   Glas Maol 1068   North Esk   South Esk   Fettercairn   Inverbervie

57°N

Blackwater Reservoir   Tilt   Glen Shee   Laurencekirk   Milton Ness

Kinlochleven   Rannoch Station   Blair Atholl   Glen Garry   Prosen Water   **ANGUS**

Glencoe   Bridge of Ericht   Tummel Bridge   Pitlochry   Brechin   Montrose Basin   Montrose

1150   Glen Etive   1108   Kinloch Rannoch   Dunalastair Reservoir   Loch Tummel   Tay   Ardle   Isla   Kirriemuir   South Esk   Lunan Bay

1

Loch Tulla   Loch an Daimh   Ben Lawers 1214   Aberfeldy   Inverquharity   Forfar   Lunan Water   Arbroath

Bridge of Orchy   Loch Lyon   Lochay   Loch Tay   Alyth   Rattray   Carnoustie

Lochan Shira   Orchy   Killin   Almond   Blairgowrie   Isla   Coupar Angus   Sidlaw Hills   Buddon Ness

Dalmally   Tyndrum   Lochearnhead   Dunkeld   Tay   **DUNDEE CITY**   Monifieth   Broughty Ferry

Crianlarich   Ben More 1174   Loch Earn   **PERTH AND KINROSS**   New Scone   **Dundee**   Tayport   Newport-on-Tay

Comrie   Crieff   **Perth**   Firth of Tay   Leuchars   Eden Mouth

Earn   Newburgh   Cupar   St. Andrews   St. Andrews Bay

E   4°W   **F**   3°W   **G**   2°W   **H**

communications

- motorway
- primary road
- A road
- railway
- canal
- major ferry route
- ✈ major airport
- ✈ other airport

settlements

- built-up area
- ■ over 1 million inhabitants
- ● more than 100 000 inhabitants
- ◉ 25 000 – 100 000 inhabitants
- • smaller towns

land height and sea depth

metres
1000
500
300
200
100
0   sea level
50
100
200

▲ spot height in metres
▼ sea depth in metres

boundaries

- international
- national
- internal
- national park

Scale 1: 1 000 000

0 10 20 30 40 50 km

© Oxford University Press

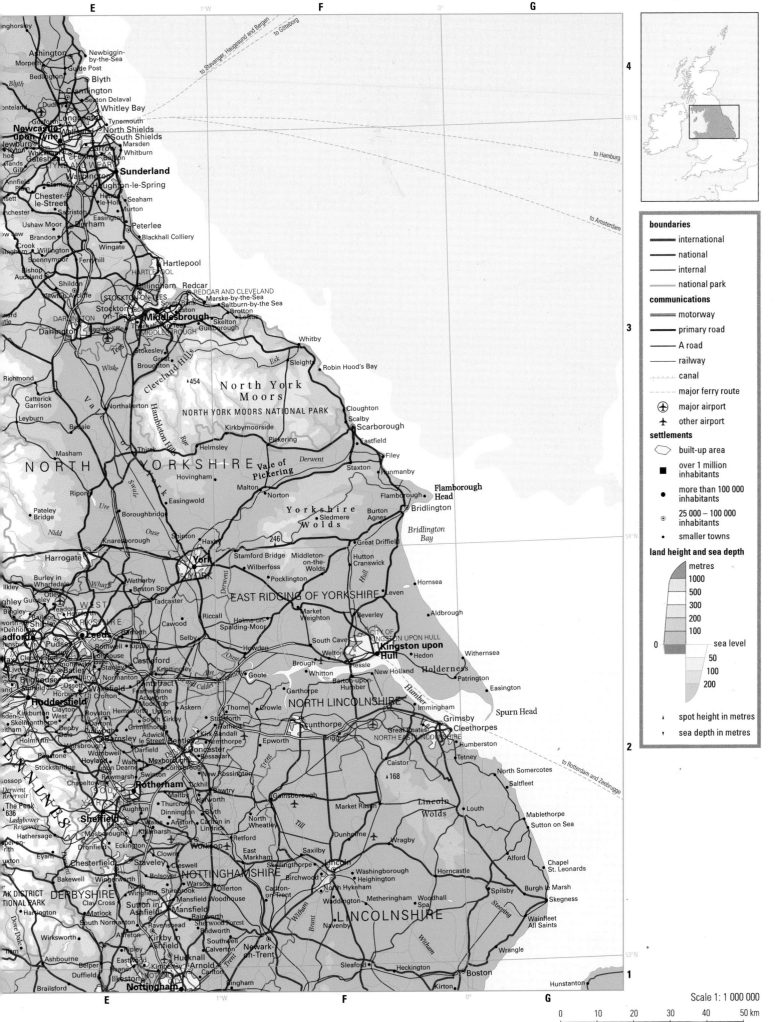

© Oxford University Press

Scale 1: 1 000 000

boundaries	
━━━	international
━━━	national
━━━	internal
━━━	national park

communications	
━━━	motorway
━━━	primary road
━━━	A road
───	railway
┄┄┄	canal
─ ─ ─	major ferry route
✈	major airport
✈	other airport

settlements	
⬡	built-up area
■	over 1 million inhabitants
●	more than 100 000 inhabitants
⊙	25 000 – 100 000 inhabitants
•	smaller towns

land height and sea depth

metres
1000
500
300
200
100
0 sea level
50
100
200

▲ spot height in metres
▼ sea depth in metres

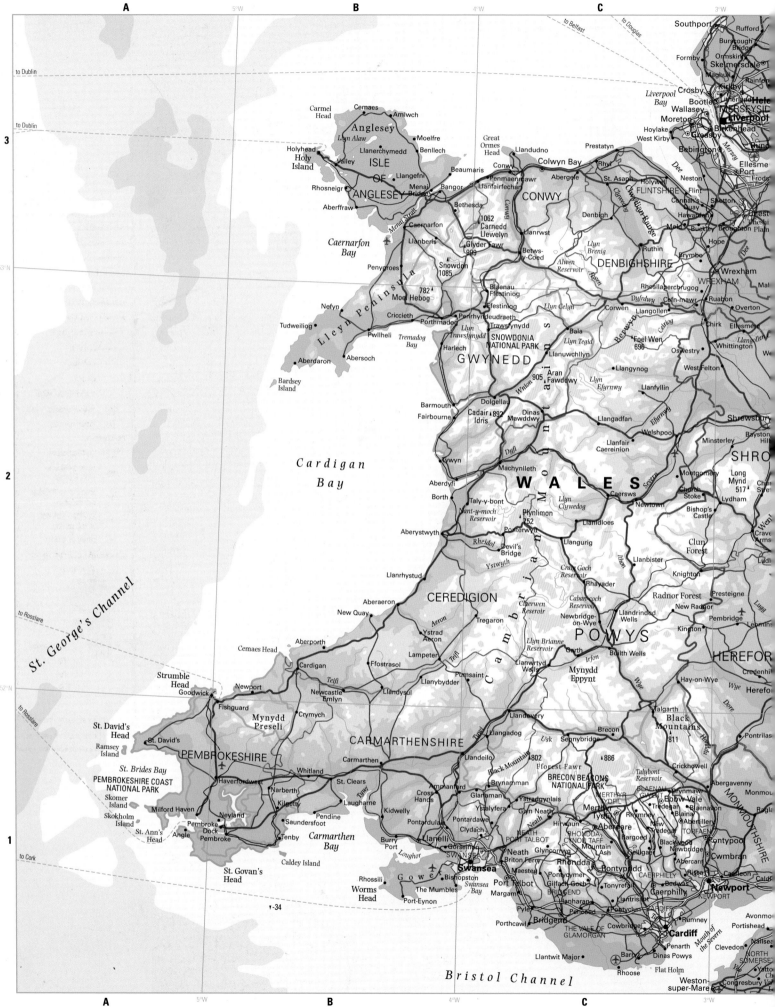

Transverse Mercator Projection   © Oxford University Press

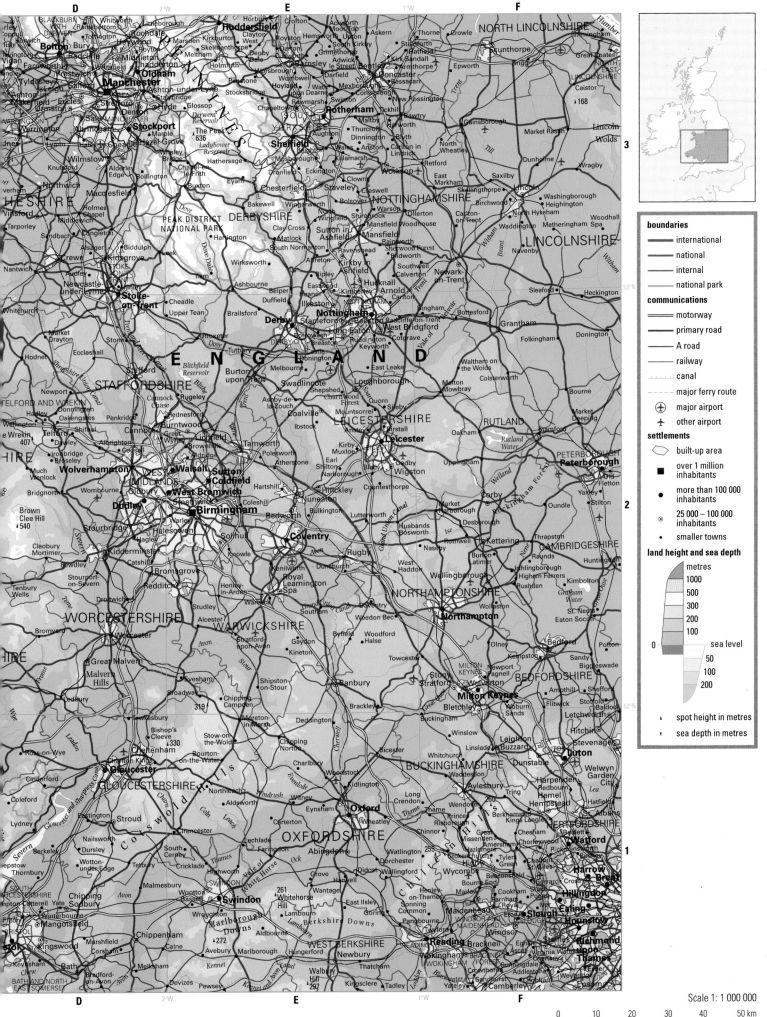

boundaries
— international
— national
— internal
— national park

communications
— motorway
— primary road
— A road
— railway
⋯ canal
- - - major ferry route
⊕ major airport
✈ other airport

settlements
⬡ built-up area
■ over 1 million inhabitants
● more than 100 000 inhabitants
⊙ 25 000 – 100 000 inhabitants
• smaller towns

land height and sea depth

metres
1000
500
300
200
100
0 — sea level
50
100
200

▲ spot height in metres
▼ sea depth in metres

Scale 1: 1 000 000

0   10   20   30   40   50 km

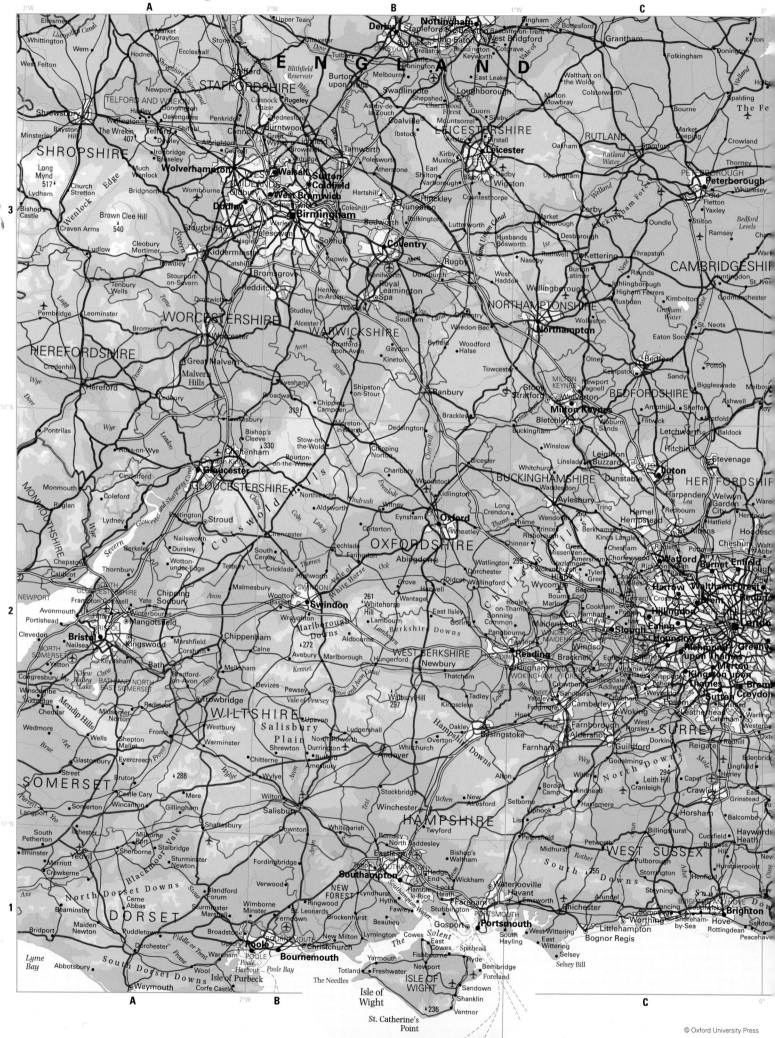

© Oxford University Press

The Wash

D

Burnham Market
Hunstanton
Heacham
Docking
Dersingham
Sandringham
King's Lynn
Wisbech
Outwell
Downham Market
Swaffham
Nar
Wissey
Watton
Breckland
Littleport
Little Ouse
Lakenheath
Brandon
Thetford
Feltwell
Ely
Lark
Cam
Isleham
Mildenhall
Soham
Fordham
Burwell
Waterbeach
Newmarket
Kentford
Cambridge
Great Shelford
Sawston
Linton
Haverhill
Great Chesterford
Saffron Walden
Newport
Thaxted
Stansted Mountfitchet
Bishop's Stortford
Great Dunmow
Sawbridgeworth
Harlow
Chipping Ongar
Ingatestone
Brentwood
Billericay
Havering
Barking
Ockendon
West Thurrock
Bexley
Dartford
Swanley
New Ash Green
Otford
Sevenoaks
Tonbridge
Royal Tunbridge Wells
Pembury
Wadhurst
Heybourough
Maresfield
Uckfield
Heathfield
EAST SUSSEX
Hailsham
Polegate
Pevensey
Eastbourne
East Dean
Beachy Head

Blakeney Point
Wells-next-the-Sea
Holt
Sheringham
Cromer
Mundesley
Saxthorpe
North Walsham
Aylsham
Reepham
Coltishall
Winterton-on-Sea
NORFOLK
East Dereham
Norwich
Taverham
Bure
Wroxham
Acle
Caister-on-Sea
Great Yarmouth
BROADS AUTHORITY
Belton
Hopton on Sea
Wymondham
Attleborough
Loddon
Yare
Lowestoft
Bungay
Beccles
Kessingland
Diss
Harleston
Waveney
Eye
Halesworth
Blyth
Southwold
Yoxford
Debenham
Framlingham
Saxmundham
Leiston
Stowmarket
Needham Market
Wickham Market
Aldeburgh
Lavenham
SUFFOLK
Claydon
Orford
Orford Ness
Woodbridge
Long Melford
Sudbury
Hadleigh
Ipswich
Bawdsey
Stour
Orwell
Felixstowe
Sible Hedingham
Halstead
Earls Colne
Manningtree
Stour
Harwich
Colne
Braintree
Coggeshall
Colchester
Thorpe-le-Soken
The Naze
Walton-on-the-Naze
Kelvedon
Abberton Reservoir
Wivenhoe
Frinton-on-Sea
Tiptree
Brightlingsea
Witham
West Mersea
Mersea Island
Clacton-on-Sea
ESSEX
Chelmsford
Hanningfield Reservoir
Maldon
Blackwater
Bradwell-on-Sea
Danbury
South Woodham Ferrers
Southminster
Hullbridge
Hockley
Foulness Point
Wickford
Basildon
Rayleigh
Rochford
Burnham-on-Crouch
Foulness Island
SOUTHEND
Southend-on-Sea
South Benfleet
Canvey Island
Shoeburyness
THURROCK
Grays
Tilbury
Thames
Swanscombe
Gravesend
MEDWAY
Grain
Sheerness
Hoo
Minster
Isle of Sheppey
Leysdown on Sea
Rochester
Queenborough
Chatham
Gillingham
Snodland
The Swale
Aylesford
Sittingbourne
Faversham
Maidstone
Bearsted
Herne Bay
Whitstable
Foreness Point
Margate
Broadstairs
North Foreland
Ramsgate
Minster
Canterbury
Ash
Sandwich
North Downs
Charing
Great Stour
Stour
Aylesham
Deal
KENT
Paddock Wood
Marden
Wye
Kennington
Ashford
Brabourne Lees
Whitfield
St. Margaret's at Cliffe
Staplehurst
Bethersden
Lymynge
South Foreland
Dover
Cranbrook
Tenterden
Hamstreet
Romney Marsh
Hythe
Folkestone
Hawkhurst
Bewl Water
Rother
Northiam
New Romney
Dymchurch
Battle
Rye
Winchelsea
Lydd
Fairlight
Hastings
Bexhill
Dungeness

E
2°E
to Göteborg
to Esbjerg
to Hamburg

to Hook of Holland
52°N

to Oostende

Strait of Dover
(Pas de Calais)

Cap Gris-Nez

F
to Hamburg

Bray-Dunes
Malo-les-Bains
Dunkerque
Gravelines
Grand Fort-Philippe
Marck
Berges
Calais
Bourbourg
Guines
Ardres
Audruicq
Esquelbecq
Wormhout
Canal de Calais
Aa
Watten
Cassel
Wimereux
Marquise
Slack
NORD-PAS-DE-CALAIS
St-Omer
Boulogne-sur-Mer
Liane
Lumbres
Hazebrouck
Desvres
FRANCE
Samer
Lys
Thérouanne
Aire-sur-la-Lys
Hardelot-Plage

51°N

to Dieppe

boundaries
— international
— national
— internal
— national park

communications
— motorway
— primary road
— A road
— railway
⊢⊣ canal
– – – major ferry route
✈ major airport
✦ other airport

settlements
⬡ built-up area
■ over 1 million inhabitants
● more than 100 000 inhabitants
⊙ 25 000 – 100 000 inhabitants
• smaller towns

land height and sea depth
metres
1000
500
300
200
100
0 — sea level
50
100
200

▲ spot height in metres
▽ sea depth in metres

Scale 1: 1 000 000

0 10 20 30 40 50 km

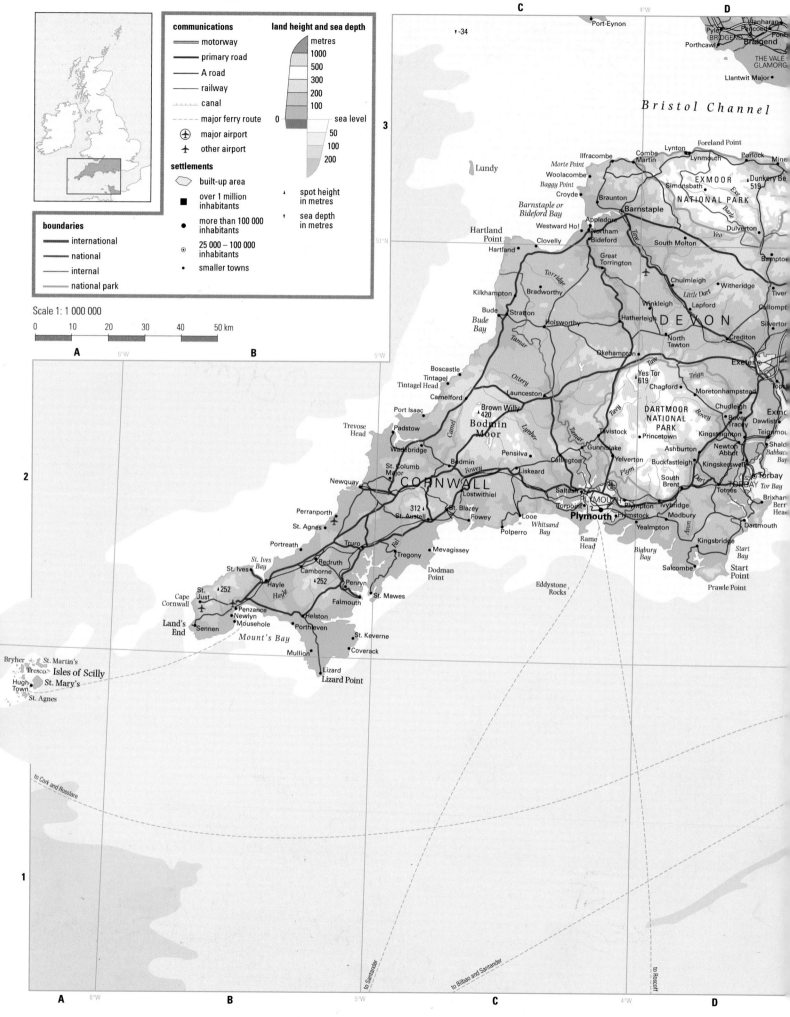

communications

- motorway
- primary road
- A road
- railway
- canal
- major ferry route
- ✈ major airport
- ✈ other airport

settlements

- built-up area
- ■ over 1 million inhabitants
- ● more than 100 000 inhabitants
- ⊙ 25 000 – 100 000 inhabitants
- • smaller towns

land height and sea depth

metres
1000
500
300
200
100
0 — sea level
50
100
200

- ▲ spot height in metres
- ▼ sea depth in metres

boundaries

- international
- national
- internal
- national park

Scale 1: 1 000 000

0   10   20   30   40   50 km

Transverse Mercator Projection   © Oxford University Press

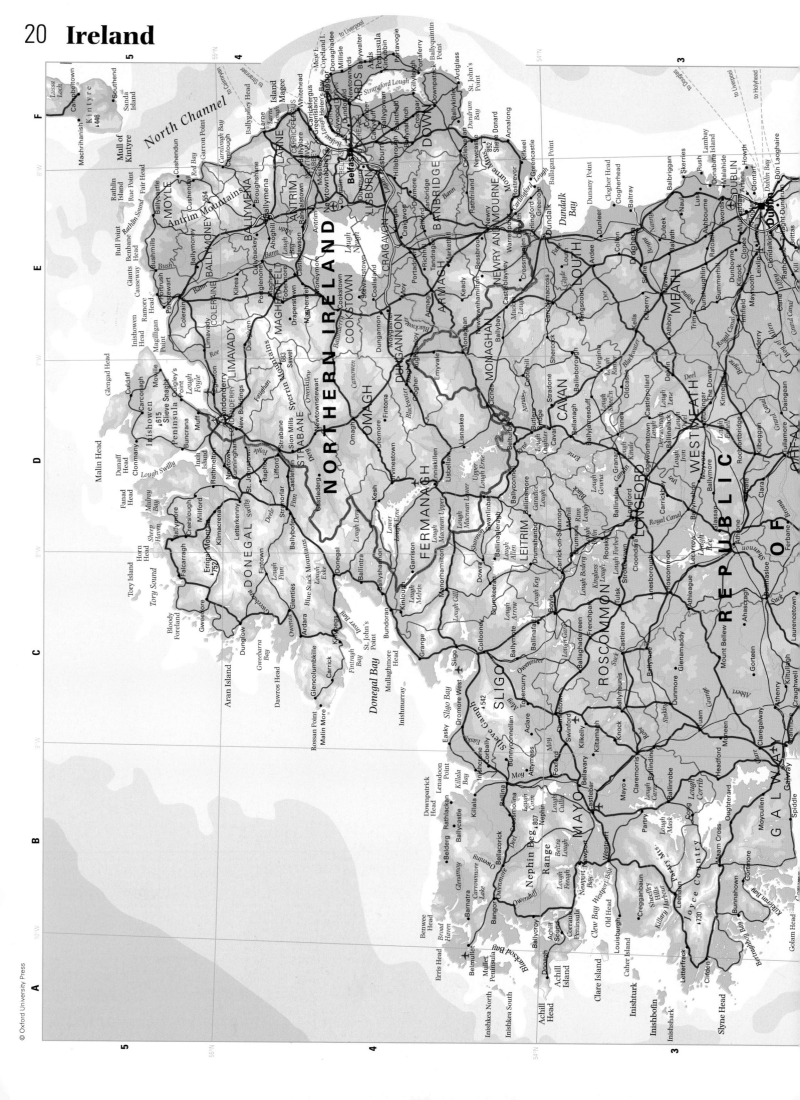

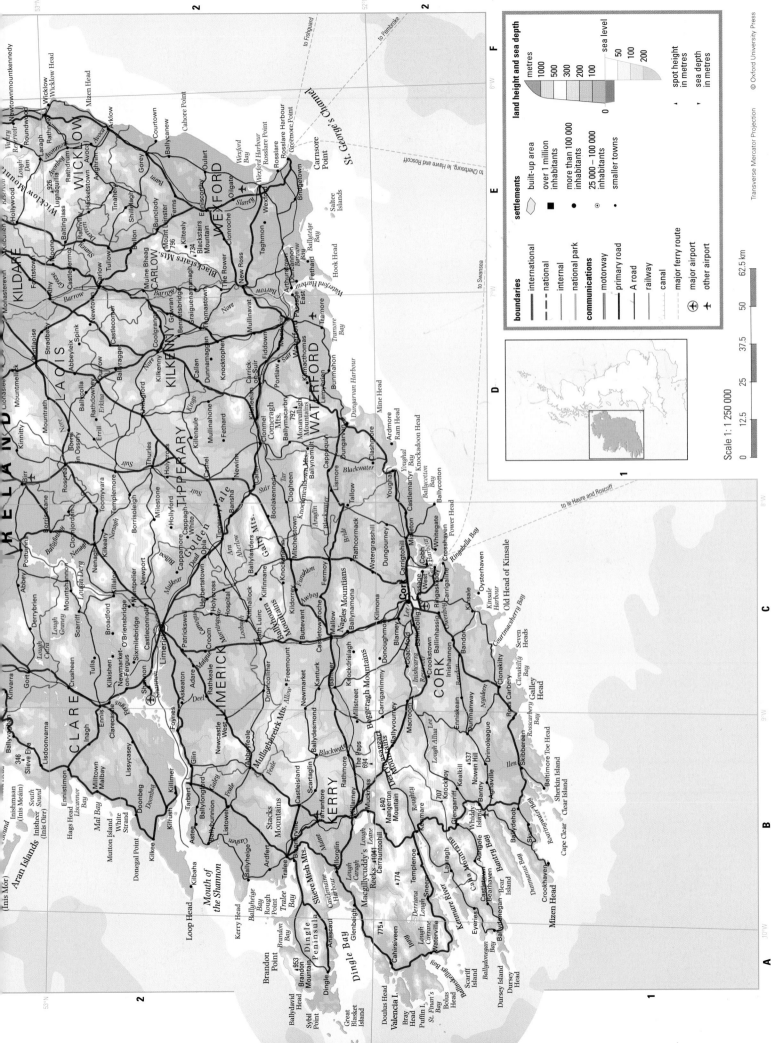

Transverse Mercator Projection

Scale 1: 1 250 000

settlements
- built-up area
- over 1 million inhabitants
- more than 100 000 inhabitants
- 25 000 – 100 000 inhabitants
- smaller towns

boundaries
- international
- national
- internal
- national park

communications
- motorway
- primary road
- A road
- railway
- canal
- major ferry route
- major airport
- other airport

land height and sea depth

metres	
1000	
500	
300	
200	
100	
sea level	
50	
100	
200	

- spot height in metres
- sea depth in metres

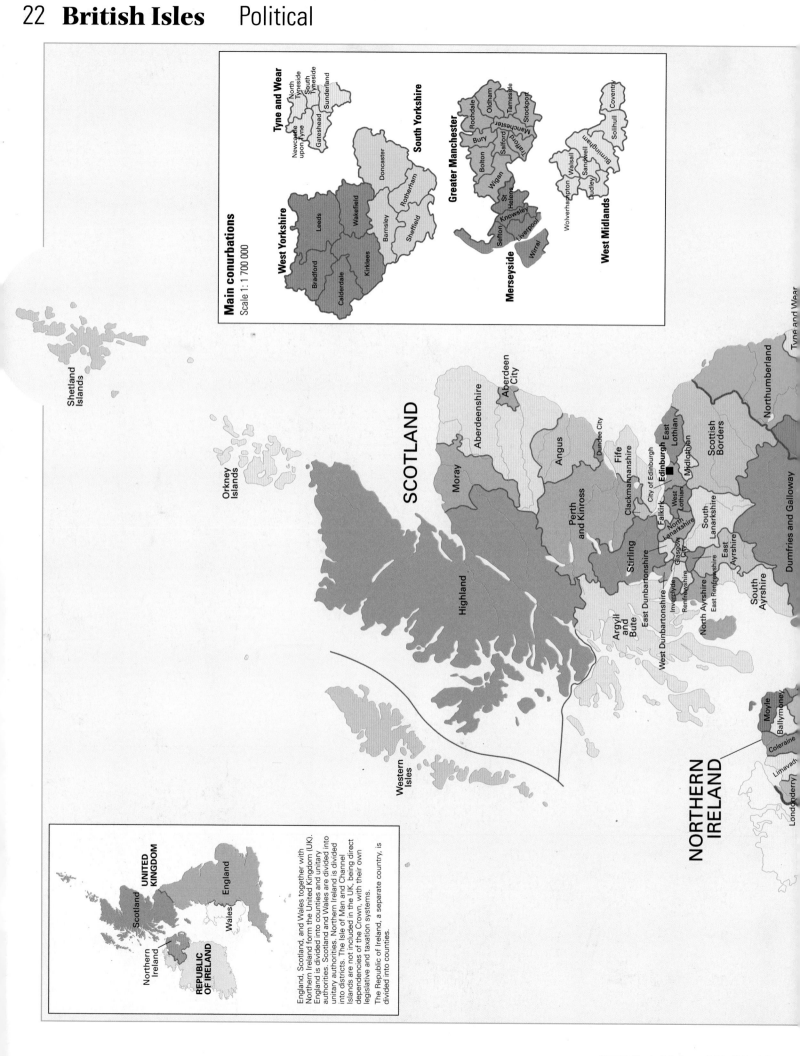

Main conurbations
Scale 1: 1 700 000

Tyne and Wear

Newcastle upon Tyne
North Tyneside
South Tyneside
Sunderland
Gateshead

South Yorkshire

Doncaster
Rotherham
Barnsley
Sheffield

West Yorkshire

Leeds
Wakefield
Bradford
Calderdale
Kirklees

Greater Manchester

Rochdale
Oldham
Tameside
Stockport
Bolton
Bury
Salford
Manchester
Trafford
Wigan

Merseyside

St Helens
Knowsley
Sefton
Liverpool
Wirral

West Midlands

Coventry
Solihull
Birmingham
Walsall
Sandwell
Dudley
Wolverhampton

Shetland Islands

Orkney Islands

SCOTLAND

Aberdeen City
Aberdeenshire
Moray
Angus
Dundee City
Fife
Perth and Kinross
Clackmannanshire
City of Edinburgh
Edinburgh
East Lothian
Midlothian
Scottish Borders
Highland
Stirling
Falkirk
West Lothian
North Lanarkshire
South Lanarkshire
Glasgow City
East Dunbartonshire
West Dunbartonshire
Inverclyde
Renfrewshire
East Renfrewshire
East Ayrshire
North Ayrshire
South Ayrshire
Argyll and Bute
Western Isles
Dumfries and Galloway
Northumberland
Tyne and Wear

NORTHERN IRELAND

Moyle
Ballymoney
Coleraine
Limavady
Londonderry

Scotland
UNITED KINGDOM
England
Wales
Northern Ireland
REPUBLIC OF IRELAND

England, Scotland, and Wales together with Northern Ireland form the United Kingdom (UK). England is divided into counties and unitary authorities. Scotland and Wales are divided into unitary authorities. Northern Ireland is divided into districts. The Isle of Man and Channel Islands are not included in the UK, being direct dependencies of the Crown, with their own legislative and taxation systems.

The Republic of Ireland, a separate country, is divided into counties.

Transverse Mercator Projection   © Oxford University Press

Scale 1 : 3 000 000 (main map)

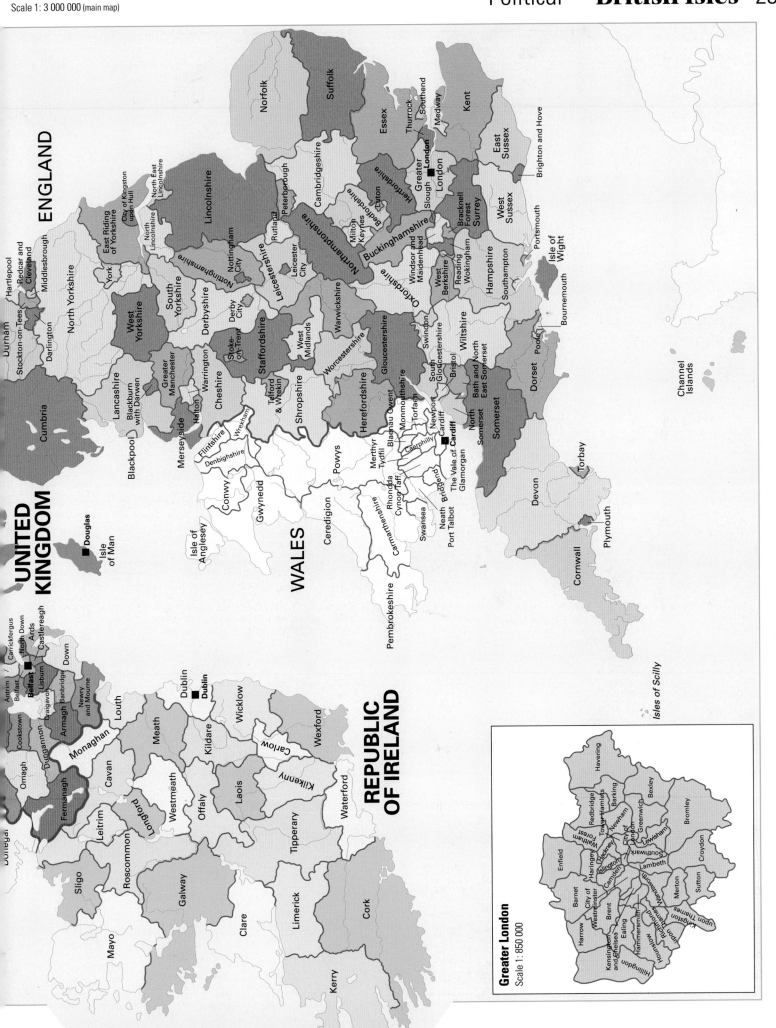

ENGLAND

UNITED KINGDOM

Durham
Hartlepool
Stockton-on-Tees
Redcar and Cleveland
Middlesbrough
Darlington
North Yorkshire
Cumbria
East Riding of Yorkshire
York
City of Kingston upon Hull
North Lincolnshire
North East Lincolnshire
Lancashire
Blackburn with Darwen
Blackpool
Greater Manchester
Merseyside
Halton
Warrington
Cheshire
Wrexham
Flintshire
Denbighshire
Conwy
Gwynedd
Isle of Anglesey
West Yorkshire
South Yorkshire
Derbyshire
Nottinghamshire
Derby City
Nottingham City
Lincolnshire
Leicestershire
Leicester City
Rutland
Peterborough
Cambridgeshire
Norfolk
Suffolk
Essex
Thurrock
Southend
Medway
Kent
East Sussex
Brighton and Hove
Greater London
Slough
London
Hertfordshire
Luton
Bedfordshire
Milton Keynes
Northamptonshire
Buckinghamshire
Bracknell Forest
Surrey
West Sussex
Portsmouth
Isle of Wight
Windsor and Maidenhead
West Berkshire
Reading
Wokingham
Hampshire
Southampton
Bournemouth
Oxfordshire
Swindon
Wiltshire
Dorset
Poole
Channel Islands
Staffordshire
Stoke-on-Trent
West Midlands
Warwickshire
Worcestershire
Gloucestershire
South Gloucestershire
Bristol
Bath and North East Somerset
North Somerset
Somerset
Torbay
Devon
Plymouth
Cornwall
Isles of Scilly
Telford & Wrekin
Shropshire
Herefordshire
Monmouthshire
Blaenau Gwent
Torfaen
Newport
Cardiff
Caerphilly
Merthyr Tydfil
Powys
Ceredigion
Carmarthenshire
Rhondda Cynor Taff
Neath Port Talbot
Swansea
Bridgend
The Vale of Glamorgan
Pembrokeshire
WALES
Douglas
Isle of Man

REPUBLIC OF IRELAND

Derry
Antrim
Carrickfergus
North Down
Ards
Castlereagh
Belfast
Lisburn
Down
Newtownabbey
Coleraine
Cookstown
Dungannon
Craigavon
Armagh
Banbridge
Newry and Mourne
Omagh
Fermanagh
Monaghan
Cavan
Leitrim
Sligo
Mayo
Roscommon
Longford
Westmeath
Meath
Louth
Dublin
Dublin
Wicklow
Kildare
Offaly
Laois
Carlow
Kilkenny
Wexford
Waterford
Tipperary
Limerick
Clare
Galway
Kerry
Cork
Donegal

Greater London
Scale 1 : 850 000

Havering
Enfield
Barnet
Harrow
Hillingdon
Hounslow
Ealing
Brent
City of Westminster
Kensington and Chelsea
Hammersmith and Fulham
Richmond upon Thames
Kingston upon Thames
Merton
Sutton
Croydon
Bromley
Bexley
Greenwich
Lewisham
Southwark
Lambeth
Wandsworth
Haringey
Waltham Forest
Redbridge
Barking
Newham
Tower Hamlets
Hackney
Islington
Camden
City of London

Scale 1 : 4 500 000

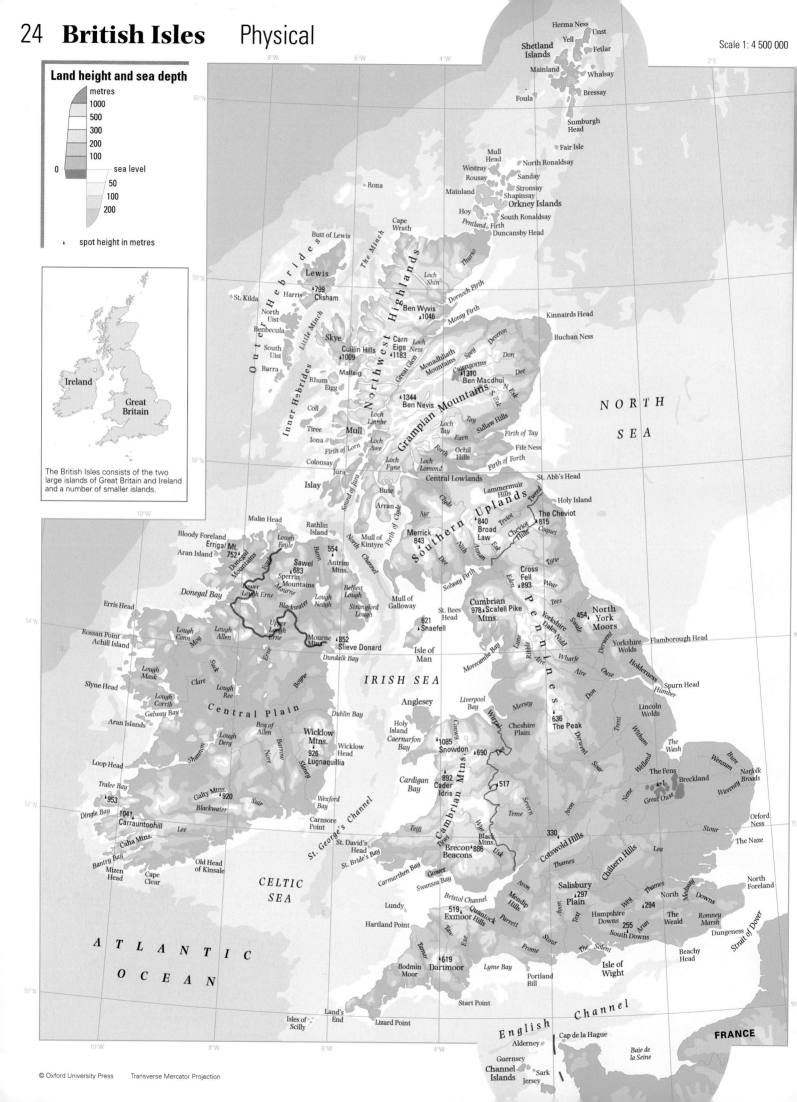

Land height and sea depth

metres
1000
500
300
200
100
0 — sea level
50
100
200

▲ spot height in metres

The British Isles consists of the two large islands of Great Britain and Ireland and a number of smaller islands.

© Oxford University Press   Transverse Mercator Projection

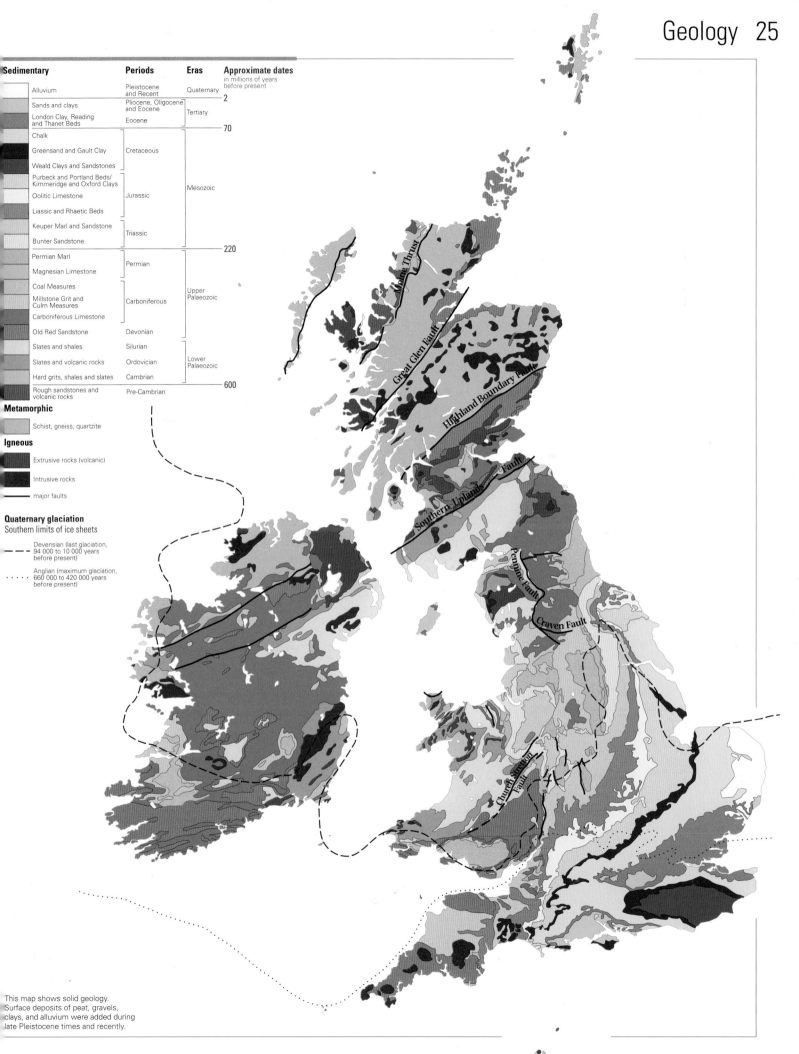

Sedimentary | **Periods** | **Eras** | **Approximate dates**
in millions of years
before present

Alluvium	Pleistocene and Recent	Quaternary	
			2
Sands and clays	Pliocene, Oligocene and Eocene	Tertiary	
London Clay, Reading and Thanet Beds	Eocene		
			70
Chalk			
Greensand and Gault Clay	Cretaceous		
Weald Clays and Sandstones			
Purbeck and Portland Beds/ Kimmeridge and Oxford Clays		Mesozoic	
Oolitic Limestone	Jurassic		
Liassic and Rhaetic Beds			
Keuper Marl and Sandstone	Triassic		
Bunter Sandstone			
			220
Permian Marl	Permian		
Magnesian Limestone			
Coal Measures		Upper Palaeozoic	
Millstone Grit and Culm Measures	Carboniferous		
Carboniferous Limestone			
Old Red Sandstone	Devonian		
Slates and shales	Silurian	Lower Palaeozoic	
Slates and volcanic rocks	Ordovician		
Hard grits, shales and slates	Cambrian		
			600
Rough sandstones and volcanic rocks	Pre-Cambrian		

Metamorphic

Schist, gneiss, quartzite

Igneous

Extrusive rocks (volcanic)

Intrusive rocks

—— major faults

Quaternary glaciation
Southern limits of ice sheets

– – – Devensian (last glaciation, 94 000 to 10 000 years before present)

· · · · · Anglian (maximum glaciation, 660 000 to 420 000 years before present)

This map shows solid geology.
Surface deposits of peat, gravels,
clays, and alluvium were added during
late Pleistocene times and recently.

© Oxford University Press   Transverse Mercator Projection

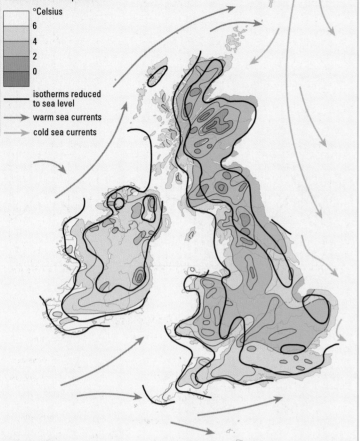

January temperature

actual surface temperature

°Celsius

6
4
2
0

— isotherms reduced to sea level

→ warm sea currents

→ cold sea currents

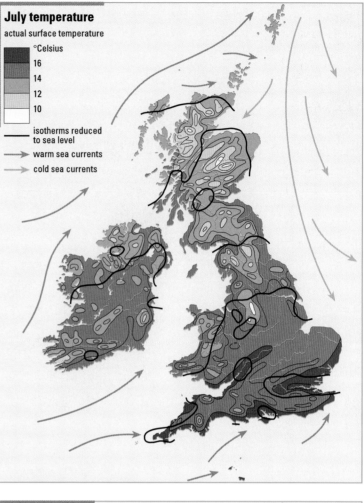

July temperature

actual surface temperature

°Celsius

16
14
12
10

— isotherms reduced to sea level

→ warm sea currents

→ cold sea currents

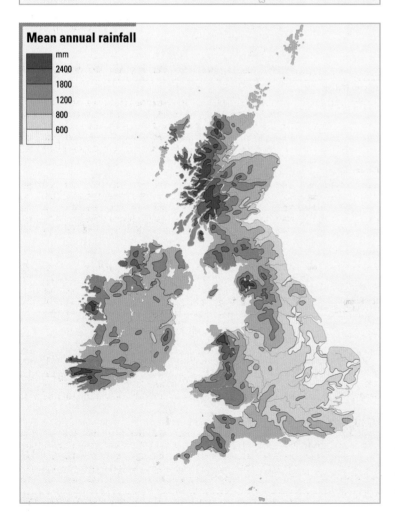

Mean annual rainfall

mm

2400
1800
1200
800
600

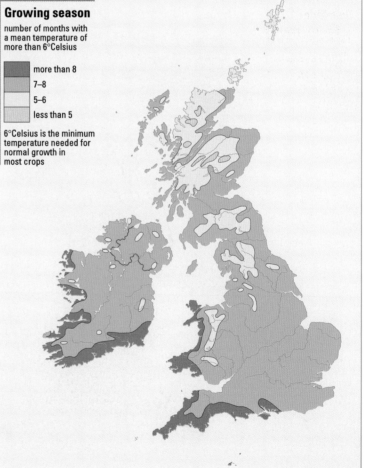

Growing season

number of months with a mean temperature of more than 6°Celsius

more than 8

7–8

5–6

less than 5

6°Celsius is the minimum temperature needed for normal growth in most crops

Transverse Mercator Projection   © Oxford University Press

Snow

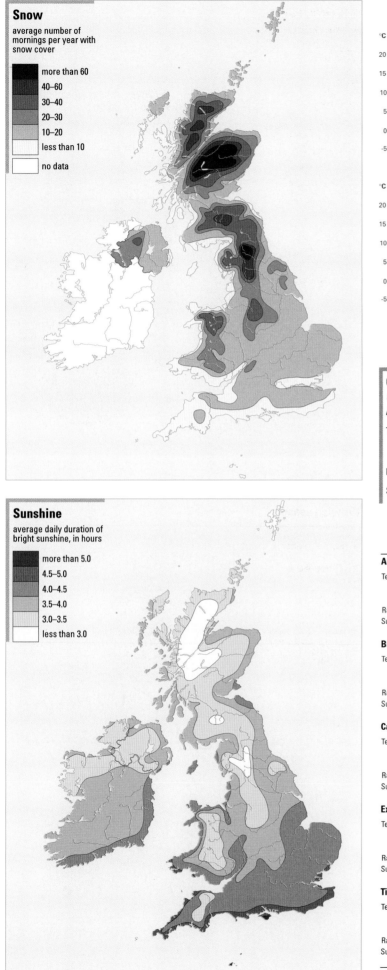

average number of mornings per year with snow cover

- more than 60
- 40–60
- 30–40
- 20–30
- 10–20
- less than 10
- no data

Sunshine

average daily duration of bright sunshine, in hours

- more than 5.0
- 4.5–5.0
- 4.0–4.5
- 3.5–4.0
- 3.0–3.5
- less than 3.0

© Oxford University Press

Climate graphs for selected British stations

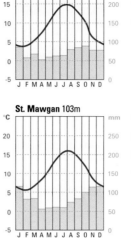

Belfast 68m

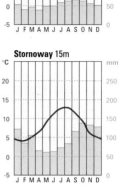

Edinburgh 26m

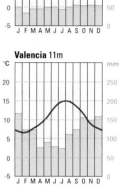

London 7m

St. Mawgan 103m

Stornoway 15m

Valencia 11m

Climate stations

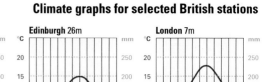

Climate data

averages are for 1961–1990

Anglesey (Valley) 10m — climate station and its height above sea level

Temperature (°C)
- high — average daily maximum temperature
- mean — average monthly temperature
- low — average daily minimum temperature

Rainfall (mm) — average monthly precipitation

Sunshine (hours) — average daily duration of bright sunshine

		Jan	Feb	Mar	Apr	May	Jun	Jul	Aug	Sep	Oct	Nov	Dec	YEAR
Anglesey (Valley) 10m														
Temperature (°C)	high	7.7	7.7	9.1	11.4	14.4	16.9	18.4	18.5	16.7	14.2	10.6	8.7	12.8
	mean	5.5	5.1	6.5	8.3	11.1	13.6	15.3	15.4	13.9	11.6	8.1	6.4	10.0
	low	3.2	2.5	3.8	5.1	7.7	10.3	12.2	12.3	11.0	8.9	5.6	4.1	7.2
Rainfall (mm)		83	56	65	53	49	52	53	74	74	91	99	94	843
Sunshine (hours)		1.8	3.0	4.0	5.9	7.2	7.0	6.4	6.0	4.7	3.3	2.2	1.6	4.4
Braemar 339m														
Temperature (°C)	high	3.8	3.9	6.0	9.2	12.8	16.2	17.5	16.9	14.0	10.8	6.3	4.6	10.1
	mean	0.8	0.6	2.7	4.9	8.1	11.4	13.0	12.5	10.2	7.3	3.2	1.8	6.3
	low	-2.2	-2.7	-0.7	0.6	3.4	6.5	8.4	8.0	6.3	3.8	0.1	-1.0	2.5
Rainfall (mm)		106	62	72	48	66	58	54	71	81	93	87	91	889
Sunshine (hours)		0.8	2.0	3.1	4.6	5.2	5.6	5.1	4.8	3.5	2.2	1.2	0.6	3.2
Cambridge 26m														
Temperature (°C)	high	6.4	6.8	9.7	12.5	16.4	19.6	21.5	21.5	18.8	14.9	9.7	7.3	13.7
	mean	3.7	3.9	6.0	8.2	11.6	14.6	16.6	16.5	14.3	11.0	6.6	4.6	9.8
	low	1.0	0.9	2.2	3.9	6.7	9.6	11.7	11.5	9.8	7.1	3.5	1.8	5.8
Rainfall (mm)		43	32	42	43	49	50	44	53	46	49	51	49	551
Sunshine (hours)		1.8	2.5	3.5	4.7	6.2	6.5	6.0	5.7	4.8	3.5	2.2	1.5	4.1
Exeter 32m														
Temperature (°C)	high	8.0	8.0	10.2	12.7	15.8	19.1	21.0	20.8	18.4	15.0	11.0	9.0	14.0
	mean	5.0	5.0	6.6	8.6	11.5	14.6	16.5	16.3	14.2	11.4	7.8	6.0	10.2
	low	2.0	2.0	2.9	4.4	7.1	10.1	12.0	11.7	9.9	7.7	4.1	2.9	6.4
Rainfall (mm)		93	71	61	50	54	47	45	54	57	73	72	87	764
Sunshine (hours)		1.7	2.4	3.5	5.1	6.0	6.3	6.2	5.6	4.4	2.9	2.3	1.6	4.0
Tiree 12m														
Temperature (°C)	high	7.3	7.1	8.3	10.1	12.6	14.7	15.8	16.0	14.5	12.5	9.5	8.1	11.3
	mean	5.1	4.9	5.8	7.3	9.7	11.9	13.3	13.5	12.2	10.3	7.2	5.6	8.9
	low	2.9	2.6	3.3	4.4	6.7	9.1	10.8	10.9	9.8	8.1	4.8	3.8	6.4
Rainfall (mm)		127	79	96	59	59	61	78	95	129	140	122	120	1165
Sunshine (hours)		1.3	2.4	3.5	5.7	6.9	6.5	5.1	5.0	3.7	2.5	1.6	1.0	3.8
		Jan	Feb	Mar	Apr	May	Jun	Jul	Aug	Sep	Oct	Nov	Dec	YEAR

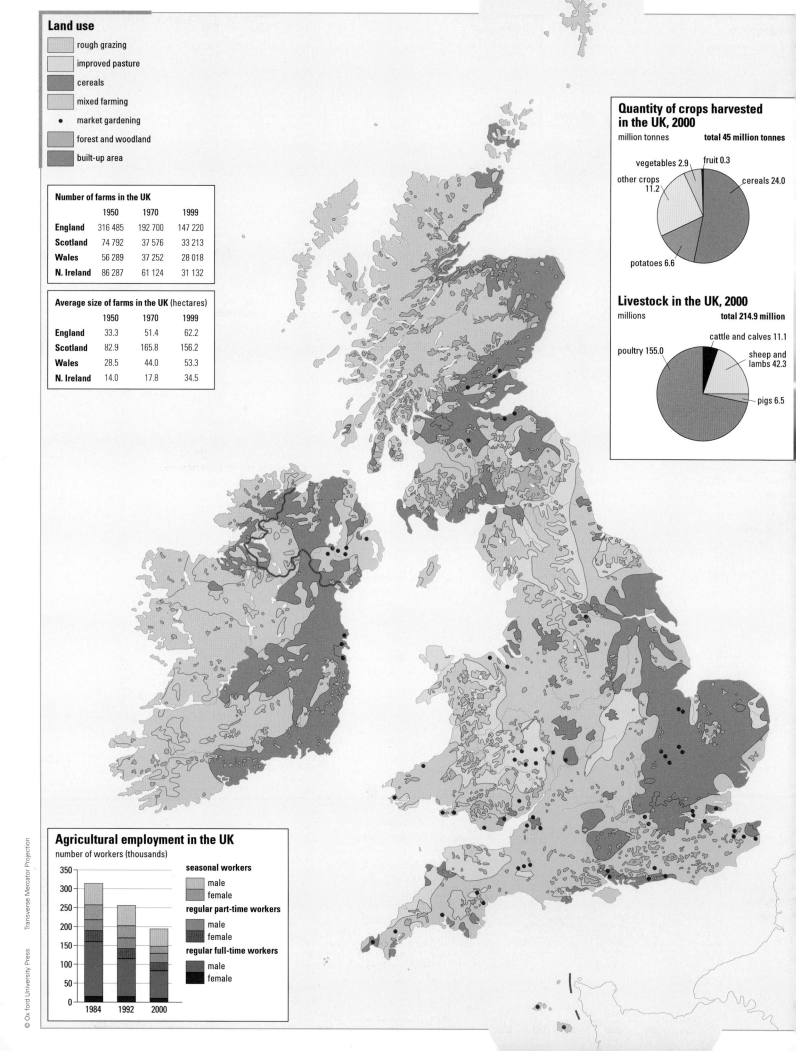

Land use

- rough grazing
- improved pasture
- cereals
- mixed farming
- • market gardening
- forest and woodland
- built-up area

Number of farms in the UK

	1950	1970	1999
England	316 485	192 700	147 220
Scotland	74 792	37 576	33 213
Wales	56 289	37 252	28 018
N. Ireland	86 287	61 124	31 132

Average size of farms in the UK (hectares)

	1950	1970	1999
England	33.3	51.4	62.2
Scotland	82.9	165.8	156.2
Wales	28.5	44.0	53.3
N. Ireland	14.0	17.8	34.5

Quantity of crops harvested in the UK, 2000

million tonnes   **total 45 million tonnes**

- vegetables 2.9
- fruit 0.3
- other crops 11.2
- cereals 24.0
- potatoes 6.6

Livestock in the UK, 2000

millions   **total 214.9 million**

- cattle and calves 11.1
- poultry 155.0
- sheep and lambs 42.3
- pigs 6.5

Agricultural employment in the UK

number of workers (thousands)

seasonal workers
- male
- female

regular part-time workers
- male
- female

regular full-time workers
- male
- female

1984 1992 2000

Transverse Mercator Projection

© Oxford University Press

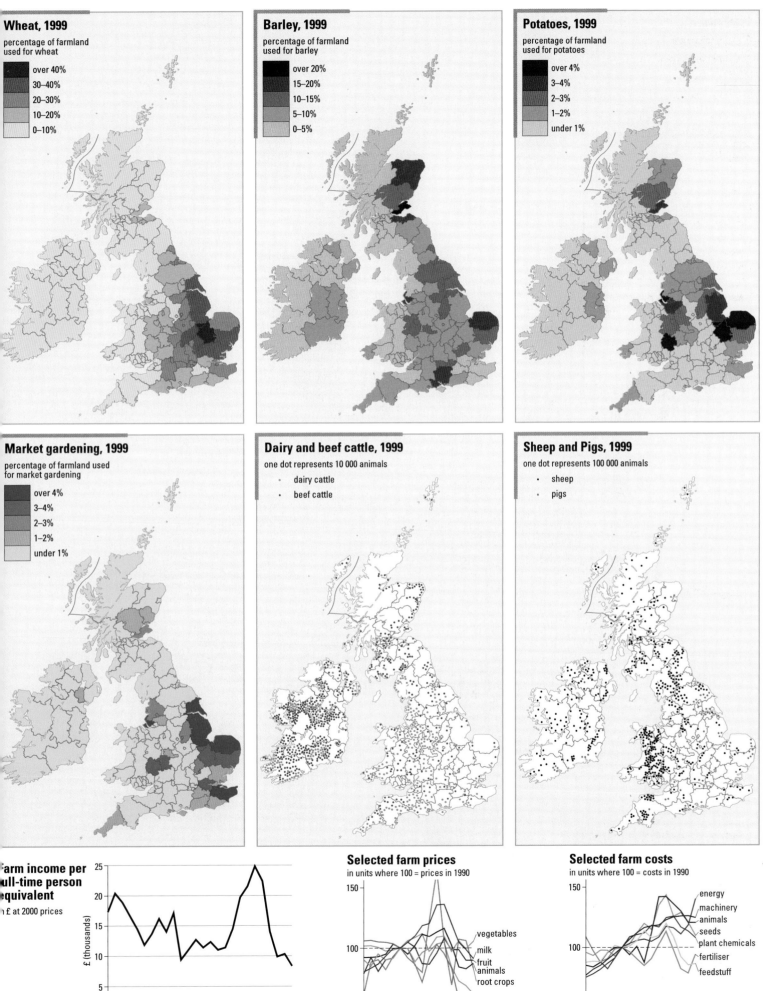

Wheat, 1999

percentage of farmland
used for wheat

- over 40%
- 30–40%
- 20–30%
- 10–20%
- 0–10%

Barley, 1999

percentage of farmland
used for barley

- over 20%
- 15–20%
- 10–15%
- 5–10%
- 0–5%

Potatoes, 1999

percentage of farmland
used for potatoes

- over 4%
- 3–4%
- 2–3%
- 1–2%
- under 1%

Market gardening, 1999

percentage of farmland used
for market gardening

- over 4%
- 3–4%
- 2–3%
- 1–2%
- under 1%

Dairy and beef cattle, 1999

one dot represents 10 000 animals

- dairy cattle
- beef cattle

Sheep and Pigs, 1999

one dot represents 100 000 animals

- sheep
- pigs

Farm income per full-time person equivalent

in £ at 2000 prices

£ (thousands)

25 / 20 / 15 / 10 / 5

1975 1980 1985 1990 1995 2000

Selected farm prices

in units where 100 = prices in 1990

150 / 100 / 50

vegetables
milk
fruit
animals
root crops
cereals
wool

1985 1990 1995 2000

Selected farm costs

in units where 100 = costs in 1990

150 / 100 / 50

energy
machinery
animals
seeds
plant chemicals
fertiliser
feedstuff

1985 1990 1995 2000

Transverse Mercator Projection

© Oxford University Press

Water supply

Scale 1 : 6 000 000

- areas of high rainfall (more than 1200mm per year)

highly productive aquifers
- porous rock
- jointed rock

reservoirs
capacity in million cubic metres
- over 100
- 50–100
- 10–50

- built-up area
- water service boundary

Minerals

- limestone
- sand and gravel
- kaolin (china clay)
- brick clay
- potash
- salt

Water pollution

- most polluted rivers and estuaries

Water use in England and Wales, 1999
total 40 100 megalitres per day

- agriculture 15.0%
- public water supply 40.6%
- industry 12.2%
- electricity generation 32.2%

Domestic water use in England and Wales, 1999
total 16 300 megalitres per day

- dish washing, garden use, others 28%
- flushing WC 25%
- washing machines 14%
- baths, showers, hand washing 33%

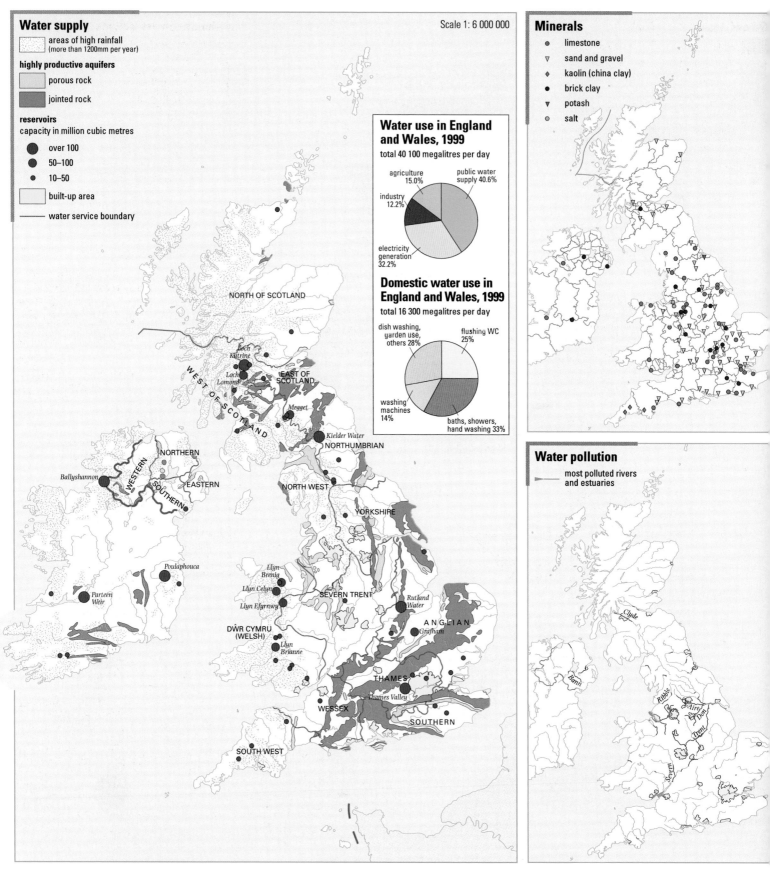

Map labels:
NORTH OF SCOTLAND
WEST OF SCOTLAND
EAST OF SCOTLAND
Loch Katrine
Loch Lomond
Megget
Kielder Water
NORTHUMBRIAN
Ballyshannon
WESTERN
NORTHERN
EASTERN
SOUTHERN
NORTH WEST
YORKSHIRE
Poulaphouca
Parteen Weir
Llyn Brenig
Llyn Celyn
Llyn Efyrnwy
SEVERN TRENT
Rutland Water
ANGLIAN
Grafham
DWR CYMRU (WELSH)
Llyn Brianne
THAMES
Thames Valley
WESSEX
SOUTHERN
SOUTH WEST

Water pollution map labels:
Clyde
Bann
Ribble
Aire
Don
Trent
Severn

Bottled water consumption, UK, 1986–2000
litres per person

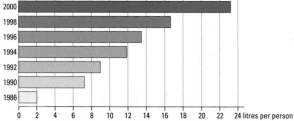

2000	~23
1998	~16
1996	~13
1994	~12
1992	~9
1990	~7
1986	~2

0 2 4 6 8 10 12 14 16 18 20 22 24 litres per person

Reservoir stocks, England and Wales, 1988–1999
percentage full

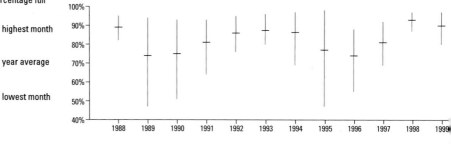

- highest month
- year average
- lowest month

100%
90%
80%
70%
60%
50%
40%

1988 1989 1990 1991 1992 1993 1994 1995 1996 1997 1998 1999

© Oxford University Press

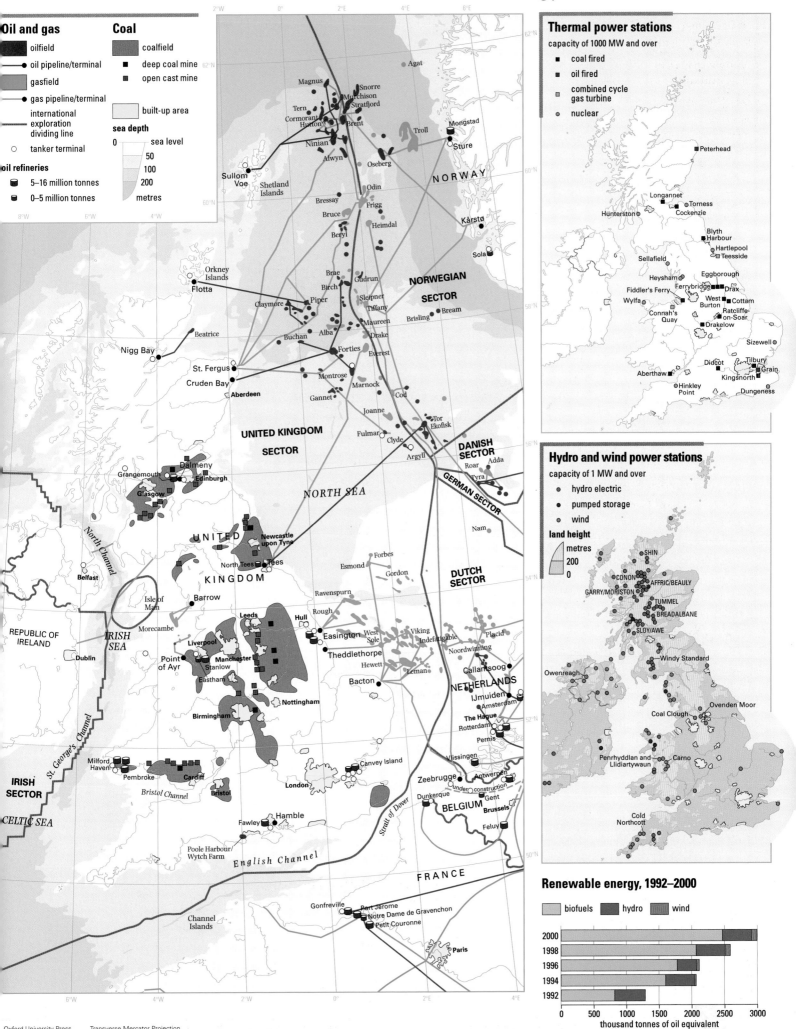

Scale 1: 4 500 000

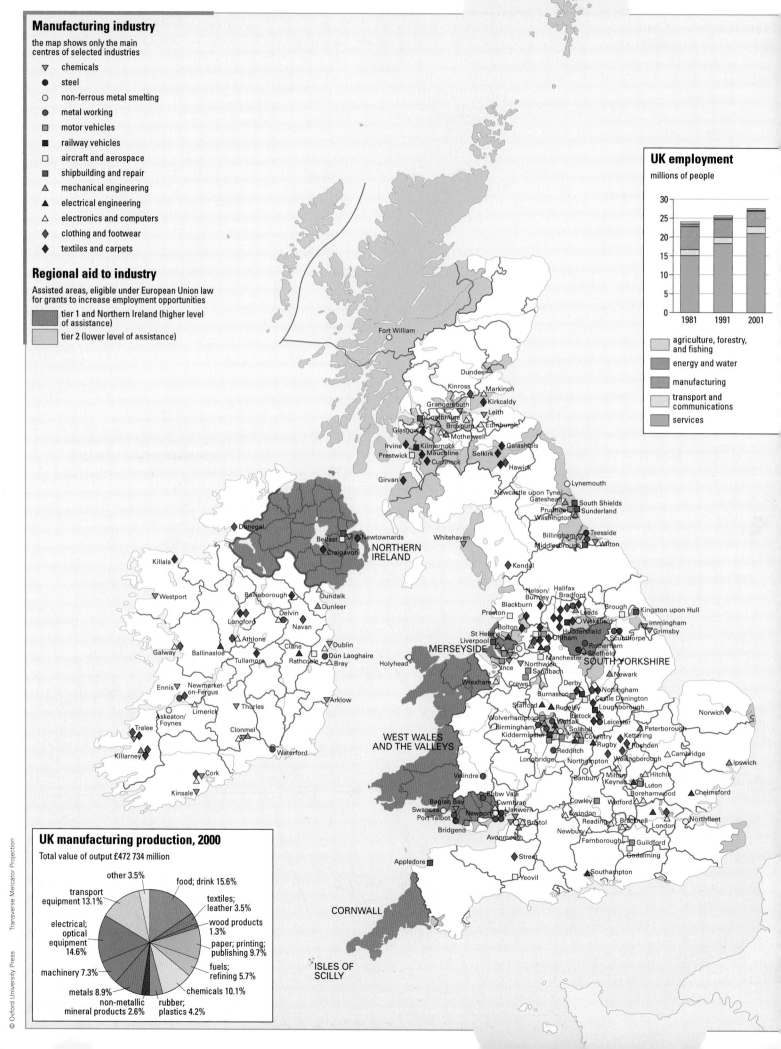

Manufacturing industry

the map shows only the main centres of selected industries

- ▽ chemicals
- ● steel
- ○ non-ferrous metal smelting
- ● metal working
- ■ motor vehicles
- ■ railway vehicles
- □ aircraft and aerospace
- ■ shipbuilding and repair
- △ mechanical engineering
- ▲ electrical engineering
- △ electronics and computers
- ◆ clothing and footwear
- ◆ textiles and carpets

Regional aid to industry

Assisted areas, eligible under European Union law for grants to increase employment opportunities

- tier 1 and Northern Ireland (higher level of assistance)
- tier 2 (lower level of assistance)

Fort William
Dundee
Kinross
Markinch
Kirkcaldy
Grangemouth
Leith
Coatbridge
Broxburn
Edinburgh
Glasgow
Motherwell
Galashiels
Irvine
Kilmarnock
Prestwick
Mauchline
Cumnock
Selkirk
Hawick
Girvan
Lynemouth
Newcastle upon Tyne
Gateshead
South Shields
Prudhoe
Sunderland
Washington
Donegal
Belfast
Newtownards
Craigavon
NORTHERN IRELAND
Whitehaven
Billingham
Teesside
Middlesbrough
Wilton
Killala
Kendal
Westport
Bailieborough
Dundalk
Dunleer
Delvin
Longford
Navan
Athlone
Galway
Ballinasloe
Clane
Dublin
Tullamore
Rathcoole
Dún Laoghaire
Bray
Holyhead
Nelson/ Burnley
Halifax
Bradford
Blackburn
Preston
Leeds
Brough
Kingston upon Hull
Bolton
Wakefield
Immingham
Grimsby
St Helens
Huddersfield
Liverpool
Oldham
Scunthorpe
MERSEYSIDE
Rotherham
Sheffield
Manchester
SOUTH YORKSHIRE
Northwich
Ince
Sandbach
Newark
Ennis
Newmarket-on-Fergus
Wrexham
Crewe
Derby
Nottingham
Arklow
Burnaston
Castle Donington
Limerick
Thurles
Stafford
Rugeley
Loughborough
Askeaton/ Foynes
Ilkeston
Norwich
Tralee
Wolverhampton
Walsall
Leicester
Clonmel
Birmingham
Solihull
Peterborough
Kidderminster
Coventry
Kettering
WEST WALES AND THE VALLEYS
Rugby
Rushden
Killarney
Waterford
Redditch
Cambridge
Longbridge
Northampton
Wellingborough
Ipswich
Cork
Velindre
Banbury
Milton Keynes
Hitchin
Luton
Kinsale
Ebbw Vale
Borehamwood
Chelmsford
Baglan Bay
Cwmbran
Cowley
Watford
Swansea
Llanwern
Port Talbot
Newport
Swindon
Bristol
Reading
Bracknell
Northfleet
Bridgend
London
Newbury
Avonmouth
Farnborough
Guildford
Godalming
Appledore
Street
Southampton
Yeovil
CORNWALL
ISLES OF SCILLY
UK employment
millions of people
30
25
20
15
10
5
0
1981
1991
2001
agriculture, forestry, and fishing
energy and water
manufacturing
transport and communications
services
UK manufacturing production, 2000
Total value of output £472 734 million
other 3.5%
food; drink 15.6%
transport equipment 13.1%
textiles; leather 3.5%
wood products 1.3%
electrical; optical equipment 14.6%
paper; printing; publishing 9.7%
fuels; refining 5.7%
machinery 7.3%
chemicals 10.1%
metals 8.9%
non-metallic mineral products 2.6%
rubber; plastics 4.2%

Transverse Mercator Projection

Employment in primary activity, 2000

percentage of the workforce employed in agriculture, forestry, fishing, mining, and quarrying, by administrative area

- over 20%
- 10–20%
- 2.5–10%
- 1–2.5%
- under 1%

Employment in secondary activity, 2000

percentage of the workforce employed in manufacturing, construction, and utilities, by administrative area

- over 30%
- 25–30%
- 20–25%
- 15–20%
- under 15%

Employment in tertiary activity, 2000

percentage of the workforce employed in services, transport, finance, and administration, by administrative area

- over 85%
- 80–85%
- 75–80%
- 70–75%
- 65–70%
- under 65%

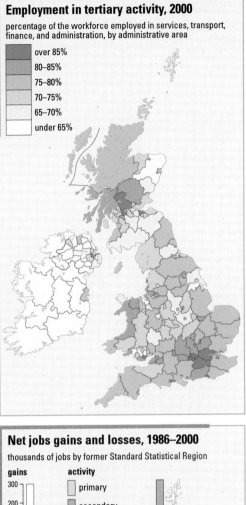

Unemployment, 2000

percentage of the workforce unemployed, by administrative area

- over 6%
- 5–6%
- 4–5%
- 3–4%
- 2–3%
- under 2%

Change in manufacturing employment, 1991–2000

percentage change in the number of people employed in manufacturing, by administrative area

gain
- over 20%
- 10–20%
- 0–10%

loss
- 0–10%
- 10–20%
- over 30%

Net jobs gains and losses, 1986–2000

thousands of jobs by former Standard Statistical Region

gains
300 — 200 — 100 — 0 — 100 — 200
losses

activity
- primary
- secondary
- tertiary

Scotland
Northern Ireland
North
East Midlands
Republic of Ireland
West Midlands
North West
Yorkshire and Humberside
East Anglia
Wales
London
South East
South West

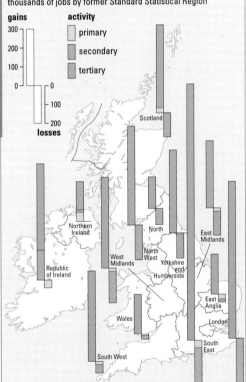

Transverse Mercator Projection

© Oxford University Press

UK workforce structure, 2000

Total workforce 29 412 000

- females aged 60 and over / males aged 65 and over 2.9%
- females aged 45–59 / males aged 45–64 31.2%
- aged 25–44 50.9%
- aged 16–24 15.1%

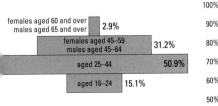

UK employment rates, 1960–2000

percentage of people of working age

males
all
females

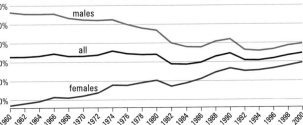

100%
90%
80%
70%
60%
50%

1960 1962 1964 1966 1968 1970 1972 1974 1976 1978 1980 1982 1984 1986 1988 1990 1992 1994 1996 1998 2000

UK unemployment structure, 2000

percentage of all economically active people

	males	Age	females
	5.8%	over 60	
	5.4%	55–59	3.1%
	4.8%	45–54	2.9%
	4.8%	25–44	4.5%
	11.8%	18–24	8.5%
	20.1%	16–17	16.9%

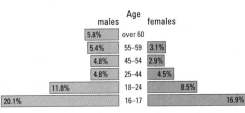

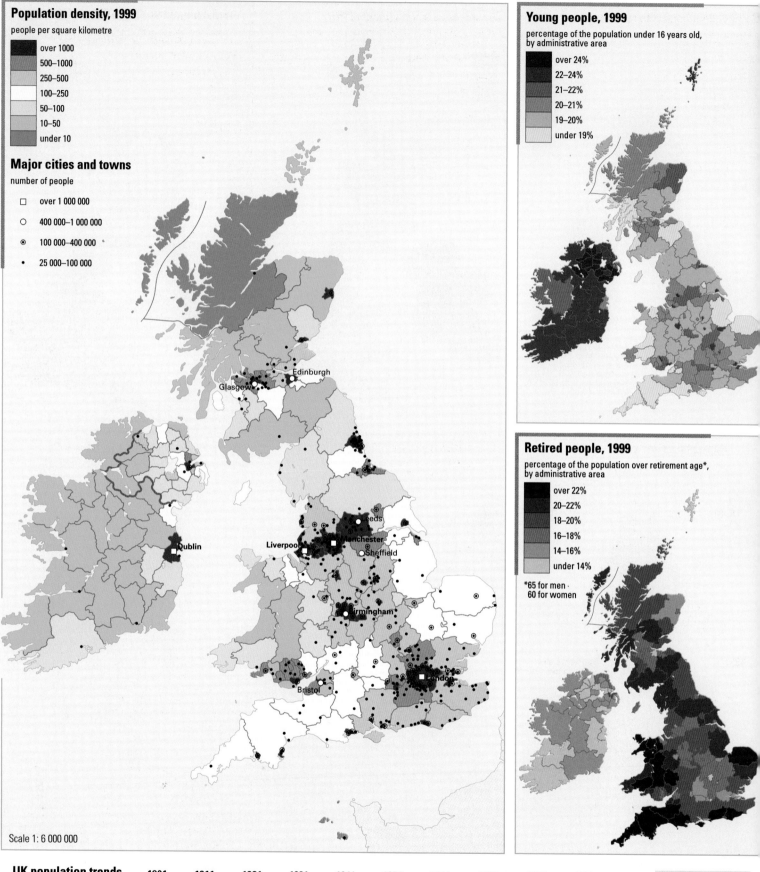

Population density, 1999

people per square kilometre

- over 1000
- 500–1000
- 250–500
- 100–250
- 50–100
- 10–50
- under 10

Major cities and towns

number of people

- ☐ over 1 000 000
- ○ 400 000–1 000 000
- ◉ 100 000–400 000
- • 25 000–100 000

Scale 1: 6 000 000

© Oxford University Press

Young people, 1999

percentage of the population under 16 years old, by administrative area

- over 24%
- 22–24%
- 21–22%
- 20–21%
- 19–20%
- under 19%

Retired people, 1999

percentage of the population over retirement age*, by administrative area

- over 22%
- 20–22%
- 18–20%
- 16–18%
- 14–16%
- under 14%

*65 for men · 60 for women

UK population trends	1901	1911	1921	1931	1941	1951	1961	1971	1981	1991	2001	2011	2021
Total population (millions)	38.24	42.08	44.03	46.04	48.22	50.23	52.81	55.93	56.35	57.65	59.62	60.93	63.64
Infant mortality (deaths per 1000 live births)	138.0	110.0	76.0	62.0	50.0	27.0	21.0	17.9	11.0	7.4	5.6	5.5	5.5
Birth rate (births per 1000 people)	28.6	24.5	22.8	16.3	14.4	15.9	17.9	16.1	13.0	13.8	12.0	11.5	11.5
Death rate (deaths per 1000 people)	16.5	14.3	11.9	12.5	13.0	12.6	12.0	11.5	11.6	11.3	10.5	10.0	10.3
Life expectancy (years)	47.0	52.2	57.3	60.0	61.0	68.5	70.9	71.9	73.8	76.0	77.5	79.5	80.5

projected

Scale 1: 12 500 000 (smallest maps)

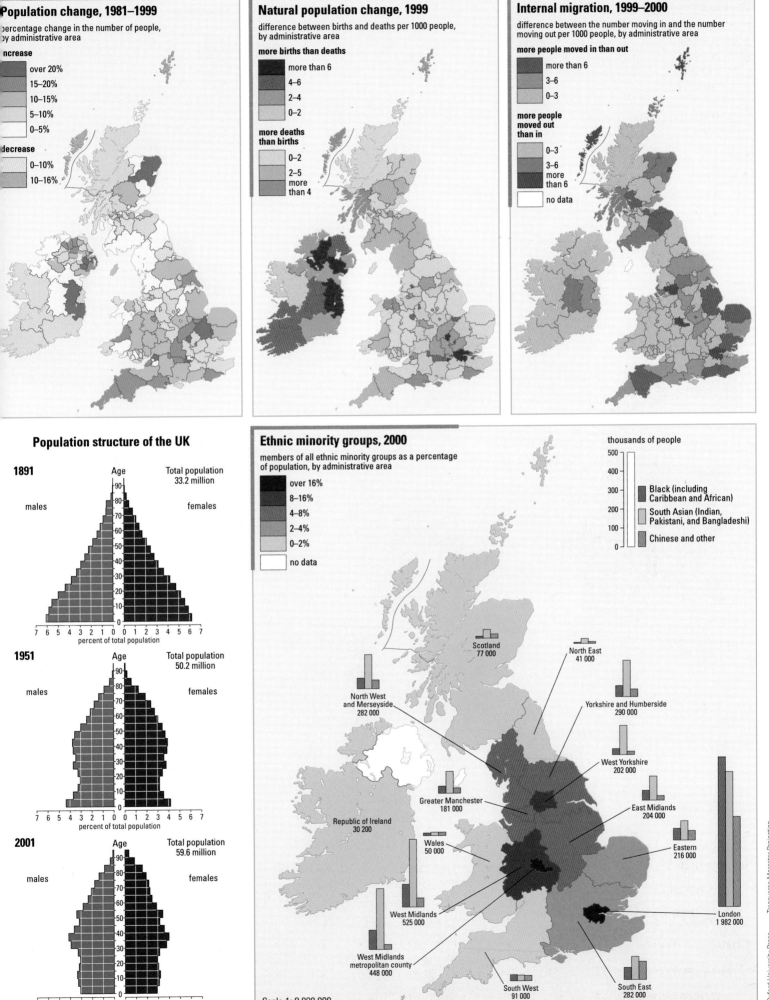

Population change, 1981–1999

percentage change in the number of people, by administrative area

increase
- over 20%
- 15–20%
- 10–15%
- 5–10%
- 0–5%

decrease
- 0–10%
- 10–16%

Natural population change, 1999

difference between births and deaths per 1000 people, by administrative area

more births than deaths
- more than 6
- 4–6
- 2–4
- 0–2

more deaths than births
- 0–2
- 2–5
- more than 4

Internal migration, 1999–2000

difference between the number moving in and the number moving out per 1000 people, by administrative area

more people moved in than out
- more than 6
- 3–6
- 0–3

more people moved out than in
- 0–3
- 3–6
- more than 6
- no data

Population structure of the UK

1891 Age Total population 33.2 million
males   females
percent of total population

1951 Age Total population 50.2 million
males   females
percent of total population

2001 Age Total population 59.6 million
males   females
percent of total population

Ethnic minority groups, 2000

members of all ethnic minority groups as a percentage of population, by administrative area

- over 16%
- 8–16%
- 4–8%
- 2–4%
- 0–2%
- no data

thousands of people
500 400 300 200 100 0

- Black (including Caribbean and African)
- South Asian (Indian, Pakistani, and Bangladeshi)
- Chinese and other

Scotland 77 000
North East 41 000
North West and Merseyside 282 000
Yorkshire and Humberside 290 000
West Yorkshire 202 000
Greater Manchester 181 000
East Midlands 204 000
Republic of Ireland 30 200
Wales 50 000
Eastern 216 000
West Midlands 525 000
West Midlands metropolitan county 448 000
London 1 982 000
South West 91 000
South East 282 000

Scale 1: 8 000 000

Transverse Mercator Projection

© Oxford University Press

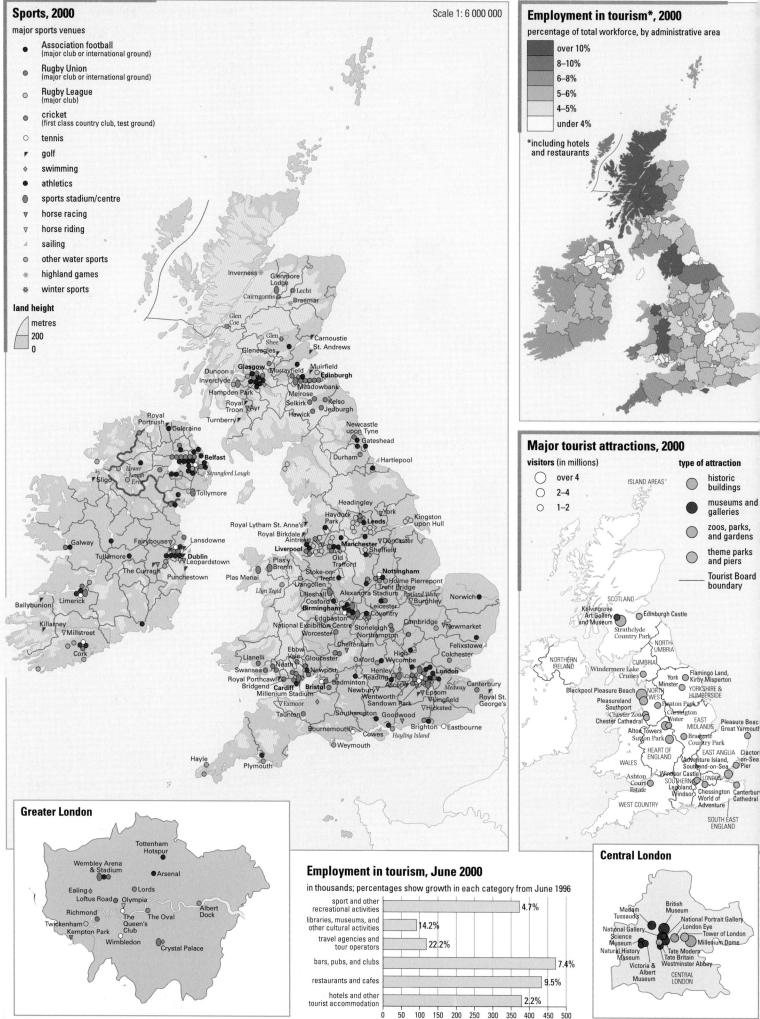

Scale 1: 12 500 000

Income, 2000

average gross weekly earnings of workers in full-time employment, by administrative area

- over £475
- £425–£475
- £400–£425
- £375–£400
- £350–£375
- under £350
- no data

Education, 2000

percentage of 16 year olds entering further or higher education, by administrative area

- over 90%
- 85–90%
- 80–85%
- 75–80%
- 70–75%
- under 70%

Index of Multiple Deprivation (IMD), 2000

IMD is calculated from a number of indicators including low income, unemployment, poor health, disability, lack of education, unsatisfactory housing, and poor access to services. The map shows the 10% most deprived areas within each part of the UK.

- England
- Wales
- Scotland
- Northern Ireland

Burglaries, 2000

per 1000 households, by administrative area

- over 40
- 30–40
- 20–30
- 10–20
- under 10

Coronary heart disease, 1992–1996

age-standardised death rates per 100 000 people, by administrative area

- over 130
- 112–129
- 97–111
- 82–96
- under 81

House prices, 2001

comparative prices for similar size and style of house in similar neighbourhoods

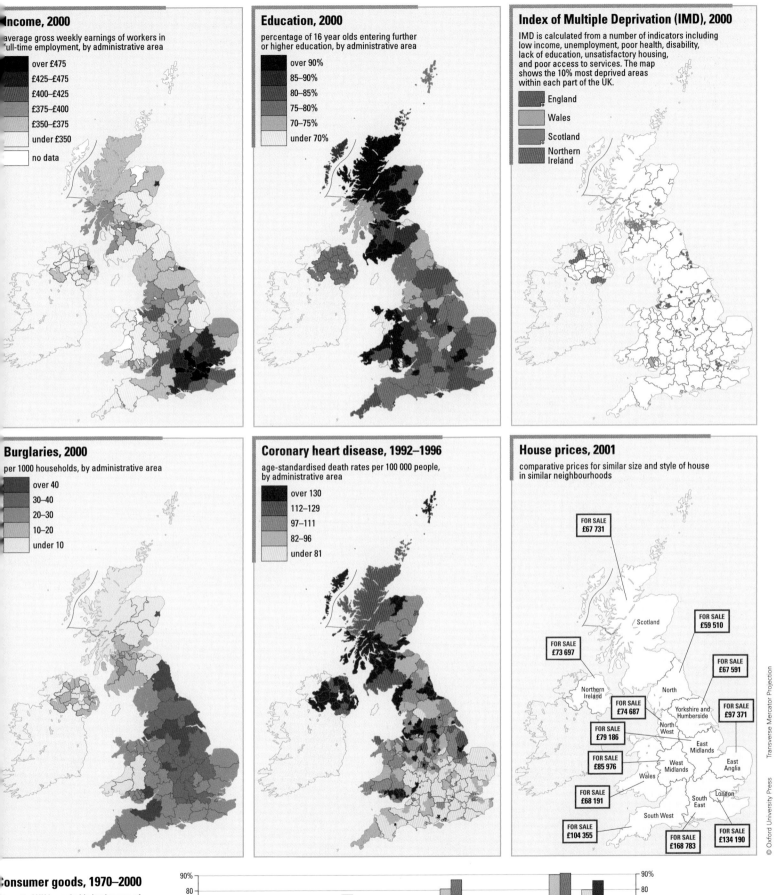

FOR SALE £67 731

FOR SALE £59 510

FOR SALE £73 697

FOR SALE £67 591

FOR SALE £74 687

FOR SALE £97 371

FOR SALE £79 186

FOR SALE £85 976

FOR SALE £68 191

FOR SALE £104 355

FOR SALE £168 783

FOR SALE £134 190

Scotland

Northern Ireland

North

Yorkshire and Humberside

North West

East Midlands

West Midlands

East Anglia

Wales

South East

London

South West

Transverse Mercator Projection

© Oxford University Press

Consumer goods, 1970–2000

percent of UK households having use of each product

- car
- central heating
- washing machine
- dishwasher
- microwave oven
- video
- PC
- CD player
- ooo no data

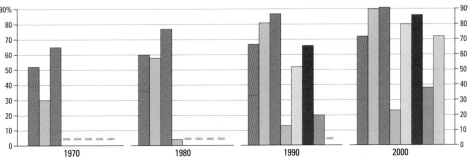

1970   1980   1990   2000

Scale 1 : 4 500 000

Conservation

- National Parks*
- Areas of Outstanding Natural Beauty (England, Wales, and Northern Ireland) National Scenic Areas (Scotland)
- Heritage Coast (England and Wales) Coastal Conservation Zone (Scotland)
- internationally recognized sites (including Special Protection Areas, 'Ramsar' Sites, and Biosphere Reserves)
- ✳ Natural Heritage Sites
- ✷ Cultural Heritage Sites
- built-up area

*National parks are designated to conserve the natural beauty and cultural heritage of areas of outstanding landscape value. There are 10 national parks in England and Wales, all designated in the 1950's following the National Parks and Access to the Countryside Act, 1949. The Broads is not officially a national park but is considered as such by the government and has had its own authority since 1989. In 2002 the government was consulting on proposals to establish the New Forest and South Downs as national parks. The National Parks (Scotland) Act was passed in July 2000, and it is expected that the Cairngorms and Loch Lomond and the Trossachs will become Scotland's first national parks in 2002/3.

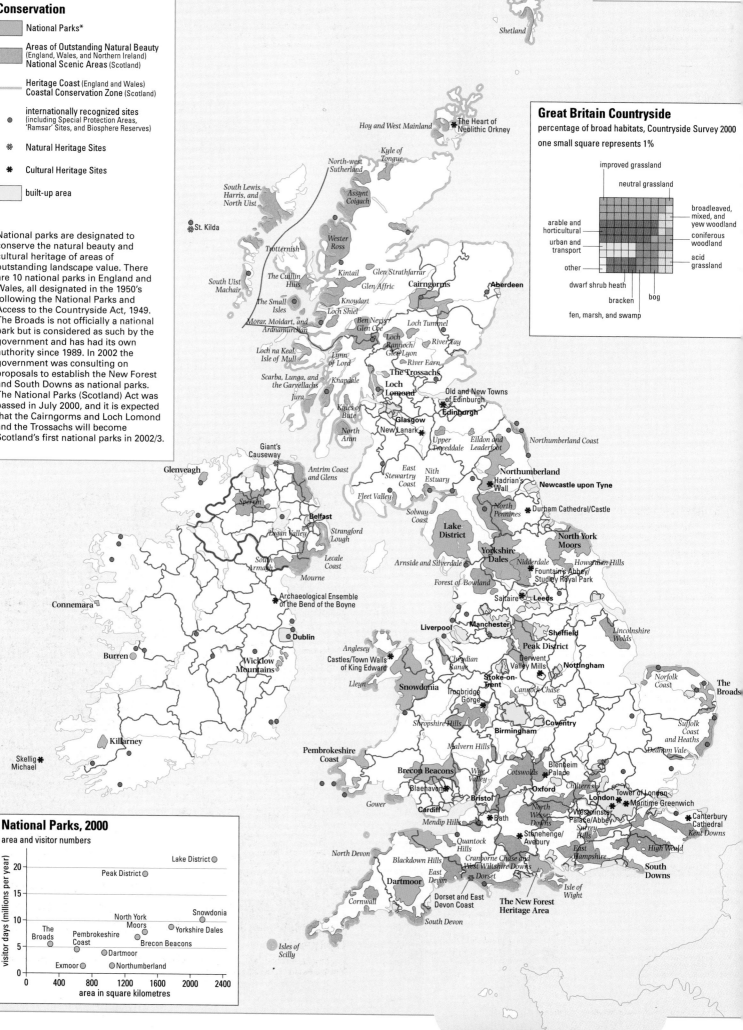

Great Britain Countryside

percentage of broad habitats, Countryside Survey 2000

one small square represents 1%

improved grassland, neutral grassland, broadleaved, mixed, and yew woodland, coniferous woodland, acid grassland, bog, bracken, dwarf shrub heath, fen, marsh, and swamp, other, urban and transport, arable and horticultural

National Parks, 2000

area and visitor numbers

y-axis: visitor days (millions per year) — 0, 5, 10, 15, 20
x-axis: area in square kilometres — 0, 400, 800, 1200, 1600, 2000, 2400

Lake District, Peak District, Snowdonia, Yorkshire Dales, North York Moors, Brecon Beacons, The Broads, Pembrokeshire Coast, Dartmoor, Exmoor, Northumberland

Acid rain

Environmental damage is more likely where acid deposition is high and soils (particularly those that are already acid) are more sensitive.

areas where potential damage to vegetation from nitrogen in acid rain is

- very high
- high
- moderate
- low

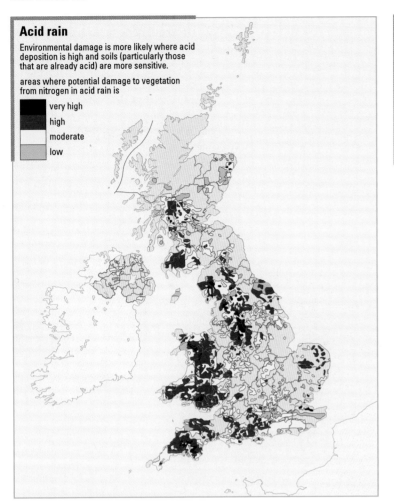

Ozone, 1996

Number of days when ozone concentration exceeded 50 parts per billion, used to assess the potential for effects on human health.

days per year

- over 45
- 35–45
- 30–35
- 25–30
- under 25

Coastal and offshore pollution

— bathing beaches heavily polluted by sewage, 1997

oil spills within UK waters, 1989–1998
tonnes

- over 5000
- 50–5000
- 0–50

Braer 86 248 tonnes
5 January 1993

ATLANTIC OCEAN

NORTH SEA

Sea Empress 72 000 tonnes
15 February 1996

English Channel

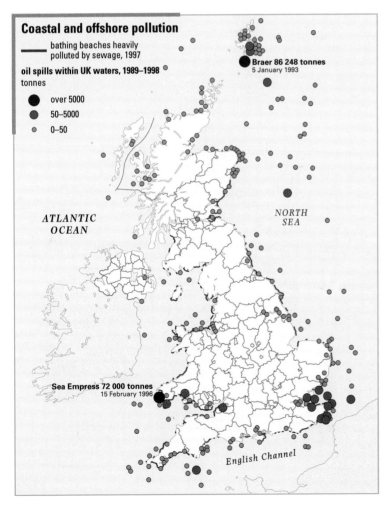

Light pollution

Image of the British Isles at night showing city lights. The patches of light in the North Sea are flares from oil rigs.

Transverse Mercator Projection

Scale 1: 7 500 000

Roads, airports, ferries

- motorway
- major road
- major ferry route

airports, 2000
passengers

- ⊕ over 10 million
- ✈ 1–10 million
- • 100–1 million

UK average distance travelled, 2000

	miles per person per year
walking	186
bicycle	38
car	5 355
motorcycle	30
local bus	199
rail	371
taxi	62
air and ferry	45

Average distance travelled, 1986–2000

percentage change per person per year, UK

walking -24%, bicycle -14%, car 41%, motorcycle -41%, local bus -23%, rail 27%, taxi 130%, air and ferry 105%

Rail network, ports

- principal railway
- • terminal or major junction
- built-up area

ports, 2000
cargo handled, tonnes

- over 40 million
- 10–40 million
- 50 000–10 million

land height
metres
200
0

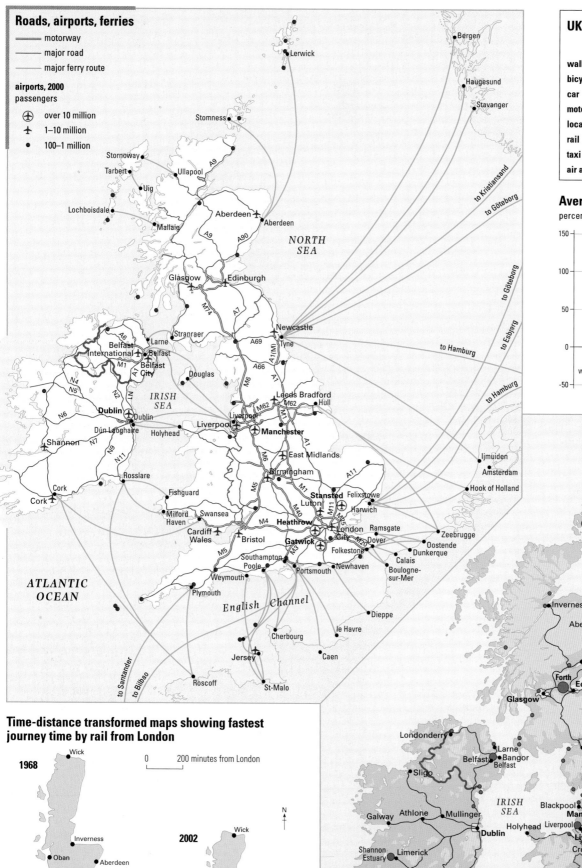
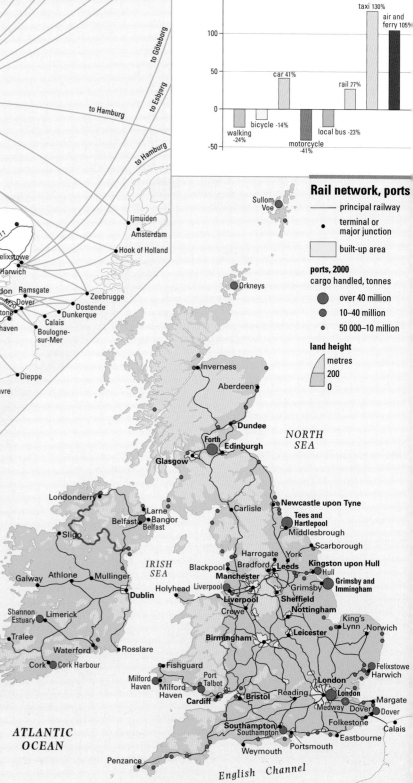

Time-distance transformed maps showing fastest journey time by rail from London

0 — 200 minutes from London

1968

2002

© Oxford University Press   Transverse Mercator Projection

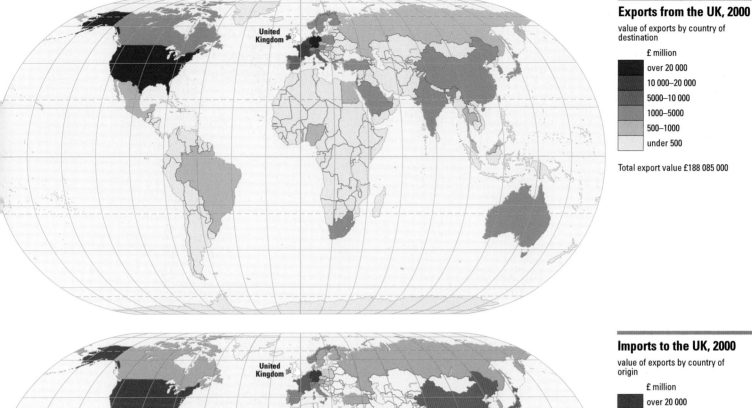

Exports from the UK, 2000

value of exports by country of destination

£ million

- over 20 000
- 10 000–20 000
- 5000–10 000
- 1000–5000
- 500–1000
- under 500

Total export value £188 085 000

Imports to the UK, 2000

value of exports by country of origin

£ million

- over 20 000
- 10 000–20 000
- 5000–10 000
- 1000–5000
- 500–1000
- under 500

Total import value £218 108 000

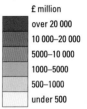

Major goods exported, 2000
percentage of total value of exports

- others 0.9%
- food and live animals (beverages and tobacco) 5.3%
- crude materials (except fuels) 1.3%
- fuels 9.1%
- chemicals 13.3%
- machinery and transport equipment 46.8%
- manufactured goods 23.3%

Major trading partners, 2000
percentage of total value of exports

- others 23.4%
- USA 15.6%
- Germany 12.1%
- France 9.9%
- Netherlands 8.1%
- Republic of Ireland 6.6%
- Belgium and Luxembourg 5.5%
- Italy 4.5%
- Spain 4.4%
- Sweden 2.2%
- China 2.2%
- Japan 2.0%
- Canada 1.9%
- Switzerland 1.6%

Major goods imported, 2000
percentage of total value of imports

- others 1.0%
- food and live animals (beverages and tobacco) 8.3%
- crude materials (except fuels) 2.7%
- fuels 4.6%
- chemicals 9.5%
- machinery and transport equipment 45.5%
- manufactured goods 28.4%

Major trading partners, 2000
percentage of total value of imports

- others 20.2%
- USA 13.1%
- Germany 12.7%
- France 8.4%
- Netherlands 6.9%
- Belgium and Luxembourg 5.3%
- China 4.9%
- Japan 4.7%
- Republic of Ireland 4.4%
- Italy 4.3%
- Spain 2.7%
- Norway 2.6%
- Switzerland 2.5%
- Sweden 2.3%
- Canada 1.8%
- Taiwan 1.6%
- South Korea 1.6%

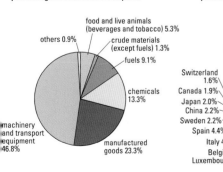
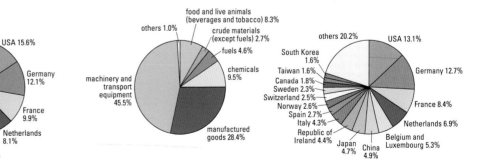

UK Balance of Trade, 1988–2000

the difference in value between exports and imports

	1988	1989	1990	1991	1992	1993	1994	1995	1996	1997	1998	1999	2000
Value of exports (£ million)	80 711	92 611	102 313	103 939	107 863	122 039	135 260	153 577	167 196	171 923	164 056	166 198	188 085
Value of imports (£ million)	102 264	117 335	121 020	114 162	120 913	135 358	146 351	165 600	180 918	184 265	185 869	193 722	218 108

Eckert IV Projection © Oxford University Press

boundaries
— international
--- disputed

physical features
river, lake
seasonal river
seasonal lake
marsh
salt lake
salt pan
ice cap
sand dunes

sea ice
unnavigable
pack ice
— autumn minimum
— spring maximum

land height and sea depth

metres
5000
3000
2000
1000
500
300
200
100
0

sea level

metres
200
3000
4000
5000
6000

spot height in metres
sea depth in metres

0 220 440 660 880 1100 km

Scale 1: 50 000 000

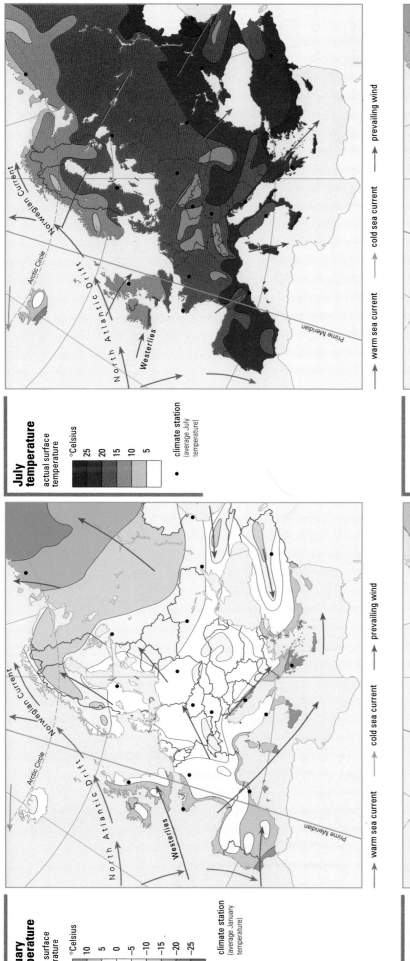

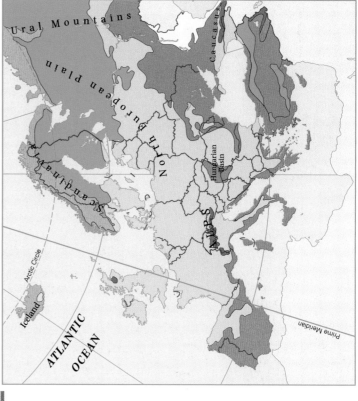

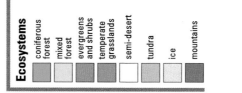

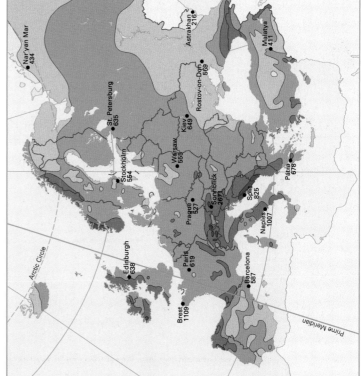

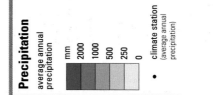

July temperature

actual surface temperature

°Celsius
25
20
15
10
5

● climate station (average July temperature)

Ecosystems

- coniferous forest
- mixed forest
- evergreens and shrubs
- temperate grasslands
- semi-desert
- tundra
- ice
- mountains

January temperature

actual surface temperature

°Celsius
10
5
0
-5
-10
-15
-20
-25

● climate station (average January temperature)

Precipitation

average annual precipitation

mm
2000
1000
500
250
0

● climate station (average annual precipitation)

prevailing wind

cold sea current

warm sea current

Norwegian Current

North Atlantic Drift

Westerlies

Arctic Circle

Prime Meridian

Ural Mountains

North European Plain

Scandinavia

C a u c a s u s

Hungarian Basin

A L P S

Iceland

ATLANTIC OCEAN

Nar'yan Mar 434

Astrakhan 216

Malaya 411

St. Petersburg 635

Rostov-on-Don 569

Kiev 649

Warsaw 555

Stockholm 564

Pátra 678

Sombrick 2671

Split 825

Prague 527

Naples 1007

Edinburgh 638

Paris 619

Barcelona 587

Brest 1109

© Oxford University Press   Conical Orthomorphic Projection

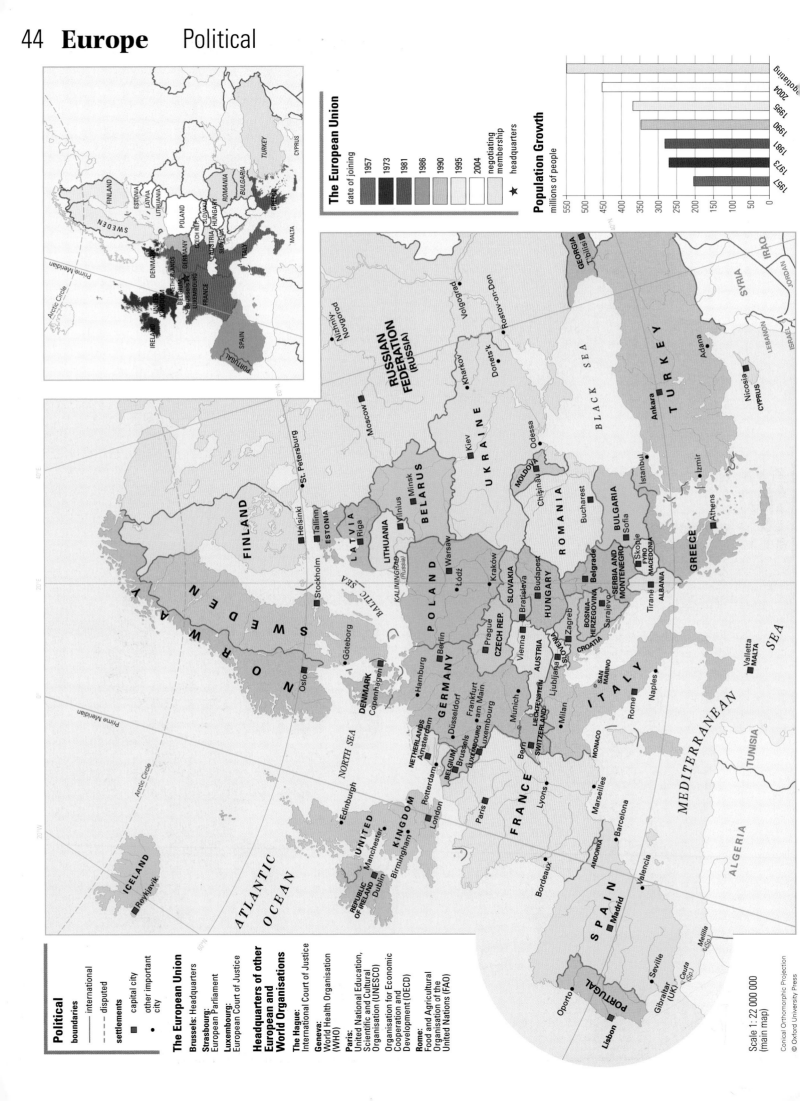

Political

boundaries
— international
-- disputed

settlements
■ capital city
• other important city

The European Union
Brussels: Headquarters
Strasbourg: European Parliament
Luxembourg: European Court of Justice

Headquarters of other European and World Organisations
The Hague: International Court of Justice
Geneva: World Health Organisation (WHO)
Paris: United National Education, Scientific and Cultural Organisation (UNESCO)
Organisation for Economic Cooperation and Development (OECD)
Rome: Food and Agricultural Organisation of the United Nations (FAO)

The European Union
date of joining
1957
1973
1981
1986
1990
1995
2004
negotiating membership
★ headquarters

Population Growth
millions of people
550 500 450 400 350 300 250 200 150 100 50 0

Scale 1: 22 000 000 (main map)
Conical Orthomorphic Projection
© Oxford University Press

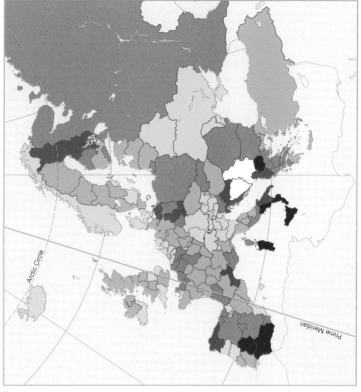

European Union budget, 2000

net contributions to and receipts from (in pounds)

contributions

over 5 billion
1–5 billion
0–1 billion

receipts

0–1 billion
1–5 billion

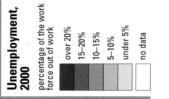

Unemployment, 2000

percentage of the work force out of work

over 20%
15–20%
10–15%
5–10%
under 5%
no data

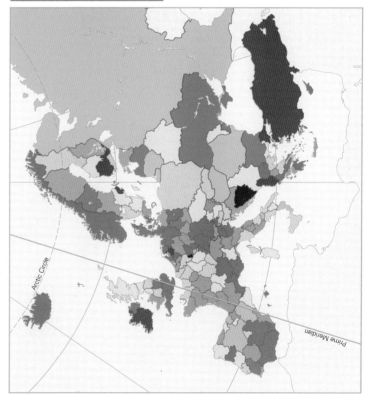

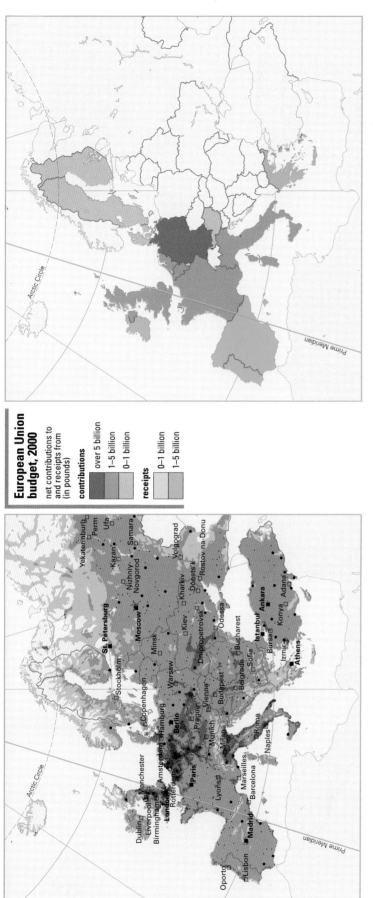

Population density

people per square kilometre

over 200
100–200
10–100
1–10
under 1

Major cities

population in millions

■ over 3
□ 1–3
● 0.5–1
· 0.1–0.5

Yekaterinburg
Perm
Ufa
Samara
Kazan
Nizhniy Novgorod
Volgograd
Rostov-na-Donu
Kharkiv
Donets'k
Kiev
Dnipropetrovsk
Odessa
Bucharest
Sofia
Belgrade
Budapest
Vienna
Warsaw
Minsk
Moscow
St. Petersburg
Stockholm
Copenhagen
Hamburg
Berlin
Prague
Munich
Milan
Rome
Naples
Athens
Bursa
Izmir
Istanbul
Ankara
Konya
Adana
Dublin
Liverpool
Manchester
Birmingham
Amsterdam
Rotterdam
London
Paris
Lyons
Marseilles
Barcelona
Madrid
Lisbon
Oporto

Population change, 1995–2000

percentage change in the number of people

increase

over 8%
4–8%
2–4%
1–2%
0–1%

decrease

0–1%
1–2%
2–4%
over 4%

Scale 1: 22 000 000

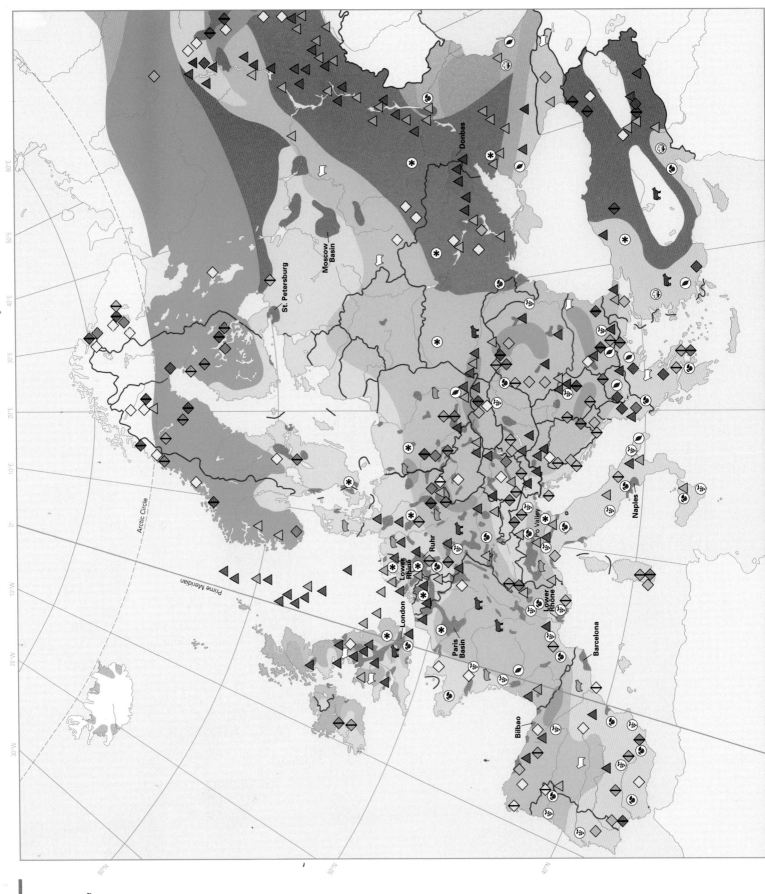

St. Petersburg

Moscow
Basin

Donbas

Ruhr

Lower
Rhine

London

Paris
Basin

Po Valley

Lower
Rhône

Barcelona

Bilbao

Naples

Arctic Circle

Prime Meridian

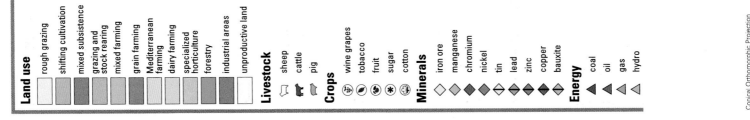

Land use

- rough grazing
- shifting cultivation
- mixed subsistence
- grazing and stock rearing
- mixed farming
- grain farming
- Mediterranean farming
- dairy farming
- specialized horticulture
- forestry
- industrial areas
- unproductive land

Livestock

- sheep
- cattle
- pig

Crops

- wine grapes
- tobacco
- fruit
- sugar
- cotton

Minerals

- iron ore
- manganese
- chromium
- nickel
- tin
- lead
- zinc
- copper
- bauxite

Energy

- coal
- oil
- gas
- hydro

Conical Orthomorphic Projection

© Oxford University Press

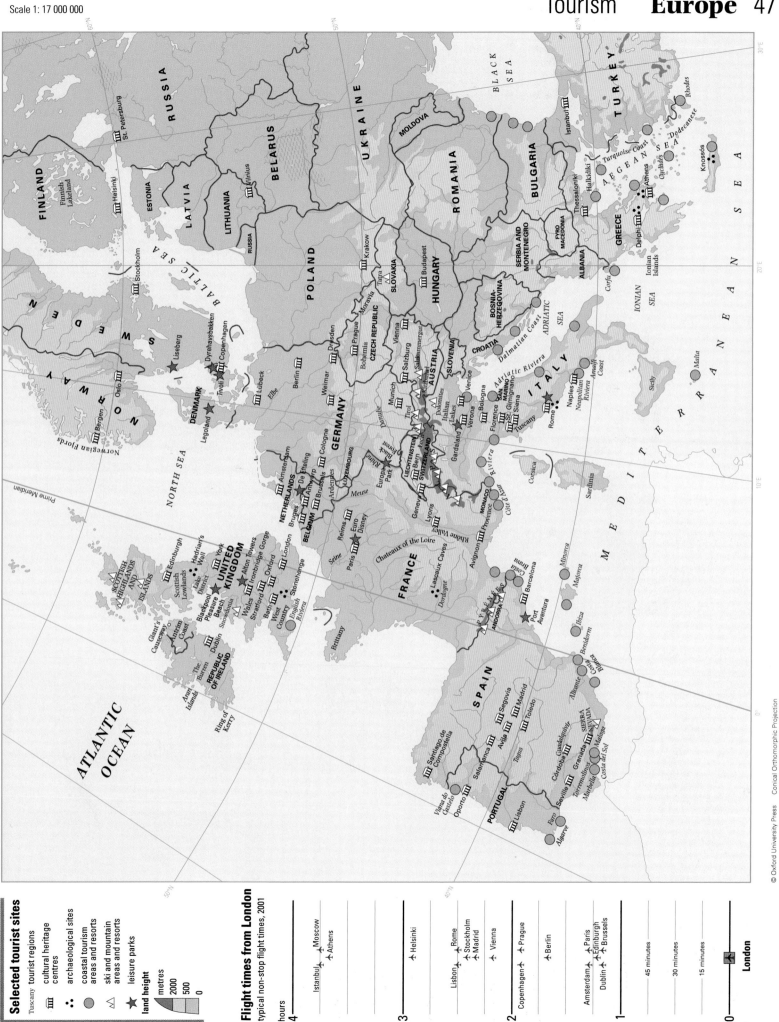

Scale 1: 2 500 000

0   25   50   75   100   125 km

Conical Orthomorphic Projection

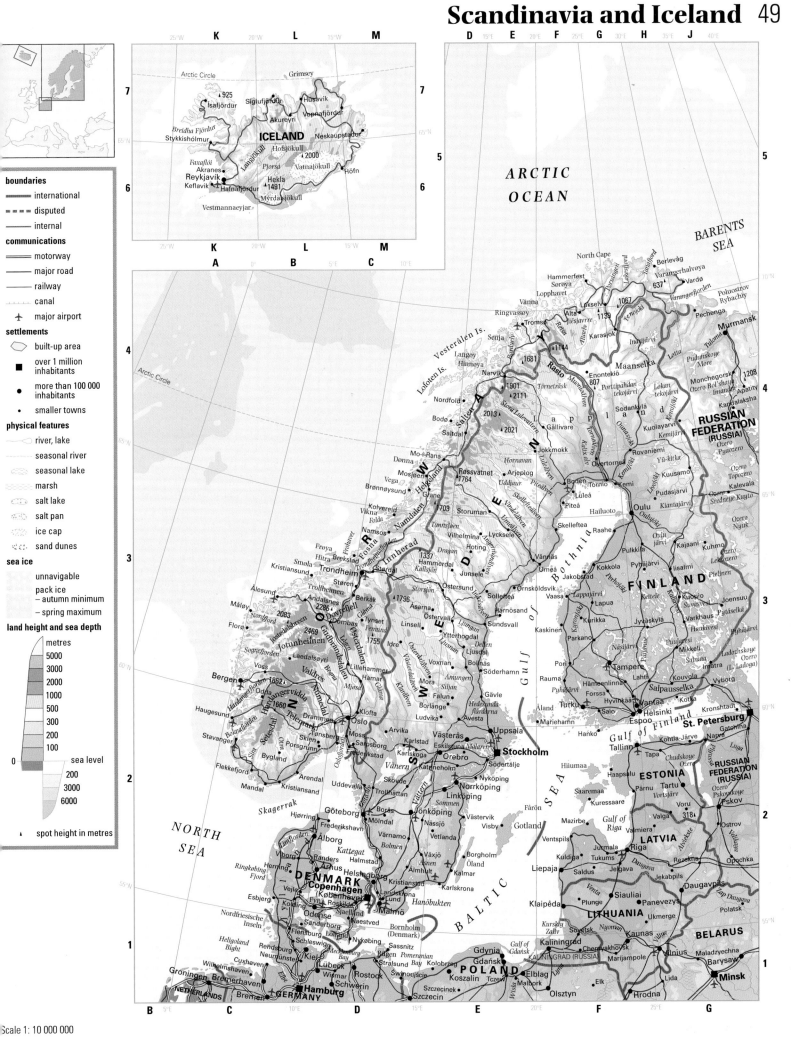

boundaries
— international
--- disputed
— internal

communications
— motorway
— major road
— railway
⊥⊥⊥ canal
✈ major airport

settlements
⬡ built-up area
■ over 1 million inhabitants
● more than 100 000 inhabitants
• smaller towns

physical features
river, lake
seasonal river
seasonal lake
marsh
salt lake
salt pan
ice cap
sand dunes

sea ice
unnavigable
pack ice
– autumn minimum
– spring maximum

land height and sea depth
metres
5000
3000
2000
1000
500
300
200
100
0   sea level
200
3000
6000

▲ spot height in metres

Scale 1: 10 000 000

0   100   200   300   400   500 km

Conical Orthomorphic Projection
© Oxford University Press

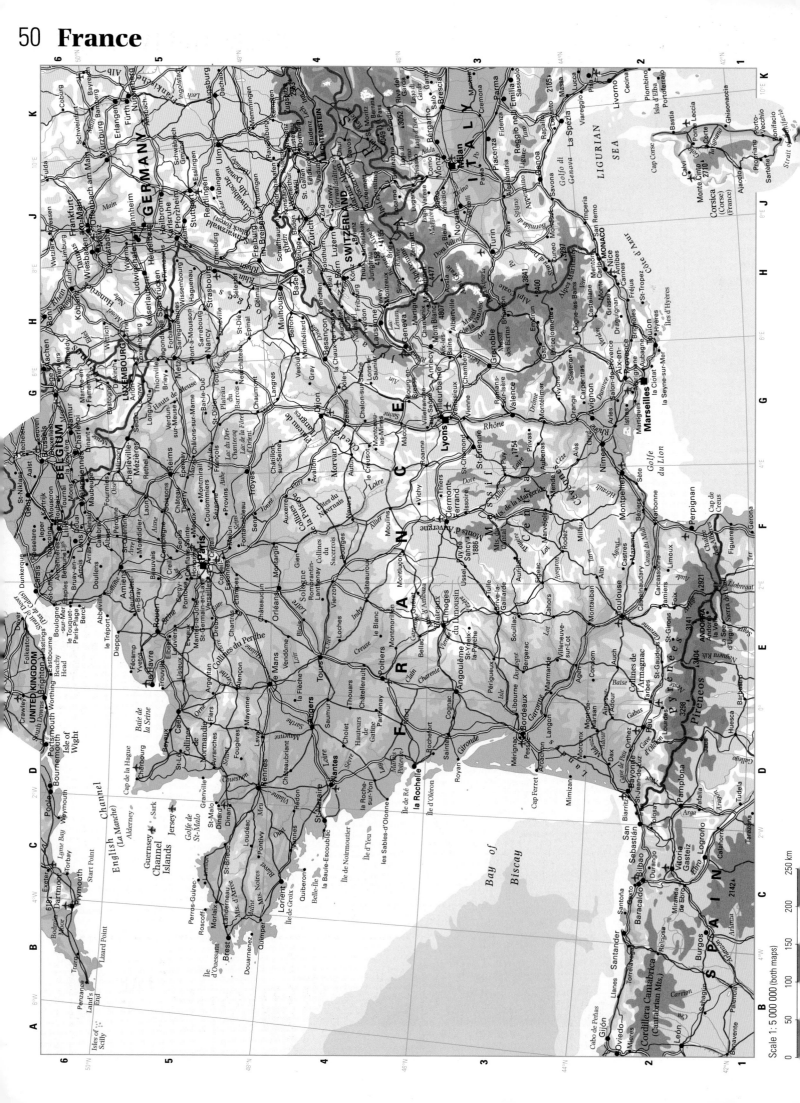

Scale 1 : 5 000 000 (both maps)

076472

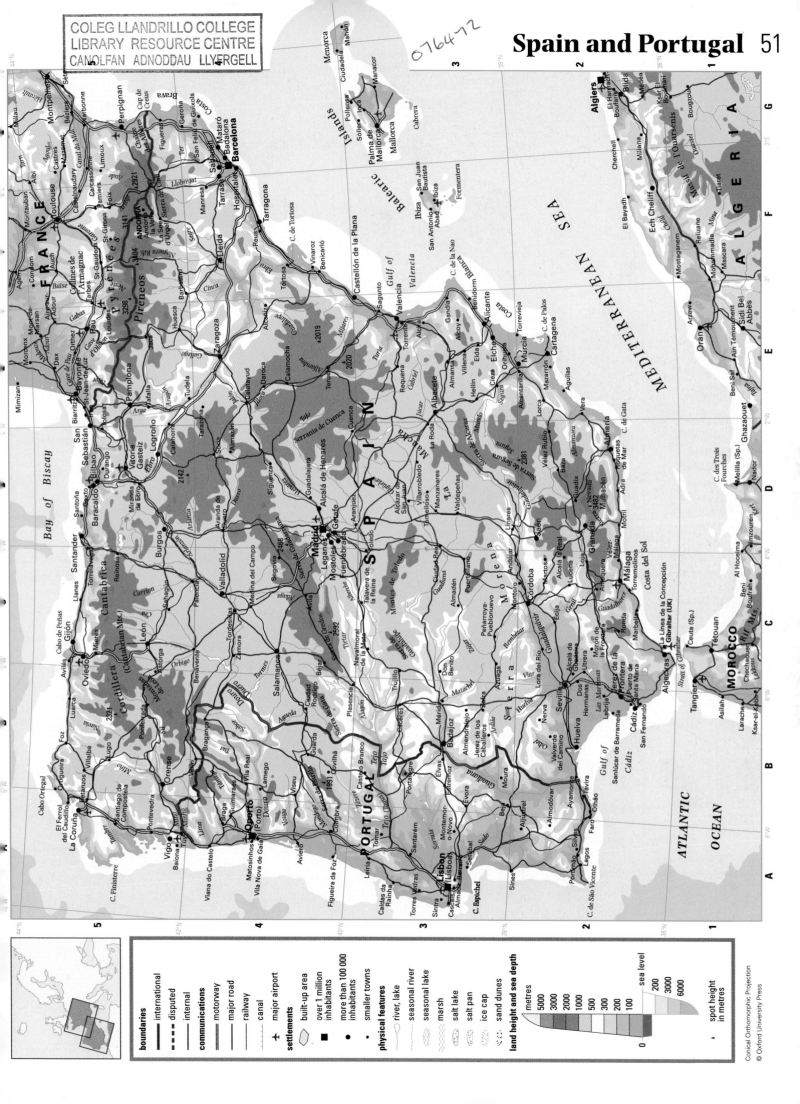

Conical Orthomorphic Projection
© Oxford University Press

boundaries
— international
--- disputed
— internal

communications
═ motorway
— major road
— railway
— canal
✦ major airport

settlements
⬡ built-up area
■ over 1 million inhabitants
● more than 100 000 inhabitants
• smaller towns

physical features
river, lake
seasonal river
seasonal lake
marsh
salt lake
salt pan
ice cap
sand dunes

land height and sea depth
metres
5000
3000
2000
1000
500
300
200
100
sea level
200
3000
6000

▲ spot height in metres

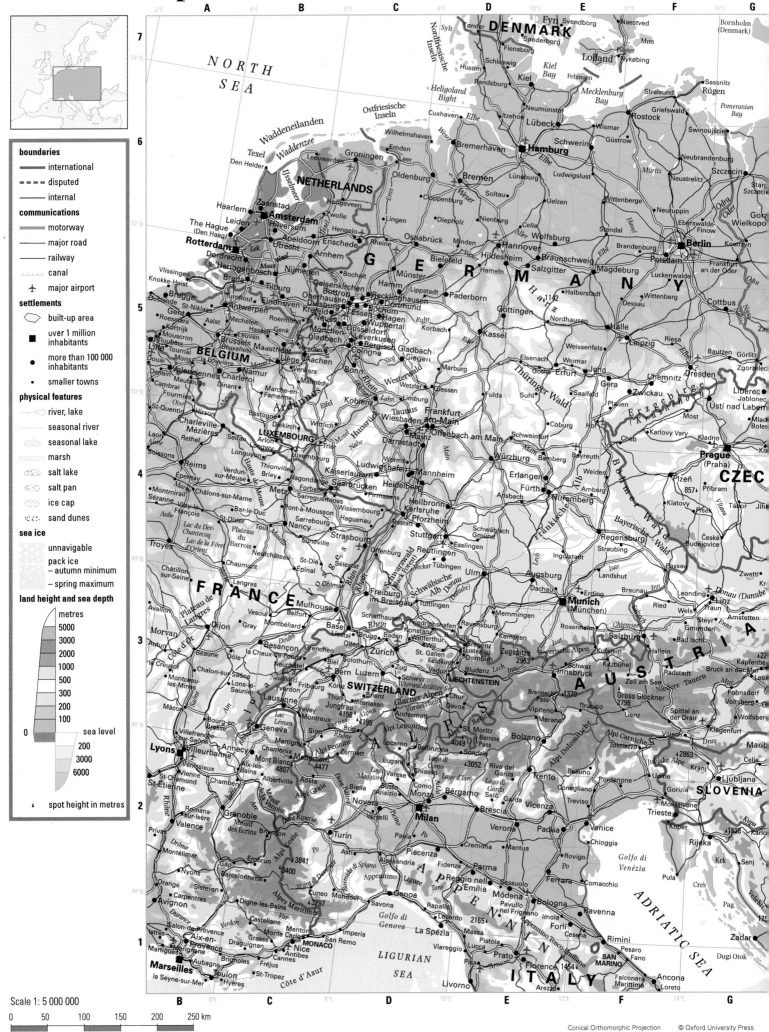

Scale 1 : 5 000 000

0   50   100   150   200   250 km

Conical Orthomorphic Projection

© Oxford University Press

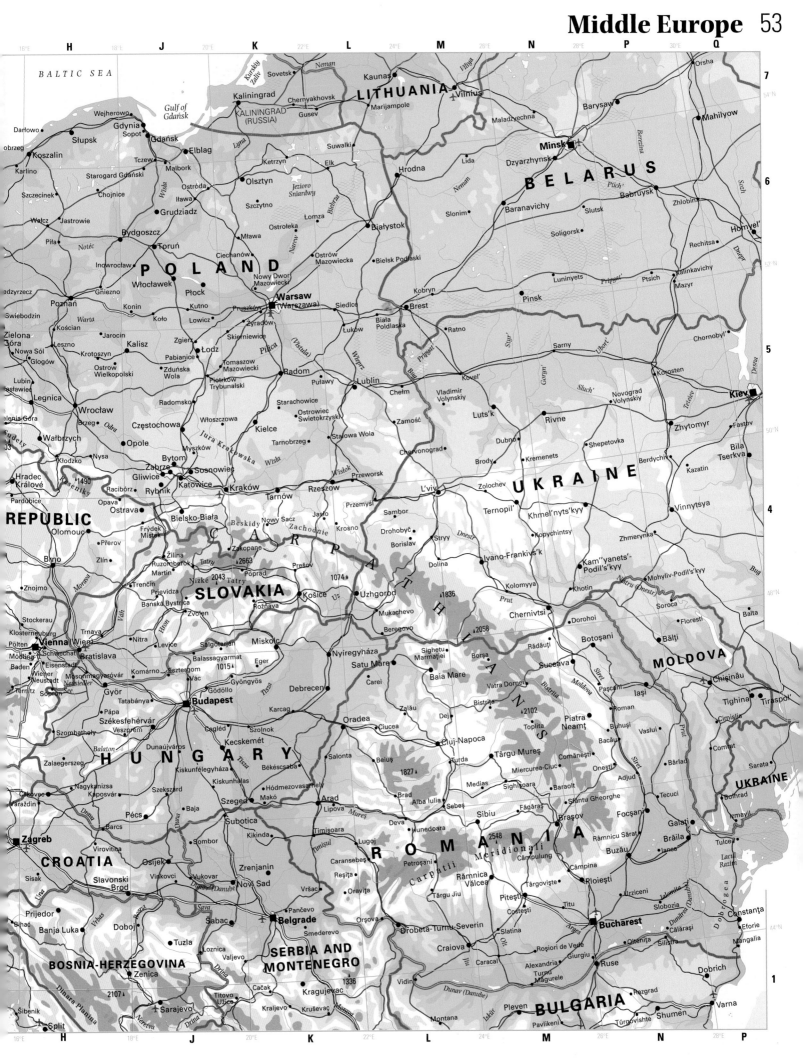

BALTIC SEA

Gulf of Gdańsk

KALININGRAD (RUSSIA)

LITHUANIA

BELARUS

POLAND

CZECH REPUBLIC

SLOVAKIA

HUNGARY

CROATIA

BOSNIA-HERZEGOVINA

SERBIA AND MONTENEGRO

UKRAINE

MOLDOVA

ROMANIA

BULGARIA

Warsaw (Warszawa)

Minsk

Kiev

Vienna (Wien)

Budapest

Bratislava

Zagreb

Belgrade

Bucharest

Chişinău

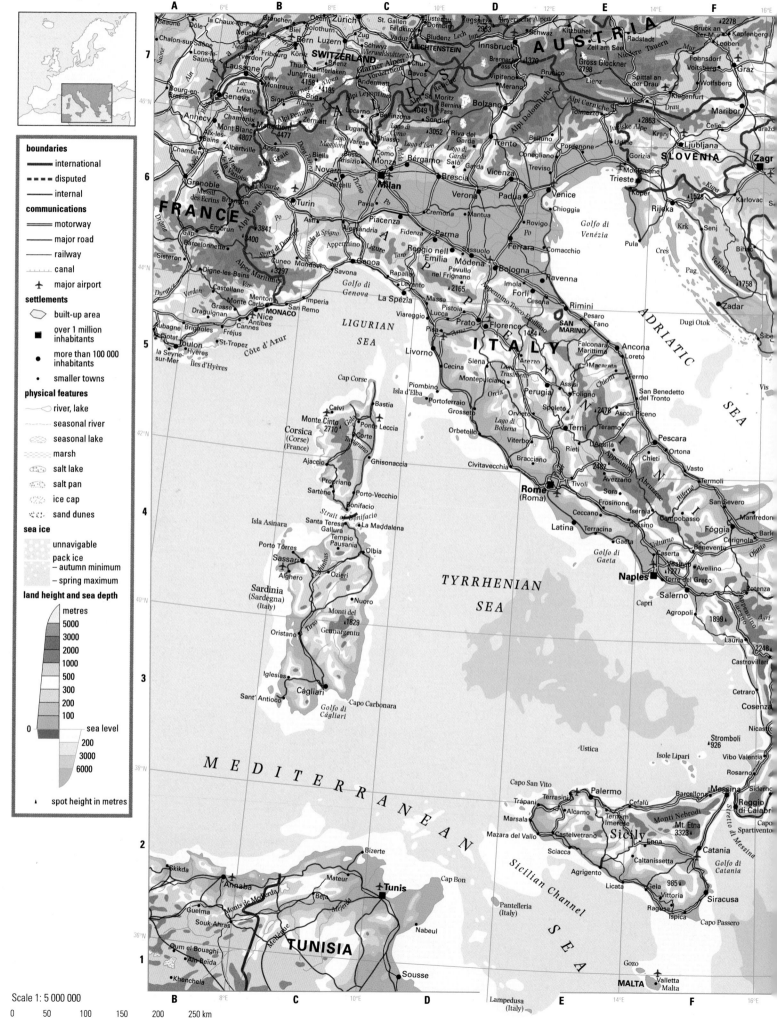

boundaries
—— international
- - - disputed
—— internal

communications
═══ motorway
—— major road
—— railway
┼┼┼ canal
✈ major airport

settlements
⬡ built-up area
■ over 1 million inhabitants
● more than 100 000 inhabitants
• smaller towns

physical features
river, lake
seasonal river
seasonal lake
marsh
salt lake
salt pan
ice cap
sand dunes

sea ice
unnavigable
pack ice
– autumn minimum
– spring maximum

land height and sea depth
metres
5000
3000
2000
1000
500
300
200
100
0 sea level
200
3000
6000
▲ spot height in metres

Scale 1: 5 000 000

0 50 100 150 200 250 km

Conical Orthomorphic Projection

© Oxford University Press

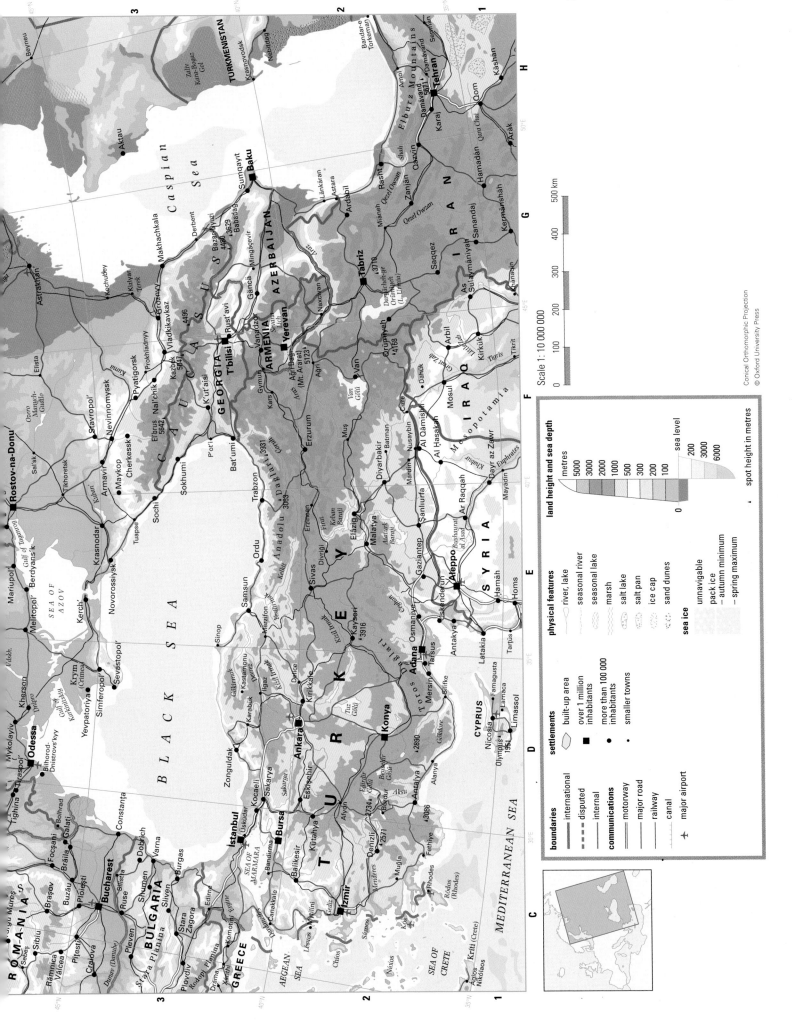

Scale 1: 10 000 000

0   100   200   300   400   500 km

Conical Orthomorphic Projection
© Oxford University Press

boundaries
international
disputed
internal

communications
motorway
major road
railway
canal
✈ major airport

settlements
built-up area
◼ over 1 million inhabitants
● more than 100 000 inhabitants
• smaller towns

physical features
river, lake
seasonal river
seasonal lake
marsh
salt lake
salt pan
ice cap
sand dunes

sea ice
unnavigable
pack ice
– autumn minimum
– spring maximum

land height and sea depth
metres
5000
3000
2000
1000
500
300
200
100
sea level
200
3000
6000
▴ spot height in metres

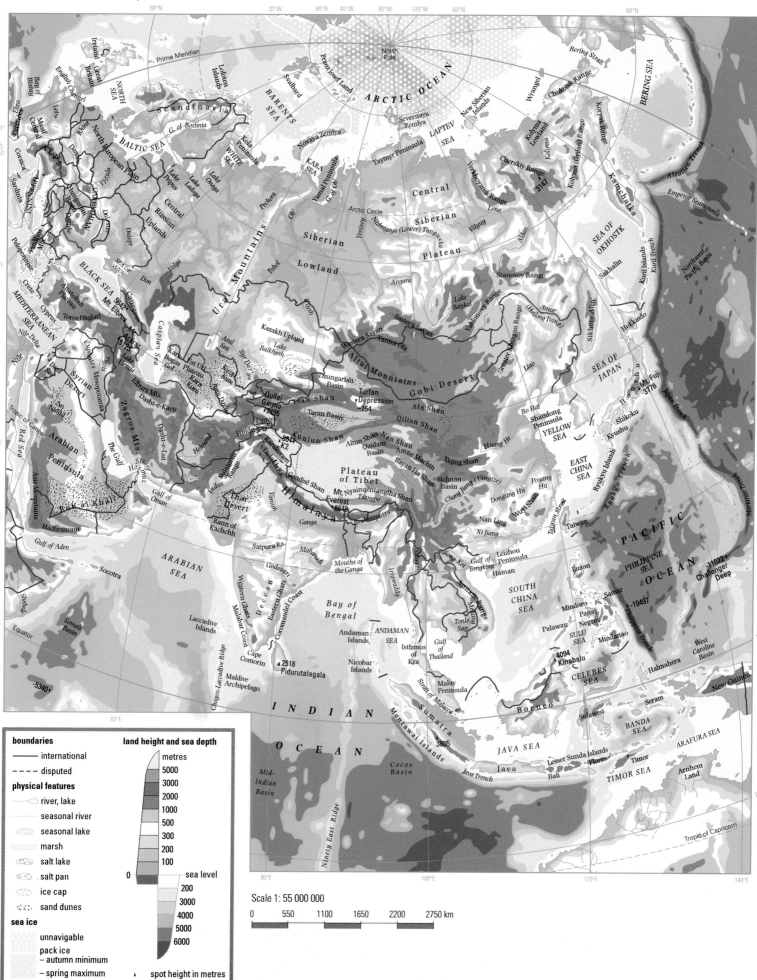

boundaries
— international
– – – disputed

physical features
~ river, lake
‑ ‑ ‑ seasonal river
seasonal lake
marsh
salt lake
salt pan
ice cap
sand dunes

sea ice
unnavigable
pack ice
– autumn minimum
– spring maximum

land height and sea depth

metres
5000
3000
2000
1000
500
300
200
100
0 — sea level
200
3000
4000
5000
6000

▲ spot height in metres
▼ sea depth in metres

Scale 1: 55 000 000

0   550   1100   1650   2200   2750 km

Zenithal equal Area Projection

© Oxford University Press

Scale 1: 60 000 000

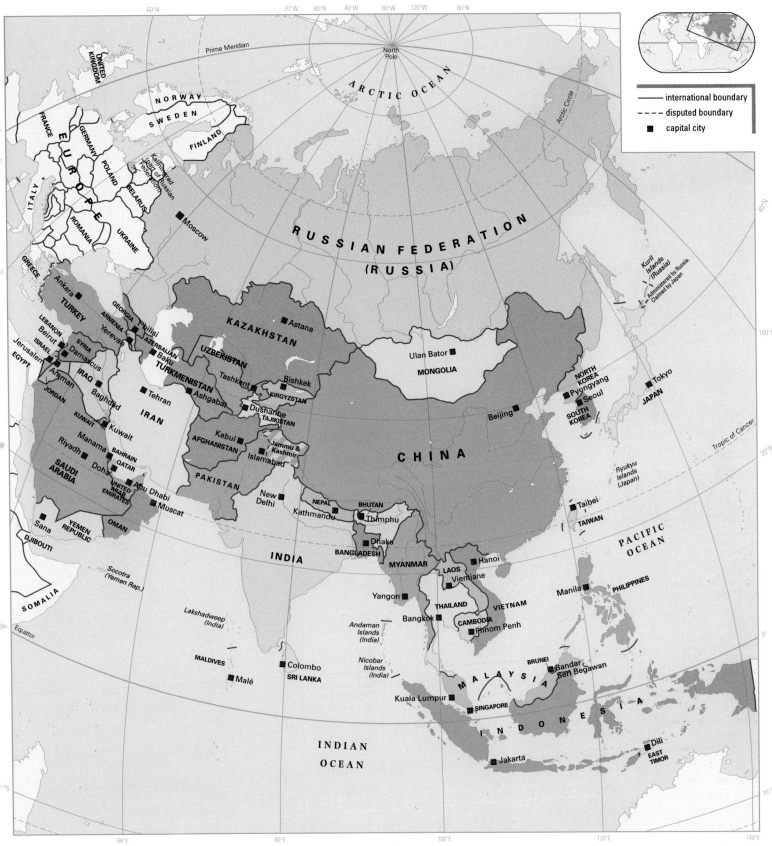

© Oxford University Press Zenithal Equal Area Projection

Asian urban and rural population, 2000

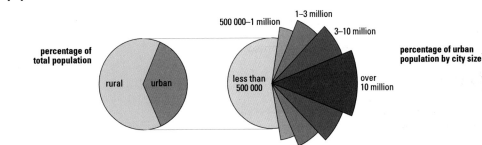

percentage of
total population

rural   urban

500 000–1 million

1–3 million

3–10 million

less than
500 000

over
10 million

percentage of urban
population by city size

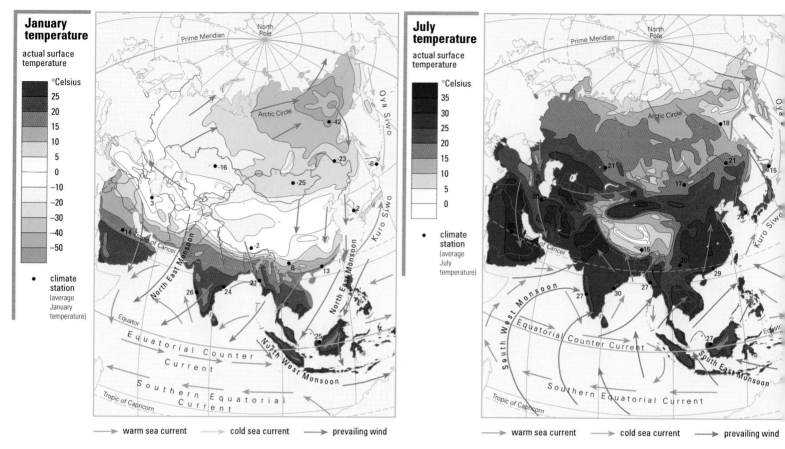

January temperature

actual surface temperature

°Celsius
25
20
15
10
5
0
−10
−20
−30
−40
−50

• climate station (average January temperature)

-42
-16
-23
-6
-25
3
-2
2
14
8
13
-2
21
26
24
25

Tropic of Cancer
North East Monsoon
North East Monsoon
Kuro Siwo
Oya Siwo
Arctic Circle
North Pole
Prime Meridian
Equator
Equatorial Counter Current
North West Monsoon
Southern Equatorial Current
Tropic of Capricorn

→ warm sea current   → cold sea current   → prevailing wind

July temperature

actual surface temperature

°Celsius
35
30
25
20
15
10
5
0

• climate station (average July temperature)

18
21
21
15
17
39
15
20
29
27
30
27
27

South West Monsoon
South East Monsoon
Equatorial Counter Current
Southern Equatorial Current
Kuro Siwo
Oya
Arctic Circle
North Pole
Prime Meridian
Tropic of Cancer
Equator
Tropic of Capricorn

→ warm sea current   → cold sea current   → prevailing wind

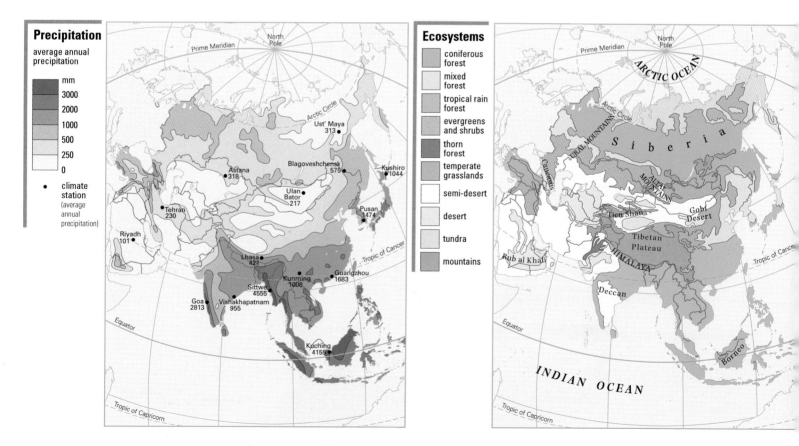

Precipitation

average annual precipitation

mm
3000
2000
1000
500
250
0

• climate station (average annual precipitation)

Ust' Maya 313
Astana 318
Blagoveshchensk 575
Kushiro 1044
Ulan Bator 217
Pusan 1474
Tehran 230
Riyadh 101
Lhasa 421
Guangzhou 1683
Kunming 1008
Sittwe 4555
Goa 2813
Vishakhapatnam 955
Kuching 4155

Prime Meridian
North Pole
Arctic Circle
Tropic of Cancer
Equator
Tropic of Capricorn

Ecosystems

coniferous forest
mixed forest
tropical rain forest
evergreens and shrubs
thorn forest
temperate grasslands
semi-desert
desert
tundra
mountains

ARCTIC OCEAN
Siberia
URAL MOUNTAINS
Caucasus
ALTAI MOUNTAINS
Tien Shan
Gobi Desert
Tibetan Plateau
HIMALAYA
Rub al Khali
Deccan
Borneo
INDIAN OCEAN

Prime Meridian
North Pole
Arctic Circle
Tropic of Cancer
Equator
Tropic of Capricorn

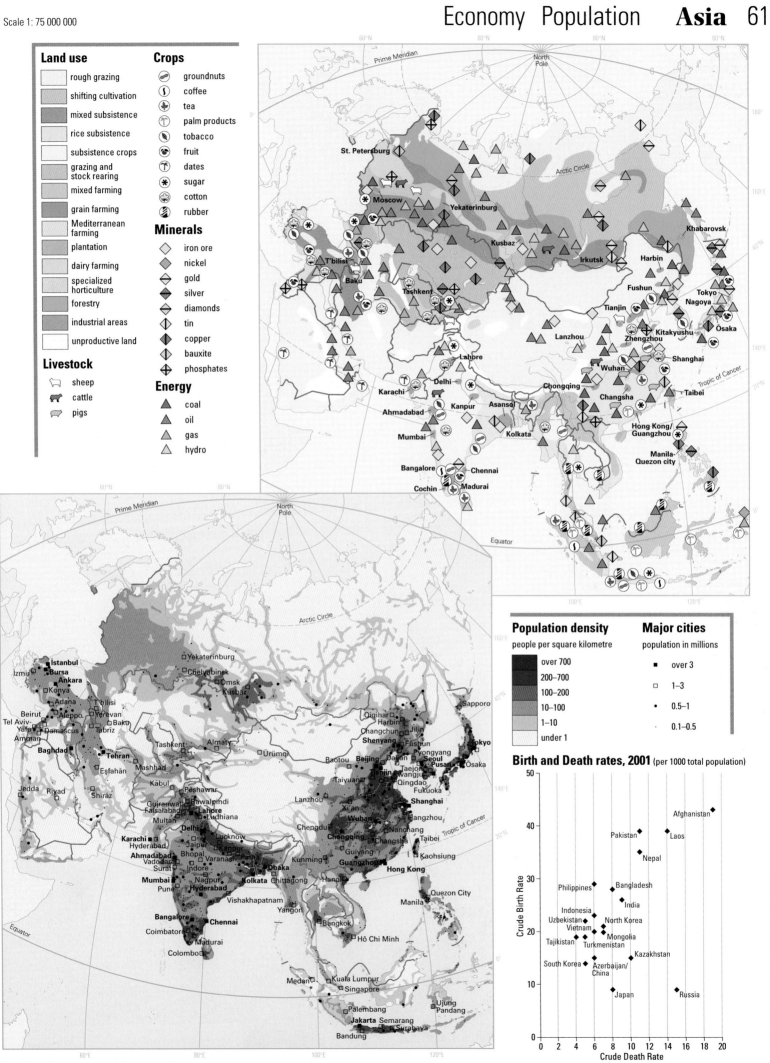

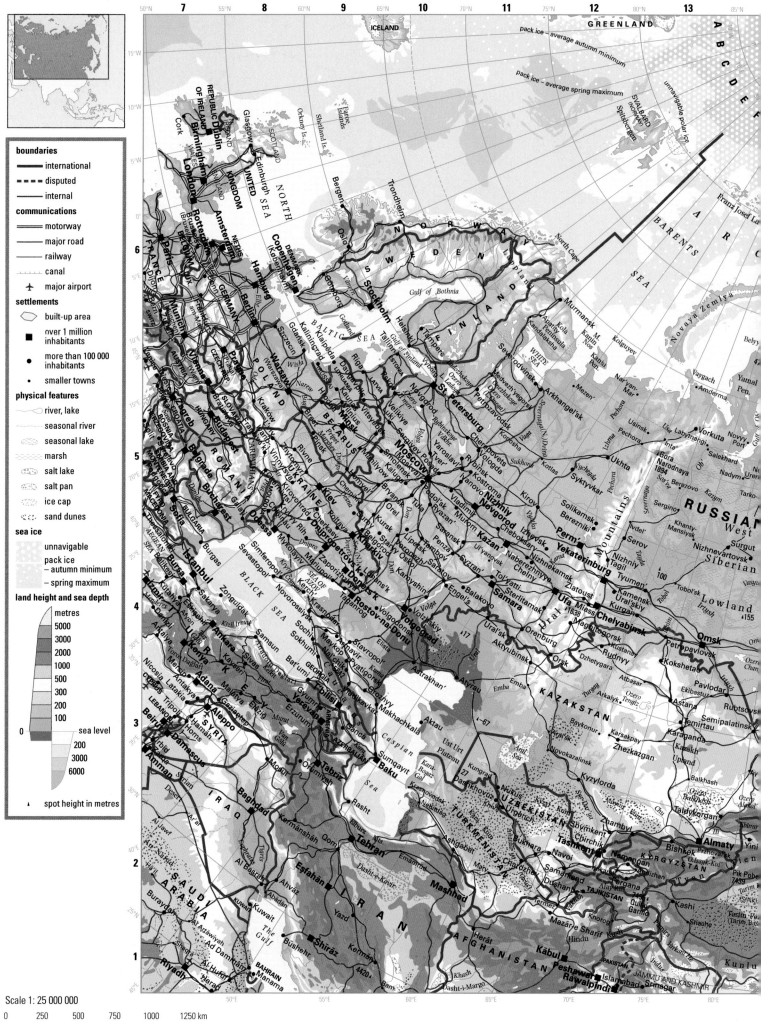

boundaries
— international
--- disputed
— internal

communications
═ motorway
— major road
— railway
⊥⊥⊥ canal
✈ major airport

settlements
⬡ built-up area
■ over 1 million inhabitants
● more than 100 000 inhabitants
• smaller towns

physical features
river, lake
seasonal river
seasonal lake
marsh
salt lake
salt pan
ice cap
sand dunes

sea ice
unnavigable
pack ice
– autumn minimum
– spring maximum

land height and sea depth
metres
5000
3000
2000
1000
500
300
200
100
0 sea level
200
3000
6000

▲ spot height in metres

Scale 1: 25 000 000

0 250 500 750 1000 1250 km

Conical Orthomorphic Projection

© Oxford University Press

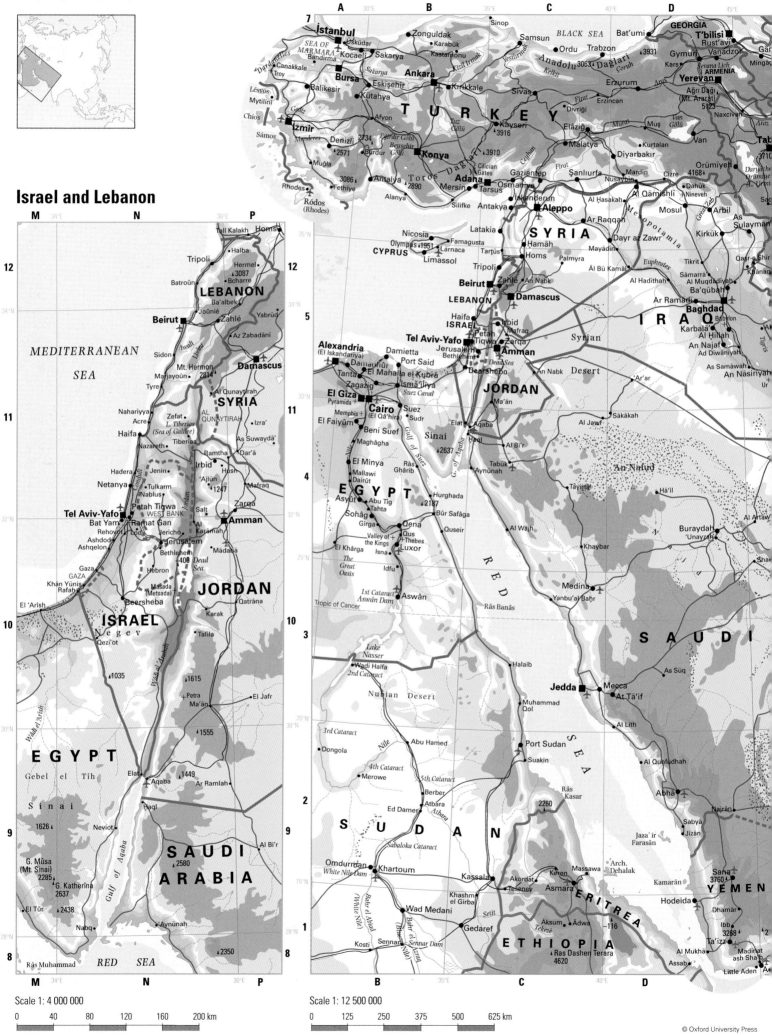

Israel and Lebanon

Scale 1 : 4 000 000

| 0 | 40 | 80 | 120 | 160 | 200 km |

Scale 1 : 12 500 000

| 0 | 125 | 250 | 375 | 500 | 625 km |

© Oxford University Press

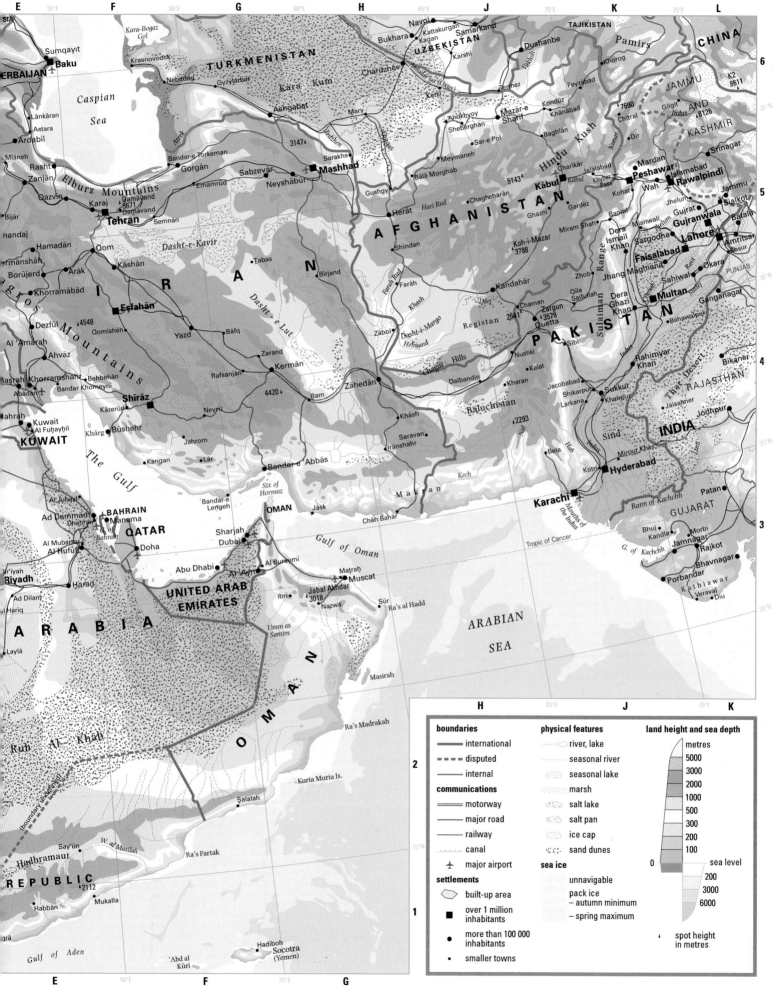

Middle East 65

boundaries
- international
- disputed
- internal

communications
- motorway
- major road
- railway
- canal
- ✈ major airport

settlements
- built-up area
- ■ over 1 million inhabitants
- ● more than 100 000 inhabitants
- • smaller towns

physical features
- river, lake
- seasonal river
- seasonal lake
- marsh
- salt lake
- salt pan
- ice cap
- sand dunes

sea ice
- unnavigable

pack ice
- – autumn minimum
- – spring maximum

land height and sea depth

metres
5000
3000
2000
1000
500
300
200
100
0 sea level
200
3000
6000

▲ spot height in metres

© Oxford University Press   Conical Orthomorphic projection

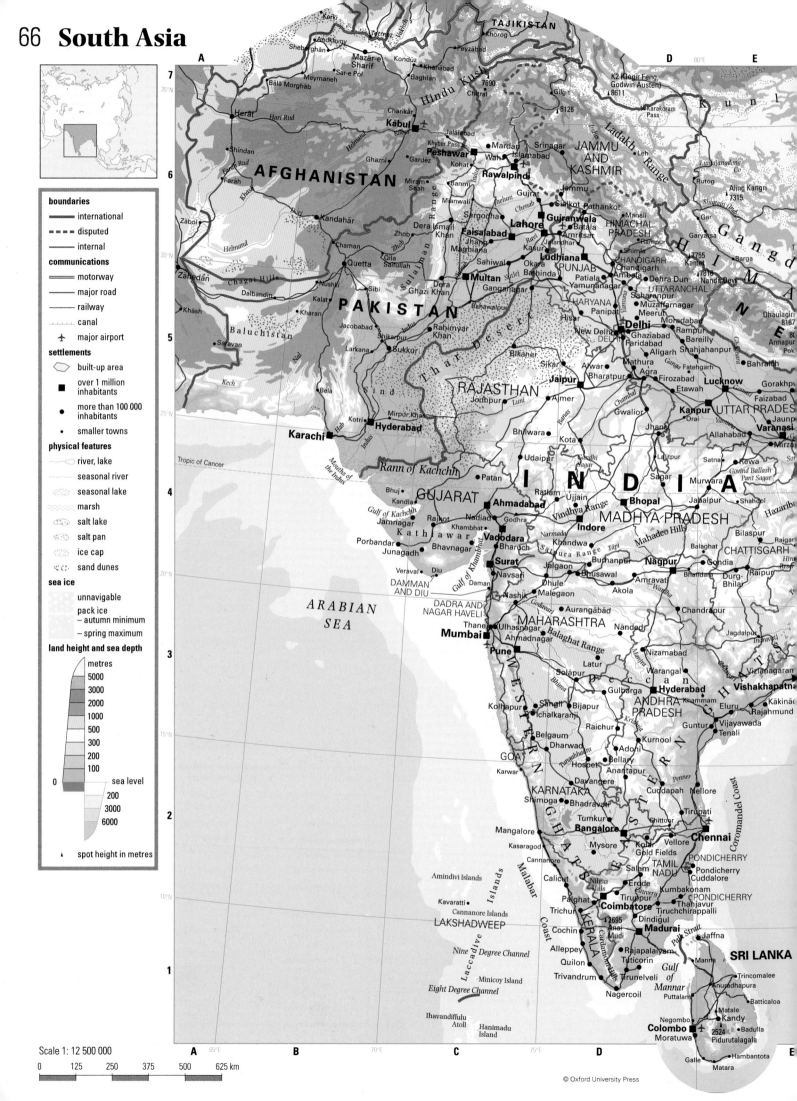

boundaries
— international
-- disputed
— internal

communications
═ motorway
— major road
— railway
┼┼┼ canal
✈ major airport

settlements
⬡ built-up area
■ over 1 million inhabitants
● more than 100 000 inhabitants
• smaller towns

physical features
⌒ river, lake
-- seasonal river
⬭ seasonal lake
marsh
salt lake
salt pan
ice cap
sand dunes

sea ice
unnavigable
pack ice
– autumn minimum
– spring maximum

land height and sea depth
metres
5000
3000
2000
1000
500
300
200
100
0   sea level
200
3000
6000

▲ spot height in metres

Scale 1: 12 500 000

0   125   250   375   500   625 km

© Oxford University Press

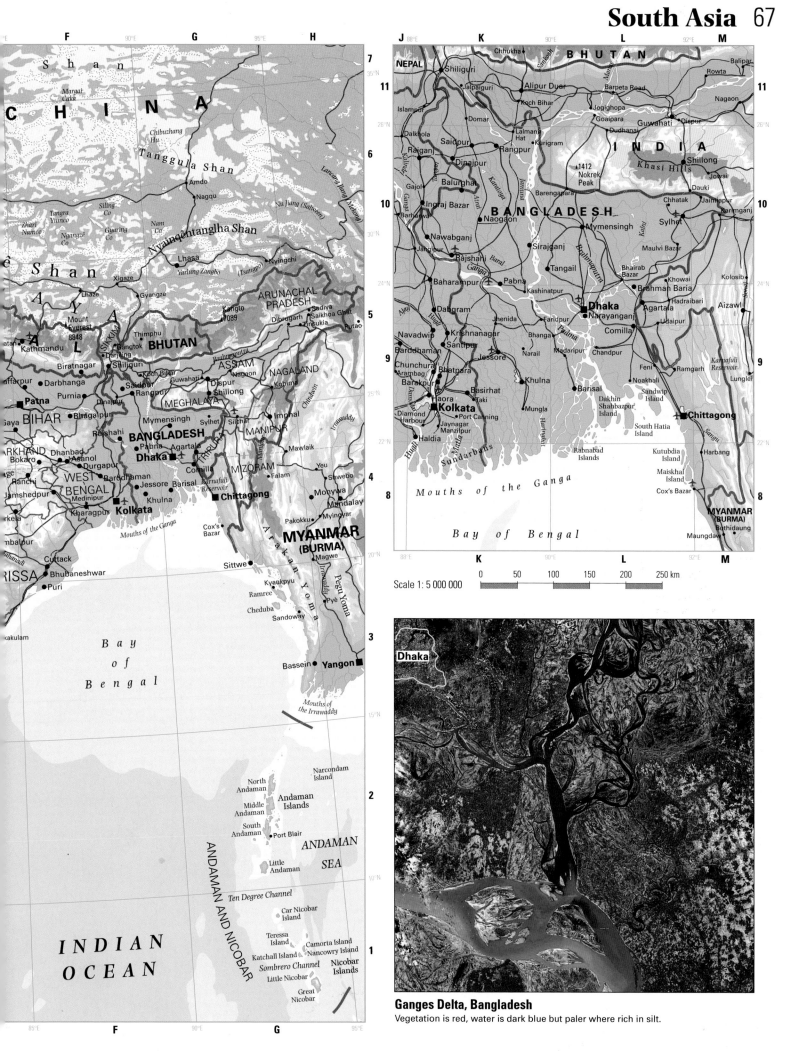

Scale 1: 5 000 000

| 0 | 50 | 100 | 150 | 200 | 250 km |

Ganges Delta, Bangladesh
Vegetation is red, water is dark blue but paler where rich in silt.

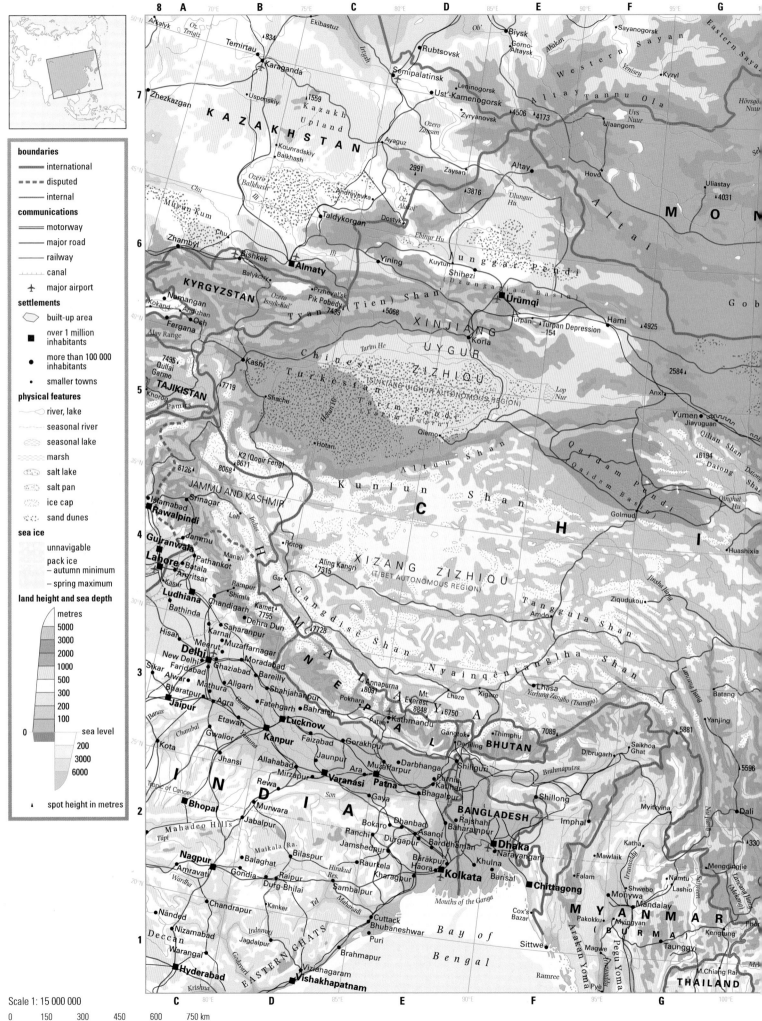

boundaries
——— international
- - - disputed
——— internal

communications
═══ motorway
——— major road
——— railway
-+-+- canal
✈ major airport

settlements
⬠ built-up area
■ over 1 million inhabitants
● more than 100 000 inhabitants
• smaller towns

physical features
river, lake
seasonal river
seasonal lake
marsh
salt lake
salt pan
ice cap
sand dunes

sea ice
unnavigable
pack ice
– autumn minimum
– spring maximum

land height and sea depth
metres
5000
3000
2000
1000
500
300
200
100
0 sea level
200
3000
6000
▲ spot height in metres

Scale 1: 15 000 000

0 150 300 450 600 750 km

Conical Orthomorphic Projection   © Oxford University Press

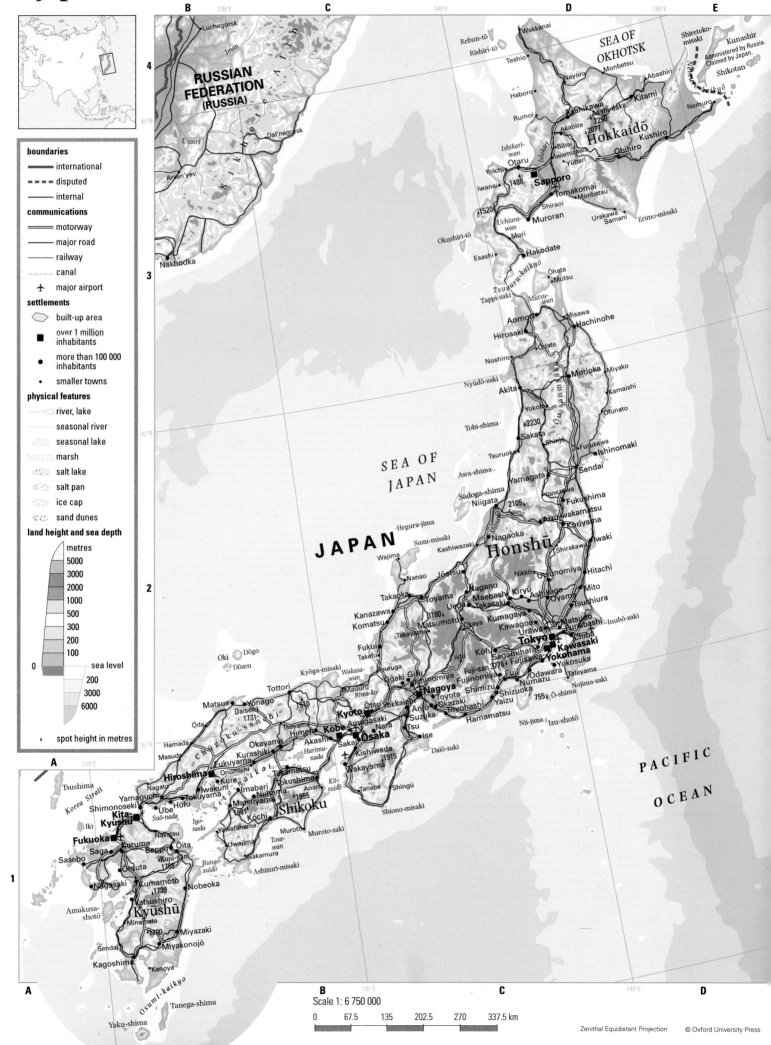

boundaries
— international
---- disputed
— internal

communications
═══ motorway
── major road
── railway
┼┼┼ canal
✈ major airport

settlements
⬡ built-up area
■ over 1 million inhabitants
● more than 100 000 inhabitants
• smaller towns

physical features
⟋⟋ river, lake
seasonal river
seasonal lake
marsh
salt lake
salt pan
ice cap
sand dunes

land height and sea depth

metres
5000
3000
2000
1000
500
300
200
100
0 — sea level
200
3000
6000

▲ spot height in metres

RUSSIAN FEDERATION (RUSSIA)

SEA OF OKHOTSK

Hokkaidō

SEA OF JAPAN

JAPAN

Honshū

Shikoku

Kyūshū

PACIFIC OCEAN

Tōkyō
Kawasaki
Yokohama
Nagoya
Kyōto
Kōbe
Ōsaka
Hiroshima
Kita-Kyūshū
Fukuoka
Sapporo

Scale 1: 6 750 000

0   67.5   135   202.5   270   337.5 km

Zenithal Equidistant Projection   © Oxford University Press

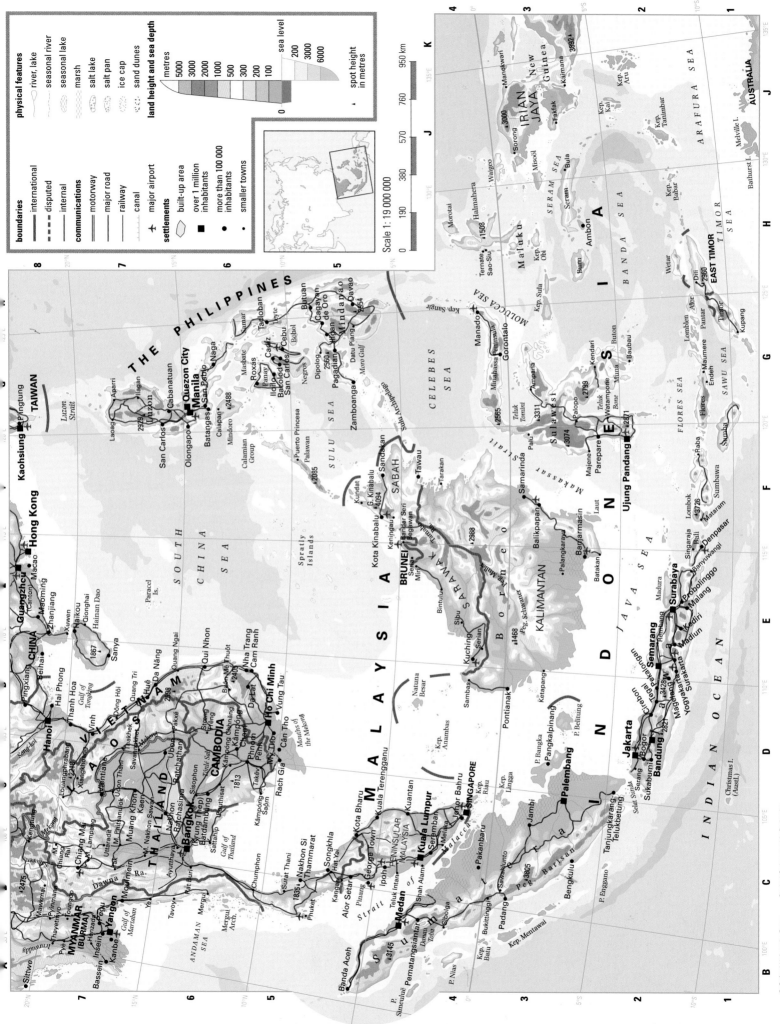

Conical Orthomorphic Projection

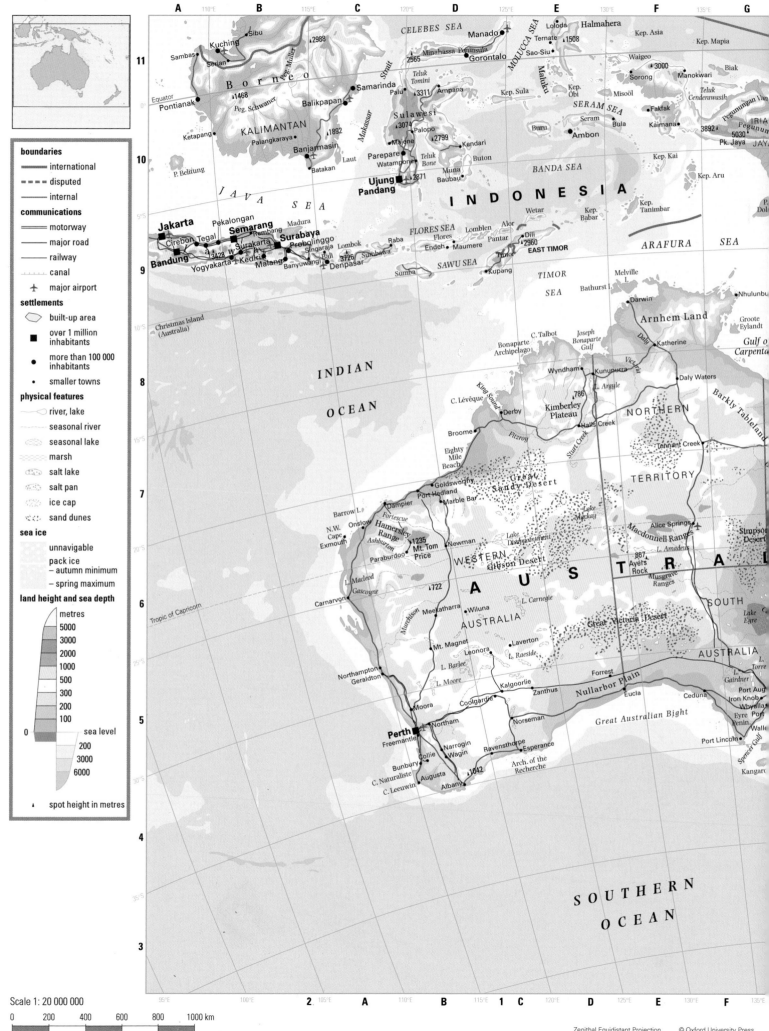

boundaries
- international
- disputed
- internal

communications
- motorway
- major road
- railway
- canal
- ✈ major airport

settlements
- ⬡ built-up area
- ■ over 1 million inhabitants
- ● more than 100 000 inhabitants
- • smaller towns

physical features
- river, lake
- seasonal river
- seasonal lake
- marsh
- salt lake
- salt pan
- ice cap
- sand dunes

sea ice
- unnavigable
- pack ice
  – autumn minimum
  – spring maximum

land height and sea depth

metres
5000
3000
2000
1000
500
300
200
100
0 — sea level
200
3000
6000

▲ spot height in metres

Scale 1: 20 000 000

0 200 400 600 800 1000 km

Zenithal Equidistant Projection

© Oxford University Press

H 145°E J 150°E K 155°E L 160°E M 165°E N 170°E P 175°E Q

Butaritari

Abaiang

Tarawa

Gilbert Islands (Kiribati)

Abemama

Equator

NAURU

Banaba (Kiribati)

Aranuka

Nonouti

Beru

Nikunau

Tabiteuea

Onotoa

KIRIBATI

Tamana

Arorae

Ninigo Group

Kaniet Is.

Hermit Is.

Saint Matthias Group

Admiralty Is.

Lyra Reef

New Ireland

Nuguria Is.

Tauu Is.

Nukumanu Is.

Ontong Java Atoll

Wuvulu

Jayapura

Sepik

BISMARCK SEA

Wewak

Madang

BISMARCK ARCHIPELAGO

Goroka

New Britain

Rabaul

Green Is.

Nanumea

Niutao

Nanumanga

New 3993

Mount Hagen

Lae

2743

Bougainville Island

Kieta

Choiseul

SOLOMON

Nui

Nukufetau

Mendi

PAPUA NEW GUINEA

Kikori

Kerema

Wau

SOLOMON SEA

New Georgia Is.

Santa Isabel

Stewart Is.

ISLANDS

Funafuti

Guinea

Daru

Gulf of Papua

Popondetta

D'Entrecasteaux Islands

Woodlark I.

Honiara 2391

Malaita

TUVALU

Weipa

Cape York Peninsula

Port Moresby

Owen Stanley Range

Guadalcanal

San Cristobal

Rennell

Duff Is.

Santa Cruz Islands

PACIFIC

Nulakita

Torres Strait

C. York

Louisiade Archipelago

Indispensable Reefs

Cherry

Mitre

OCEAN

C. Melville

CORAL SEA

Banks Islands

Rotuma I.

Cooktown

CORAL SEA ISLANDS TERRITORY

Espiritu Santo

Maéwo

Cairns

Innisfail

Ingham

VANUATU

Aoba

Pentecost I.

Ambrym

Épi

Vanua Levu

Labassa

Townsville

Bowen

Malekula

Vila

Éfaté

Lautoka

Viti Levu

1324

FIJI

Charters Towers

Îles Chesterfield

Erromango

Suva

Kadavu

QUEENSLAND

Mackay

Tanna

Îs. Loyauté

Lifou

Anatom

Ceva-i-Ra

Longreach

Emerald

Yeppoon

Rockhampton

Capricorn Channel

New Caledonia (Fr.)

Mare

Tropic of Capricorn

Barcaldine

Mount Morgan

Gladstone

Nouméa

Matthew

Minerva Reefs

Blackall

Springsure

Monto

Bundaberg

Walpole

Hunter

Taroom

Maryborough

Gympie

A

Charleville

Mitchell

Roma

Toowoomba

Darling Downs

Chinchilla

Dalby

Brisbane

Gold Coast

Cunnamula

Goondiwindi

Warwick

Norfolk I. (Aust.)

Wompah

Bourke

Moree

Lismore

Grafton

NEW SOUTH

Cobar

Nyngan

Armidale

Tamworth

Port Macquarie

Lord Howe I. (Aust.)

WALES

Dubbo

Taree

Broken Hill

Orange

Maitland

Great Dividing Range

Newcastle

Bathurst

Lithgow

Adelaide

Mildura

Sydney

Wagga Wagga

Wollongong

Canberra

Queanbeyan

ACT

Albury

Wangaratta

Snowy Mts.

2230

Mt. Kosciusko

Kermadec Is. (NZ)

Raoul

Macauley I.

Curtis I.

Bendigo

VICTORIA

Melbourne

Gippsland

Cape Howe

TASMAN

Three Kings Is.

North Cape

Mount Gambier

Geelong

Portland

Moe

SEA

Kaitaia

Warrnambool

Dargaville

Whangarei

King I.

Bass Strait

Furneaux Group

Auckland

Takapuna

North Island

Burnie

Devenport

Launceston

1617

Hamilton

New Plymouth

Tauranga

East Cape

Queenstown

Mt. Ossa

2518

Rotorua

1754

TASMANIA

Hobart

2997

Gisborne

S.E. Cape

Wanganui

Napier

Hastings

South Island

Mt. Cook

Greymouth

Nelson

2885

Picton

Cook Strait

Porirua

Lower Hutt

Wellington

Palmerston North

3764

Southern Alps

Christchurch

NEW ZEALAND

Timaru

C. Providence

Chatham Is. (NZ)

Stewart I.

Dunedin

Invercargill

Pitt I.

11

10

9

8

7

6

5

4

3

2

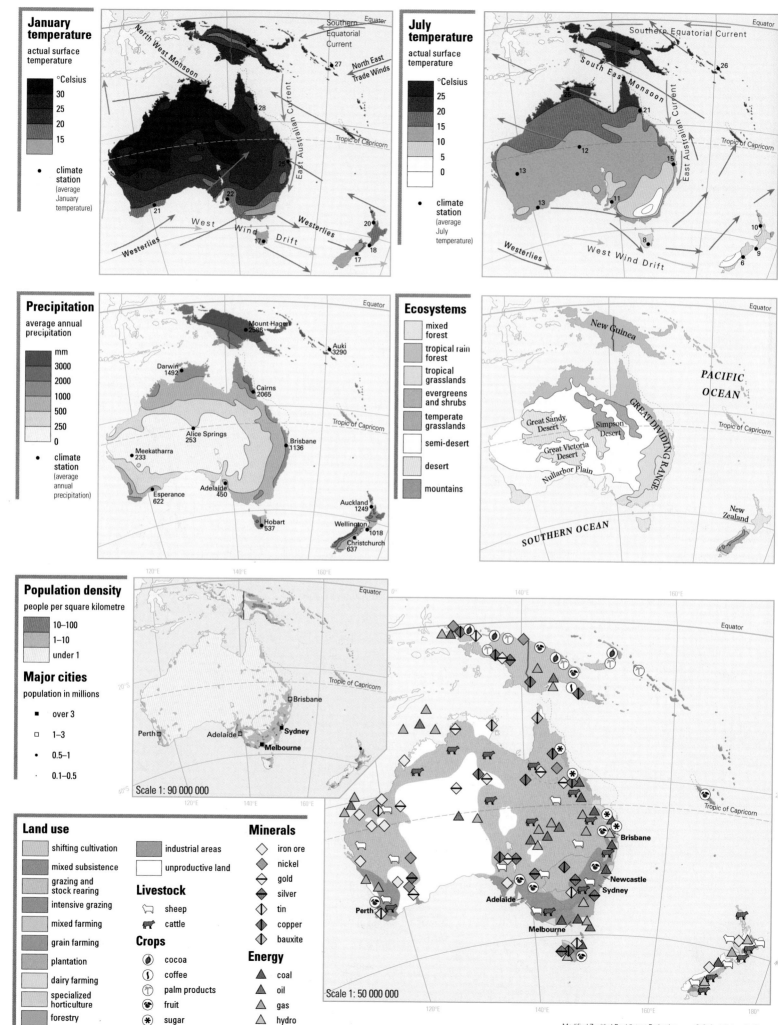

January temperature

actual surface temperature

°Celsius
- 30
- 25
- 20
- 15

• climate station (average January temperature)

Southern Equatorial Current
North West Monsoon
North East Trade Winds
East Australian Current
Tropic of Capricorn
West Wind Drift
Westerlies
Westerlies
Equator

July temperature

actual surface temperature

°Celsius
- 25
- 20
- 15
- 10
- 5
- 0

• climate station (average July temperature)

Southern Equatorial Current
South East Monsoon
East Australian Current
Tropic of Capricorn
Westerlies
West Wind Drift
Equator

Precipitation

average annual precipitation

mm
- 3000
- 2000
- 1000
- 500
- 250
- 0

• climate station (average annual precipitation)

Mount Hagen 2586
Auki 3290
Darwin 1492
Cairns 2065
Alice Springs 253
Brisbane 1136
Meekatharra 233
Esperance 622
Adelaide 450
Hobart 537
Auckland 1249
Wellington 1018
Christchurch 637

Equator
Tropic of Capricorn

Ecosystems

- mixed forest
- tropical rain forest
- tropical grasslands
- evergreens and shrubs
- temperate grasslands
- semi-desert
- desert
- mountains

New Guinea
PACIFIC OCEAN
Great Sandy Desert
Simpson Desert
Great Victoria Desert
GREAT DIVIDING RANGE
Nullarbor Plain
SOUTHERN OCEAN
New Zealand
Equator
Tropic of Capricorn

Population density

people per square kilometre
- 10–100
- 1–10
- under 1

Major cities

population in millions
- ■ over 3
- □ 1–3
- • 0.5–1
- · 0.1–0.5

Brisbane
Perth
Adelaide
Sydney
Melbourne

Scale 1: 90 000 000

Tropic of Capricorn

Land use

- shifting cultivation
- mixed subsistence
- grazing and stock rearing
- intensive grazing
- mixed farming
- grain farming
- plantation
- dairy farming
- specialized horticulture
- forestry
- industrial areas
- unproductive land

Livestock

- 🐑 sheep
- 🐂 cattle

Crops

- cocoa
- coffee
- palm products
- fruit
- ✳ sugar

Minerals

- ◇ iron ore
- ◆ nickel
- ◈ gold
- ◈ silver
- ◧ tin
- ◧ copper
- ◧ bauxite

Energy

- ▲ coal
- ▲ oil
- △ gas
- △ hydro

Brisbane
Newcastle
Sydney
Adelaide
Perth
Melbourne

Scale 1: 50 000 000

Modified Zenithal Equidistant Projection

© Oxford University Press

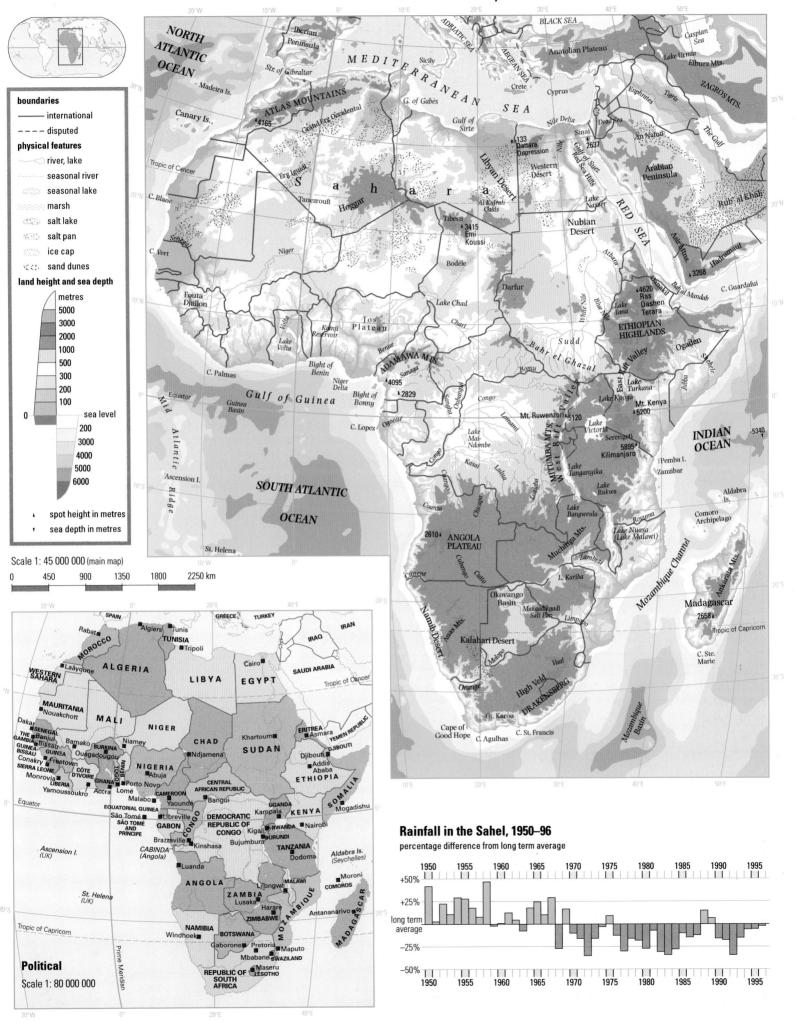

boundaries
— international
--- disputed

physical features
river, lake
seasonal river
seasonal lake
marsh
salt lake
salt pan
ice cap
sand dunes

land height and sea depth
metres
5000
3000
2000
1000
500
300
200
100
0
sea level
200
3000
4000
5000
6000

▲ spot height in metres
▼ sea depth in metres

Scale 1: 45 000 000 (main map)

0   450   900   1350   1800   2250 km

Political

Scale 1: 80 000 000

© Oxford University Press   Zenithal Equal Area Projection

Rainfall in the Sahel, 1950–96
percentage difference from long term average

1950   1955   1960   1965   1970   1975   1980   1985   1990   1995

+50%
+25%
long term average
-25%
-50%

1950   1955   1960   1965   1970   1975   1980   1985   1990   1995

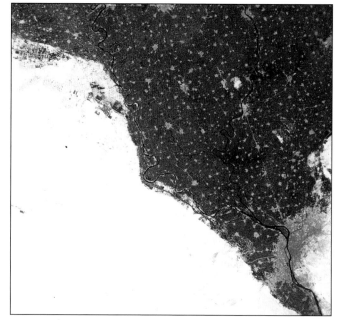

Nile River Delta

Cairo is shown by the blue/grey area to lower right of the image. The city has grown in size from 1.5 million people in 1947 to more than 6 million in 1991. Other blue areas show rapid urban development in the delta. Yellow areas at top left of the image show the spread of agriculture in the desert, assisted by centre pivot irrigation.

Kenya crop cover

Remote sensing can be used to predict food shortages. Dark green areas on the satellite image of Kenya for April, 2000 show the newly sown 'long rains' cereal crop. However, gaps in the dark green pattern indicate a poor harvest and in June, $88 million of international food aid was agreed. By August, low rainfall had led to widespread crop failure in the south, shown as light green, and spread of bare soil in the north, shown as orange and yellow.

April, 2000

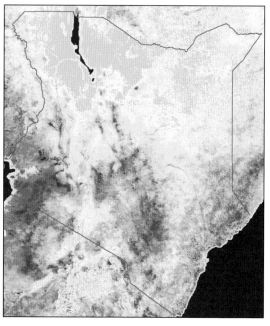

August, 2000

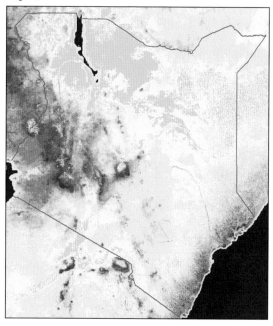

Mozambique floods
Before flooding, August, 1999.

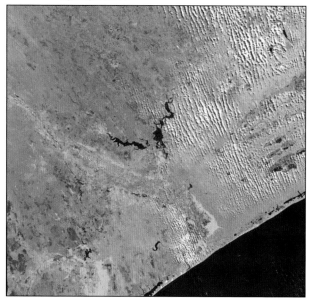

After flooding, March 2000.

These images from the Landsat 7 satellite show the Limpopo river before and after flooding. Torrential rain between 4 and 7 February, 2000 added to already high levels of seasonal rainfall. Tropical cyclone Eline hit the southern coast of Mozambique on 21 February bringing even more rain. Over a million people were made homeless and 100 000 hectares of agricultural land flooded. 620 miles of roads were swept away.

Scale 1: 90 000 000

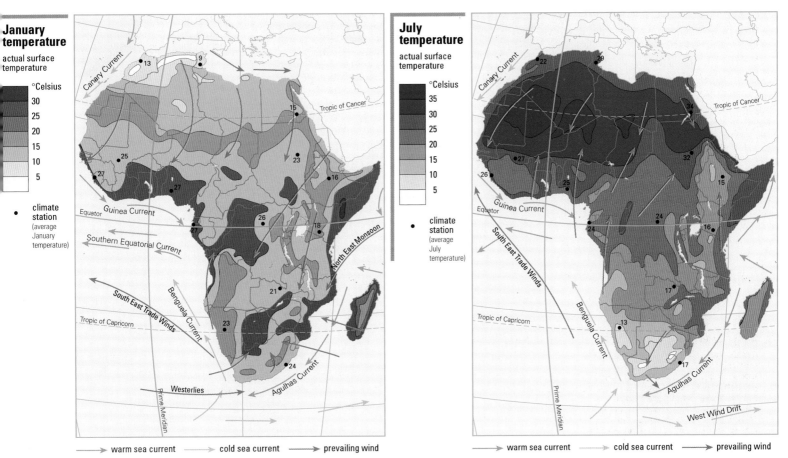

January temperature

actual surface temperature

°Celsius
30
25
20
15
10
5

• climate station
(average January temperature)

Canary Current
13   9
15
25
23
27
16
27
Guinea Current
Equator
26
27
18
Southern Equatorial Current
North East Monsoon
South East Trade Winds
Benguela Current
21
Tropic of Capricorn
23
24
Westerlies
Agulhas Current
Prime Meridian
Tropic of Cancer

→ warm sea current   → cold sea current   → prevailing wind

July temperature

actual surface temperature

°Celsius
35
30
25
20
15
10
5

• climate station
(average July temperature)

Canary Current
22   29
27
34
26
32
25
15
Guinea Current
Equator
24
24
16
South East Trade Winds
17
Benguela Current
13
Tropic of Capricorn
17
Agulhas Current
Prime Meridian
West Wind Drift
Tropic of Cancer

→ warm sea current   → cold sea current   → prevailing wind

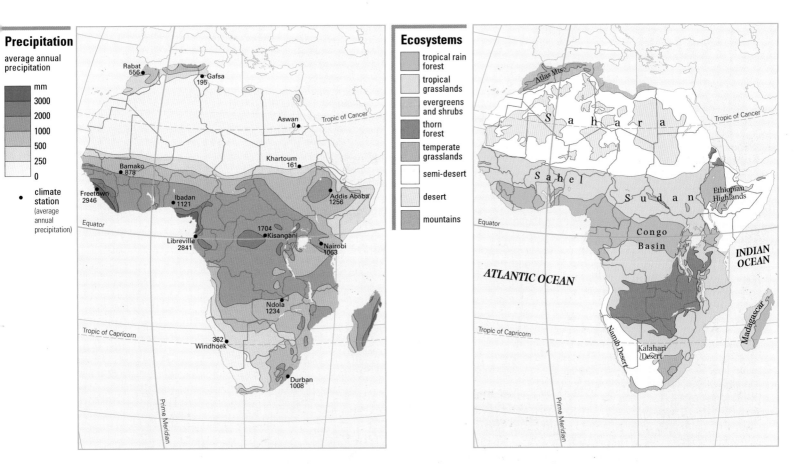

Precipitation

average annual precipitation

mm
3000
2000
1000
500
250
0

• climate station
(average annual precipitation)

Rabat 556
Gafsa 195
Aswan 0
Tropic of Cancer
Khartoum 161
Bamako 878
Freetown 2946
Ibadan 1121
Addis Ababa 1256
Equator
Libreville 2841
Kisangani 1704
Nairobi 1063
Ndola 1234
Tropic of Capricorn
362 Windhoek
Durban 1008
Prime Meridian

Ecosystems

tropical rain forest
tropical grasslands
evergreens and shrubs
thorn forest
temperate grasslands
semi-desert
desert
mountains

Atlas Mts.
S a h a r a
Tropic of Cancer
S a h e l
S u d a n
Ethiopian Highlands
Equator
Congo Basin
INDIAN OCEAN
ATLANTIC OCEAN
Tropic of Capricorn
Namib Desert
Kalahari Desert
Madagascar
Prime Meridian

Scale 1:55 000 000

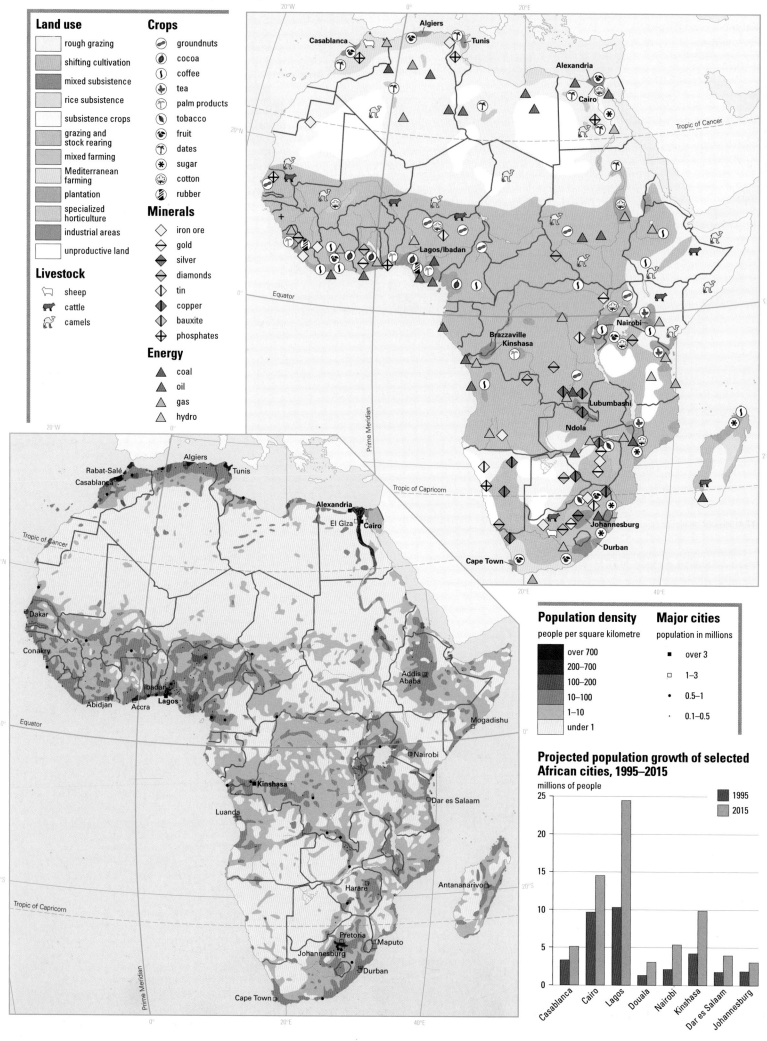

Land use

- rough grazing
- shifting cultivation
- mixed subsistence
- rice subsistence
- subsistence crops
- grazing and stock rearing
- mixed farming
- Mediterranean farming
- plantation
- specialized horticulture
- industrial areas
- unproductive land

Livestock

- sheep
- cattle
- camels

Crops

- groundnuts
- cocoa
- coffee
- tea
- palm products
- tobacco
- fruit
- dates
- sugar
- cotton
- rubber

Minerals

- iron ore
- gold
- silver
- diamonds
- tin
- copper
- bauxite
- phosphates

Energy

- coal
- oil
- gas
- hydro

Population density

people per square kilometre

- over 700
- 200–700
- 100–200
- 10–100
- 1–10
- under 1

Major cities

population in millions

- over 3
- 1–3
- 0.5–1
- 0.1–0.5

Projected population growth of selected African cities, 1995–2015

millions of people

- 1995
- 2015

Cities: Casablanca, Cairo, Lagos, Douala, Nairobi, Kinshasa, Dar es Salaam, Johannesburg

© Oxford University Press

Zenithal Equal Area Projection

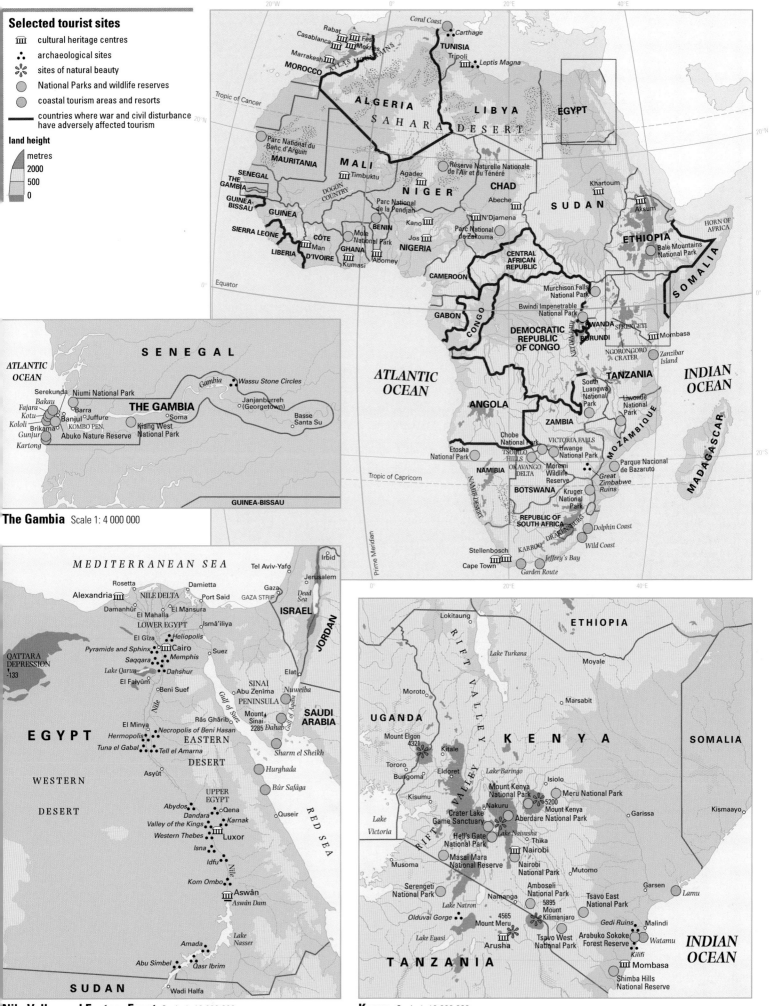

Scale 1: 55 000 000 (main map)

The Gambia Scale 1: 4 000 000

Nile Valley and Eastern Egypt Scale 1: 10 000 000

Kenya Scale 1: 10 000 000

Zenithal Equal Area Projection

© Oxford University Press

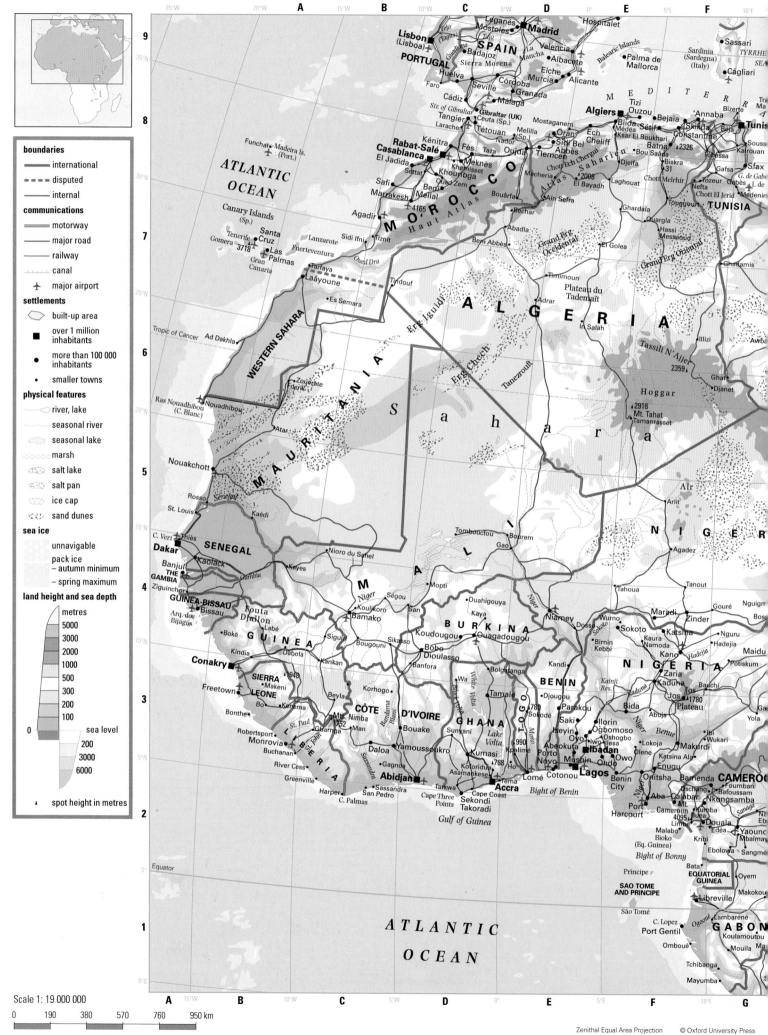

boundaries
— international
--- disputed
— internal
communications
— motorway
— major road
— railway
⊥⊥⊥ canal
✈ major airport
settlements
⬡ built-up area
■ over 1 million inhabitants
● more than 100 000 inhabitants
• smaller towns
physical features
~ river, lake
--- seasonal river
⬭ seasonal lake
⬭ marsh
⬭ salt lake
⬭ salt pan
⬭ ice cap
⬭ sand dunes
sea ice
unnavigable
pack ice
— autumn minimum
— spring maximum
land height and sea depth

metres
5000
3000
2000
1000
500
300
200
100
0   sea level
200
3000
6000

▲ spot height in metres

Scale 1: 19 000 000

0   190   380   570   760   950 km

A   B   C   D   E   F   G

Zenithal Equal Area Projection

© Oxford University Press

Scale 1: 19 000 000

0   190   380   570   760   950 km

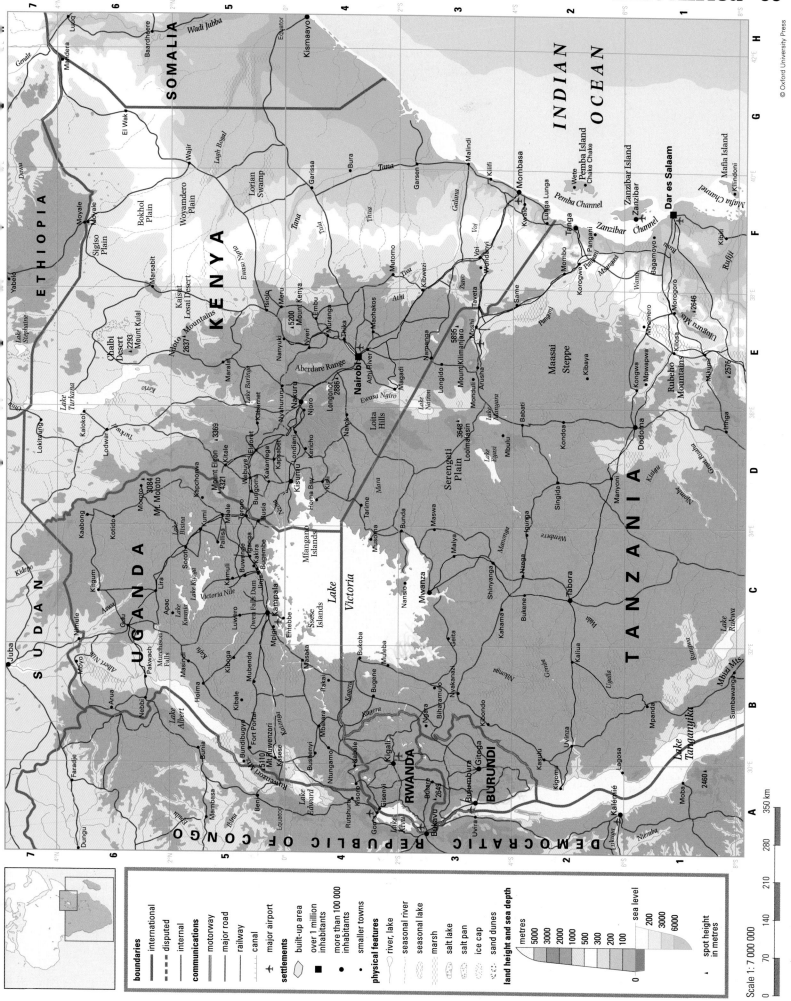

Scale 1:7 000 000

boundaries
—— international
---- disputed
—— internal

communications
||| motorway
—— major road
—— railway
—— canal
✈ major airport

settlements
⬡ built-up area
■ over 1 million inhabitants
● more than 100 000 inhabitants
• smaller towns

physical features
river, lake
seasonal river
seasonal lake
marsh
salt lake
salt pan
ice cap
sand dunes

land height and sea depth

metres	
5000	
3000	
2000	
1000	
500	
300	
200	
100	
sea level	
200	
3000	
6000	

▲ spot height in metres

0 70 140 210 280 350 km

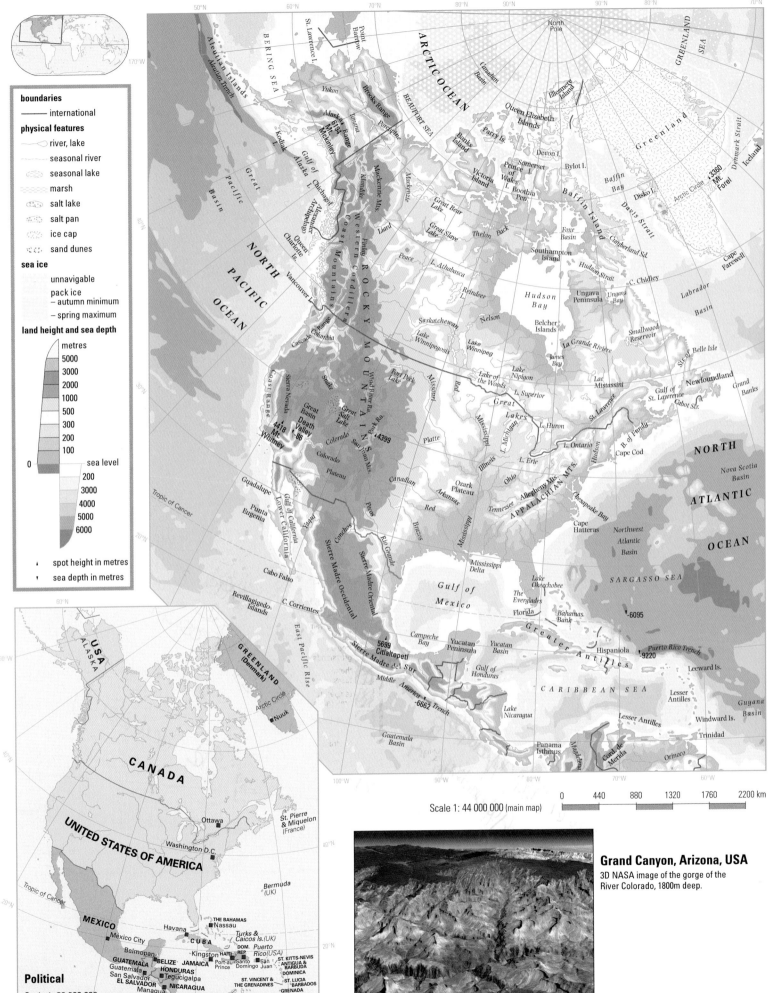

Grand Canyon, Arizona, USA
3D NASA image of the gorge of the River Colorado, 1800m deep.

Scale 1: 44 000 000 (main map)

Scale 1: 80 000 000

Oblique Mercator Projection   © Oxford University Press

Scale 1: 80 000 000

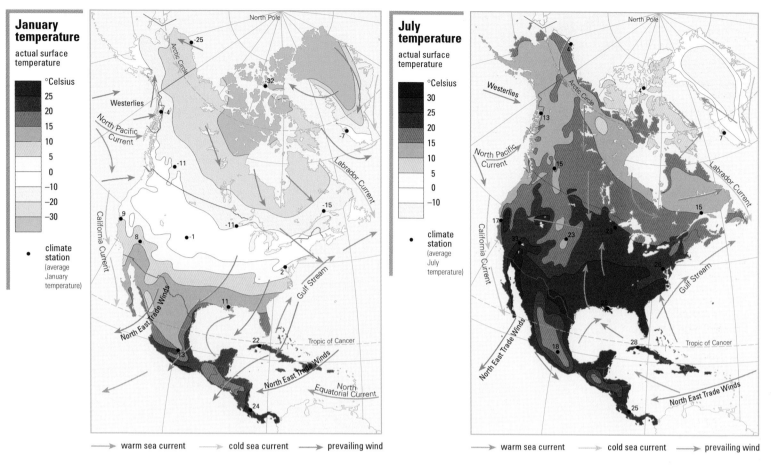

January temperature

actual surface temperature

°Celsius

25
20
15
10
5
0
−10
−20
−30

● climate station (average January temperature)

North Pole
−25
Arctic Circle
−32
Westerlies
−4
North Pacific Current
−7
Labrador Current
−11
−15
−11
California Current
9
8
−1
2
Gulf Stream
North East Trade Winds
11
22
13
North East Trade Winds
Tropic of Cancer
North East Trade Winds
North Equatorial Current
24

→ warm sea current → cold sea current → prevailing wind

July temperature

actual surface temperature

°Celsius

30
25
20
15
10
5
0
−10

● climate station (average July temperature)

North Pole
Westerlies
Arctic Circle
13
4
North Pacific Current
7
15
Labrador Current
17
15
33
23
23
California Current
26
North East Trade Winds
18
28
Gulf Stream
Tropic of Cancer
North East Trade Winds
25

→ warm sea current → cold sea current → prevailing wind

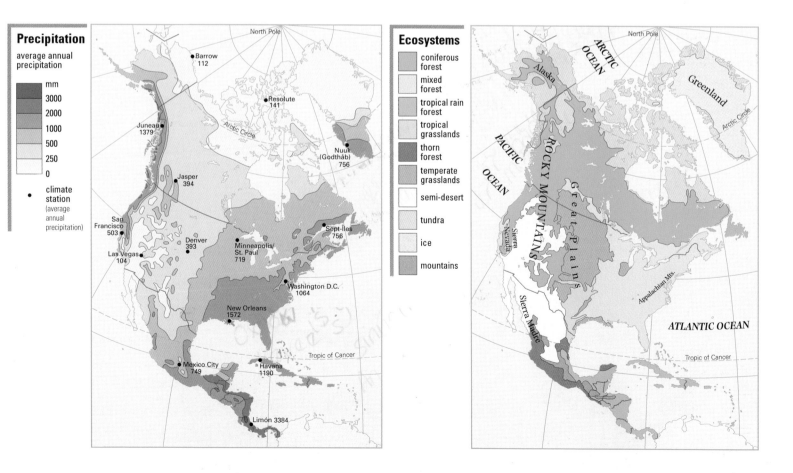

Precipitation

average annual precipitation

mm

3000
2000
1000
500
250
0

● climate station (average annual precipitation)

North Pole
Barrow 112
Resolute 141
Juneau 1379
Arctic Circle
Nuuk (Godthåb) 756
Jasper 394
San Francisco 503
Denver 393
Minneapolis/ St. Paul 719
Sept-Îles 756
Las Vegas 104
Washington D.C. 1064
New Orleans 1572
Mexico City 749
Havana 1190
Tropic of Cancer
Limón 3384

Ecosystems

■ coniferous forest
■ mixed forest
■ tropical rain forest
■ tropical grasslands
■ thorn forest
■ temperate grasslands
□ semi-desert
■ tundra
■ ice
■ mountains

North Pole
ARCTIC OCEAN
Alaska
Greenland
Arctic Circle
PACIFIC OCEAN
ROCKY MOUNTAINS
Great Plains
Sierra Nevada
Sierra Madre
Appalachian Mts.
ATLANTIC OCEAN
Tropic of Cancer

Oblique Mercator rojection

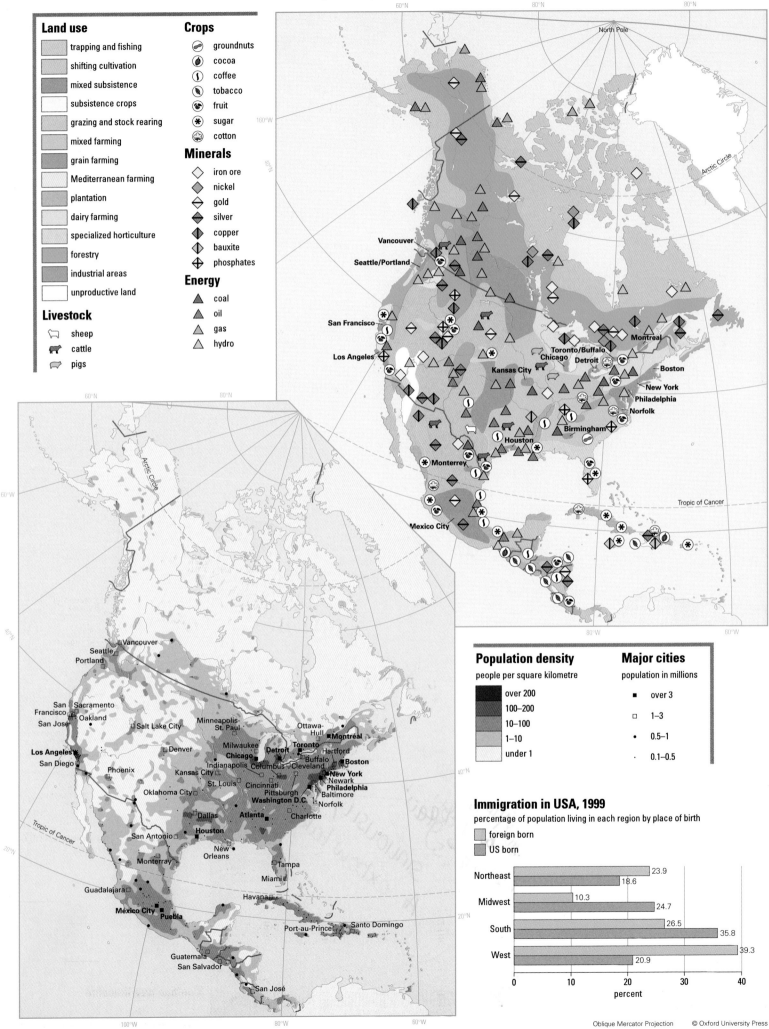

Land use

- trapping and fishing
- shifting cultivation
- mixed subsistence
- subsistence crops
- grazing and stock rearing
- mixed farming
- grain farming
- Mediterranean farming
- plantation
- dairy farming
- specialized horticulture
- forestry
- industrial areas
- unproductive land

Livestock

- sheep
- cattle
- pigs

Crops

- groundnuts
- cocoa
- coffee
- tobacco
- fruit
- sugar
- cotton

Minerals

- iron ore
- nickel
- gold
- silver
- copper
- bauxite
- phosphates

Energy

- coal
- oil
- gas
- hydro

Population density

people per square kilometre

- over 200
- 100–200
- 10–100
- 1–10
- under 1

Major cities

population in millions

- over 3
- 1–3
- 0.5–1
- 0.1–0.5

Immigration in USA, 1999

percentage of population living in each region by place of birth

- foreign born
- US born

Region	foreign born	US born
Northeast	23.9	18.6
Midwest	10.3	24.7
South	26.5	35.8
West	39.3	20.9

percent

Oblique Mercator Projection   © Oxford University Press

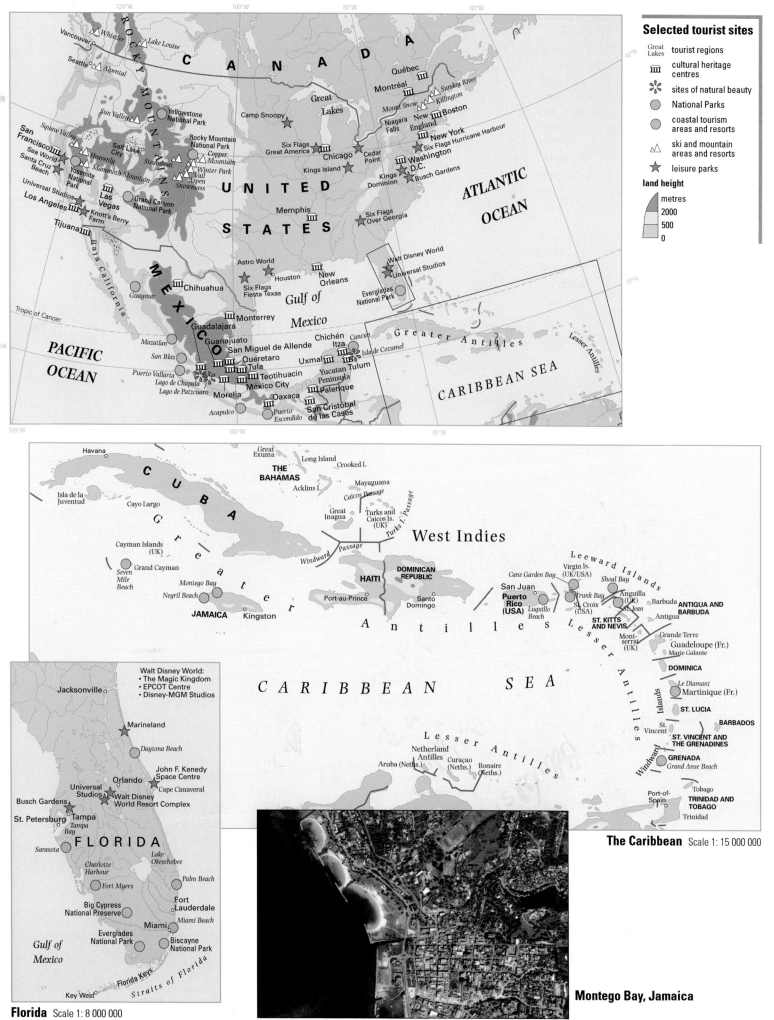

Scale 1: 40 000 000 (main map)

Florida Scale 1: 8 000 000

The Caribbean Scale 1: 15 000 000

Montego Bay, Jamaica

Oblique Mercator Projection   © Oxford University Press

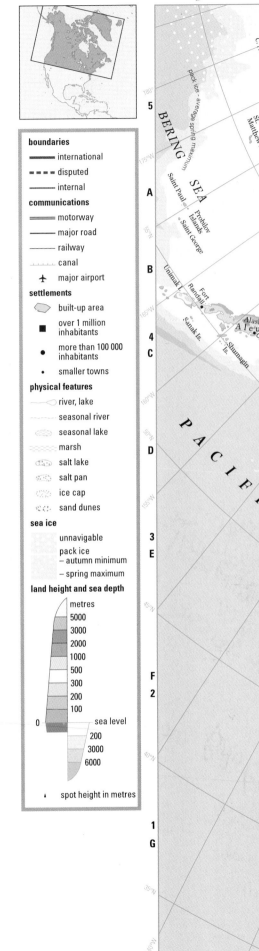

boundaries

▬▬▬	international
▬ ▬ ▬	disputed
▬▬▬	internal

communications

═══	motorway
▬▬	major road
▬▬	railway
┼┼┼┼	canal
✈	major airport

settlements

⬡	built-up area
■	over 1 million inhabitants
●	more than 100 000 inhabitants
•	smaller towns

physical features

⬳	river, lake
	seasonal river
	seasonal lake
	marsh
	salt lake
	salt pan
	ice cap
	sand dunes

sea ice

	unnavigable
	pack ice – autumn minimum
	– spring maximum

land height and sea depth

metres
5000
3000
2000
1000
500
300
200
100
0 sea level
200
3000
6000

▲ spot height in metres

Scale 1: 19 000 000

0   190   380   570   760   950 km

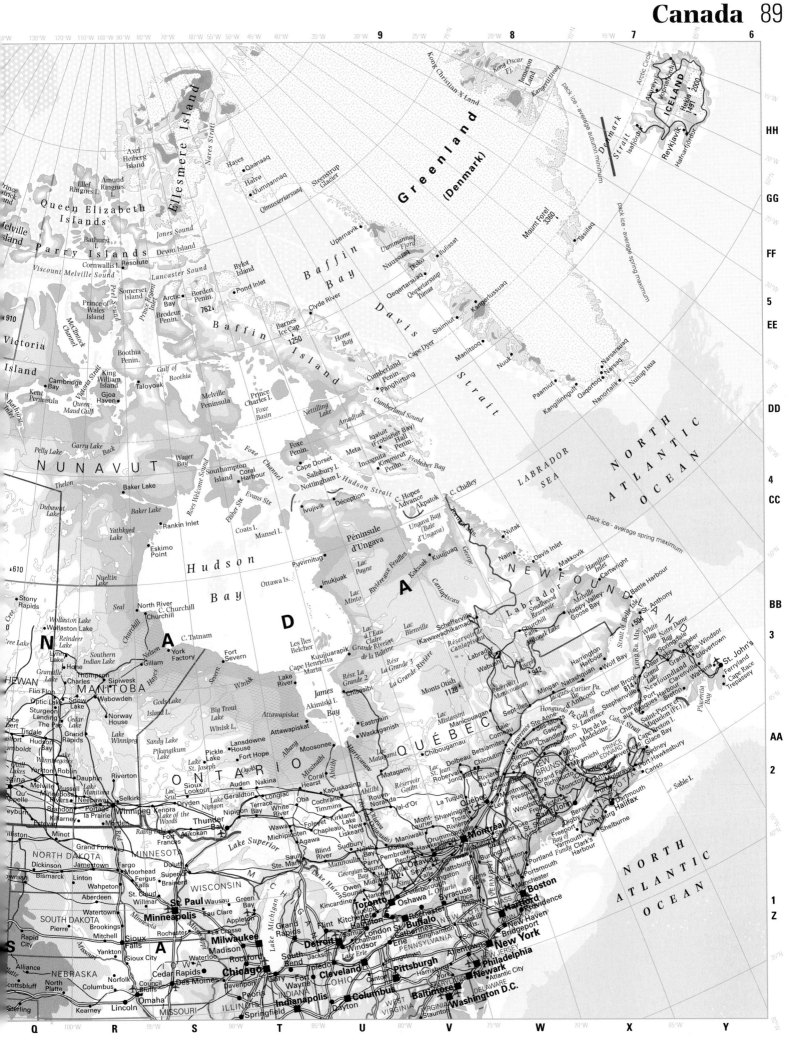

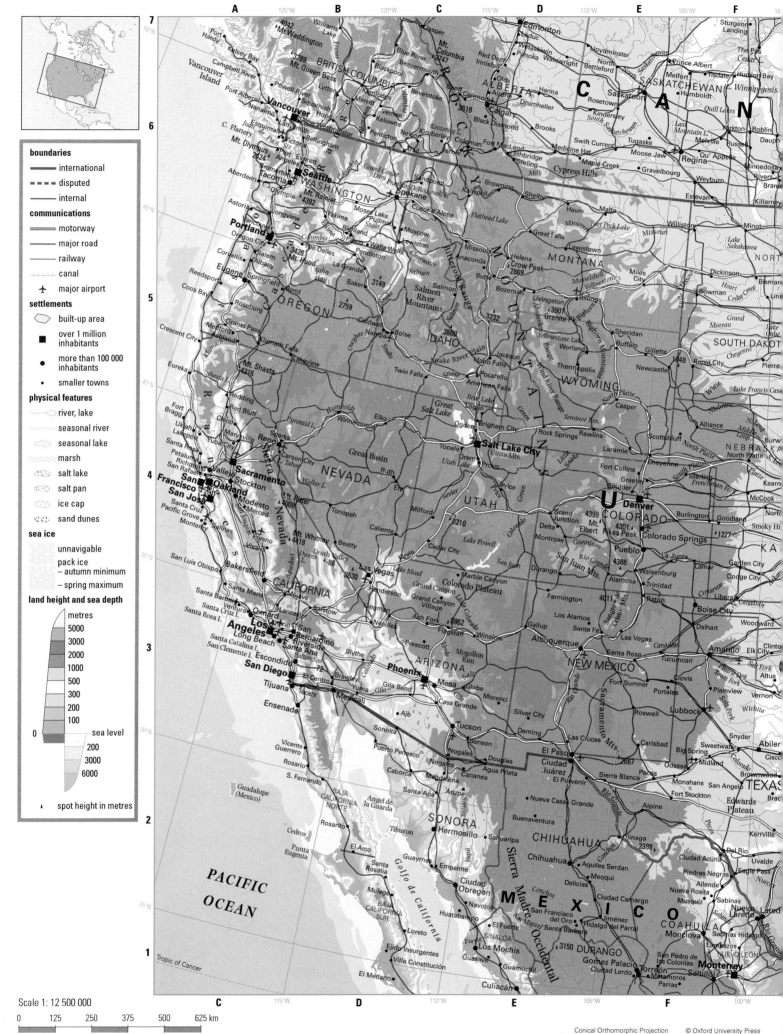

boundaries

— international
--- disputed
— internal

communications

═ motorway
— major road
— railway
+++ canal
✈ major airport

settlements

⬡ built-up area
■ over 1 million inhabitants
● more than 100 000 inhabitants
• smaller towns

physical features

river, lake
seasonal river
seasonal lake
marsh
salt lake
salt pan
ice cap
sand dunes

sea ice

unnavigable
pack ice
— autumn minimum
— spring maximum

land height and sea depth

metres
5000
3000
2000
1000
500
300
200
100
0 sea level
200
3000
6000

▲ spot height in metres

Scale 1: 12 500 000

0   125   250   375   500   625 km

Conical Orthomorphic Projection   © Oxford University Press

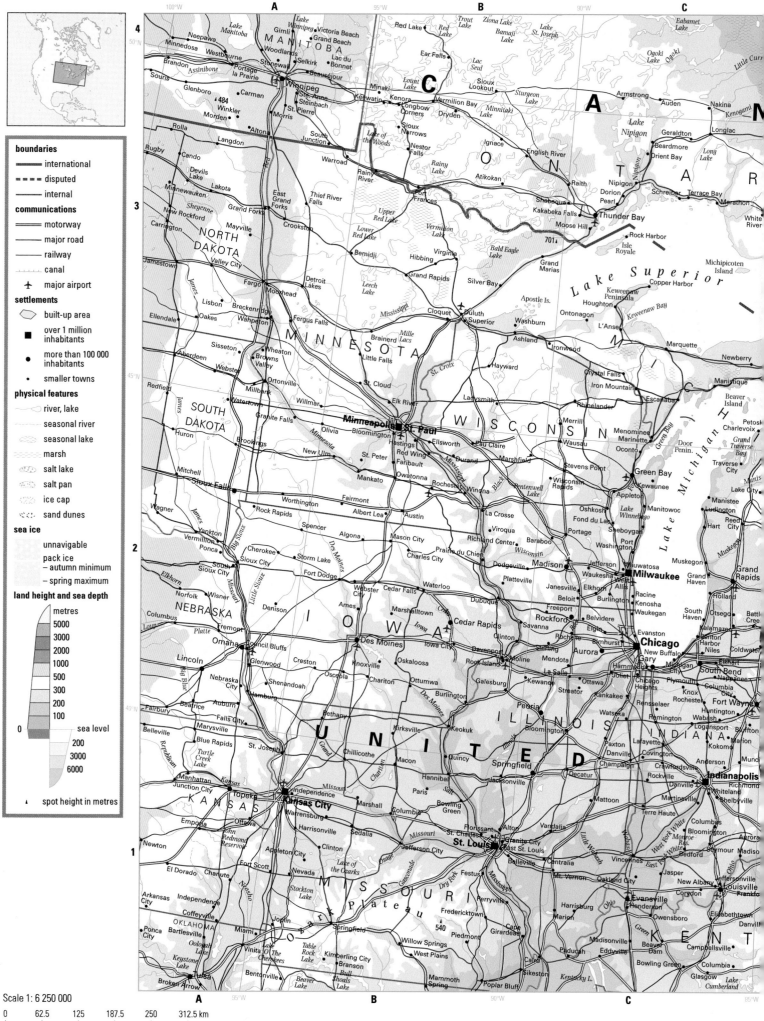

Scale 1: 6 250 000

0   62.5   125   187.5   250   312.5 km

Conical Orthomorphic Projection

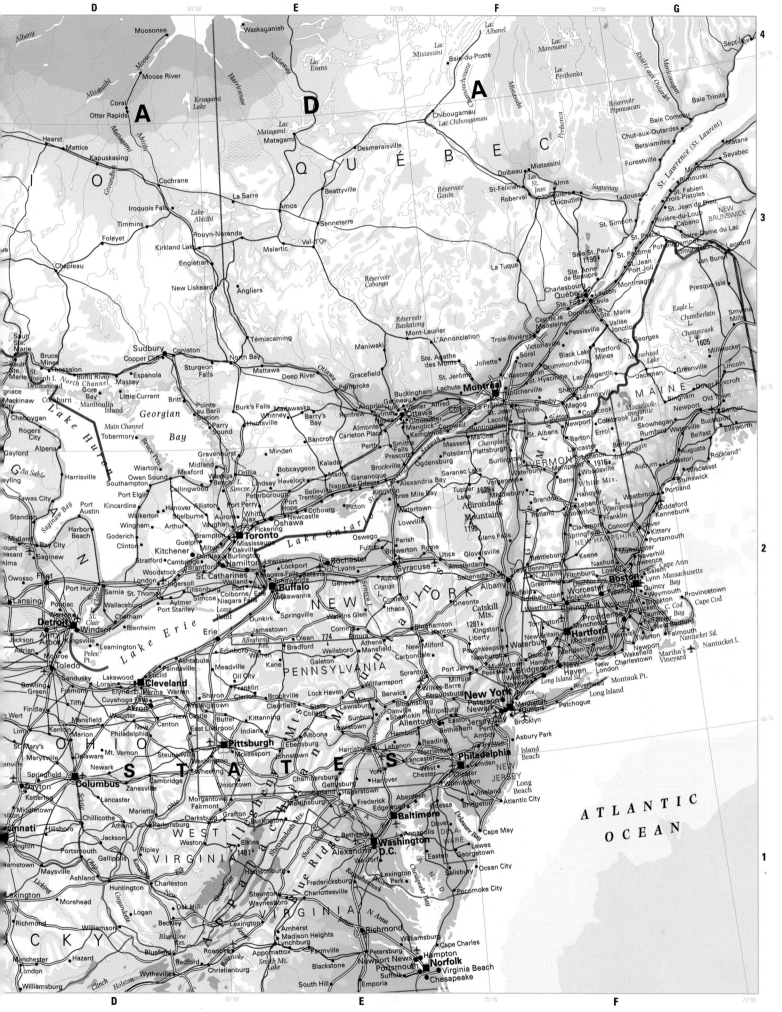

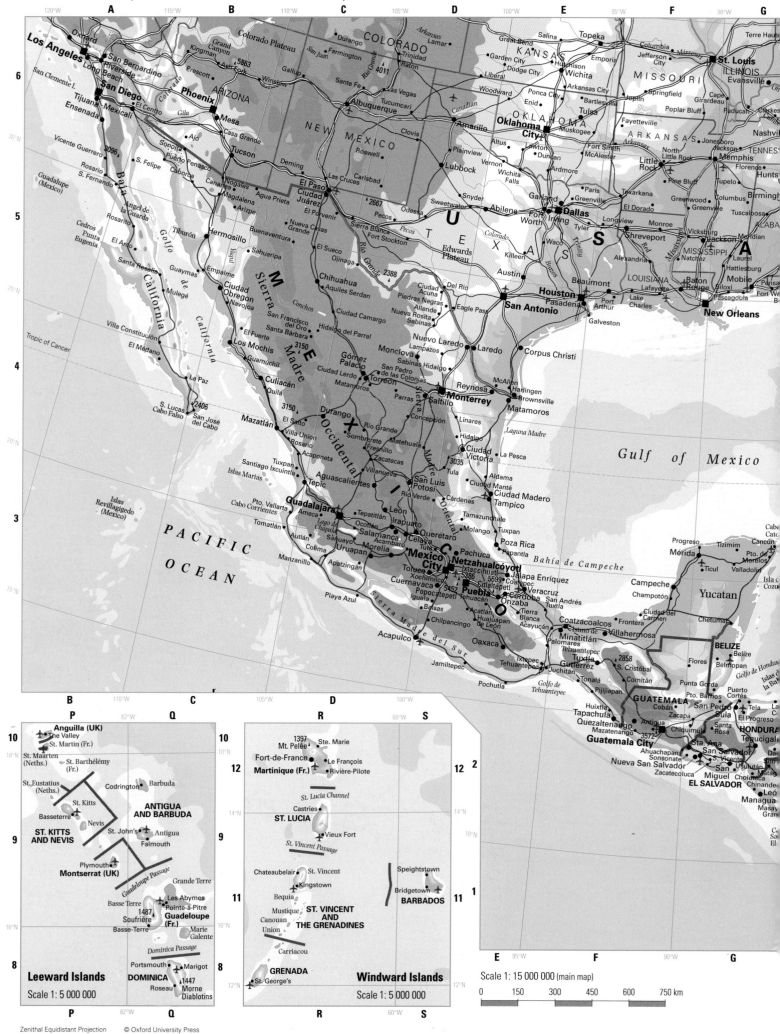

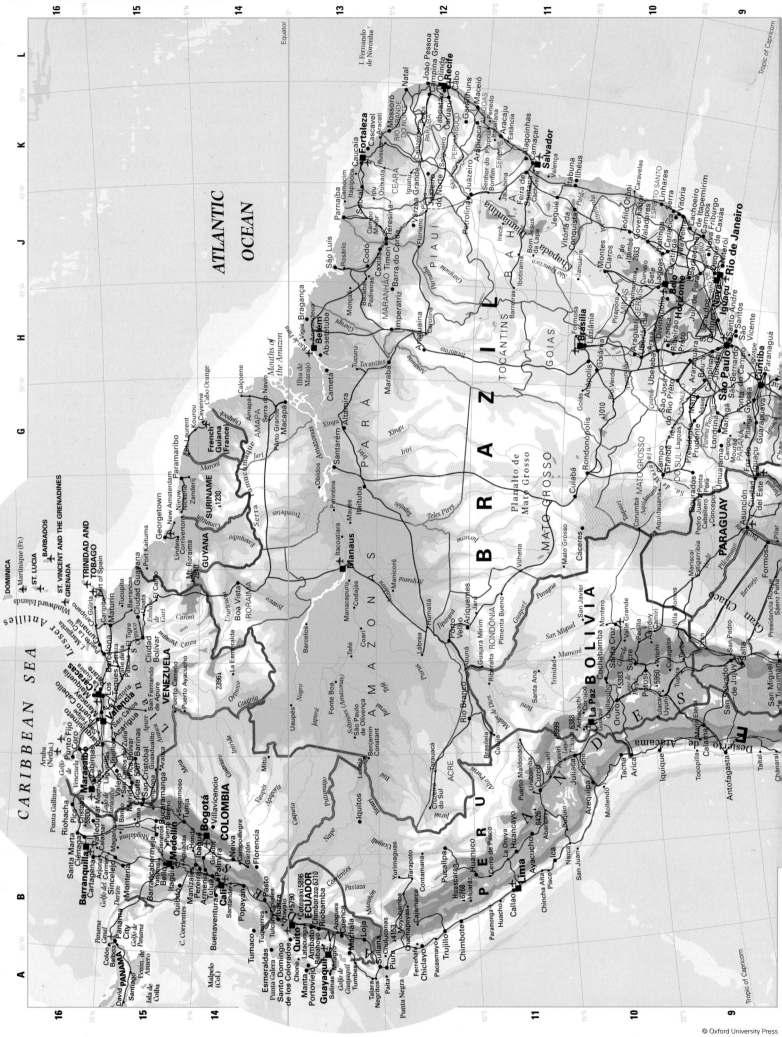

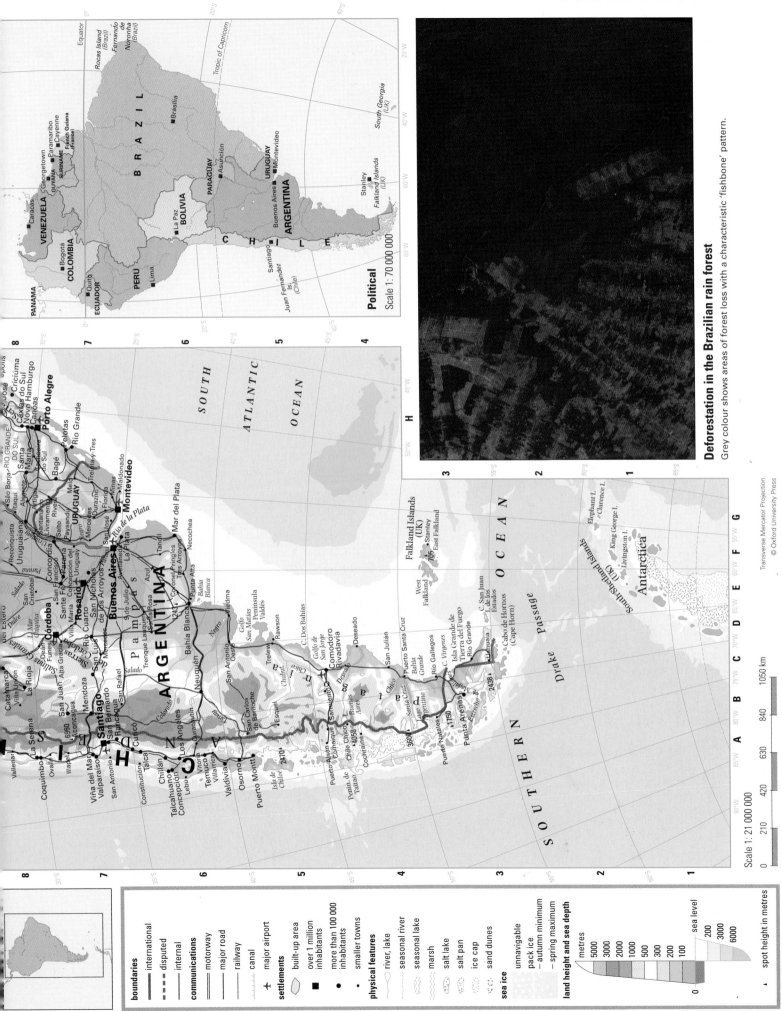

Deforestation in the Brazilian rain forest

Grey colour shows areas of forest loss with a characteristic 'fishbone' pattern.

Political
Scale 1: 70 000 000

Scale 1: 21 000 000

Transverse Mercator Projection

© Oxford University Press

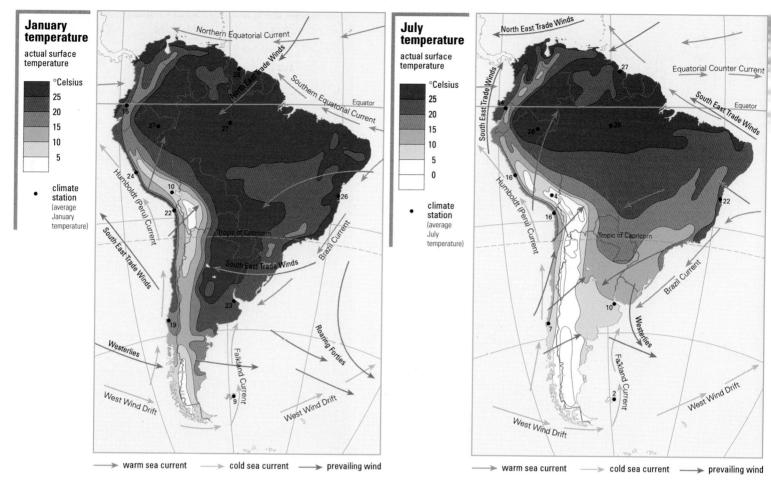

January temperature

actual surface temperature

°Celsius
25
20
15
10
5

• climate station (average January temperature)

Northern Equatorial Current
North East Trade Winds
Southern Equatorial Current
Equator
Humboldt (Peru) Current
South East Trade Winds
Westerlies
West Wind Drift
Tropic of Capricorn
Brazil Current
Roaring Forties
Falkland Current
West Wind Drift

26
15
27
27
24
10
22
26
23
19
9

→ warm sea current   → cold sea current   → prevailing wind

July temperature

actual surface temperature

°Celsius
25
20
15
10
5
0

• climate station (average July temperature)

North East Trade Winds
South East Trade Winds
Equatorial Counter Current
Equator
South East Trade Winds
Humboldt (Peru) Current
Tropic of Capricorn
Brazil Current
Westerlies
Falkland Current
West Wind Drift
West Wind Drift

27
14
26
28
16
4
16
22
10
7
2

→ warm sea current   → cold sea current   → prevailing wind

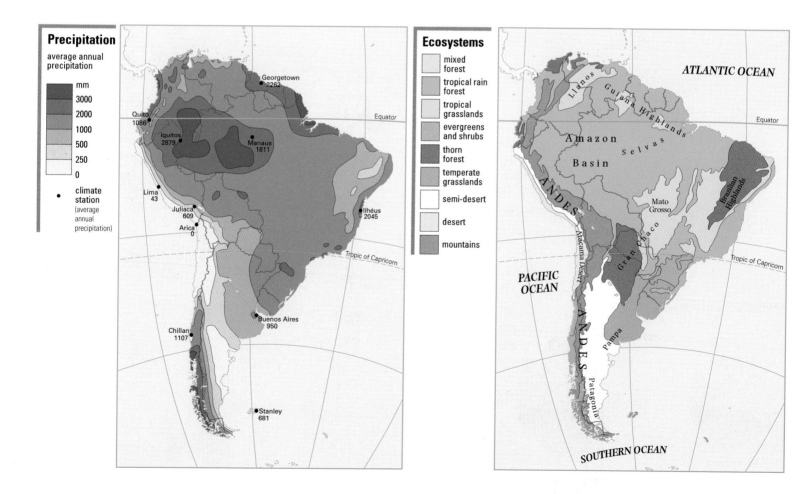

Precipitation

average annual precipitation

mm
3000
2000
1000
500
250
0

• climate station (average annual precipitation)

Georgetown 2262
Quito 1086
Iquitos 2879
Manaus 1811
Lima 43
Juliaca 609
Arica 0
Ilhéus 2045
Buenos Aires 950
Chillan 1107
Stanley 681
Equator
Tropic of Capricorn

Ecosystems

mixed forest
tropical rain forest
tropical grasslands
evergreens and shrubs
thorn forest
temperate grasslands
semi-desert
desert
mountains

ATLANTIC OCEAN
Llanos
Guiana Highlands
Amazon Basin
Selvas
ANDES
Atacama Desert
Mato Grosso
Brazilian Highlands
Gran Chaco
PACIFIC OCEAN
Pampa
ANDES
Patagonia
Equator
Tropic of Capricorn
SOUTHERN OCEAN

Oblique Mercator Projection

© Oxford University Press

Scale 1: 45 000 000

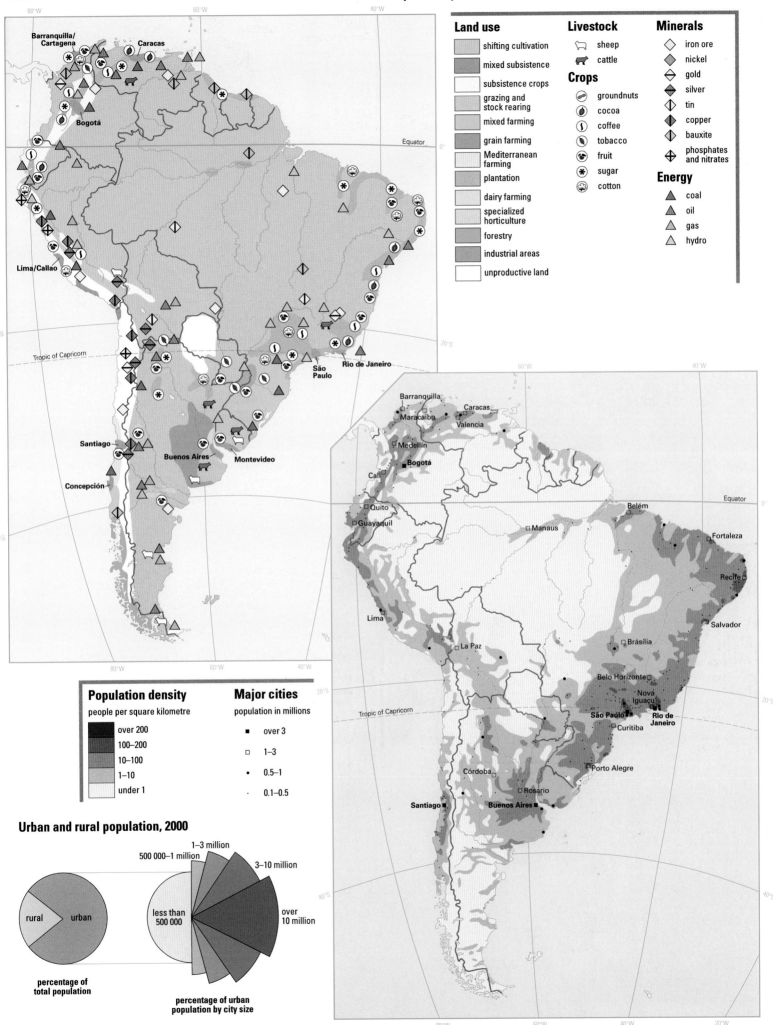

Land use

shifting cultivation

mixed subsistence

subsistence crops

grazing and stock rearing

mixed farming

grain farming

Mediterranean farming

plantation

dairy farming

specialized horticulture

forestry

industrial areas

unproductive land

Livestock

sheep

cattle

Crops

groundnuts

cocoa

coffee

tobacco

fruit

sugar

cotton

Minerals

iron ore

nickel

gold

silver

tin

copper

bauxite

phosphates and nitrates

Energy

coal

oil

gas

hydro

Population density

people per square kilometre

over 200

100–200

10–100

1–10

under 1

Major cities

population in millions

over 3

1–3

0.5–1

0.1–0.5

Urban and rural population, 2000

rural / urban

percentage of total population

less than 500 000

500 000–1 million

1–3 million

3–10 million

over 10 million

percentage of urban population by city size

© Oxford University Press   Oblique Mercator Projection

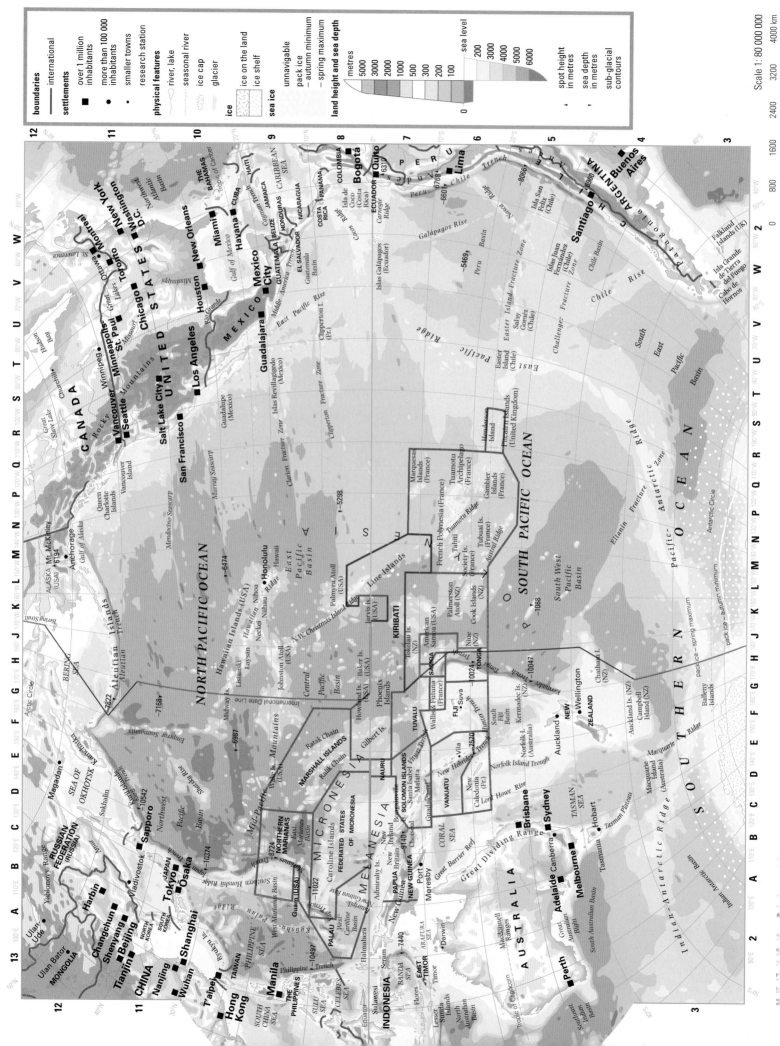

Scale 1:80 000 000

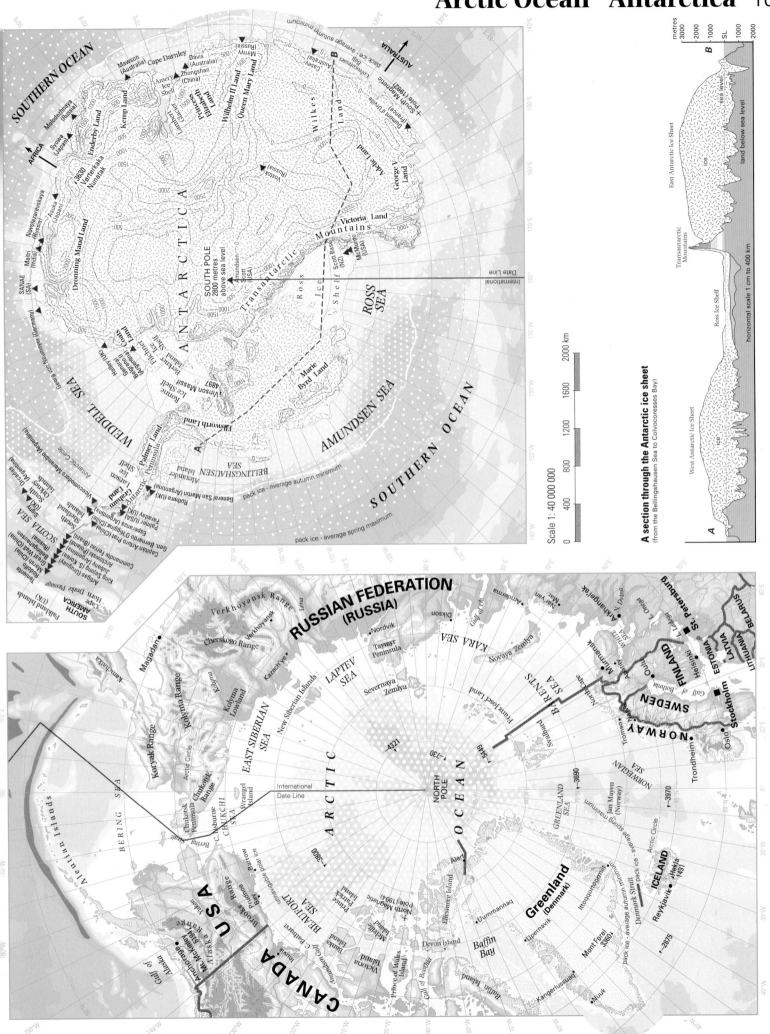

Antarctica (top map)

SOUTHERN OCEAN

Mawson (Australia) Cape Darnley Davis (Australia) Casey (Australia)
Molodezhnaya (Russia) Zhongshan (China) Mirny (Russia)
Amery Ice Shelf Wilhelm II Land Queen Mary Land
Enderby Land Kemp Land
Syowa (Japan) pack ice - average autumn minimum
AFRICA Wilkes Land

Novolazarevskaya (Russia) Asuka (Japan) Vostok (Russia)
·3630 Vorterkaka Nunatak Wilhelm II Land Adélie Land
Maitri (India) Dronning Maud Land George V Land

SANAE (SA) Victoria Land
Mountains
Neumayer (Germany) A N T A R C T I C A
WEDDELL SEA McMurdo (USA) Scott Base (NZ)
Halley (UK) Coats Land Amundsen· Scott (USA)
General Belgrano II (Argentina) Filchner Ice Shelf SOUTH POLE 2800 metres above sea level
Berkner Island Transantarctic Ross Ice Shelf ROSS SEA
International Date Line

·4897 Vinson Massif
Ronne Ice Shelf Marie Byrd Land
Ellsworth Land
Alexander Island Larsen Ice Shelf AMUNDSEN SEA
Palmer Land
BELLINGSHAUSEN SEA SOUTHERN OCEAN

Graham Land Antarctic Peninsula
Rothera (UK) General San Martín (Argentina)
Esperanza (Argentina) Faraday (UK)
pack ice - average spring maximum

Vicecomodoro Marambio (Argentina)
Antarctic Circle
South Orkney Islands
South Shetland Islands
SCOTIA SEA Signy (UK)
Bellingshausen (Russia) Great Wall (China)
Artigas (Uruguay) Rodolfo Marsh (Chile) Teniente
Arturo Prat (Chile) Gen. Bernardo O'Higgins (Chile) Comandante Ferraz (Brazil)
Arctowski (Poland) Jubany (Argentina) King George I. (S. Korea)
SOUTH AMERICA Cape Horn Drake Passage
Falkland Islands (UK)

Scale 1 : 40 000 000
0 400 800 1200 1600 2000 km

A section through the Antarctic ice sheet
(from the Bellingshausen Sea to Colvocoresses Bay)

A West Antarctic Ice Sheet Ross Ice Shelf Transantarctic Mountains East Antarctic Ice Sheet B

metres 3000 2000 1000 SL sea level 1000 2000
ice land below sea level
horizontal scale 1 cm to 400 km

Arctic Ocean (bottom map)

RUSSIAN FEDERATION (RUSSIA)

Verkhoyansk Range Lena Ob
Verkhoyansk Nordvik Dikson Nar'yan-Mar
Cherskogo Range Taymyr Peninsula KARA SEA Novaya Zemlya
Magadan Kazach'ye LAPTEV SEA Severnaya Zemlya Franz Josef Land
Kamchatka New Siberian Islands BARENTS SEA Svalbard Murmansk
Kolyma Range Kolyma Lowland Severnaya Zemlya North Cape
Koryak Range EAST SIBERIAN SEA ·4321 ·-730 Spitsbergen Tromsø NORWAY
Chukotsk Peninsula Wrangel Island ·-5449 WHITE SEA Arkhangel'sk
Chukotsk Range CHUKCHI SEA International Date Line NORTH POLE ARCTIC OCEAN Jan Mayen (Norway) NORWEGIAN SEA L. Ladoga FINLAND St. Petersburg
C. Asburne Bering Strait ·-730 GREENLAND SEA ·-3690 SWEDEN ESTONIA LATVIA LITHUANIA BELARUS
BERING SEA ·-3800 Gulf of Bothnia Stockholm
Aleutian Islands Barrow BEAUFORT SEA North Magnetic Pole (1994) Greenland (Denmark) ·-3970 Oslo Trondheim
USA Prudhoe Bay Banks Island Prince Patrick Island Alert Arctic Circle
Alaska Anchorage Mt. McKinley Brooks Range Melville Island Ellesmere Island Upernavik pack ice - average spring maximum ICELAND Hekla ·1491
Alaska Range Yukon Amundsen Gulf Victoria Island Ummannaq Mont Forel ·3360 Reykjavík ·-2875
CANADA Inuvik Banks Island Prince of Wales Island Gulf of Boothia Devon Island Baffin Bay pack ice - average autumn minimum Denmark Strait
Gulf of Alaska Prince Patrick Island Baffin Island Kangerlussuaq Nuuk Ittoqqortoormiit

Zenithal Equidistant Projection © Oxford University Press

Equatorial scale 1: 95 000 000 (main map)

Legend:
- international boundary
- • capital city

Grid references (top): 10 A 180° 160°W B 140°W C 120°W D 100°W E 80°W F 60°W G 40°W H 20°W J

80°N
9 Arctic Circle 60°N
USA
8
CANADA
Ottawa
40°N
7
UNITED STATES OF AMERICA
Washington D.C.
Tropic of Cancer
Hawaiian Islands (USA)
20°N
MEXICO
THE BAHAMAS
Havana
Mexico City
CUBA
JAMAICA HAITI DOMINICAN REPUBLIC
BELIZE Kingston Puerto Rico ANTIGUA AND BARBUDA
GUATEMALA Belmopan (USA) DOMINICA
Guatemala City HONDURAS ST. KITTS AND NEVIS
San Salvador Tegucigalpa ST. LUCIA
EL SALVADOR NICARAGUA ST. VINCENT AND BARBADOS
Managua THE GRENADINES GRENADA
COSTA San José TRINIDAD AND TOBAGO
6 RICA Caracas
PANAMA Panama City
VENEZUELA Georgetown
COLOMBIA GUYANA SURINAME
Bogotá Paramaribo Cayenne
French Guiana
(France)
Equator 0°
Galapagos Islands Quito
(Ecuador) ECUADOR
KIRIBATI
PERU BRAZIL
5
American Lima
Samoa
SAMOA Brasília
Cook Islands La Paz
(New Zealand) BOLIVIA
20°S
TONGA PARAGUAY
Tropic of Capricorn Asunción
Pitcairn CHILE
Island (UK)
Easter Island SOUTH
(Chile)
4
Santiago URUGUAY
Buenos Aires Montevideo
ARGENTINA ATLANTI
Chatham Islands
(NZ) 40°S
3 Falkland Islands (UK) OCEAN
South Georgia (UK)

North Atlantic Ocean labels:
NORTH ATLANTIC OCEAN
Greenland (Denmark)
Jan M... (Norw...)
Nuuk Reykjavik ICELAND Faeroe (Den...
REPUBLIC OF IRELAND UN... KING...
Dublin Lo...
Azores PORTUGAL U...
(Portugal) Lisbon SP...
Bermuda (UK)
Madeira Raba...
(Portugal)
Canary MOROCC...
Islands
(Spain)
Laayoune
WESTERN
SAHARA
MAURITANIA
Nouakchott
CAPE VERDE Dakar SENEGAL
THE GAMBIA Bamako BU...
GUINEA-BISSAU GUINEA
Conakry CÔTE
SIERRA LEONE D'IVOI...
Freetown Yamousso...
Monrovia
LIBERIA
Ascension Island
St. Helena (UK)
Tristan da Cunha (UK)

PACIFIC OCEAN

Antarctic Circle
ANTA... A N T A

Grid references (bottom): A 160°W B 140°W C 120°W D 100°W E 80°W F 60°W G 40°W H 20°W J

Antarctica inset:
40°W 20°W undefined
NORWAY
UNITED KINGDOM
ARGENTINA
Prime Meridien
Antarctic Circle
CHILE
60°W
80°W
ANTARCTICA
AUSTRALIA
100°W 100°E
120°W FRANCE
AUSTRALIA 120°E
NEW ZEALAND
140°W 180° 160°E 140°E
80°E

World inset map:
Europe
Asia North America
Africa
Oceania South America
Antarctica

The main map on this page is centred on the Greenwich meridian. World maps used in Oceania usually have the Pacific Ocean at the centre.

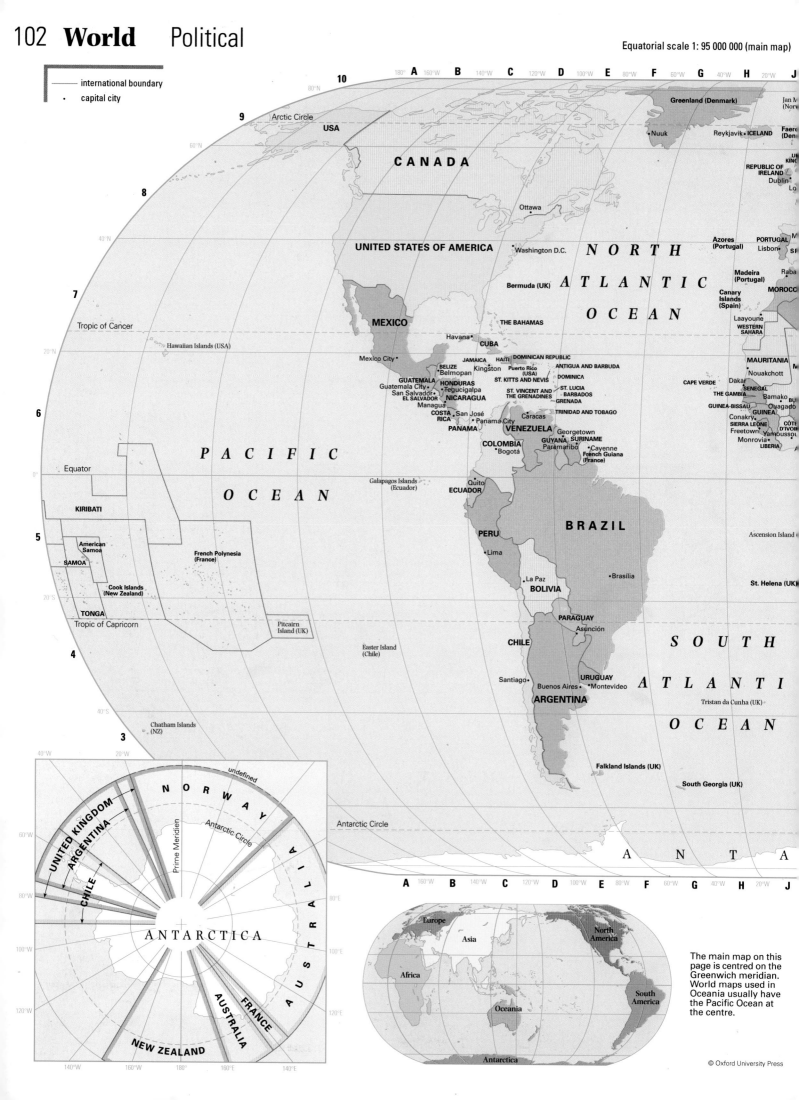

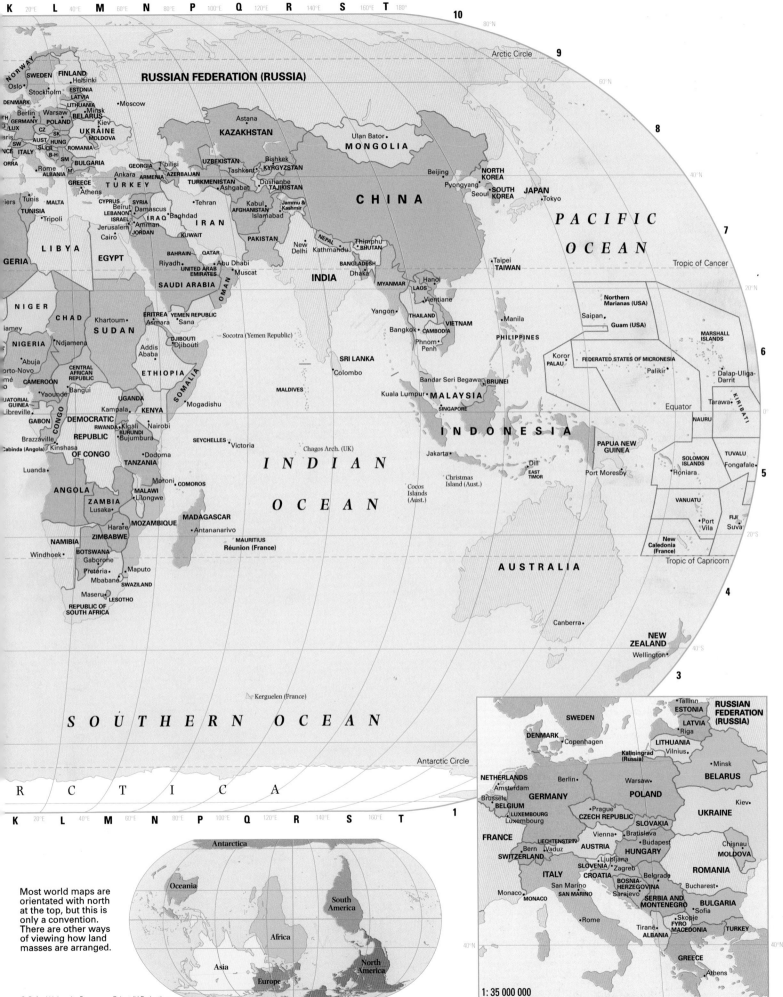

Most world maps are orientated with north at the top, but this is only a convention. There are other ways of viewing how land masses are arranged.

© Oxford University Press   Eckert IV Projection

Equatorial scale 1: 95 000 000

boundaries
— international
········· disputed

physical features
river, lake
seasonal river
seasonal lake
marsh
salt lake
salt pan
ice cap
sand dunes

land height and sea depth
metres
5000
2000
1000
500
200
0
sea level
200
4000
7000

▲ spot height in metres
▼ sea depth in metres

Continental drift
land areas
continental shelf
sea areas

ARCTIC OCEAN
BEAUFORT SEA
Greenland
Baffin Bay
Baffin Island
Davis Strait
Denmark Strait
Iceland
Yukon
Mt. McKinley 6194
Mackenzie
Great Bear Lake
Great Slave Lake
Hudson Bay
Lake Winnipeg
Missouri
ROCKY MOUNTAINS
Great Lakes
St. Lawrence
Newfoundland Basin
NORTH ATLANTIC OCEAN
Grand Banks
Ohio
Appalachian Mts.
Mississippi
Northwestern Atlantic Basin
Mt. Whitney 4418
Sierra Madre
Rio Grande
Gulf of Mexico
Greater Antilles
Puerto Rico Trench
Mid Atlantic Ridge
Canary Basin
Cape Verde Basin
Cabo Falso
Hawaiian Islands
CARIBBEAN SEA
Lesser Antilles
Great
Pacific
Basin
PACIFIC OCEAN
Llanos
Orinoco
Guiana Highlands
Negro
Galapagos Islands
Chimborazo 6310
Selvas
Amazon
Madeira
Peru Basin
Toquntins
Brazilian Highlands
SOUTH ATLANTIC OCEAN
Mid Atlantic Ridge
ANDES
Lake Titicaca
Atacama Desert
East Pacific Ridge
Polynesia
Paraguay
Paraná
Rio Grande Rise
Aconcagua 6960
Pampas
Argentine Basin
Southwest Pacific Basin
Chile Rise
Patagonia
Falkland Islands
Scotia Ridge
Southeast Pacific Basin
Cape Horn

Present day

100 million years ago (Cretaceous period)

200 million years ago (Triassic period)

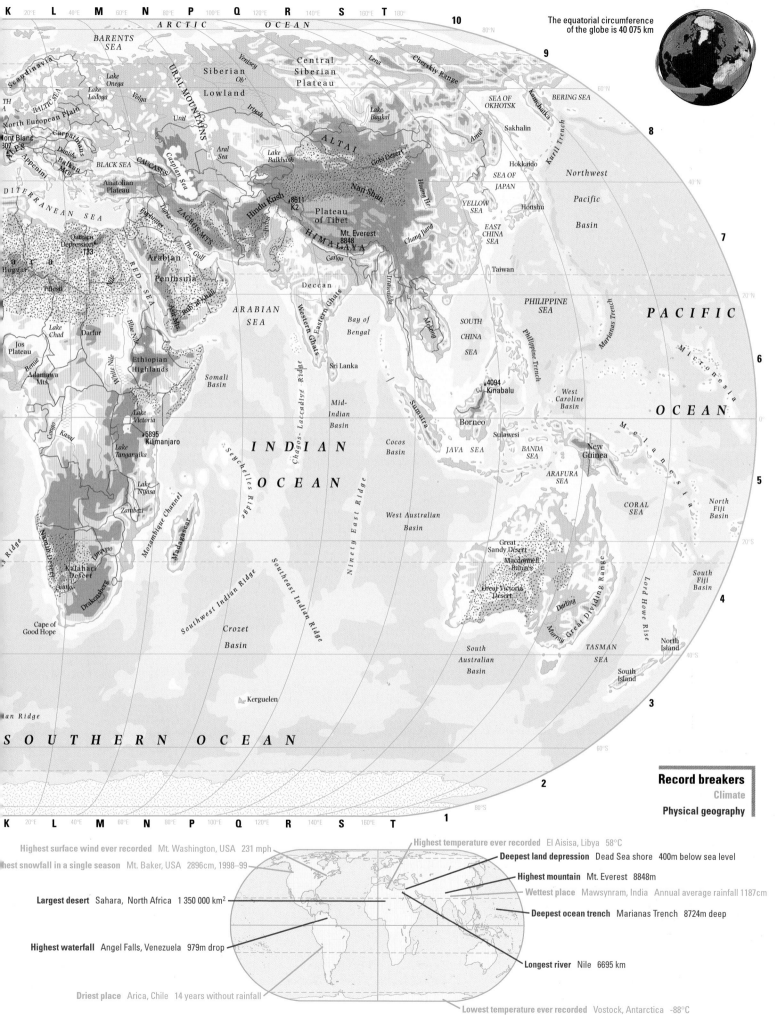

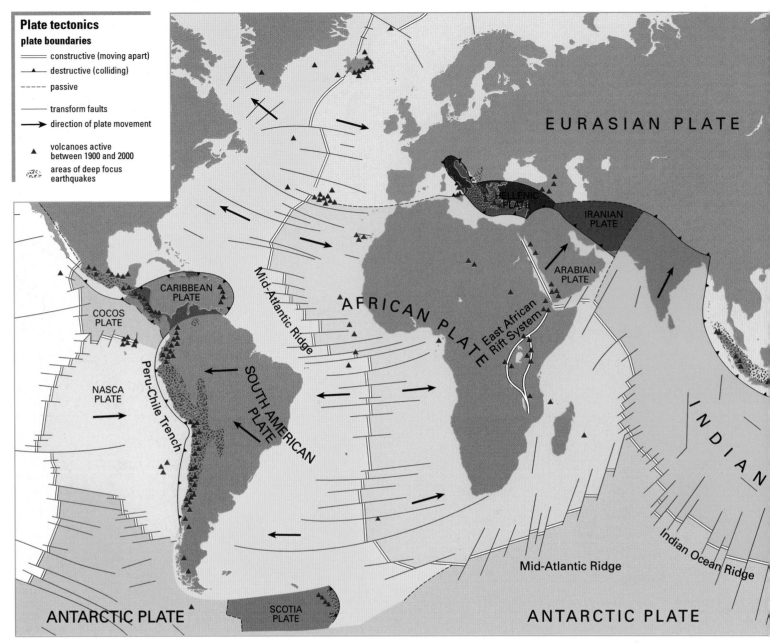

Plate tectonics

plate boundaries

- constructive (moving apart)
- ▲ destructive (colliding)
- passive
- transform faults
- → direction of plate movement
- ▲ volcanoes active between 1900 and 2000
- areas of deep focus earthquakes

EURASIAN PLATE

HELLENIC PLATE

IRANIAN PLATE

ARABIAN PLATE

AFRICAN PLATE

East African Rift System

CARIBBEAN PLATE

COCOS PLATE

NASCA PLATE

Peru-Chile Trench

SOUTH AMERICAN PLATE

Mid-Atlantic Ridge

INDIAN

Indian Ocean Ridge

Mid-Atlantic Ridge

ANTARCTIC PLATE

SCOTIA PLATE

ANTARCTIC PLATE

Structure of the Earth

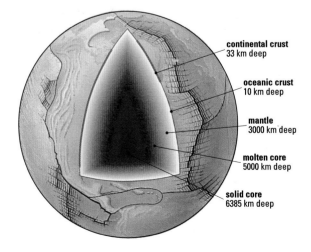

continental crust
33 km deep

oceanic crust
10 km deep

mantle
3000 km deep

molten core
5000 km deep

solid core
6385 km deep

Mt. St. Helens

A digital elevation model (DEM) of the stratovolcano which erupted on 18 May, 1980 in Washington State, USA.

Deadliest earthquakes, 1990–2000

force measured on the Richter scale

Year	Place	Force	Deaths
1990	Northwestern Iran	7.7	37 000
1990	Luzon, Philippines	7.7	1660
1991	Afghanistan/Pakistan	6.8	1000
1991	Uttar Pradesh, India	6.1	1500
1992	Erzincan, Turkey	6.7	2000
1992	Flores Island, Indonesia	7.5	2500
1993	Maharashtra, India	6.3	9800
1994	Cauca, Colombia	6.8	1000
1995	Kobe, Japan	7.2	5500
1995	Sakhalin Island, Russia	7.6	2000
1997	Ardabil, Iran	unknown	>1000
1997	Khorash, Iran	7.1	>1600
1998	Takhar, Afghanistan	6.1	>3800
1998	Northeastern Afghanistan	7.1	>3000
1999	Western Colombia	6.0	1124
1999	Izmit, Turkey	7.4	>17 000
1999	Central Taiwan	7.6	2295
1999	Ducze, Turkey	7.2	>700

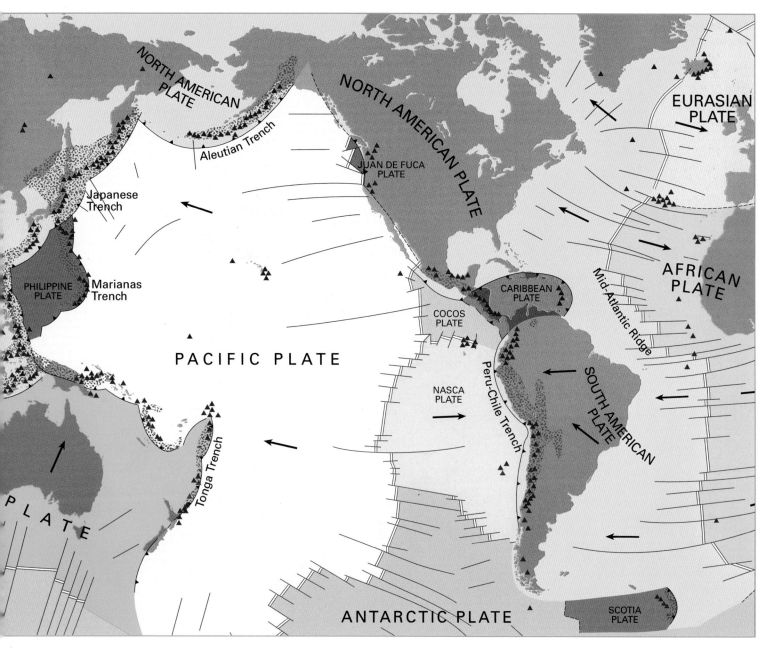

NORTH AMERICAN PLATE

NORTH AMERICAN PLATE

EURASIAN PLATE

AFRICAN PLATE

Aleutian Trench

JUAN DE FUCA PLATE

Japanese Trench

PHILIPPINE PLATE

Marianas Trench

PACIFIC PLATE

Mid-Atlantic Ridge

CARIBBEAN PLATE

COCOS PLATE

NASCA PLATE

Peru-Chile Trench

SOUTH AMERICAN PLATE

Tonga Trench

PLATE

ANTARCTIC PLATE

SCOTIA PLATE

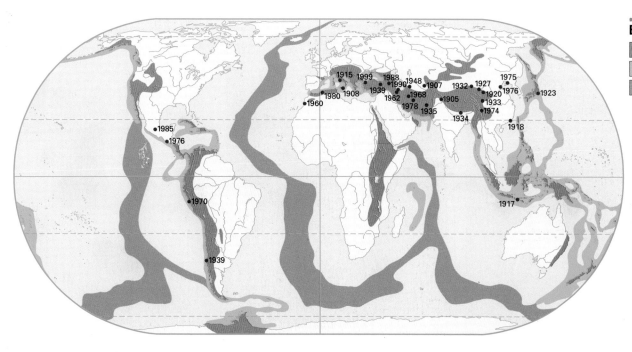

1915 1999 1988 1948 1975
1990 1907 1932 1927 1976
1980 1939 1962 1968 1905 1920 1923
1908 1978 1935 1933 1974
1960 1934 1918

1985
1976

1970

1917

1939

Earthquakes

■	mobile areas (on land)
■	mobile areas (under sea)
■	mid-oceanic ridges
•	earthquakes causing more than 10 000 deaths, 1900–2000

Eckert IV Projection

Scale 1: 240 000 000

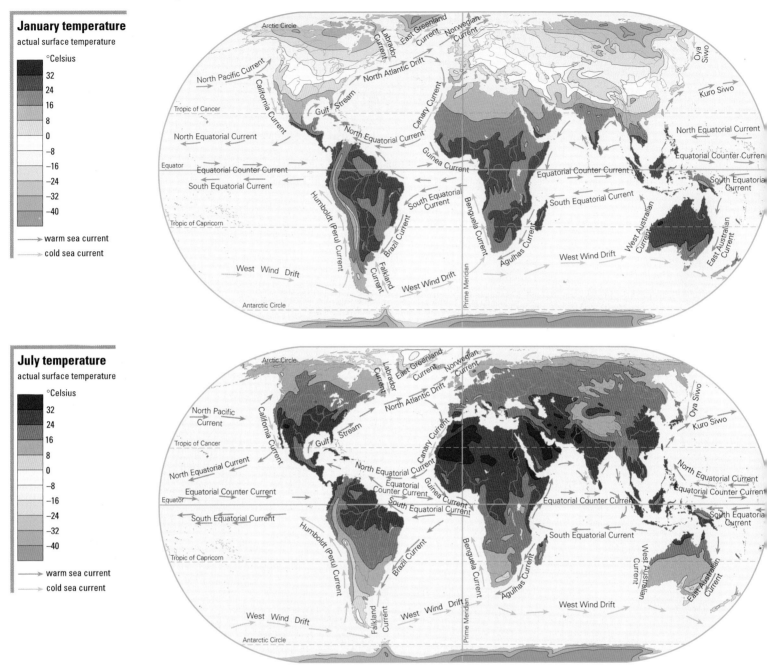

January temperature

actual surface temperature

°Celsius
- 32
- 24
- 16
- 8
- 0
- −8
- −16
- −24
- −32
- −40

→ warm sea current
→ cold sea current

July temperature

actual surface temperature

°Celsius
- 32
- 24
- 16
- 8
- 0
- −8
- −16
- −24
- −32
- −40

→ warm sea current
→ cold sea current

Antarctic ozone 'hole'

Three dimensional image of ozone depletion over Antarctica in September, 1998. The lowest ozone concentration is shown in blue.

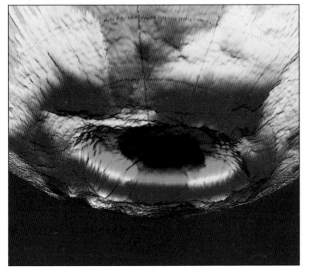

Global warming

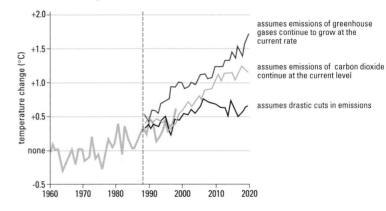

temperature change (°C)

assumes emissions of greenhouse gases continue to grow at the current rate

assumes emissions of carbon dioxide continue at the current level

assumes drastic cuts in emissions

- - - - predictions made in 1988
——— actual temperature change

© Oxford University Press

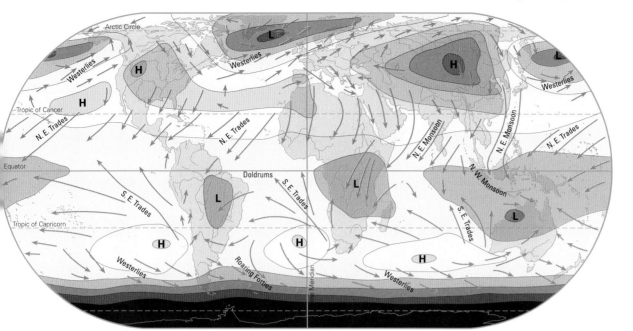

January pressure and winds

pressure reduced to sea level

millibars
1035
1030
1025
1020
1015
1010
1005
1000
995

H high pressure cell
L low pressure cell
→ prevailing wind

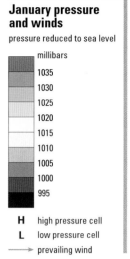

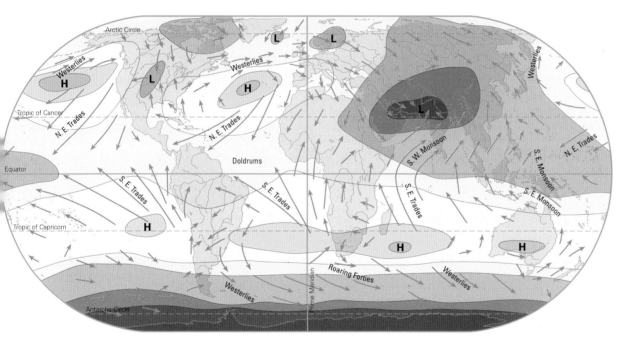

July pressure and winds

pressure reduced to sea level

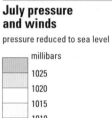

millibars
1025
1020
1015
1010
1005
1000
995

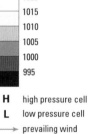

H high pressure cell
L low pressure cell
→ prevailing wind

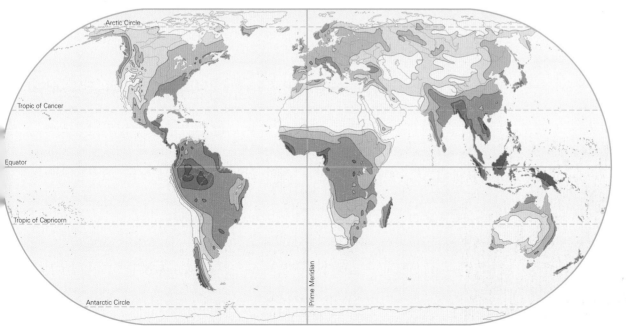

Precipitation

average annual precipitation

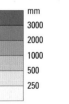

mm
3000
2000
1000
500
250

Equatorial scale 1: 95 000 000

Climate regions

Hot tropical rainy climates
- rain all year
- monsoon
- dry in winter

Very dry climates
- with no reliable rain
- with a little rain

**Climates influenced by the sea:
warm summers, mild winters**
- with dry summers (Mediterranean climate)
- with dry winters
- with no dry season

Cool climates
- with dry winters
- rain all year

Cold polar climates
- no warm season and fairly dry

Mountain climates
- height of the land strongly affects the climate

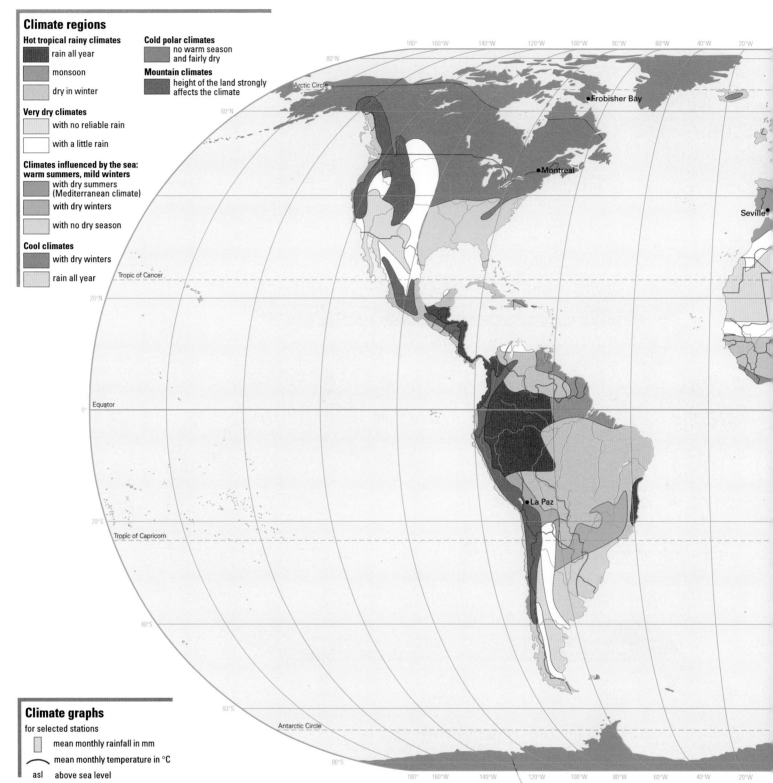

Climate graphs

for selected stations

- mean monthly rainfall in mm
- mean monthly temperature in °C
- asl   above sea level

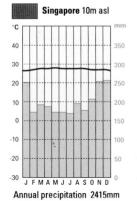

Singapore 10m asl

Annual precipitation 2415mm

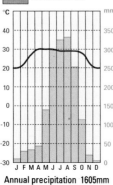

Kolkata 5m asl

Annual precipitation 1605mm

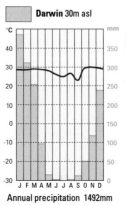

Darwin 30m asl

Annual precipitation 1492mm

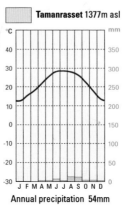

Tamanrasset 1377m asl

Annual precipitation 54mm

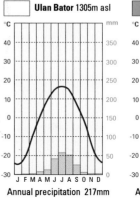

Ulan Bator 1305m asl

Annual precipitation 217mm

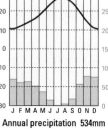

Seville 8m asl

Annual precipitation 534mm

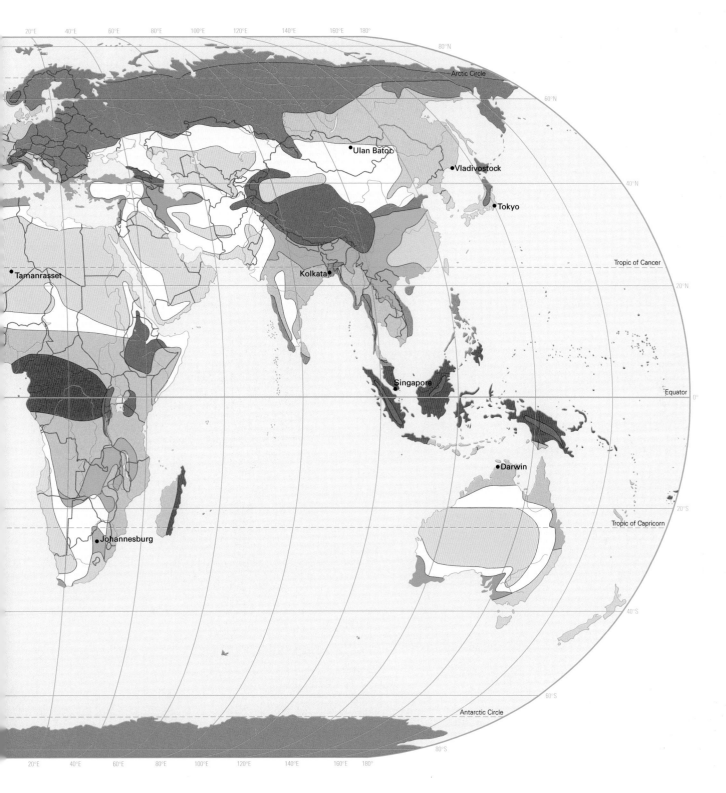

Ulan Bator

Vladivostock

Tokyo

Tropic of Cancer

Tamanrasset

Kolkata

Arctic Circle

80°N

60°N

40°N

20°N

Singapore

Equator

Darwin

20°S

Johannesburg

Tropic of Capricorn

40°S

60°S

Antarctic Circle

80°S

20°E 40°E 60°E 80°E 100°E 120°E 140°E 160°E 180°

| | Johannesburg 1665m asl | | Tokyo 6m asl | | Montreal 57m asl | | Vladivostock 29m asl | | Frobisher Bay 21m asl | | La Paz 3632m asl |

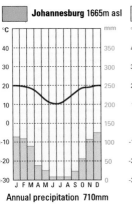
Annual precipitation 710mm

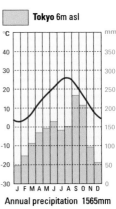
Annual precipitation 1565mm

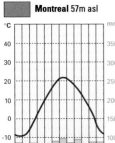
Annual precipitation 1047mm

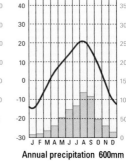
Annual precipitation 600mm

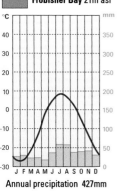
Annual precipitation 427mm

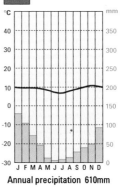
Annual precipitation 610mm

Climate data

Averages are for 1961–1990

Denver 1626m   climate station and its height above sea level

Temperature (°C) **high** average daily maximum temperature
 mean average monthly temperature
 low average daily minimum temperature

Rainfall (mm) average monthly precipitation

	Jan	Feb	Mar	Apr	May	Jun	Jul	Aug	Sep	Oct	Nov	Dec	YEAR
Denver 1626m													
Temperature (°C) high	6.2	8.1	11.2	16.6	21.6	27.4	31.2	29.9	24.9	19.1	11.4	6.9	17.9
mean	-1.3	0.8	3.9	9.0	14.0	19.4	23.1	21.9	16.8	10.8	3.9	-0.6	10.1
low	-8.8	-6.6	-3.4	1.4	6.4	11.3	14.8	13.8	8.7	2.4	-3.7	-8.1	2.4
Rainfall (mm)	13	15	33	43	61	46	49	38	32	25	22	16	393
Georgetown 2m													
Temperature (°C) high	28.6	28.9	29.2	29.5	29.4	29.2	29.6	30.2	30.8	30.8	30.2	29.1	29.6
mean	26.1	26.4	26.7	27.0	26.8	26.5	26.6	27.0	27.5	27.6	27.2	26.4	26.8
low	23.6	23.9	24.2	24.4	24.3	23.8	23.5	23.8	24.2	24.4	24.2	23.8	24.0
Rainfall (mm)	185	89	111	141	286	328	268	201	98	107	186	262	2262
Guangzhou 42m													
Temperature (°C) high	18.3	18.4	21.6	25.5	29.4	31.3	32.7	32.6	31.4	28.6	24.4	20.5	26.2
mean	13.3	14.3	17.7	21.9	25.6	27.3	28.5	28.3	27.1	24.0	19.4	15.0	21.9
low	5.0	6.6	10.7	16.1	20.7	23.5	25.7	25.2	22.6	17.6	11.9	6.5	16.0
Rainfall (mm)	43	65	85	182	284	258	228	221	172	79	42	24	1683
Havana 50m													
Temperature (°C) high	25.8	26.1	27.6	28.6	29.8	30.5	31.3	31.6	31.0	29.2	27.7	26.5	28.8
mean	22.2	22.4	23.7	24.8	26.1	26.9	27.6	27.8	27.4	26.2	24.5	23.0	25.2
low	18.6	18.6	19.7	20.9	22.4	23.4	23.8	24.1	23.8	23.0	21.3	19.5	21.6
Rainfall (mm)	64	69	46	54	98	182	106	100	144	181	88	58	1190
Juliaca 3827m													
Temperature (°C) high	16.7	16.7	16.5	16.8	16.6	16.0	16.0	17.0	17.6	18.6	18.8	17.7	17.1
mean	10.2	10.1	9.9	8.7	6.4	4.5	4.3	5.8	8.1	9.5	10.2	10.4	8.2
low	3.6	3.5	3.2	0.6	-3.8	-7.0	-7.5	-5.4	-1.4	0.3	1.5	3.0	-0.8
Rainfall (mm)	133	109	99	43	10	3	3	6	22	41	55	86	609
Khartoum 380m													
Temperature (°C) high	30.8	33.0	36.8	40.1	41.9	41.3	38.4	37.3	39.1	39.3	35.2	31.8	37.1
mean	23.2	25.0	28.7	31.9	34.5	34.3	32.1	31.5	32.5	32.4	28.1	24.5	29.9
low	15.6	17.0	20.5	23.6	27.1	27.3	25.9	25.3	26.0	25.5	21.0	17.1	22.7
Rainfall (mm)	0	0	0	0.5	4	5	46	75	25	5	1	0	161
Lhasa 3650m													
Temperature (°C) high	6.9	9.0	12.1	15.6	19.3	22.7	22.1	21.1	19.7	16.3	11.2	7.7	15.3
mean	-2.1	1.1	4.6	8.1	11.9	15.5	15.3	14.5	12.8	8.1	2.2	-1.7	7.5
low	-10.1	-6.8	-3.0	0.9	5.0	9.3	10.1	9.4	7.5	1.3	-4.9	-9.0	0.8
Rainfall (mm)	1	1	2	5	27	72	119	123	58	10	2	1	421
Libreville 15m													
Temperature (°C) high	29.5	30.0	30.2	30.1	29.4	27.6	26.4	26.8	27.5	28.0	28.4	29.0	28.6
mean	26.8	27.0	27.1	26.6	26.7	25.4	24.3	24.3	25.4	25.7	25.9	26.2	26.0
low	24.1	24.0	23.9	23.1	24.0	23.2	22.1	21.8	23.4	23.4	23.4	23.4	23.3
Rainfall (mm)	250	243	363	339	247	54	1	14	104	427	490	303	2841
Limón 3m													
Temperature (°C) high	27.9	28.6	29.6	29.6	28.5	27.5	27.7	27.7	27.2	27.0	27.1	27.7	28.0
mean	24.0	24.3	25.0	25.8	26.1	25.9	25.2	25.6	25.7	25.4	25.1	24.3	25.2
low	20.3	20.3	20.9	21.6	22.2	22.3	22.1	22.1	22.2	21.9	21.6	20.9	21.5
Rainfall (mm)	319	201	193	287	281	276	408	289	163	198	367	402	3384
Malatya 849m													
Temperature (°C) high	2.9	5.3	11.1	18.2	23.5	29.2	33.8	33.4	28.9	20.9	11.8	5.7	18.7
mean	-0.4	1.5	6.9	13.0	17.8	22.9	27.0	26.5	22.0	14.8	7.6	2.4	13.5
low	-3.2	-1.7	2.4	7.7	11.8	16.1	19.8	19.4	15.2	9.5	3.7	-0.3	8.4
Rainfall (mm)	42	36	60	61	50	22	3	2	6	40	47	42	411
Manaus 84m													
Temperature (°C) high	30.5	30.4	30.6	30.7	30.8	31.0	31.3	32.6	32.9	32.8	32.1	31.3	31.4
mean	26.1	26.0	26.1	26.3	26.3	26.4	26.5	27.0	27.5	27.6	27.3	26.7	26.7
low	23.1	23.1	23.2	23.3	23.3	23.0	22.7	23.0	23.5	23.7	23.7	23.5	23.3
Rainfall (mm)	260	288	314	300	256	114	88	58	83	126	183	217	2287

	Jan	Feb	Mar	Apr	May	Jun	Jul	Aug	Sep	Oct	Nov	Dec	YEAR
Meekatharra 518m													
Temperature (°C) high	38.1	36.5	34.5	29.2	23.6	19.7	18.9	21.0	25.4	29.4	33.1	36.5	28.8
mean	31.2	30.1	28.0	23.2	17.8	14.3	13.2	14.8	18.4	22.2	25.9	29.3	22.4
low	24.3	23.7	21.5	17.1	11.9	8.9	7.5	8.5	11.4	15.0	18.6	22.1	15.9
Rainfall (mm)	26	30	22	17	27	36	25	12	6	7	14	11	233
Minneapolis-St. Paul 255m													
Temperature (°C) high	-6.3	-3.0	4.0	13.6	20.8	26.0	28.9	27.1	21.5	14.9	5.0	-3.6	12.4
mean	-11.2	-7.8	-0.6	8.0	14.7	20.1	23.1	21.4	15.8	9.3	0.7	-7.8	7.1
low	-16.2	-12.7	-5.2	2.3	8.7	14.2	17.3	15.7	10.2	3.8	-3.8	-12.1	1.9
Rainfall (mm)	24	22	49	62	86	103	90	92	69	56	39	27	719
Ndola 1270m													
Temperature (°C) high	26.6	26.9	27.4	27.5	26.6	25.1	25.2	27.5	30.5	31.5	29.4	27.0	27.6
mean	20.8	20.8	21.0	20.5	18.6	16.5	16.7	19.2	22.5	23.7	22.5	21.0	20.3
low	17.1	17.1	16.5	14.4	10.8	7.9	7.8	10.2	13.6	16.2	17.1	17.2	13.8
Rainfall (mm)	293	249	170	46	4	1	0	0	3	32	130	306	1234
Nuuk 70m													
Temperature (°C) high	-4.4	-4.5	-4.8	-0.8	3.5	7.7	10.6	9.9	6.3	1.7	-1.0	-3.3	1.7
mean	-7.4	-7.8	-8.0	-3.9	0.6	3.9	6.5	6.1	3.5	-0.6	-3.6	-6.2	-1.4
low	-10.1	-10.6	-10.6	-6.1	-1.5	1.3	3.8	3.8	1.6	-2.5	-5.8	-8.7	-3.8
Rainfall (mm)	39	47	50	46	55	62	82	89	88	70	74	54	756
Paris 65m													
Temperature (°C) high	6.0	7.6	10.8	14.4	18.2	21.5	24.0	23.8	20.8	16.0	10.1	6.8	15.0
mean	3.4	4.2	6.6	9.5	13.2	16.4	18.4	18.0	15.3	11.4	6.7	4.2	10.6
low	0.9	1.3	2.9	4.9	8.3	11.2	12.9	12.7	10.6	7.7	3.8	1.7	6.6
Rainfall (mm)	54	46	54	47	63	58	84	52	54	56	56	56	650
Qiqihar 148m													
Temperature (°C) high	-12.7	-7.8	2.3	12.9	21.0	26.2	27.8	26.1	20.1	11.1	-1.3	-10.4	9.6
mean	-19.2	-14.8	-4.5	6.1	14.4	20.3	22.8	20.9	14.0	4.8	-7.1	-16.2	3.5
low	-24.5	-20.9	-11.0	-0.9	7.3	14.2	17.9	16.2	8.5	-0.7	-12.0	-21.2	-2.3
Rainfall (mm)	1	2	5	15	31	64	138	94	45	19	4	3	421
Rabat Sale 75m													
Temperature (°C) high	17.2	17.7	19.2	20.0	22.1	24.1	26.8	27.1	26.4	24.0	20.6	17.7	21.9
mean	12.6	13.1	14.2	15.2	17.4	19.8	22.2	22.4	21.5	19.0	15.9	13.2	17.2
low	8.0	8.6	9.2	10.4	12.7	15.4	17.6	17.7	16.7	14.1	11.1	8.7	12.5
Rainfall (mm)	77	74	61	62	25	7	1	1	6	44	97	101	556
Sittwe 5m													
Temperature (°C) high	28.0	29.4	31.4	34.1	31.5	29.5	28.9	28.9	30.1	31.1	30.3	28.5	30.1
mean	21.4	22.7	24.8	28.9	28.3	27.1	26.8	26.7	27.4	27.6	25.7	22.6	25.8
low	14.7	15.9	18.2	23.6	25.1	24.6	24.7	24.5	24.6	24.0	21.0	16.6	21.5
Rainfall (mm)	11	8	5	44	268	1091	1155	1025	537	289	105	17	4555
Stockholm 52m													
Temperature (°C) high	-0.7	-0.6	3.0	8.6	15.7	20.7	21.9	20.4	15.1	9.9	4.5	1.1	10.0
mean	-2.8	-3.0	0.1	4.6	10.7	15.6	17.2	16.2	11.9	7.5	2.6	-1.0	6.6
low	-5.0	-5.3	-2.7	1.1	6.3	11.3	13.4	12.7	9.0	5.3	0.7	-3.2	3.6
Rainfall (mm)	39	27	26	30	30	45	72	66	55	50	53	46	539
Tehran 1191m													
Temperature (°C) high	7.2	9.9	15.4	21.9	28.0	34.1	36.8	35.4	31.5	24.0	16.5	9.8	22.5
mean	3.0	5.3	10.3	16.4	22.1	27.5	30.4	29.2	25.3	18.5	11.6	5.6	17.1
low	-1.1	0.7	5.2	10.9	16.1	20.9	24.0	23.0	19.2	12.9	6.7	1.3	11.7
Rainfall (mm)	37	34	37	28	15	3	3	1	1	14	21	36	230
Wellington 8m													
Temperature (°C) high	21.3	21.1	19.8	17.3	14.8	12.8	12.0	12.7	14.2	15.9	17.8	19.6	16.6
mean	17.8	17.7	16.6	14.3	11.9	10.1	9.2	9.8	11.2	12.8	14.5	16.3	13.5
low	14.4	14.3	13.5	11.3	9.1	7.3	6.4	6.9	8.3	9.7	11.3	13.2	10.5
Rainfall (mm)	67	48	76	87	99	113	111	106	82	81	74	74	1018

Tropical revolving storms

temperature 27°C and over at mean sea level

August–September
Maximum frequency in
northern hemisphere

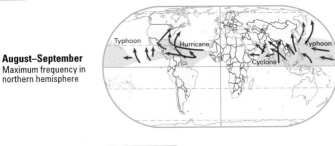

January–March
Maximum frequency in
southern hemisphere

Hurricane Floyd, Florida
Winds in this hurricane reached 225km per hour and caused 40 deaths.
US NOAA satellite image, 15 September, 1999.

Drought and flood

areas where severe drought may occur

major river flood plains susceptible to flooding

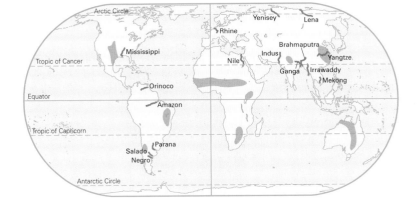

Dust storms, South West Africa
Dust streaming from SW African coastal
deserts into the Atlantic Ocean.
NASA SeaWiFS image, 6 June, 2000.

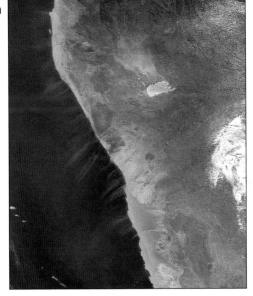

El Niño

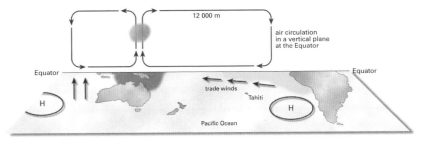

Normal year
The Humboldt current carries cold water north along the coast of Peru.
High temperatures in S.E. Asia draw in the S.E. Trade Winds which
push the surface waters west. Rainfall in S.E. Asia is high. Cold water
continues to flow north along the coast of S. America and this is rich in
plankton and fish.

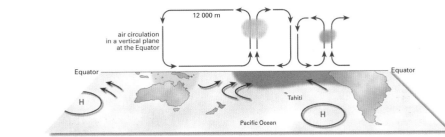

El Niño year
Weaker S.E. Trade Winds allow hot water from the western Pacific to
drift eastwards. Warm waters appear in Peru at about Christmas time.
Arid coastal areas in S. America suffer torrential rains. Coastal fish
stocks move to deeper cold water out of reach of small boats.
Drought occurs in S.E. Asia.

Equatorial scale 1: 105 000 000

Ecosystems

vegetation types are those which would occur naturally without interference by people

coniferous forest
cone bearing trees

deciduous and mixed forest
leaf shedding and coniferous trees

tropical rain forest
many species of lush, tall trees

tropical grasslands (savannah)
tall grass parkland with scattered trees

evergreen trees and shrubs
plants and small trees with leathery leaves

thorn forest
low trees and shrubs with spines or thorns

temperate grasslands
prairies, steppes, pampas, and veld

semi-desert
short grasses and drought-resistant scrub

desert
sand and stones, very little vegetation

tundra
moss and lichen, with few trees

ice
no vegetation

mountains
thin soils, steep slopes,
and high altitude
affects type of
vegetation

ice
Aerial view of Jameson Land, towards
Liverpool Land, Greenland

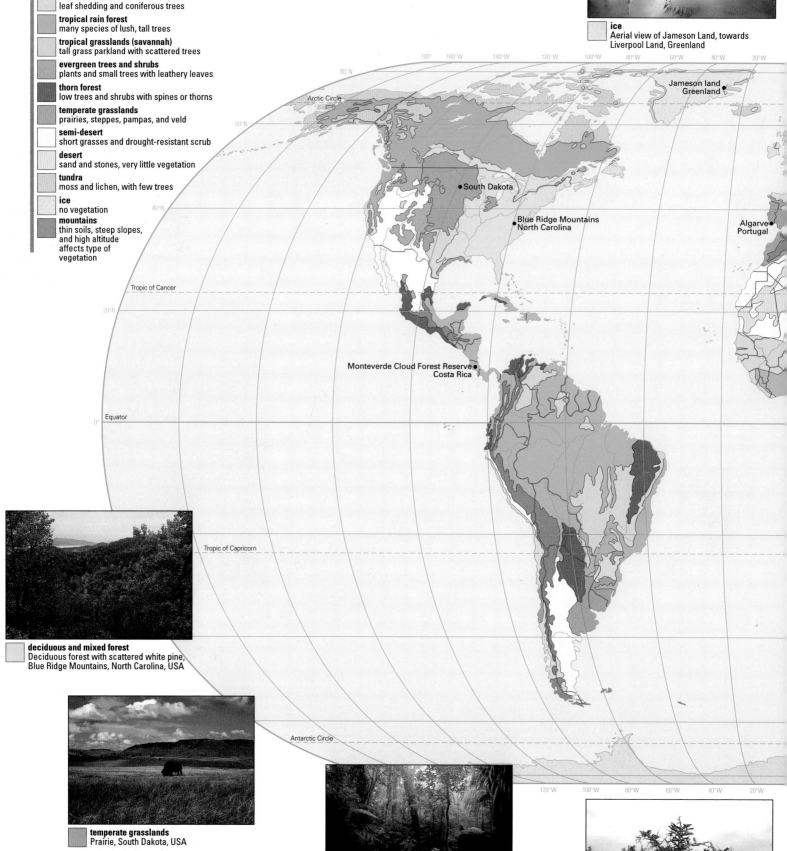

deciduous and mixed forest
Deciduous forest with scattered white pine,
Blue Ridge Mountains, North Carolina, USA

temperate grasslands
Prairie, South Dakota, USA

tropical rain forest
Monteverde Cloud Forest Reserve,
Costa Rica

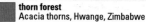

thorn forest
Acacia thorns, Hwange, Zimbabwe

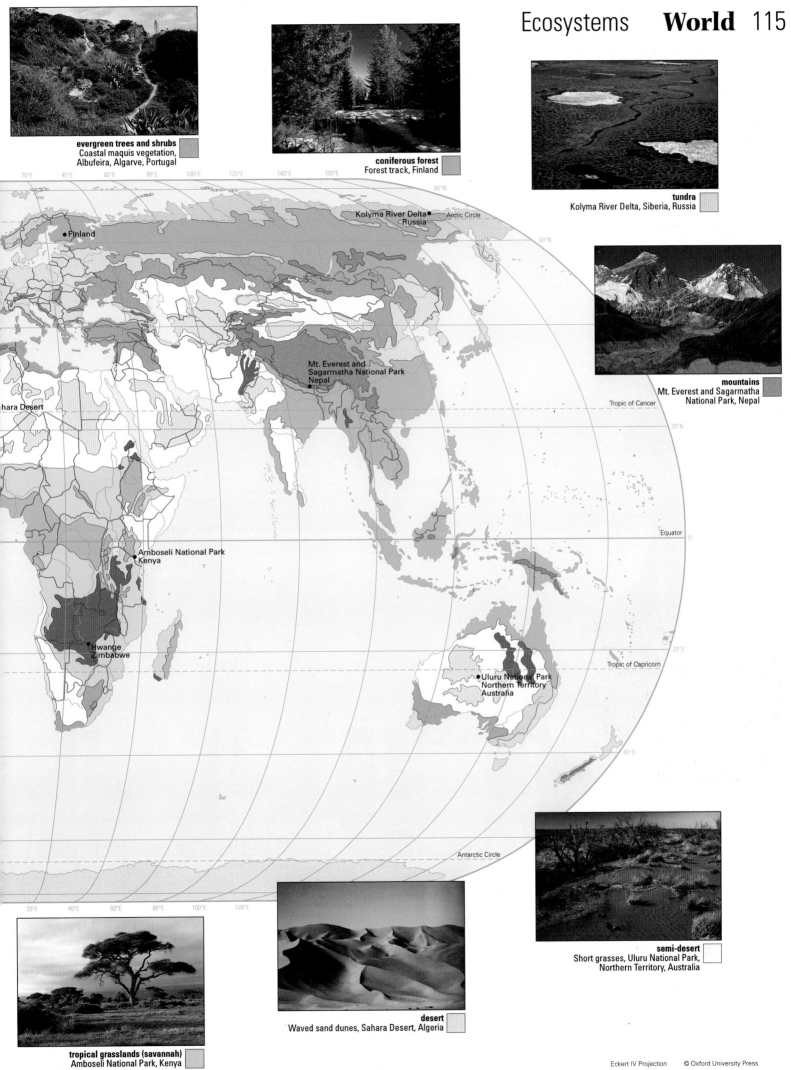

evergreen trees and shrubs
Coastal maquis vegetation,
Albufeira, Algarve, Portugal

coniferous forest
Forest track, Finland

tundra
Kolyma River Delta, Siberia, Russia

mountains
Mt. Everest and Sagarmatha
National Park, Nepal

semi-desert
Short grasses, Uluru National Park,
Northern Territory, Australia

desert
Waved sand dunes, Sahara Desert, Algeria

tropical grasslands (savannah)
Amboseli National Park, Kenya

Kolyma River Delta
Russia

Arctic Circle

Finland

Mt. Everest and
Sagarmatha National Park
Nepal

hara Desert

Amboseli National Park
Kenya

Hwange
Zimbabwe

Uluru National Park
Northern Territory
Australia

Tropic of Cancer

Equator

Tropic of Capricorn

Antarctic Circle

80°N
60°N
20°N
0°
20°S
40°S

20°E 40°E 60°E 80°E 100°E 120°E 140°E 160°E

20°E 40°E 60°E 80°E 100°E 120°E

Eckert IV Projection   © Oxford University Press

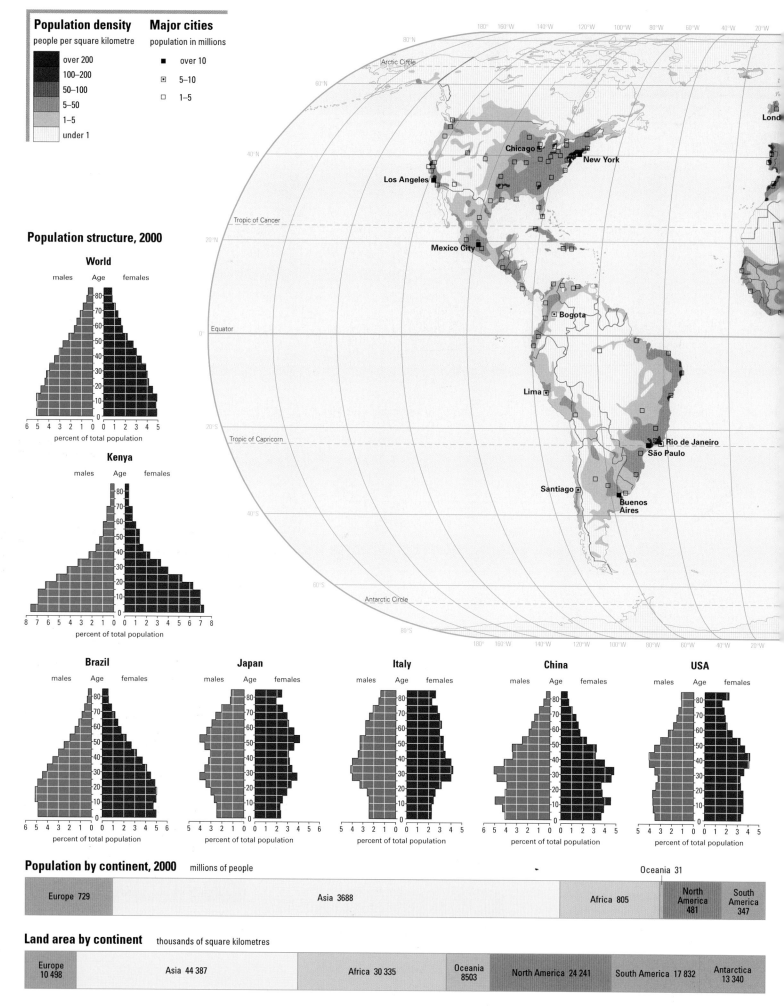

Population density

people per square kilometre

- over 200
- 100–200
- 50–100
- 5–50
- 1–5
- under 1

Major cities

population in millions

- ■ over 10
- ◙ 5–10
- □ 1–5

Population structure, 2000

World

males / Age / females

percent of total population

Kenya

males / Age / females

percent of total population

Brazil

males / Age / females

percent of total population

Japan

males / Age / females

percent of total population

Italy

males / Age / females

percent of total population

China

males / Age / females

percent of total population

USA

males / Age / females

percent of total population

Population by continent, 2000   millions of people

Europe 729	Asia 3688	Africa 805	Oceania 31	North America 481	South America 347

Land area by continent   thousands of square kilometres

Europe 10 498	Asia 44 387	Africa 30 335	Oceania 8503	North America 24 241	South America 17 832	Antarctica 13 340

Eckert IV Projection   © Oxford University Press

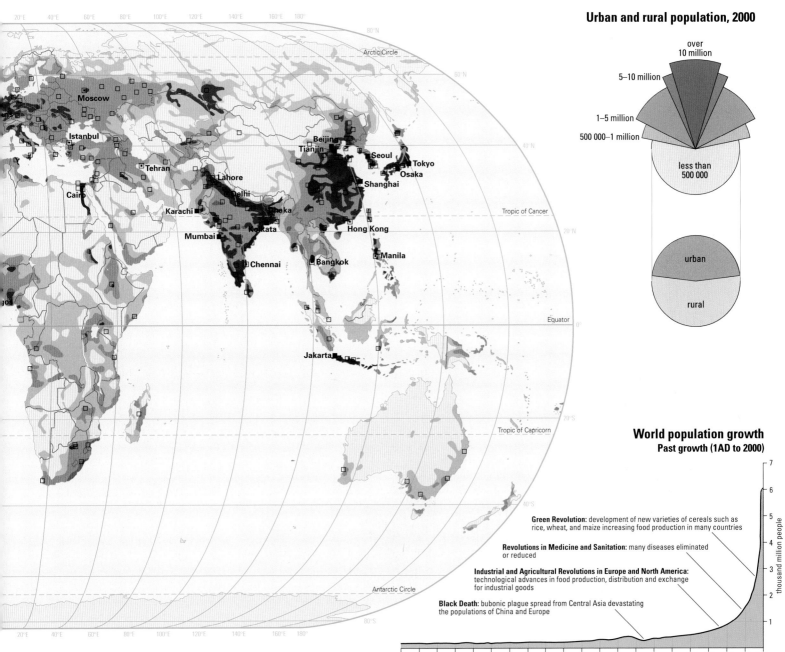

Urban and rural population, 2000

over 10 million
5–10 million
1–5 million
500 000–1 million
less than 500 000

urban
rural

World population growth
Past growth (1AD to 2000)

Green Revolution: development of new varieties of cereals such as rice, wheat, and maize increasing food production in many countries

Revolutions in Medicine and Sanitation: many diseases eliminated or reduced

Industrial and Agricultural Revolutions in Europe and North America: technological advances in food production, distribution and exchange for industrial goods

Black Death: bubonic plague spread from Central Asia devastating the populations of China and Europe

thousand million people

1AD 100 200 300 400 500 600 700 800 900 1000 1100 1200 1300 1400 1500 1600 1700 1800 1900 2000

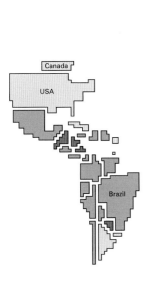

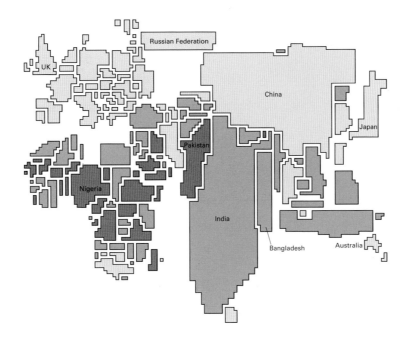

Population cartogram

the size of each country represents the number of people living there

100 million
25 million
1 million

Population change

average annual increase or decrease

very high increase (over 2.6%)
increase above world average (1.3–2.6%)
increase below world average (0–1.3%)
decrease (by less than 1%)

Population change, 1990–2000

percentage population gain or loss

- over 40% gain
- 30–40% gain
- 20–30% gain
- 10–20% gain
- under 10% gain
- 0–10% loss

Highest population gain
Afghanistan 75.5%
Qatar 54.6%
Jordan 53.2%
French Guiana 48.9%
Marshall Islands 47.3%

United Kingdom 3.3%

Highest population loss
Kuwait -7.9%
Georgia -8%
Latvia -10%
Bulgaria -12.3%
Bosnia-Herzegovina -13.3%

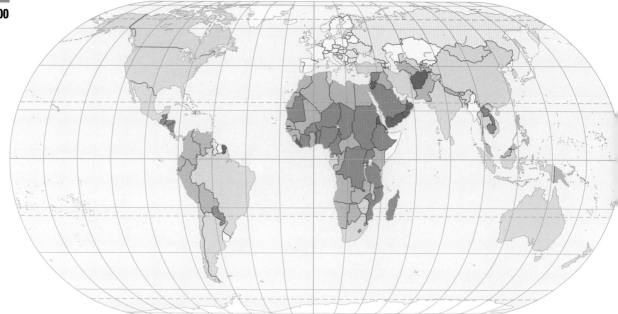

Urban population, 2000

percentage of the population living in urban areas

- over 80%
- 60–80%
- 40–60%
- 20–40%
- under 20%

Most urban
Kuwait 100%
Monaco 100%
Nauru 100%
Singapore 100%
Belgium 97%

United Kingdom 90%

Least urban
Bhutan 15%
Solomon Islands 13%
Nepal 11%
Burundi 8%
Rwanda 5%

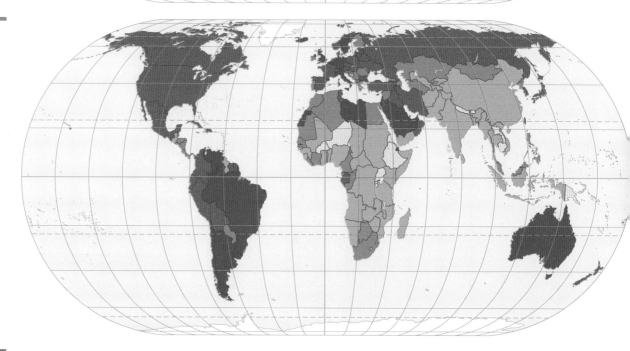

Fertility rate, 2000

average number of children born to childbearing women

- over 6 children
- 5–5.9 children
- 4–4.9 children
- 3–3.9 children
- 2–2.9 children
- 1–1.9 children

Largest families
Niger 7.5 children
Yemen 7.2 children
Mali 7.0 children
Angola 6.9 children
Uganda 6.9 children

United Kingdom 1.7 children

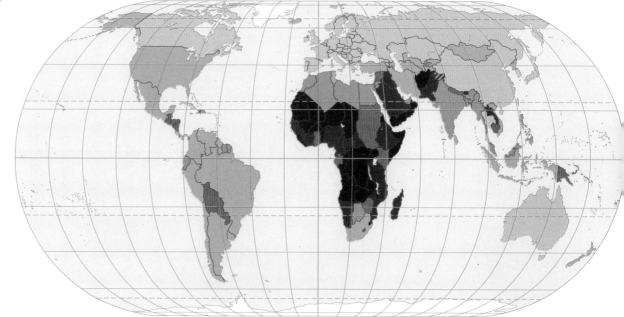

Eckert IV Projection   © Oxford University Press

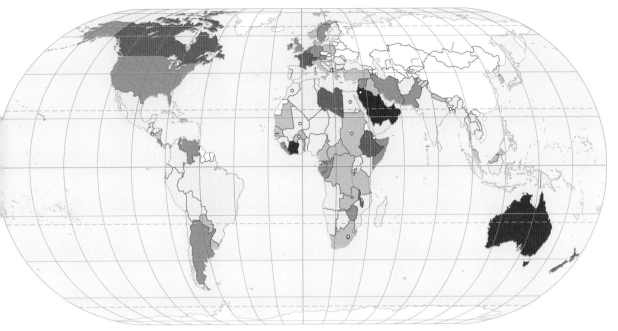

International migration

percentage of total population
foreign born

over 20%

10–20%

5–10%

2–5%

under 2%

no data

○ countries where more than
20% of foreign earnings is sent
home as payments from
workers abroad

Highest percentage of foreign born
United Arab Emirates 90.2%
Oman 33.6%
Israel 30.9%
Côte d'Ivoire 29.3%
Jordan 26.4%

United Kingdom 6.5%

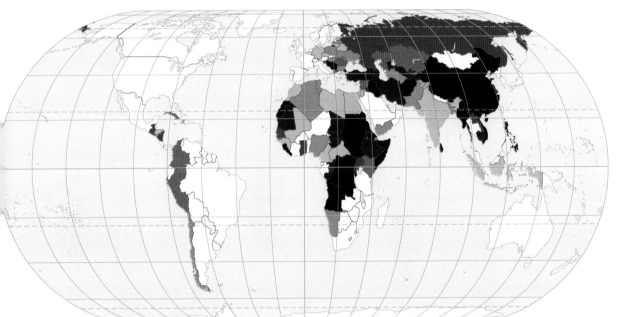

Refugees by country of origin, 1999

number of applications for refugee
status submitted during 1999

over 100 000

25 000–100 000

10 000–25 000

2500–10 000

500–2500

under 500

no data

**Countries from which most refugees
fled, 1999**
Iraq 572 500
Burundi 525 500
Sierra Leone 487 200
Sudan 467 700
Somalia 451 600

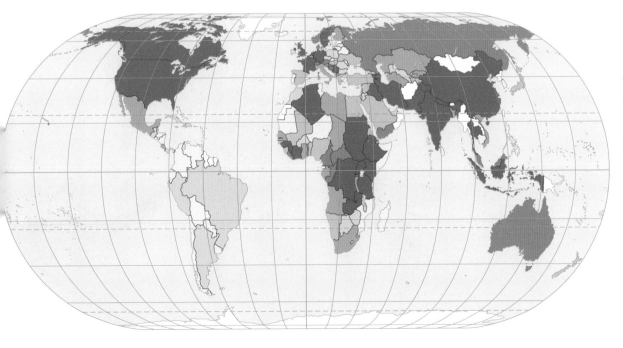

Refugees by country of asylum, 1999

number of applications for refugee
status submitted during 1999

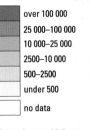

over 100 000

25 000–100 000

10 000–25 000

2500–10 000

500–2500

under 500

no data

**Countries to which most refugees
fled, 1999**
Iran 1 835 700
Pakistan 1 202 000
Germany 975 500
Tanzania 622 200
USA 513 000

United Kingdom 137 000

Purchasing power, 1999

Purchasing Power Parity (PPP) in US$
Based on Gross Domestic Product (GDP)
per person, adjusted for the local cost
of living

- over 25 000
- 10 000–25 000
- 5000–10 000
- 2500–5000
- 1000–2500
- under 1000

Highest purchasing power
Luxembourg $42 769
United States $31 872
Norway $28 433
Iceland $27 835
Switzerland $27 171

United Kingdom $22 093

Lowest purchasing power
Ethiopia $628
Malawi $586
Burundi $578
Tanzania $501
Sierra Leone $448

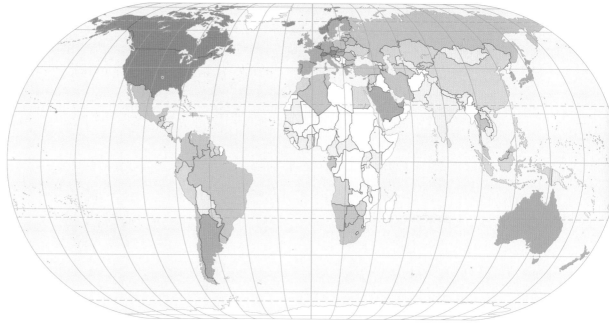

Literacy and schooling, 1999

percentage of the population over 15 years
able to read and write

- over 95%
- 85–95%
- 75–85%
- 60–75%
- 40–60%
- under 40%

Highest literacy levels
Latvia 99.8%
Poland 99.7%
Georgia 99.6%
Slovenia 99.6%
Ukraine 99.6%

United Kingdom 99%

Lowest literacy levels
Gambia 35.7%
Guinea 35%
Sierra Leone 32%
Burkina 23%
Niger 15.3%

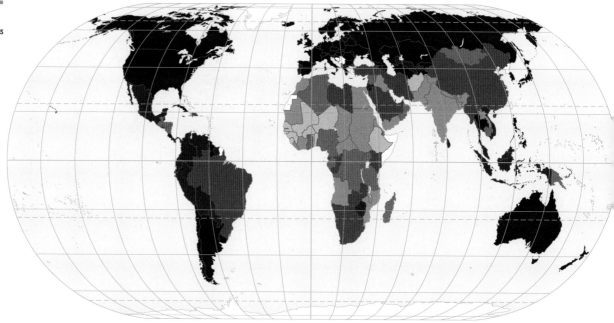

Life expectancy

average expected lifespan of babies
born in 2000

- over 75 years
- 70–75 years
- 65–70 years
- 60–65 years
- 55–60 years
- 50–55 years
- under 50 years

Highest life expectancy
Japan 81 years
San Marino 80 years
Sweden 80 years
Switzerland 80 years

United Kingdom 77 years

Lowest life expectancy
Malawi 39 years
Rwanda 39 years
Angola 38 years
Zambia 37 years

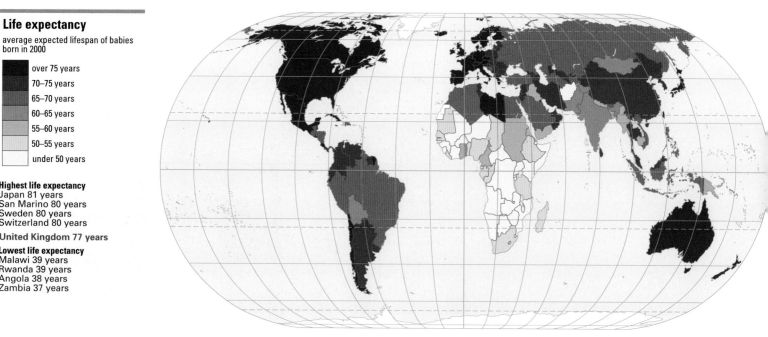

Eckert IV Projection   © Oxford University Press

Human Development Index (HDI), 1999

HDI measures the relative social and economic progress of a country. It combines life expectancy, adult literacy, average number of years of schooling, and purchasing power.

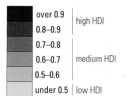

over 0.9	high HDI
0.8–0.9	
0.7–0.8	
0.6–0.7	medium HDI
0.5–0.6	
under 0.5	low HDI

Highest HDI
Norway 0.939
Australia 0.936
Canada 0.936
Sweden 0.936
Belgium 0.935

United Kingdom 0.923

Lowest HDI
Ethiopia 0.321
Burkina 0.320
Burundi 0.309
Niger 0.274
Sierra Leone 0.258

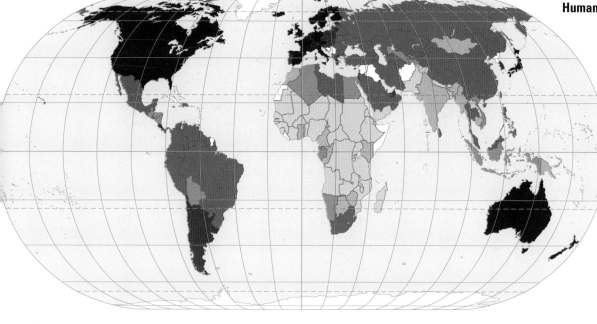

Medical care, 1990–1999

number of doctors per 100 000 people

over 300
200–300
100–200
10–100
under 10

Most doctors per 100 000 people
Italy 554
Belarus 443
Georgia 436
Spain 424
Russian Federation 421

United Kingdom 164

Fewest doctors per 100 000 people
Central African Republic 4
Gambia 4
Nepal 4
Niger 4
Tanzania 4
Burkina 3
Chad 3
Gambia 3

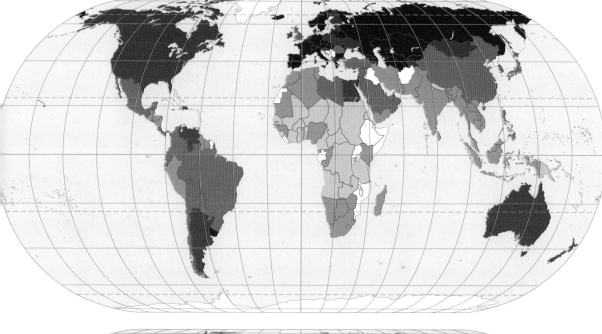

Food consumption, 1997

average daily food intake in calories per person

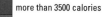

more than 3500 calories
3000–3500 calories
2500–3000 calories
2000–2500 calories
less than 2000 calories
○ average food consumption per head declining by more than 1%, 1988–1997

Highest food consumption
United States 3699
Portugal 3667
Greece 3649
Belgium 3619
Ireland 3565

United Kingdom 3276

Lowest food consumption
Comoros 1858
Ethiopia 1858
Congo, Democratic Republic 1755
Burundi 1685
Eritrea 1622

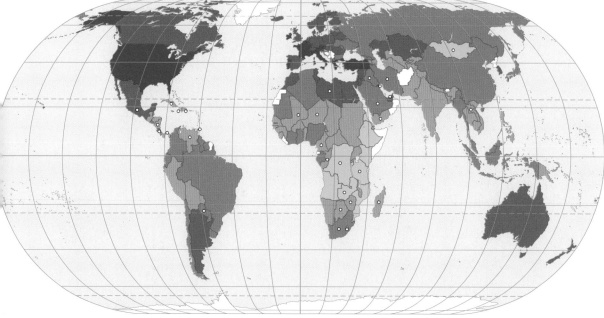

Employment in agriculture
percentage of the labour force

- over 80%
- 60–80%
- 30–60%
- 10–30%
- under 10%
- no data

Highest employment in agriculture
Bhutan 94%
Nepal 94%
Burkina 92%
Burundi 92%
Rwanda 92%

Lowest employment in agriculture
Bahrain 2%
Brunei 2%
United Kingdom 2%
Kuwait 1%
Singapore 0%

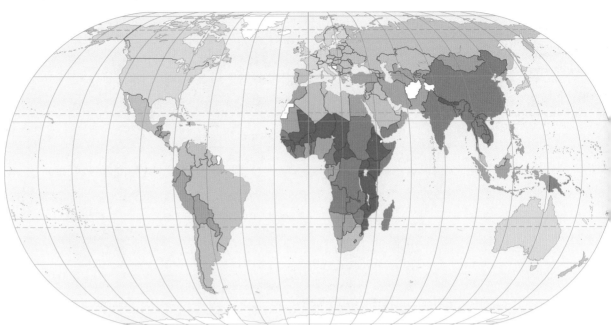

Employment in industry
percentage of the labour force

- over 80%
- 60–80%
- 30–60%
- 10–30%
- under 10%
- no data

Highest employment in industry
Bulgaria 48%
Romaina 47%
Slovenia 46%
Czech Republic 45%
Armenia 43%
Mauritius 43%

United Kingdom 29%

Lowest employment in industry
Bhutan 2%
Burkina 2%
Ethiopia 2%
Guinea 2%
Guinea-Bissau 2%
Mali 2%
Nepal 0%

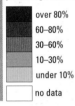

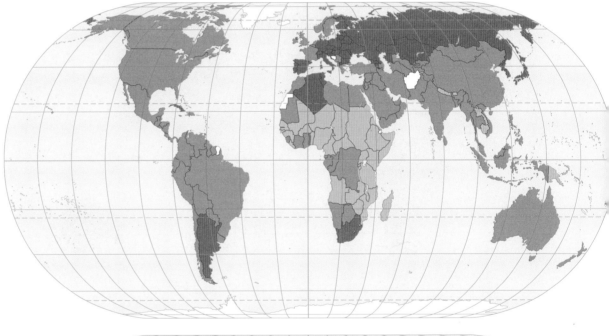

Employment in services
percentage of the labour force

- over 80%
- 60–80%
- 30–60%
- 10–30%
- under 10%
- no data

Highest employment in service
Bahamas 79%
Brunei 74%
Kuwait 74%
Sweden 74%
Canada 72%

United Kingdom 69%

Lowest employment in services
Burkina 6%
Nepal 6%
Niger 6%
Burundi 5%
Rwanda 5%
Bhutan 4%

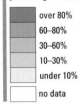

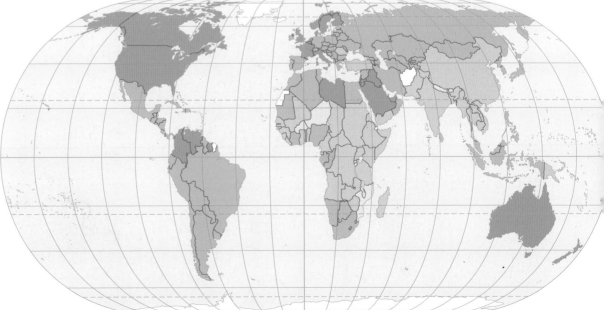

Sector

Sector	includes
Primary	Farming, fishing, forestry, mining and quarrying
Secondary	Manufacturing industry, building and construction
Tertiary	Transport and distribution, wholesale and retail, administration and finance, public services

Employment by economic sector

△ Low income economies

○ Middle income economies

□ High income economies

◇ European Union

■ UK (selected dates)

average for country categories

selected countries

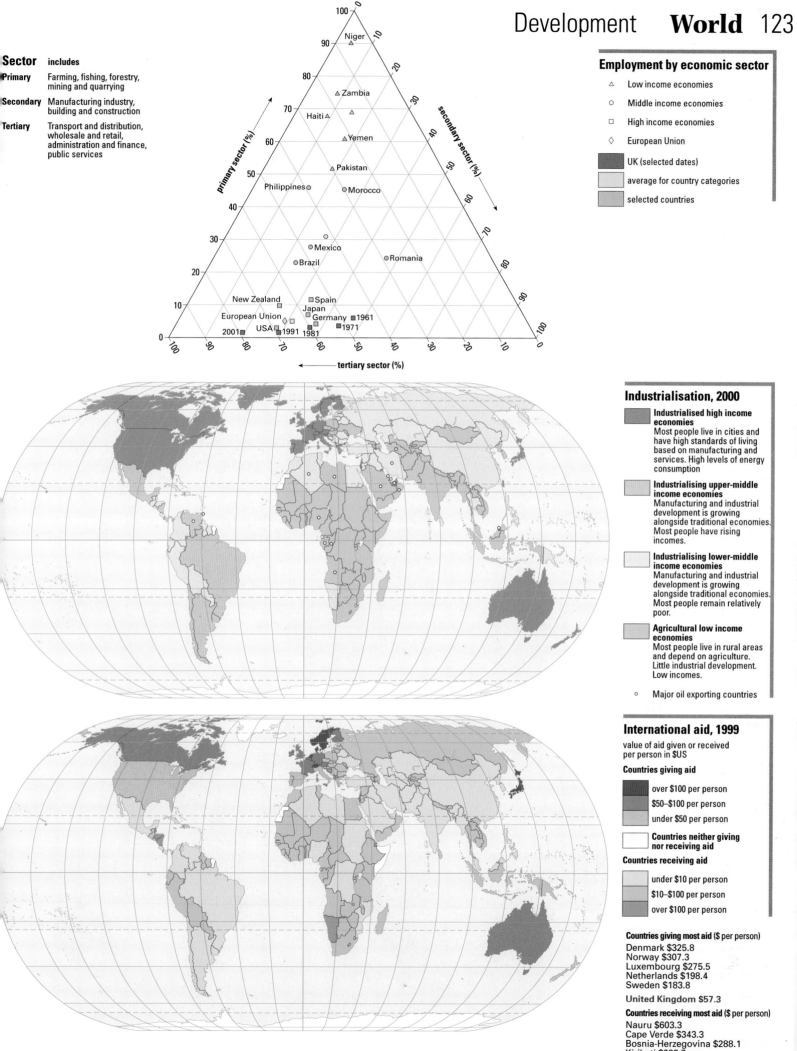

Industrialisation, 2000

Industrialised high income economies
Most people live in cities and have high standards of living based on manufacturing and services. High levels of energy consumption

Industrialising upper-middle income economies
Manufacturing and industrial development is growing alongside traditional economies. Most people have rising incomes.

Industrialising lower-middle income economies
Manufacturing and industrial development is growing alongside traditional economies. Most people remain relatively poor.

Agricultural low income economies
Most people live in rural areas and depend on agriculture. Little industrial development. Low incomes.

○ Major oil exporting countries

International aid, 1999

value of aid given or received per person in $US

Countries giving aid

over $100 per person

$50–$100 per person

under $50 per person

Countries neither giving nor receiving aid

Countries receiving aid

under $10 per person

$10–$100 per person

over $100 per person

Countries giving most aid ($ per person)
Denmark $325.8
Norway $307.3
Luxembourg $275.5
Netherlands $198.4
Sweden $183.8

United Kingdom $57.3

Countries receiving most aid ($ per person)
Nauru $603.3
Cape Verde $343.3
Bosnia-Herzegovina $288.1
Kiribati $233.7
Tonga $209.0

Energy production, 1999

kg oil equivalent per person

- over 25 000
- 2500–25 000
- 1000–2500
- 100–1000
- under 100

Highest energy producers
kg oil equivalent per person

Qatar 84 909
United Arab Emirates 67 071
Brunei 61 623
Kuwait 60 047
Norway 53 532

United Kingdom 5057

Lowest energy producers
these countries do not produce energy

Belize	Guinea-Bissau
Cyprus	Lesotho
Chad	Liberia
Djibouti	Namibia
Eritrea	Sierra Leone
Gambia	Somalia

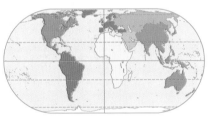

- North America
- Central and South America
- Europe
- former USSR
- Middle East
- Africa
- Asia Pacific

Oil reserves
Proven recoverable reserves
World total: 142 100 000 000 tonnes

Gas reserves
Proven recoverable reserves
World total: 150 000 000 000 000 m³

Coal reserves
Proven recoverable reserves
World total: 984 211 000 000 tonnes

Oil consumption
World total: 3503 600 000 tonnes

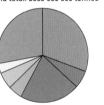

Gas consumption
World total: 2404 600 000 000 m³

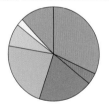

Coal consumption
World total: 2186 000 000 tonnes oil equivalent

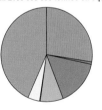

Energy consumption, 1999

kg oil equivalent per person

- over 10 000
- 2500–10 000
- 1000–2500
- 250–1000
- under 250

Highest energy consumers
kg oil equivalent per person

Qatar 24 222
United Arab Emirates 20 162
Bahrain 14 695
Iceland 11576
Luxembourg 10 888

United Kingdom 4177

Lowest energy consumers
kg oil equivalent per person

Afghanistan 25
Burkina 24
Ethiopia 22
Cambodia 16
Chad 8

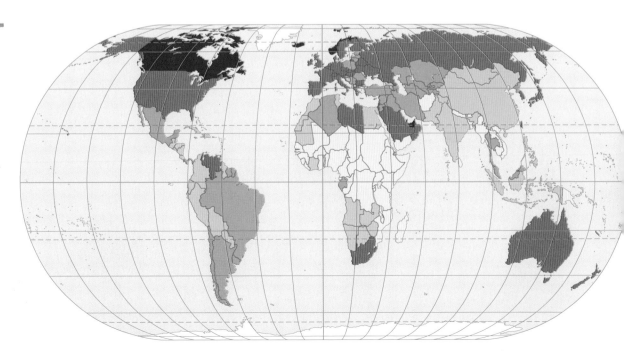

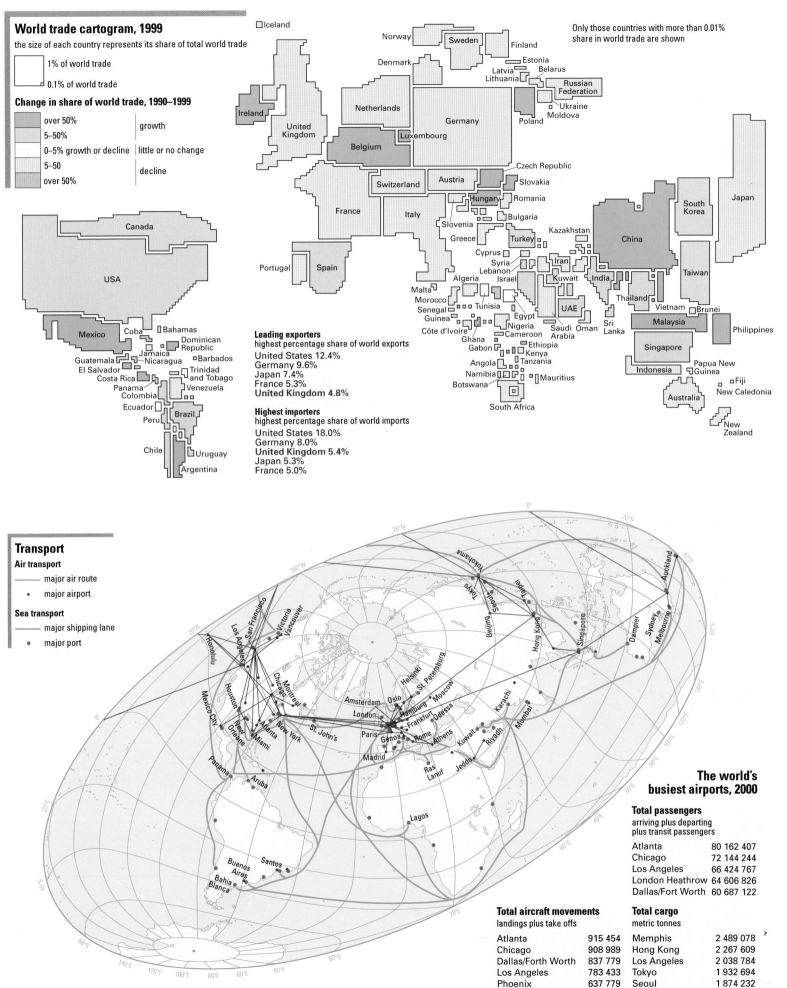

World trade cartogram, 1999

the size of each country represents its share of total world trade

◻ 1% of world trade

▫ 0.1% of world trade

Change in share of world trade, 1990–1999

over 50%	growth
5–50%	
0–5% growth or decline	little or no change
5–50	decline
over 50%	

Only those countries with more than 0.01% share in world trade are shown

Leading exporters
highest percentage share of world exports
United States 12.4%
Germany 9.6%
Japan 7.4%
France 5.3%
United Kingdom 4.8%

Highest importers
highest percentage share of world imports
United States 18.0%
Germany 8.0%
United Kingdom 5.4%
Japan 5.3%
France 5.0%

Transport

Air transport

— major air route

• major airport

Sea transport

— major shipping lane

• major port

The world's busiest airports, 2000

Total passengers
arriving plus departing
plus transit passengers

Atlanta	80 162 407
Chicago	72 144 244
Los Angeles	66 424 767
London Heathrow	64 606 826
Dallas/Fort Worth	60 687 122

Total aircraft movements
landings plus take offs

Atlanta	915 454
Chicago	908 989
Dallas/Forth Worth	837 779
Los Angeles	783 433
Phoenix	637 779

Total cargo
metric tonnes

Memphis	2 489 078
Hong Kong	2 267 609
Los Angeles	2 038 784
Tokyo	1 932 694
Seoul	1 874 232

© Oxford University Press   Oblique Aitoff Projection

Scale 1: 240 000 000

Desertification and tropical deforestation

existing areas of desert

areas with a high risk of desertification

areas with a moderate risk of desertification

existing areas of tropical rain forest

former areas of tropical rain forest

Countries losing greatest areas of forest ('000 hectares)

Brazil	2554
Indonesia	1084
Congo, Dem. Rep.	740
Bolivia	581
Mexico	508

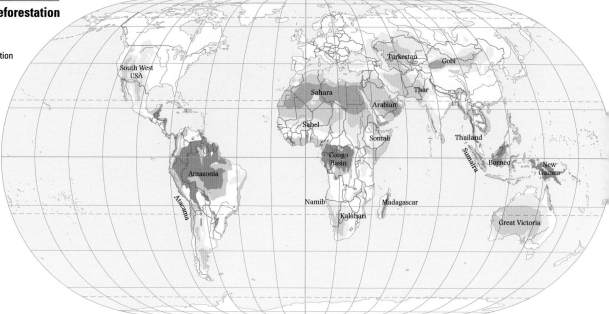

Lake Chad, West Africa, 1973–1997

Lake Chad was once the sixth-largest lake in the world, but persistent drought since the 1960's has shrunk it to about one tenth of its former size. Wetland marsh (shown on the satellite images as red) has now largely replaced open water (shown in blue). The lake is shallow and very responsive to the high variability on rainfall in the region. People living around Lake Chad do not have secure food supplies. Farming and irrigation projects have been affected by fluctuations in the level of the lake.

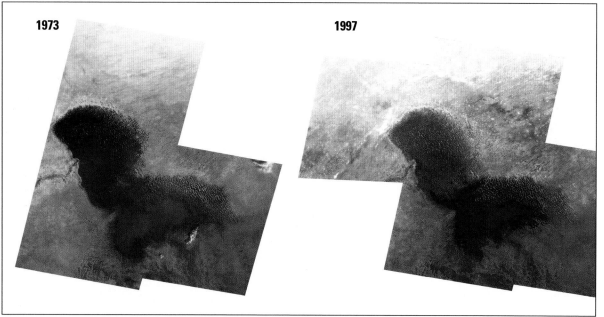

Acid rain

Sulphur and nitrogen emissions
Oxides of sulphur and nitrogen produced by burning fossil fuel react with rain to form dilute sulphuric and nitric acids

areas with high levels of fossil fuel burning

• cities where sulphur dioxide emissions are recorded and exceed World Health Organization recommended levels

Areas of acid rain deposition
Annual mean values of pH in precipitation

▬▬ pH less than 4.2 (most acidic)

── pH 4.2–4.6

── pH 4.6–5.0

⌒ other areas where acid rain is becoming a problem

Lower pH values are more acidic. 'Clean' rain water is slightly acidic with a pH of 5.6. The pH scale is logarithmic, so that a value of 4.6 is ten times as acidic as normal rain.

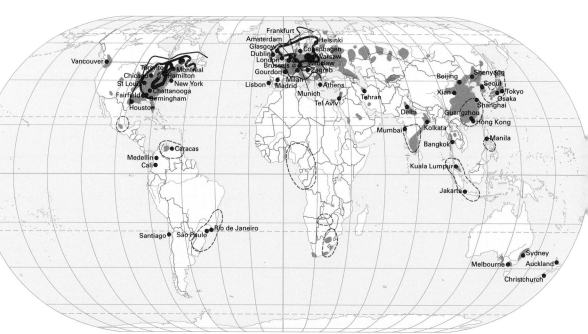

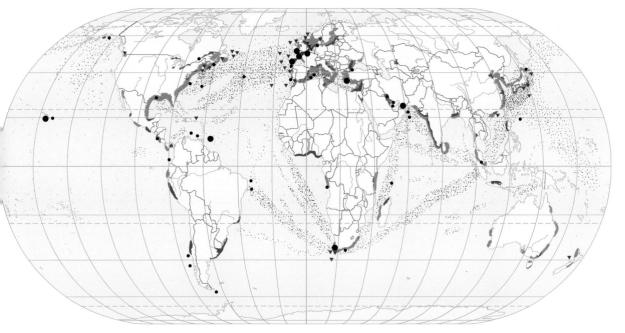

Sea pollution

Major oil spills

- ●   over 100 000 tonnes
- ·   under 100 000 tonnes
- ░░░   frequent oil slicks from shipping

Other sea pollution

- ▬   severe pollution
- ▬   moderate pollution
- ▼   deep sea dump sites

Major oil spills ('000 tonnes)

1977	*Ekofisk* well blow-out, North Sea	270
1979	*Ixtoc 1* well blow-out, Gulf of Mexico	600
1979	Collision of *Atlantic Empress* and *Aegean Captain*, off Tobago, Caribbean	370
1983	*Nowruz* well blow-out, The Gulf	600
1991	Release of oil by Iraqi troops, *Sea Island* terminal, The Gulf	799

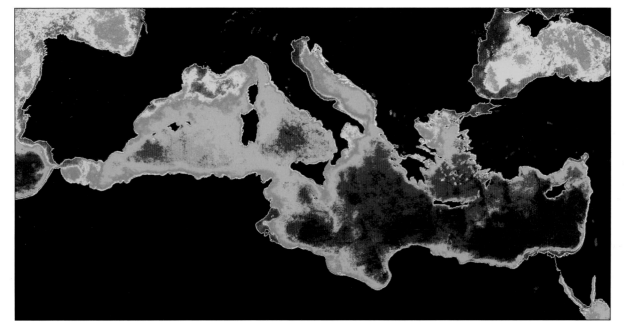

Phytoplankton in the Mediterranean Sea

Phytoplankton are micro-organisms that thrive in shallow, polluted sea areas. In this false colour satellite image red, orange, and yellow show the highest densities of phytoplankton. Green and blue show the lowest densities.

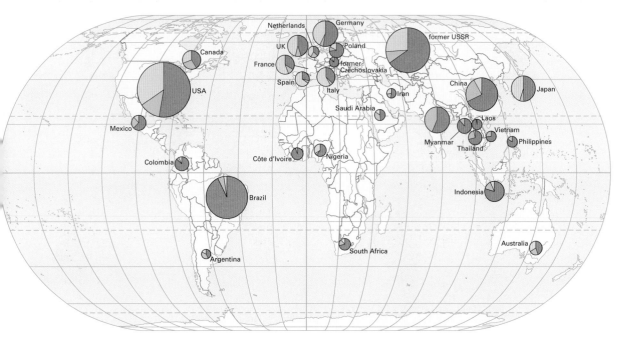

Greenhouse gases

Highest total emissions by country
thousand tonnes of carbon

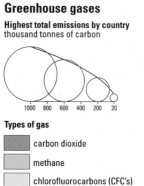

1000   800   600   400   200   20

Types of gas

- ▬   carbon dioxide
- ▬   methane
- ▬   chlorofluorocarbons (CFC's)

   Eckert IV Projection

Scale 1: 125 000 000 (main map)

Selected tourist destinations

- 🏛 cultural heritage sites
- ✳ natural heritage sites
- 🔘 resorts
- 🔘 tourist cities
- —— main cruise routes

land height
metres
2000
500
0

Top tourist destinations, 2000

	arrivals (000's)	% change 1999–2000
France	75 500	3.4
USA	50 900	4.9
Spain	48 200	3.0
Italy	41 200	12.8
China	31 200	15.5
United Kingdom	25 200	-0.8
Russian Federation	21 200	14.5
Mexico	20 600	8.4
Canada	20 400	4.9
Germany	19 000	10.9

Market share, 2000

percent of all international tourist arrivals

France	10.8%
USA	7.3%
Spain	6.9%
Italy	5.9%
China	4.5%
UK	3.6%
Russia	3.0%
Mexico	3.0%
Canada	2.9%
Germany	2.7%

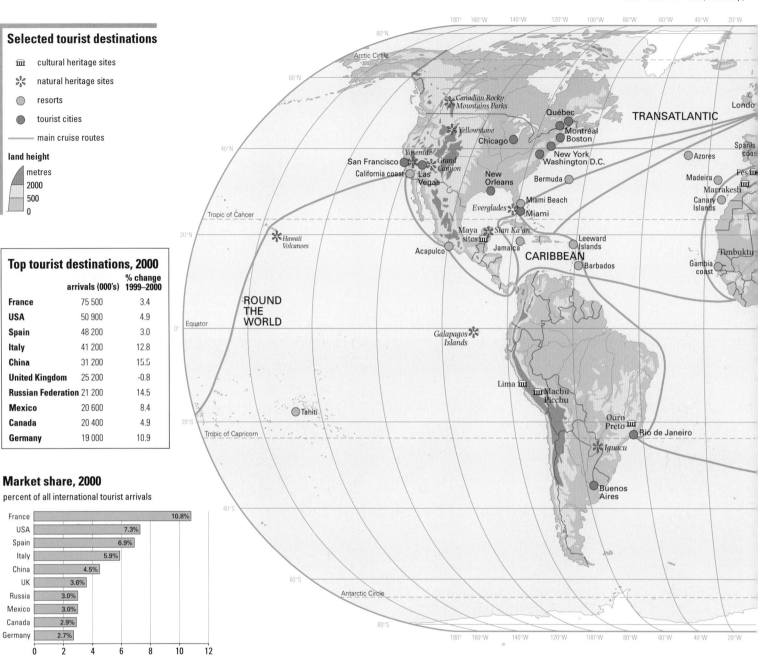

Earnings from tourism, 1998

tourist receipts in million $US

- over 5000
- 1000–5000
- 250–1000
- 100–250
- under 100
- no data

Highest tourist earnings (millions)
USA $71 250
France $29 931
Italy $29 866
Spain $29 737
United Kingdom $20 978

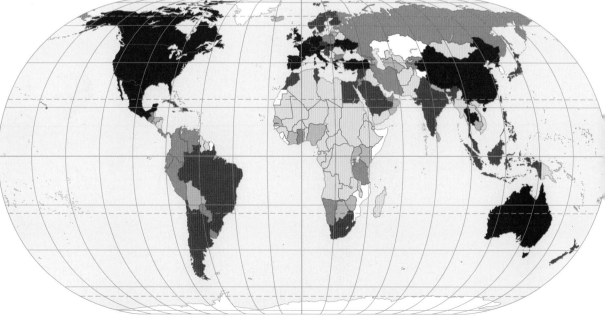

Eckert IV Projection   © Oxford University Press

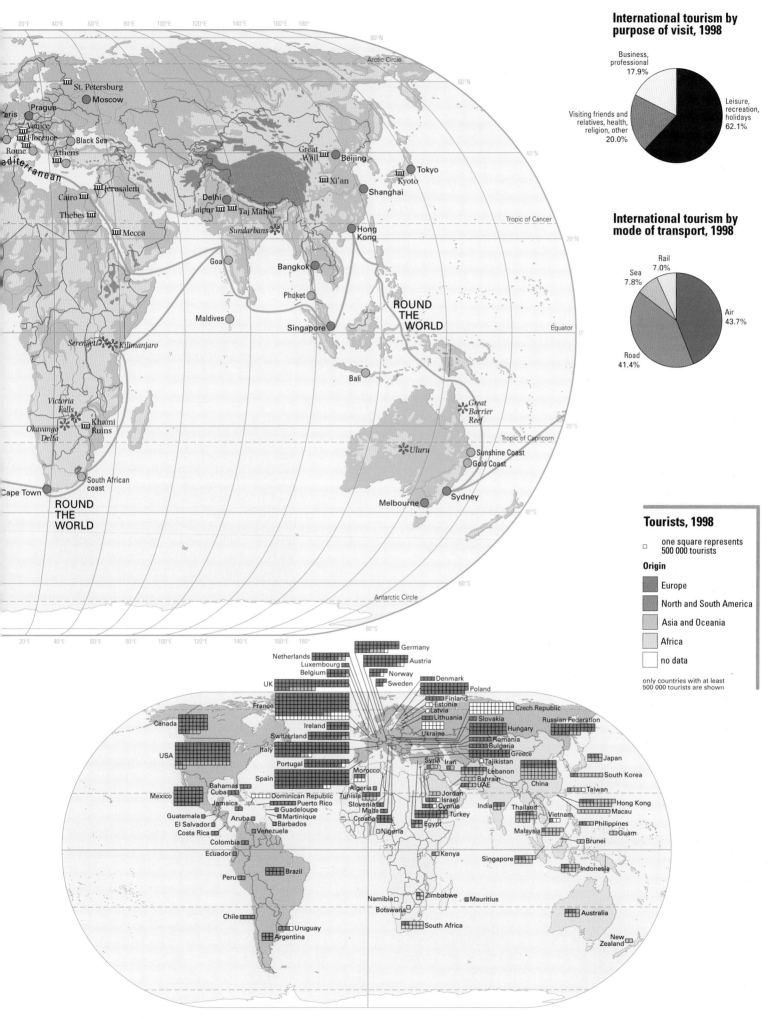

International tourism by purpose of visit, 1998

Business, professional 17.9%

Leisure, recreation, holidays 62.1%

Visiting friends and relatives, health, religion, other 20.0%

International tourism by mode of transport, 1998

Rail 7.0%

Sea 7.8%

Air 43.7%

Road 41.4%

Tourists, 1998

□ one square represents 500 000 tourists

Origin

Europe

North and South America

Asia and Oceania

Africa

no data

only countries with at least 500 000 tourists are shown

Time zones, 2001

Minus numbers show hours behind Greeenwich Mean Time (GMT).
Plus numbers show hours ahead of GMT.

- even numbers of hours difference from GMT
- odd numbers of hours difference from GMT
- half an hour difference from adjacent zone
- less than half an hour difference from adjacent zone

Longitude is measured from the **prime meridian** which passes through Greenwich. There are 24 standard time zones, each of 15° of longitude. The edges of these time zones usually follow international boundaries.

The **international date line** marks the point where one calendar day ends and another begins. A traveller crossing from east to west moves forward one day. Crossing from west to east the calendar goes back one day.

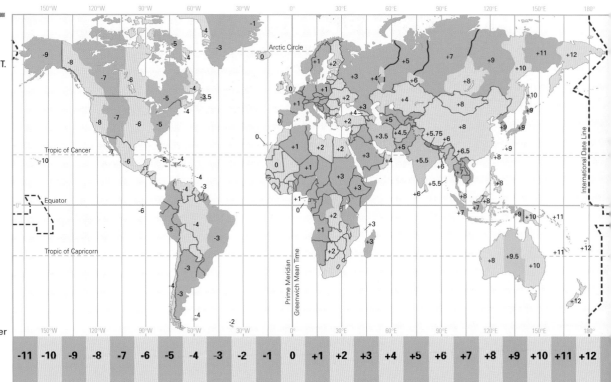

-11 | -10 | -9 | -8 | -7 | -6 | -5 | -4 | -3 | -2 | -1 | 0 | +1 | +2 | +3 | +4 | +5 | +6 | +7 | +8 | +9 | +10 | +11 | +12

The Earth rotates from west to east

The Earth rotates on its axis once in every 24 hours.

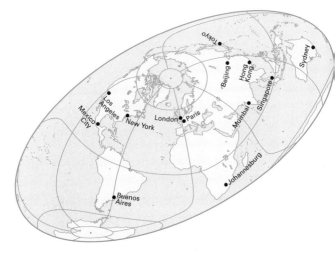

daytime

night time

Distance

Flight distance between cities in kilometres
to convert kilometres to miles multiply by 0.62

Beijing												
19 307	**Buenos Aires**											
1983	18 484	**Hong Kong**										
11 710	8088	10 732	**Johannesburg**									
8145	11 161	9645	9071	**London**								
10 081	9871	11 678	16 676	8774	**Los Angeles**							
12 468	7468	14 162	14 585	8936	2484	**Mexico City**						
4774	14 952	4306	8274	7193	14 033	15 678	**Mumbai**					
11 000	8548	12 984	12 841	5580	3951	3371	12 565	**New York**				
8226	11 097	9613	8732	338	9032	9210	7032	5839	**Paris**			
4468	15 904	2661	8860	10 871	14 146	16 630	3919	15 533	10 758	**Singapore**		
8949	11 800	7374	11 040	16 992	12 073	12 969	9839	15 989	16 962	6300	**Sydney**	
2113	18 388	2903	13 547	9581	8823	11 355	6758	10 871	9726	5322	7823	**Tokyo**

Flying time

Typical flight times by air between cities in hours and minutes
ooo means there is no direct flight available, early 2002

Beijing												
ooo	**Buenos Aires**											
3.00	ooo	**Hong Kong**										
ooo	ooo	13.00	**Johannesburg**									
10.25	14.50	13.30	10.50	**London**								
13.30	16.40	14.50	ooo	13.00	**Los Angeles**							
ooo	13.10	ooo	ooo	11.05	4.15	**Mexico City**						
ooo	ooo	7.45	20.15	10.30	ooo	ooo	**Mumbai**					
25.20	13.25	19.25	16.25	7.20	6.00	6.00	20.05	**New York**				
10.20	13.50	12.45	10.55	1.10	12.30	12.20	12.10	7.40	**Paris**			
6.15	ooo	4.05	10.30	14.40	18.45	ooo	6.30	22.05	14.15	**Singapore**		
12.55	16.35	8.50	14.30	22.45	14.35	ooo	14.40	21.45	22.25	8.55	**Sydney**	
3.35	ooo	4.55	ooo	12.40	10.40	15.50	12.35	15.55	12.50	7.05	10.00	**Tokyo**

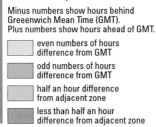

Gall Projection (Timezones)   Oblique Aitoff Projection   © Oxford University Press

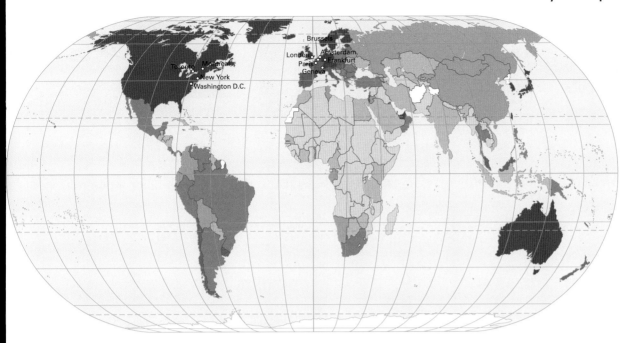

Internet users, 2000

per 10 000 people

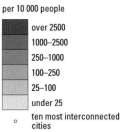

- over 2500
- 1000–2500
- 250–1000
- 100–250
- 25–100
- under 25
- ○ ten most interconnected cities

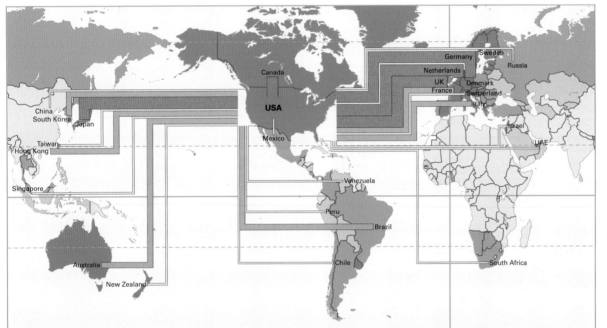

Internet traffic, 2000

internet providers
per 10 000 people

- over 100
- 10–100
- 1–10
- under 1

internet bandwidth
megabits per second (Mbps)

- over 5000
- 1000–5000
- under 1000

Internet traffic flow

The 'arc map' shows internet traffic between 50 countries. Arcs are coloured to show internet traffic between countries. The height of each arc is proportional to the volume of internet traffic flowing over a link, so the highest arcs represent the greatest volume of traffic.

Europe

Albania

Andorra

Austria

Belarus

Belgium

Bosnia-Herzegovina

Bulgaria

Greece

Hungary

Iceland

Ireland

Italy

Latvia

Liechtenstein

Norway

Poland

Portugal

Romania

Russian Federation

San Marino

Serbia and Montenegro

Asia

Afghanistan

Armenia

Azerbaijan

Bahrain

Bangladesh

Bhutan

Brunei

Iran

Iraq

Israel

Japan

Jordan

Kazakhstan

Kuwait

Nepal

North Korea

Oman

Pakistan

Papua New Guinea

Philippines

Qatar

Tajikistan

Thailand

Turkey

Turkmenistan

United Arab Emirates

Uzbekistan

Vietnam

Oceania

Australia

Fiji

Kiribati

Marshall Islands

Micronesia

Nauru

New Zealand

Africa

Algeria

Angola

Benin

Botswana

Burkina

Burundi

Cameroon

Djibouti

Egypt

Equatorial Guinea

Eritrea

Ethiopia

Gabon

Gambia

Madagascar

Malawi

Mali

Mauritania

Mauritius

Morocco

Mozambique

Somalia

South Africa

Sudan

Swaziland

Tanzania

Togo

Tunisia

North America

Antigua and Barbuda

Bahamas

Barbados

Belize

Canada

Costa Rica

Cuba

Honduras

Jamaica

Mexico

Nicaragua

Panama

St. Kitts and Nevis

St. Lucia

S. America

Argentina

Bolivia

Brazil

Chile

Colombia

Ecuador

French Guiana

Europe

Croatia | Czech Republic | Denmark | Estonia | Finland | France | Germany

Lithuania | Luxembourg | Macedonia, FYRO | Malta | Moldova | Monaco | Netherlands

Slovakia | Slovenia | Spain | Sweden | Switzerland | Ukraine | United Kingdom

Asia

Cambodia | China | Cyprus | East Timor | Georgia | India | Indonesia

Kyrgyzstan | Laos | Lebanon | Malaysia | Maldives | Mongolia | Myanmar

Saudi Arabia | Seychelles | Singapore | South Korea | Sri Lanka | Syria | Taiwan

Yemen

Oceania

Northern Marianas | Palau | Samoa | Solomon Islands | Tonga | Tuvalu | Vanuatu

Africa

Cape Verde | Central African Republic | Chad | Comoros | Congo | Congo, Dem. Rep. | Côte d'Ivoire

Ghana | Guinea | Guinea-Bissau | Kenya | Lesotho | Liberia | Libya

Namibia | Niger | Nigeria | Rwanda | Sao Tomé and Pirncipe | Senegal | Sierra Leone

Uganda | Zambia | Zimbabwe

North America

Dominica | Dominican Republic | El Salvador | Greenland | Grenada | Guatemala | Haiti

St. Vincent & the Grenadines | Trinidad and Tobago | United States of America

S. America

Guyana | Paraguay | Peru | Suriname | Uruguay | Venezuela

	ooo	no data
	per capita	for each person

	Land		Population									Employment		
	Area	Arable and permanent crops	Total	Density	Change	Births	Deaths	Fertility	Infant mortality	Life expectancy	Urban	Agriculture	Industry	Services
	2002		2002	2002	1990–2000	2002	2002	2001	2001	2001	2001	1990	1990	1990
	thousand km²	% of total	millions	persons per km²	%	births per 1000	deaths per 1000	children per mother	per 1000 live births	years	%	%	%	%
Afghanistan	652	12.4	27.8	42.6	75.5	41	17	6.0	145	45	22	ooo	ooo	ooo
Albania	29	24.3	3.5	120.7	7.1	19	6	2.1	26	73	43	55	23	22
Algeria	2382	3.5	32.3	13.6	23.1	22	5	2.8	39	69	58	26	31	43
Andorra	0.5	2.2	0.07	136.0	26.5	10	6	1.2	4	ooo	93	ooo	ooo	ooo
Angola	1247	2.8	10.6	8.5	25.9	46	26	6.8	154	40	35	75	8	17
Antigua and Barbuda	0.4	18.2	0.07	167.5	6.0	19	6	2.4	12	74	37	ooo	ooo	ooo
Argentina	2780	9.8	38.3	13.8	13.2	18	8	2.6	16	74	88	12	32	56
Armenia	30	18.8	3.3	110.0	-0.6	12	10	1.1	31	72	67	18	43	39
Australia	7741	6.2	19.5	2.5	12.6	13	7	1.7	6	79	91	6	26	68
Austria	84	17.6	8.2	97.6	5.4	10	10	1.3	5	78	67	8	38	54
Azerbaijan	87	22.9	7.8	89.7	7.6	19	10	1.9	74	72	52	31	29	40
Bahamas, The	14	0.7	0.3	21.4	14.7	19	9	2.1	13	67	89	5	16	79
Bahrain	0.7	8.7	0.7	937.1	26.7	20	4	2.8	13	74	93	2	30	68
Bangladesh	144	58.6	135.7	942.4	17.6	30	9	3.3	51	61	26	65	16	19
Barbados	0.4	39.5	0.3	690.0	4.4	13	9	1.8	12	77	51	14	30	56
Belarus	208	30.4	10.3	49.5	1.5	10	14	1.3	17	70	70	20	40	40
Belgium	33	25.2	10.3	312.1	2.7	11	10	1.7	5	79	97	3	28	69
Belize	23	3.9	0.3	11.3	30.5	31	6	3.7	34	72	48	33	19	48
Benin	113	16.4	6.8	60.2	37.4	44	14	5.6	94	51	43	63	8	29
Bhutan	47	3.4	2.1	44.7	25.5	35	14	4.7	74	63	7	94	2	4
Bolivia	1099	2.0	8.4	7.6	24.0	26	8	4.1	60	63	63	47	18	35
Bosnia-Herzegovina	51	12.7	4.0	77.7	-13.3	13	8	1.6	15	74	43	ooo	ooo	ooo
Botswana	582	0.6	1.6	2.7	20.9	26	29	3.9	80	45	49	46	20	34
Brazil	8547	7.6	179.9	21.0	14.4	18	6	2.2	31	68	82	23	23	54
Brunei	6	1.2	0.4	58.3	30.3	20	3	2.7	6	76	73	2	24	74
Bulgaria	111	40.7	7.6	68.5	-12.3	8	14	1.3	14	71	68	13	48	39
Burkina	274	12.6	12.9	47.1	32.2	45	19	6.8	104	46	17	92	2	6
Burundi	28	39.5	6.0	213.0	14.6	40	18	6.8	114	40	9	92	3	5
Cambodia	181	21.0	12.9	71.2	36.2	27	9	4.0	97	57	17	74	8	18
Cameroon	475	15.1	15.4	32.4	31.1	36	15	4.9	96	48	50	70	9	21
Canada	9971	4.6	31.9	3.2	12.6	11	8	1.5	5	79	79	3	25	72
Cape Verde	4	10.2	0.4	100.0	14.9	28	7	4.0	29	70	63	30	30	40
Central African Republic	623	3.2	3.6	5.8	25.3	36	19	5.1	115	40	42	80	3	17
Chad	1284	2.8	9.0	7.0	40.0	48	16	6.6	117	45	24	83	4	13
Chile	757	3.0	15.5	20.5	15.4	16	6	2.4	10	76	86	19	25	56
China	9598	14.1	1286.5	134.0	10.8	13	7	1.8	31	71	37	72	15	13
Colombia	1139	3.8	41.0	36.0	20.8	22	6	2.6	19	72	76	27	23	50
Comoros	2	52.9	0.6	307.0	34.8	39	9	6.8	59	60	34	78	9	13
Congo	342	0.6	2.9	8.5	27.7	30	14	6.3	81	49	66	49	15	36
Congo, Dem. Rep.	2345	3.4	55.0	23.5	36.8	46	15	6.9	129	41	29	68	13	19
Costa Rica	51	9.9	3.8	74.5	22.6	20	4	2.5	9	78	60	26	27	47
Côte d'Ivoire	322	22.8	16.6	51.6	34.1	40	18	5.2	102	42	44	60	10	30
Croatia	57	28.1	4.4	77.2	-5.0	13	11	1.4	7	74	58	16	34	50
Cuba	111	40.3	11.2	100.9	5.7	12	7	1.5	7	77	76	19	30	51
Cyprus	9	15.5	0.8	85.2	11.3	13	8	1.7	5	78	70	14	30	56
Czech Republic	79	42.2	10.3	130.4	-0.4	9	11	1.1	4	75	75	11	45	44
Denmark	43	53.4	5.4	125.6	3.8	12	11	1.7	4	76	85	6	28	66
Djibouti	23	ooo	0.5	19.4	22.1	41	19	5.9	100	46	84	ooo	ooo	ooo
Dominica	0.8	20.0	0.07	87.5	-1.6	17	7	1.8	14	73	71	ooo	ooo	ooo
Dominican Republic	49	32.2	8.6	175.5	18.9	24	7	3.1	41	67	66	25	29	46
Ecuador	284	10.6	13.4	47.2	25.2	25	5	3.3	24	71	63	33	19	48
Egypt	1001	3.3	73.3	73.2	21.8	25	5	3.5	35	68	43	40	22	38
El Salvador	21	38.5	6.4	304.8	20.1	28	6	3.5	33	70	61	36	21	43
Equatorial Guinea	28	8.2	0.5	17.9	28.8	37	13	5.9	101	49	49	66	11	23
Eritrea	118	4.3	4.3	36.4	40.5	40	13	5.9	72	53	19	80	5	15

© Oxford University Press

Wealth

Energy and trade

Quality of life

GNP	Purchasing power	Growth of PP	Energy consumption	Imports	Exports	Aid received (given)	Human Development Index	Health care	Food consumption	Safe water	Illiteracy male	Illiteracy female	Higher education	Cars	
2001	2001	1990–2000	2000	2001	2001	2000	2001	1990–2002	2001	2000	2000	2000	1996	2000	
billion US$	US$	%	kg oil equivalent per capita	US$ per capita	US$ per capita	million US$		doctors per 100 000 people	daily calories per capita	% access	%	%	students per 100 000 people	people per car	
ooo	ooo	ooo	ooo	ooo	ooo	142	ooo	ooo	ooo	13	ooo	ooo	165	644	Afghanistan
4.2	3880	2.7	521	378	88	319	0.735	133	2900	76	8	23	1087	36	Albania
50.4	5150	-0.1	956	315	651	162	0.704	85	2987	94	24	43	1238	34	Algeria
ooo	ooo	ooo	ooo	ooo	ooo	ooo	ooo	ooo	ooo	100	ooo	ooo	ooo	2	Andorra
6.7	1550	-1.8	584	293	544	307	0.377	5	1953	38	ooo	ooo	ooo	111	Angola
0.6	9870	2.8	ooo	ooo	ooo	10	0.798	17	2381	91	ooo	ooo	ooo	ooo	Antigua and Barbuda
261.0	11 690	3.0	1660	542	711	76	0.849	294	3171	79	3	3	3317	7	Argentina
2.1	2880	-2.5	542	234	88	216	0.729	305	1991	84	1	2	1886	1900	Armenia
383.3	25 780	2.9	5744	3310	3284	(987)	0.939	260	3126	100	ooo	ooo	5682	2	Australia
194.5	27 080	1.7	3524	9118	8678	(423)	0.929	302	3799	100	ooo	ooo	2988	2	Austria
5.3	3020	-7.3	1454	213	304	139	0.744	357	2474	ooo	ooo	ooo	2289	30	Azerbaijan
4.5	16 400	0.1	ooo	ooo	ooo	6	0.812	106	2777	96	6	4	ooo	4	Bahamas, The
6.2	14 410	1.7	9858	ooo	ooo	49	0.839	169	ooo	ooo	9	17	1402	5	Bahrain
49.9	1680	3.0	142	58	45	1172	0.502	20	2187	97	51	70	397	2808	Bangladesh
2.5	15 020	1.7	ooo	ooo	ooo	0	0.888	121	2992	100	0	0	2535	7	Barbados
11.9	8030	-1.4	2432	815	732	40	0.804	457	2925	100	0	0	3168	9	Belarus
239.8	28 210	1.8	5776	17 641	18 336	(820)	0.937	395	3682	ooo	ooo	ooo	3551	2	Belgium
0.7	5350	1.6	ooo	ooo	ooo	15	0.776	55	2886	76	7	7	ooo	29	Belize
2.3	1030	1.8	377	103	58	239	0.411	10	2455	63	48	76	256	260	Benin
0.5	1530	3.4	ooo	ooo	ooo	53	0.511	16	ooo	62	ooo	ooo	ooo	ooo	Bhutan
8.0	2380	1.6	592	197	148	477	0.672	130	2267	79	8	21	ooo	65	Bolivia
5.0	ooo	ooo	1096	ooo	ooo	1063	0.777	140	2845	ooo	ooo	ooo	ooo	34	Bosnia-Herzegovina
5.9	8810	2.3	ooo	1475	1444	31	0.614	26	2292	70	26	20	587	59	Botswana
528.5	7450	1.5	1077	338	337	322	0.777	158	3002	83	13	13	1424	11	Brazil
ooo	16 779	-0.7	5870	ooo	ooo	1	0.872	85	2814	ooo	5	12	516	2	Brunei
12.6	5950	-1.5	2299	926	649	311	0.795	344	2626	100	1	2	3110	5	Bulgaria
2.4	1020	2.4	ooo	45	18	336	0.330	3	2485	ooo	66	86	83	744	Burkina
0.7	590	-4.7	ooo	22	5	93	0.337	1	1612	52	44	60	ooo	650	Burundi
3.3	1520	2.0	ooo	110	114	399	0.556	30	1967	30	20	43	85	788	Cambodia
8.7	1670	-0.8	427	99	116	380	0.499	7	2242	62	21	36	ooo	152	Cameroon
661.9	27 870	1.9	8156	7363	8459	(1744)	0.937	186	3176	100	ooo	ooo	5953	2	Canada
0.6	4870	3.3	ooo	ooo	ooo	94	0.727	17	3308	74	16	34	ooo	133	Cape Verde
1.0	1180	-0.5	ooo	32	39	76	0.363	4	1949	60	40	65	ooo	422	Central African Republic
1.6	930	-0.8	ooo	44	22	131	0.376	3	2245	27	48	66	51	853	Chad
66.9	9420	5.2	1604	1116	1147	49	0.831	115	2868	94	4	4	2546	15	Chile
307.2	4260	9.2	905	188	206	1735	0.721	167	2963	75	8	22	473	369	China
82.0	5980	1.1	681	303	290	187	0.779	109	2580	91	8	8	1640	43	Colombia
0.2	1610	-2.4	ooo	ooo	ooo	19	0.528	7	1735	96	37	51	ooo	1	Comoros
2.2	580	-3.4	296	303	773	33	0.502	25	2221	51	13	26	ooo	119	Congo
5.0	765	-8.2	292	6	8	184	0.363	7	1535	45	27	50	212	525	Congo, Dem. Rep.
15.3	8080	3.0	861	1601	1222	12	0.832	178	2761	98	5	4	2830	22	Costa Rica
10.3	1470	0.4	433	174	235	352	0.396	9	2594	77	41	63	568	88	Côte d'Ivoire
19.9	8440	1.8	1775	1924	991	66	0.818	229	2678	95	1	3	1911	5	Croatia
ooo	ooo	3.7	1180	ooo	ooo	44	0.806	590	2643	95	3	3	1013	574	Cuba
9.4	20 780	3.1	3203	ooo	ooo	55	0.891	269	3302	100	1	5	1193	4	Cyprus
54.1	14 550	1.0	3931	3544	3240	438	0.861	308	3097	ooo	ooo	ooo	2009	3	Czech Republic
166.3	27 950	2.1	3644	8595	9776	(1664)	0.930	339	3454	100	ooo	ooo	3349	3	Denmark
0.6	2120	-3.9	ooo	ooo	ooo	71	0.462	13	2218	100	24	46	26	55	Djibouti
0.2	5040	ooo	ooo	ooo	ooo	16	0.776	49	2995	97	ooo	ooo	ooo	23	Dominica
19.0	5870	4.2	932	1044	653	62	0.737	216	2333	79	16	16	2223	53	Dominican Republic
16.0	3070	-0.3	647	411	347	147	0.731	138	2792	71	7	10	ooo	123	Ecuador
99.4	3790	2.5	726	189	59	1328	0.648	218	3385	95	33	56	1895	52	Egypt
13.1	4500	2.6	651	785	448	180	0.719	121	2512	74	19	24	1935	67	El Salvador
0.3	5640	18.9	ooo	ooo	ooo	21	0.664	25	ooo	43	8	26	ooo	143	Equatorial Guinea
0.8	970	1.1	ooo	ooo	ooo	176	0.446	5	1690	46	33	56	90	760	Eritrea

The datasets below are explained on pages 140/1◄

	○○○	no data
per capita		for each person

	Land		Population										Employment		
	Area	Arable and permanent crops	Total	Density	Change	Births	Deaths	Fertility	Infant mortality	Life expectancy	Urban	Agriculture	Industry	Services
	2002	2002	2002	2002	1990–2000	2002	2002	2001	2001	2001	2001	1990	1990	1990
	thousand km²	% of total	millions	persons per km²	%	births per 1000	deaths per 1000	children per mother	per 1000 live births	years	%	%	%	%
Estonia	45	25.2	1.4	31.1	-9.0	9	13	1.3	11	71	69	14	41	45
Ethiopia	1104	9.7	65.3	59.1	32.7	40	20	5.9	116	46	16	86	2	12
Fiji	18	15.6	0.9	47.6	12.8	23	6	3.3	18	69	50	46	15	39
Finland	338	6.4	5.2	15.4	3.6	11	10	1.7	4	78	59	8	31	61
France	552	35.4	59.9	108.5	4.6	13	9	1.9	4	79	76	5	29	66
French Guiana	91	0.1	0.2	2.0	48.9	22	5	3.6	○○○	76	79	○○○	○○○	○○○
Gabon	268	1.8	1.3	4.9	13.0	37	11	4.3	60	57	82	51	16	33
Gambia, The	11	17.7	1.5	136.4	42.2	41	13	5.8	91	54	31	82	8	10
Georgia	70	15.3	5.0	70.9	-8.0	11	15	1.2	24	73	57	26	31	43
Germany	357	33.7	82.4	230.8	4.3	9	10	1.3	4	78	88	4	38	58
Ghana	239	22.2	20.2	84.5	27.2	27	10	4.3	57	58	36	59	13	28
Greece	132	29.3	10.6	80.3	4.4	10	10	1.3	5	78	60	23	27	50
Greenland	342	○○○	0.06	0.2	1.1	16	8	○○○	○○○	○○○	○○○	○○○	○○○	○○○
Grenada	0.3	32.4	0.09	296.7	-3.3	23	8	2.4	20	65	39	○○○	○○○	○○○
Guatemala	109	17.5	13.5	123.9	31.2	36	7	4.6	43	65	40	52	17	31
Guinea	246	6	8.8	35.8	25.8	43	16	5.5	109	49	28	87	2	11
Guinea-Bissau	36	9.7	1.3	36.1	29.1	39	17	6.0	130	45	32	85	2	13
Guyana	215	2.3	0.7	3.3	-6.0	18	9	2.5	54	63	37	22	25	53
Haiti	28	32.8	7.4	264.3	13.9	34	14	4.7	79	49	36	68	9	23
Honduras	112	16.3	6.5	58.0	31.0	32	6	4.4	31	69	54	41	20	39
Hungary	93	54.2	10.1	108.6	-2.3	9	13	1.3	8	72	65	15	38	47
Iceland	103	0.07	0.3	2.7	8.5	14	7	2.0	3	80	93	○○○	○○○	○○○
India	3288	51.6	1034.2	314.5	19.2	24	9	3.2	67	63	28	64	16	20
Indonesia	1905	16.3	231.3	121.4	19.2	22	6	2.6	33	66	42	55	14	31
Iran	1633	11.8	67.5	41.3	17.8	17	6	2.5	35	70	65	39	23	38
Iraq	438	12.2	24.0	54.8	25.0	34	6	5.4	104	59	68	16	18	66
Ireland	70	15.4	3.9	55.7	8.2	15	8	1.9	6	77	59	14	29	57
Israel	21	20.9	6.0	285.7	29.5	19	6	2.9	6	79	92	4	29	67
Italy	301	37.9	57.9	192.4	1.6	9	10	1.3	4	79	67	9	31	60
Jamaica	11	24.9	2.7	245.5	7.7	18	5	2.4	17	76	57	25	23	52
Japan	378	12.9	127.1	336.2	2.4	10	8	1.3	3	81	79	7	34	59
Jordan	89	4.3	5.3	59.6	53.2	25	3	3.6	27	71	79	15	23	62
Kazakhstan	2717	11.1	16.7	6.1	0.2	18	11	1.8	61	66	56	22	32	46
Kenya	580	7.8	31.2	53.8	27.7	30	16	4.4	78	46	34	80	7	13
Kiribati	0.7	50.7	0.1	137.1	28.9	32	9	4.5	53	62	37	○○○	○○○	○○○
Kuwait	18	0.4	2.1	116.7	-7.9	22	2	4.3	9	76	96	1	25	74
Kyrgyzstan	199	7.2	4.8	24.1	6.7	26	9	2.4	52	68	34	32	27	41
Laos	237	4.0	5.5	24.5	30.6	37	13	4.9	87	54	20	78	6	16
Latvia	65	29.1	2.4	36.9	-10.0	8	15	1.2	17	71	60	16	40	44
Lebanon	10	29.6	3.7	370.0	13.7	20	6	2.4	28	73	90	7	31	62
Lesotho	30	10.7	1.9	63.3	23.7	28	24	4.3	91	39	29	40	28	32
Liberia	111	2.9	3.3	29.7	44.5	46	18	6.6	157	50	45	○○○	○○○	○○○
Libya	1760	1.2	5.4	3.1	23.6	28	4	3.7	16	72	88	11	23	66
Liechtenstein	0.2	25.0	0.03	150.0	11.8	11	7	1.4	10	○○○	23	○○○	○○○	○○○
Lithuania	65	46.0	3.6	55.4	-2.2	10	13	1.3	8	72	69	18	41	41
Luxembourg	3	○○○	0.4	133.3	14.5	12	9	1.8	5	78	92	○○○	○○○	○○○
Macedonia, FYRO	26	24.7	2.1	80.8	7.8	13	8	1.9	22	73	60	21	40	39
Madagascar	587	5.3	16.5	28.1	34.6	42	12	5.8	84	53	30	78	7	15
Malawi	118	16.9	11.4	96.6	12.7	45	22	6.5	114	39	15	87	5	8
Malaysia	330	23.1	22.7	68.8	24.5	24	5	3.2	8	73	58	27	23	50
Maldives	0.3	10.0	0.3	1066.7	39.3	37	8	3.4	58	67	28	32	31	37
Mali	1240	3.8	11.3	9.1	29.9	48	19	6.8	141	48	31	86	2	12
Malta	0.3	28.1	0.4	1333.3	9.1	13	8	1.7	5	78	91	○○○	○○○	○○○
Marshall Islands	0.2	16.7	0.06	300.0	47.3	34	5	5.7	63	65	65	○○○	○○○	○○○
Mauritania	1026	0.5	2.8	2.7	34.4	43	13	4.7	120	52	59	55	10	35

Wealth   Energy and trade   Quality of life

GNP	Purchasing power	Growth of PP	Energy consumption	Imports	Exports	Aid received (given)	Human Development Index	Health care	Food consumption	Safe water	Illiteracy male	Illiteracy female	Higher education	Cars	
2001	2001	1990–2000	2000	2001	2001	2000	2001	1990–2002	2001	2000	2000	2000	1996	2000	
billion US$	US$	%	kg oil equivalent per capita	US$ per capita	US$ per capita	million US$		doctors per 100 000 people	daily calories per capita	% access	%	%	students per 100 000 people	people per car	
5.2	10 020	1.0	3303	3250	2504	64	0.833	307	3048	ooo	0	0	2965	3	Estonia
6.8	710	2.4	291	ooo	6	693	0.359	3	2037	24	53	69	74	1433	Ethiopia
1.8	5140	0.7	ooo	ooo	ooo	29	0.754	36	2789	47	5	9	757	17	Fiji
124.2	25 180	2.4	6409	6162	8328	(371)	0.930	306	3202	100	ooo	ooo	4418	3	Finland
377.4	25 280	1.3	4366	5427	5369	(4105)	0.925	303	3629	100	ooo	ooo	3541	2	France
ooo	ooo	ooo	ooo	ooo	ooo	ooo	ooo	ooo	ooo	ooo	ooo	ooo	ooo	7	French Guiana
4.0	5460	0.1	1271	ooo	ooo	12	0.653	ooo	2602	70	ooo	ooo	649	7	Gabon
0.4	1730	-0.3	ooo	ooo	ooo	49	0.463	4	2300	62	56	70	148	186	Gambia, The
3.1	2860	-12.4	533	156	56	170	0.746	487	2247	76	ooo	ooo	3149	12	Georgia
948.0	25 530	1.2	4131	6013	6946	(5030)	0.921	354	3567	ooo	ooo	ooo	2603	2	Germany
5.7	1980	1.8	400	154	86	609	0.567	6	2670	64	20	37	ooo	214	Ghana
124.6	17 860	1.8	2635	2581	827	(226)	0.892	392	3754	ooo	2	4	3138	4	Greece
ooo	ooo	ooo	ooo	ooo	ooo	ooo	ooo	ooo	ooo	ooo	ooo	ooo	ooo	ooo	Greenland
0.4	6720	2.9	ooo	ooo	ooo	17	0.738	50	2749	94	ooo	ooo	ooo	ooo	Grenada
19.6	3850	1.4	628	482	208	264	0.652	90	2203	92	24	39	804	84	Guatemala
3.0	1980	1.7	ooo	144	96	153	0.425	13	2362	48	ooo	ooo	112	488	Guinea
0.2	710	-1.1	ooo	ooo	ooo	80	0.373	17	2481	49	46	77	ooo	267	Guinea-Bissau
0.6	3750	5.0	ooo	ooo	ooo	108	0.740	48	2515	94	1	2	956	32	Guyana
3.9	1450	-2.7	256	125	17	208	0.467	25	2045	46	48	52	ooo	252	Haiti
5.9	2450	0.3	469	453	192	449	0.667	83	2406	90	25	25	985	165	Honduras
48.9	12 570	1.9	2448	3427	3109	252	0.837	361	3520	99	1	1	1903	4	Hungary
8.2	29 830	1.8	12 246	ooo	ooo	0	0.942	326	3231	ooo	ooo	ooo	2918	2	Iceland
474.3	2450	4.1	494	49	43	1487	0.590	48	2487	88	32	55	638	218	India
144.7	2940	2.5	706	145	264	1731	0.682	16	2904	76	8	18	1157	86	Indonesia
112.9	6230	1.9	1771	230	369	130	0.719	110	2931	95	17	31	1763	44	Iran
ooo	ooo	ooo	1190	ooo	ooo	76	ooo	ooo	2619	85	45	77	ooo	35	Iraq
88.4	27 460	6.5	3854	13 401	21 957	(235)	0.930	226	3666	ooo	ooo	ooo	3702	3	Ireland
104.1	19 330	2.2	3241	5665	4680	800	0.905	378	3512	99	3	7	3571	5	Israel
1123.5	24 340	1.4	2974	4065	4196	(1376)	0.916	567	3680	ooo	1	2	3299	2	Italy
7.3	3650	0.4	1524	1311	493	10	0.757	140	2705	71	17	9	768	23	Jamaica
4574.2	27 430	1.1	4136	2750	3179	(13 508)	0.932	197	2746	96	ooo	ooo	3131	3	Japan
8.8	4080	1.0	1061	970	437	552	0.743	205	2769	96	5	16	ooo	28	Jordan
20.1	6370	-3.1	2594	400	543	189	0.765	339	2477	91	0	1	2859	ooo	Kazakhstan
10.3	1020	-0.5	515	92	57	512	0.489	14	2058	49	11	24	ooo	174	Kenya
0.08	ooo	ooo	ooo	ooo	ooo	21	ooo	ooo	2922	47	ooo	ooo	ooo	ooo	Kiribati
35.8	18 690	-1.4	10 529	3482	8117	3	0.820	160	3170	100	16	20	1750	3	Kuwait
1.4	2710	-5.1	497	95	112	215	0.727	288	2882	77	ooo	ooo	1088	36	Kyrgyzstan
1.6	1610	3.9	ooo	81	59	281	0.525	61	2309	90	24	47	260	540	Laos
7.6	7870	-2.3	1541	1473	846	91	0.811	313	2809	ooo	0	0	2248	5	Latvia
17.6	4640	4.2	1169	2025	247	197	0.752	274	3184	100	8	20	2712	5	Lebanon
1.1	2670	2.1	ooo	357	124	42	0.510	7	2320	91	27	6	234	350	Lesotho
ooo	ooo	ooo	ooo	ooo	ooo	94	ooo	ooo	1946	ooo	30	63	ooo	310	Liberia
ooo	7570	ooo	3107	ooo	ooo	15	0.783	120	3333	72	9	32	ooo	11	Libya
ooo	ooo	ooo	ooo	ooo	ooo	ooo	ooo	ooo	ooo	ooo	ooo	ooo	ooo	2	Liechtenstein
11.4	7610	-2.9	2032	1672	1251	99	0.824	394	3384	ooo	0	1	2251	4	Lithuania
18.6	48 080	4.1	8409	ooo	ooo	(127)	0.930	253	ooo	ooo	ooo	ooo	640	2	Luxembourg
3.4	4860	-1.5	ooo	815	585	252	0.784	300	2552	99	ooo	ooo	1557	7	Macedonia, FYRO*
4.2	870	-0.9	ooo	48	19	322	0.468	11	2072	47	26	40	188	288	Madagascar
1.8	620	1.8	ooo	47	27	445	0.387	ooo	2168	57	26	54	58	644	Malawi
86.5	8340	4.4	2126	3291	3917	45	0.790	68	2927	95	9	17	1048	6	Malaysia
0.6	4520	5.4	ooo	ooo	ooo	19	0.751	40	2587	100	3	3	ooo	ooo	Maldives
2.3	810	1.3	ooo	66	41	360	0.337	5	2376	65	64	84	134	557	Mali
3.6	16 530	4.0	2088	ooo	ooo	21	0.856	263	3496	100	9	7	2183	2	Malta
0.1	ooo	ooo	ooo	ooo	ooo	63	ooo	ooo	ooo	ooo	ooo	ooo	ooo	ooo	Marshall Islands
1.0	1680	1.2	ooo	125	100	212	0.454	14	2764	37	49	70	365	280	Mauritania

The datasets below are explained on pages 140/1

ooo	no data
per capita	for each person

	Land		Population									Employment		
	Area	Arable and permanent crops	Total	Density	Change	Births	Deaths	Fertility	Infant mortality	Life expectancy	Urban	Agriculture	Industry	Services
	2002		2002	2002	1990–2000	2002	2002	2001	2001	2001	2001	1990	1990	1990
	thousand km²	% of total	millions	persons per km²	%	births per 1000	deaths per 1000	children per mother	per 1000 live births	years	%	%	%	%
Mauritius	2	52.0	1.2	600.0	9.9	16	7	1.9	17	72	42	17	43	40
Mexico	1958	13.9	103.4	52.8	18.8	22	5	2.9	24	73	75	28	24	48
Micronesia, Fed. States	0.7	51.4	0.1	142.9	22.6	31	6	4.9	20	66	27	ooo	ooo	ooo
Moldova	34	64.4	4.4	129.4	0.8	14	13	1.3	27	69	42	33	30	37
Monaco	0.002	ooo	0.03	15 000	5.7	10	13	ooo	5	ooo	100	ooo	ooo	ooo
Mongolia	1567	0.8	2.7	1.7	18.0	21	7	2.5	61	63	57	32	22	46
Morocco	447	21.2	31.2	69.8	22.0	24	6	3.1	39	68	56	45	25	30
Mozambique	802	4.2	17.3	21.6	33.8	39	29	5.6	125	39	33	83	8	9
Myanmar	677	15.0	42.3	62.5	8.4	20	12	3.1	77	57	28	73	10	17
Namibia	824	1.0	1.9	2.3	25.7	35	18	4.9	55	47	31	49	15	36
Nauru	0.02	ooo	0.01	500.0	24.8	27	7	4.4	25	61	100	ooo	ooo	ooo
Nepal	147	20.2	25.9	176.2	27.8	33	10	4.1	66	59	12	94	0	6
Netherlands	41	22.9	16.1	392.7	6.3	12	9	1.7	5	78	90	5	26	69
New Zealand	271	12.1	3.9	14.4	13.7	14	8	2.0	6	78	86	10	25	65
Nicaragua	130	21.1	5.0	38.5	32.1	27	5	4.1	36	69	57	28	26	46
Niger	1267	4.0	10.8	8.5	32.1	50	22	8.0	156	46	21	90	4	6
Nigeria	924	33.3	130.5	141.2	33.4	39	14	5.8	110	52	45	43	7	50
Northern Marianas	0.5	17.4	0.08	154.0	6.3	20	2	ooo	ooo	ooo	ooo	ooo	ooo	ooo
North Korea	121	16.6	22.2	183.5	8.3	19	7	2.1	23	70	59	38	32	30
Norway	324	2.7	4.5	13.9	5.6	12	10	1.8	4	79	75	6	25	69
Oman	213	0.4	2.7	12.7	42.9	38	4	4.7	12	72	77	44	24	32
Pakistan	796	27.5	147.7	185.6	24.2	30	9	4.8	84	60	33	52	19	29
Palau	0.5	21.7	0.02	40.0	23.4	19	7	2.6	28	67	71	ooo	ooo	ooo
Panama	76	8.7	2.9	38.2	17.6	21	6	2.6	19	74	57	26	16	58
Papua New Guinea	463	1.5	5.2	11.2	28.8	32	8	4.8	70	57	18	79	7	14
Paraguay	407	5.6	5.9	14.5	31.9	31	5	4.2	26	71	57	39	22	39
Peru	1285	3.3	27.9	21.7	22.9	23	6	2.9	30	69	73	36	18	46
Philippines	300	33.5	83.0	276.7	24.8	27	6	3.5	29	70	59	46	15	39
Poland	323	44.6	38.6	119.5	1.4	10	10	1.3	8	74	63	27	36	37
Portugal	92	29.4	10.1	109.8	1.3	12	10	1.5	5	76	66	18	34	48
Qatar	11	1.9	0.8	72.1	54.6	16	4	3.9	11	72	93	3	32	65
Romania	238	41.3	22.3	93.7	-2.0	11	12	1.2	19	71	55	24	47	29
Russian Federation	17 075	7.4	145.0	8.5	-1.4	10	14	1.3	18	67	73	14	42	44
Rwanda	26	42.4	7.7	296.2	3.8	40	22	5.8	96	38	6	92	3	5
St. Kitts and Nevis	0.4	22.2	0.04	100.0	-6.3	19	9	2.4	20	70	34	ooo	ooo	ooo
St. Lucia	0.6	27.4	0.2	333.3	12.0	21	5	2.0	17	72	38	ooo	ooo	ooo
St. Vincent & the Grenadines	0.4	28.2	0.1	250.0	8.4	18	6	2.3	22	74	56	ooo	ooo	ooo
Samoa	3.0	43.0	0.2	66.7	5.3	16	6	4.5	20	70	22	ooo	ooo	ooo
San Marino	0.06	16.7	0.03	500.0	14.8	11	8	1.2	6	80	89	ooo	ooo	ooo
Sao Tome and Principe	1.0	42.7	0.2	170.0	33.9	42	7	6.1	57	69	48	ooo	ooo	ooo
Saudi Arabia	2150	1.8	23.5	10.9	39.0	37	6	5.7	23	72	87	19	20	61
Senegal	197	11.5	10.3	52.3	25.7	37	11	5.2	79	52	48	77	8	15
Serbia and Montenegro	102	36.5	10.7	104.9	9.2	13	11	1.7	20	72	52	ooo	ooo	ooo
Seychelles	0.5	15.6	0.08	160.0	8.0	17	7	2.1	13	73	65	ooo	ooo	ooo
Sierra Leone	72	7.5	5.6	77.8	23.8	44	21	6.5	182	35	37	68	15	17
Singapore	1	1.6	4.5	4500.0	37.6	13	4	1.4	3	78	100	0	36	64
Slovakia	49	32.5	5.4	110.2	2.8	10	9	1.2	8	73	58	12	32	56
Slovenia	20	10.0	1.9	95.0	1.7	9	10	1.3	4	76	49	6	46	48
Solomon Islands	29	2.1	0.5	17.2	39.4	33	4	5.7	20	69	20	77	7	16
Somalia	638	1.7	7.8	12.2	8.7	47	18	7.2	125	46	28	ooo	ooo	ooo
South Africa	1221	12.9	42.7	35.0	13.7	19	17	2.9	56	51	58	14	32	54
South Korea	99	19.1	48.0	484.8	10.7	13	6	1.5	5	75	82	18	35	47
Spain	506	36.6	40.2	79.4	1.6	10	9	1.2	4	79	78	12	33	55
Sri Lanka	66	29.0	19.6	297.0	11.9	16	6	2.0	17	72	23	48	21	31
Sudan	2506	6.7	37.1	14.8	31.7	37	10	4.9	65	55	37	70	8	22

Wealth | Energy and trade | Quality of life

GNP	Purchasing power	Growth of PP	Energy consumption	Imports	Exports	Aid received (given)	Human Development Index	Health care	Food consumption	Safe water	Illiteracy male	Illiteracy female	Higher education	Cars	
2001	2001	1990–2000	2000	2001	2001	2000	2001	1990–2002	2001	2000	2000	2000	1996	2000	
million US$	US$	%	kg oil equivalent per capita	US$ per capita	US$ per capita	million US$		doctors per 100 000 people	daily calories per capita	% access	%	%	students per 100 000 people	people per car	
4.6	10 410	4.0	ooo	ooo	ooo	20	0.779	85	2995	100	12	19	632	26	Mauritius
550.5	8770	1.4	1567	1755	1579	-54	0.800	130	3160	86	7	11	1739	11	Mexico
0.3	ooo	ooo	ooo	ooo	ooo	108	ooo	ooo	ooo	ooo	ooo	ooo	ooo	ooo	Micronesia, Fed. States
1.4	2420	-9.5	671	213	131	123	0.700	325	2712	100	1	2	2143	25	Moldova
ooo	ooo	ooo	ooo	ooo	ooo	ooo	ooo	ooo	ooo	100	ooo	ooo	ooo	2	Monaco
1.0	1800	-0.3	ooo	177	96	218	0.661	254	1974	60	1	2	1767	104	Mongolia
34.6	3690	0.6	359	356	234	419	0.606	49	3046	82	38	64	1167	29	Morocco
3.7	1000	3.9	403	55	26	876	0.356	6	1980	60	40	71	40	233	Mozambique
ooo	1027	4.8	262	51	36	107	0.549	30	2822	68	11	20	590	1274	Myanmar
3.5	6700	1.8	587	956	906	152	0.627	29	2745	77	17	19	735	31	Namibia
ooo	ooo	ooo	ooo	ooo	ooo	7	ooo	ooo	ooo	ooo	ooo	ooo	ooo	ooo	Nauru
5.9	1450	2.4	343	52	27	390	0.499	4	2459	81	41	76	485	ooo	Nepal
385.4	26 440	2.2	4762	13 073	14 455	(3135)	0.938	251	3282	100	ooo	ooo	3018	3	Netherlands
47.6	19 130	1.8	4864	3509	3619	(113)	0.917	226	3235	ooo	ooo	ooo	3318	2	New Zealand
2.1	2366	0.6	542	342	117	562	0.643	61	2256	79	34	33	1209	98	Nicaragua
2.0	770	-1.0	ooo	38	24	211	0.292	4	2118	59	76	92	ooo	590	Niger
37.1	830	-0.4	710	88	164	185	0.463	19	2747	57	28	44	ooo	151	Nigeria
ooo	ooo	ooo	ooo	ooo	ooo	0	ooo	ooo	ooo	ooo	ooo	ooo	ooo	ooo	Northern Marianas
ooo	ooo	ooo	2071	ooo	ooo	201	ooo	ooo	2201	100	ooo	ooo	ooo	ooo	North Korea
160.6	30 440	3.1	5704	7191	12 857	(1264)	0.944	413	3382	100	ooo	ooo	4239	3	Norway
ooo	13 356	0.3	4046	ooo	ooo	46	0.755	137	ooo	39	20	38	695	13	Oman
59.6	1920	1.2	463	70	64	703	0.499	68	2457	88	43	72	ooo	161	Pakistan
0.1	ooo	ooo	ooo	ooo	ooo	29	ooo	ooo	ooo	79	ooo	ooo	ooo	ooo	Palau
9.5	5720	2.3	892	1040	335	17	0.788	117	2386	87	8	9	3025	15	Panama
3.0	2150	1.4	ooo	219	368	275	0.548	7	2193	42	29	43	ooo	136	Papua New Guinea
7.3	4400	-0.4	715	383	174	82	0.751	117	2576	79	6	8	948	66	Paraguay
52.1	4680	2.9	489	332	734	401	0.752	117	2610	77	5	15	3268	48	Peru
80.8	4360	1.1	554	407	436	578	0.751	124	2372	87	5	5	2958	110	Philippines
163.9	9280	4.5	2328	1296	920	1396	0.841	233	3397	ooo	0	0	1865	5	Poland
109.2	17 270	2.5	2459	3766	2373	(271)	0.896	312	3751	82	5	10	3242	3	Portugal
ooo	18 789	ooo	26 773	ooo	ooo	1	0.826	220	ooo	ooo	20	17	1518	4	Qatar
38.4	6980	-0.4	1619	693	511	432	0.773	191	3407	58	1	3	1819	10	Romania
253.4	8660	-4.6	4218	370	713	1565	0.779	423	3014	99	0	1	3006	9	Russian Federation
1.9	1000	-2.1	ooo	33	10	322	0.422	ooo	2086	41	26	40	ooo	889	Rwanda
0.3	11 730	4.7	ooo	ooo	ooo	4	0.808	117	2997	98	ooo	ooo	ooo	8	St. Kitts and Nevis
0.6	5200	0.9	ooo	ooo	ooo	11	0.775	518	2849	98	ooo	ooo	ooo	21	St. Lucia
0.3	5250	2.6	ooo	ooo	ooo	6	0.755	88	2609	93	ooo	ooo	ooo	16	St. Vincent & the Grenadines
0.3	5450	1.9	ooo	ooo	ooo	27	0.775	70	ooo	99	1	2	ooo	56	Samoa
ooo	ooo	ooo	ooo	ooo	ooo	ooo	ooo	ooo	ooo	ooo	ooo	ooo	ooo	1	San Marino
0.04	1792	-0.8	ooo	ooo	ooo	35	0.639	47	2567	ooo	ooo	ooo	ooo	3	Sao Tome and Principe
149.9	11 390	-1.2	5081	1529	3248	31	0.769	153	2841	95	17	33	1455	11	Saudi Arabia
4.7	1560	0.9	324	156	111	424	0.430	10	2277	78	53	72	297	104	Senegal
ooo	ooo	ooo	1289	461	181	638	ooo	ooo	2778	ooo	16	31	1625	5	Serbia and Montenegro
0.6	12 508	1.1	ooo	ooo	ooo	18	0.840	132	2461	ooo	ooo	ooo	ooo	12	Seychelles
0.7	480	-6.5	ooo	36	6	182	0.275	9	1913	28	ooo	ooo	ooo	131	Sierra Leone
99.4	24 910	4.7	6120	28 283	29 690	1	0.884	135	ooo	100	4	12	2730	10	Singapore
20.0	11 610	1.9	3234	2734	2339	113	0.836	322	2894	100	ooo	ooo	1897	4	Slovakia
19.4	18 160	2.8	3288	5093	4666	61	0.881	215	2935	100	0	0	2657	3	Slovenia
0.3	1680	-1.0	ooo	ooo	ooo	68	0.632	13	2272	71	ooo	ooo	ooo	ooo	Solomon Islands
ooo	ooo	ooo	ooo	ooo	ooo	ooo	ooo	ooo	ooo	ooo	ooo	ooo	ooo	876	Somalia
125.5	9510	-0.2	2514	655	669	488	0.684	443	2921	86	14	15	1841	11	South Africa
447.7	18 110	4.7	4119	2996	3199	-198	0.879	173	3055	92	1	4	6106	6	South Korea
586.9	20 150	2.3	3084	3621	2778	(1195)	0.918	436	3422	ooo	2	3	4254	2	Spain
16.3	3560	3.9	437	319	257	276	0.730	41	2274	83	6	11	474	87	Sri Lanka
10.3	1610	5.6	521	ooo	ooo	225	0.503	16	2288	75	31	54	ooo	398	Sudan

	no data
ooo	no data
per capita	for each person

	Land		Population									Employment		
	Area	Arable and permanent crops	Total	Density	Change	Births	Deaths	Fertility	Infant mortality	Life expectancy	Urban	Agriculture	Industry	Services
			2002	2002	1990–2000	2002	2002	2001	2001	2001	2001	1990	1990	1990
	thousand km²	% of total	millions	persons per km²	%	births per 1000	deaths per 1000	children per mother	per 1000 live births	years	%	%	%	%
Suriname	163	0.4	0.4	2.5	9.2	20	7	2.8	26	71	75	21	18	61
Swaziland	17	10.4	1.2	70.6	27.1	30	19	5.9	106	38	27	40	22	38
Sweden	450	6.1	8.9	19.8	3.7	10	11	1.6	3	80	83	ooo	ooo	ooo
Switzerland	41	10.6	7.3	178.0	6.2	10	9	1.4	5	79	68	6	35	59
Syria	185	29.7	17.2	93.0	31.1	30	5	4.1	23	72	52	33	24	43
Taiwan	36	ooo	22.5	625.0	9.4	13	6	1.4	ooo	75	77	ooo	ooo	ooo
Tajikistan	143	6.0	6.7	46.9	20.8	33	9	2.4	53	68	28	41	23	36
Tanzania	945	4.9	35.3	37.4	34.6	40	17	5.6	104	44	33	84	5	11
Thailand	513	35.1	63.6	124.0	11.2	17	7	1.8	24	69	20	64	14	22
Togo	57	40.5	5.3	93.0	36.0	36	11	5.8	79	50	34	66	10	24
Tonga	0.8	64.0	0.1	125.0	11.1	24	6	4.2	18	71	32	ooo	ooo	ooo
Trinidad and Tobago	5	23.8	1.1	220.0	-1.9	13	8	1.7	17	72	75	11	31	58
Tunisia	164	31.2	9.8	59.8	16.9	17	5	2.1	21	73	66	28	33	39
Turkey	775	34.4	67.3	86.8	17.1	18	6	2.5	36	70	66	53	18	29
Turkmenistan	488	3.5	4.7	9.6	23.2	28	9	2.2	76	67	45	37	23	40
Tuvalu	0.02	ooo	0.01	500.0	18.2	21	7	2.4	40	67	18	ooo	ooo	ooo
Uganda	241	28.3	24.9	103.3	35.7	47	17	6.9	79	45	15	85	5	10
Ukraine	604	55.7	48.4	80.1	-4.9	10	16	1.1	17	69	68	20	40	40
United Arab Emirates	84	1.6	2.4	28.6	21.5	18	4	3.5	8	74	87	8	27	65
United Kingdom	245	24.6	59.9	244.5	3.3	11	10	1.6	6	78	90	2	29	69
United States of America	9364	18.6	287.7	30.7	10.3	14	9	2.1	7	77	77	3	28	69
Uruguay	177	7.4	3.4	19.2	7.4	17	9	2.2	14	75	92	14	27	59
Uzbekistan	447	10.8	25.6	57.3	20.0	26	8	2.7	52	69	37	34	25	41
Vanuatu	12	9.8	0.2	16.7	23.3	25	8	5.3	34	68	22	ooo	ooo	ooo
Venezuela	912	3.8	24.3	26.6	21.8	20	5	2.8	19	74	87	12	27	61
Vietnam	332	22.2	80.6	242.8	18.8	20	6	2.3	30	69	25	71	14	15
Western Sahara	252	0.008	0.3	1.2	28.1	46	17	6.8	ooo	ooo	95	ooo	ooo	ooo
Yemen	528	3.2	18.7	35.4	45.4	43	9	7.2	79	59	25	61	17	22
Zambia	753	7.0	10.2	13.4	22.1	40	24	5.7	112	33	40	75	8	17
Zimbabwe	391	8.6	12.5	32.0	12.3	31	21	4.0	76	35	36	68	8	24

Explanation of datasets

Land

Area does not include areas of lakes and seas

Arable and permanent crops percentage of total land area used for arable and permanent crops

Population

Total estimate for mid 2002

Density the total population of a country divided by its land area

Change percentage change in population between 1990 and 2000. Negative numbers indicate a decrease

Births number of births per one thousand people in one year

Deaths number of deaths per one thousand people in one year

Fertility average number of children born to child bearing women

Infant mortality number of deaths of children under one year per 1000 live births

Life expectancy number of years a baby born now can expect to live

Urban percentage of the population living in towns and cities

Employment

Agriculture percentage of the labour force employed in agriculture

Industry percentage of the labour force employed in industry

Services percentage of the labour force employed in services

Macedonia, FYRO*   Former Yugoslav Republic of Macedonia

Wealth | Energy and trade | Quality of life

GNP	Purchasing power	Growth of PP	Energy consumption	Imports	Exports	Aid received (given)	Human Development Index	Health care	Food consumption	Safe water	Illiteracy male	Illiteracy female	Higher education	Cars	
2001	2001	1990–2000	2000	2001	2001	2000	2001	1990–2002	2001	2000	2000	2000	1996	2000	
billion US$	US$	%	kg oil equivalent per capita	US$ per capita	US$ per capita	million US$		doctors per 100 000 people	daily calories per capita	% access	%	%	students per 100 000 people	people per car	
0.7	3310	3.0	○○○	○○○	○○○	34	0.762	45	2643	95	○○○	○○○	○○○	8	Suriname
1.4	4690	0.2	○○○	○○○	○○○	13	0.547	15	2593	○○○	19	21	630	38	Swaziland
225.9	24 670	1.6	5354	7099	8545	(1799)	0.941	311	3164	100	○○○	○○○	3116	2	Sweden
266.5	31 320	0.2	3704	11 677	11 398	(890)	0.932	336	3440	100	○○○	○○○	2072	2	Switzerland
16.6	3440	2.8	1137	258	326	158	0.685	142	3038	80	12	40	1559	107	Syria
○○○	○○○	○○○	○○○	4766	5462	0	○○○	○○○	○○○	○○○	○○○	○○○	○○○	5	Taiwan
1.1	1150	-11.8	470	127	94	0142	0.677	207	1662	69	0	1	1895	○○○	Tajikistan
9.2	540	0.1	457	46	22	1045	0.400	4	1997	54	16	34	57	735	Tanzania
120.9	6550	3.3	1212	946	1010	641	0.768	24	2486	80	3	6	2252	37	Thailand
1.3	1420	-0.4	338	132	92	70	0.501	8	2287	54	28	58	315	174	Togo
0.2	○○○	○○○	○○○	○○○	○○○	21	○○○	○○○	○○○	100	○○○	○○○	○○○	19	Tonga
7.2	9080	2.3	6660	○○○	○○○	-2	0.802	79	2756	86	1	2	787	6	Trinidad and Tobago
20.1	6450	3.0	825	990	689	223	0.740	70	3293	99	19	39	1341	24	Tunisia
168.3	6640	2.1	1181	598	462	325	0.734	127	3343	83	7	24	2301	17	Turkey
5.0	4580	-8.0	2627	439	533	32	0.748	300	2738	58	○○○	○○○	2072	○○○	Turkmenistan
○○○	○○○	○○○	○○○	○○○	○○○	7	○○○	○○○	○○○	100	○○○	○○○	○○○	○○○	Tuvalu
6.3	1250	3.8	○○○	60	22	819	0.489	5	2398	50	23	43	179	923	Uganda
35.2	4150	-8.8	2820	328	338	541	0.766	299	3008	55	0	1	2996	10	Ukraine
○○○	17 935	-1.6	10 175	○○○	○○○	4	0.816	177	3340	○○○	25	21	801	7	United Arab Emirates
451.4	24 460	2.2	3962	5589	4596	(4501)	0.930	164	3368	100	○○○	○○○	3237	2	United Kingdom
9900.7	34 870	2.2	8148	4129	2556	(9955)	0.937	276	3766	100	○○○	○○○	5341	2	United States of America
19.0	8710	2.6	923	917	614	17	0.834	375	2848	98	3	2	2458	11	Uruguay
13.8	2470	-2.4	2027	107	105	186	0.729	300	2197	85	0	1	○○○	○○○	Uzbekistan
0.2	2710	-0.9	○○○	○○○	○○○	46	0.568	12	2565	88	○○○	○○○	○○○	50	Vanuatu
117.2	5890	-0.6	2452	763	1163	77	0.775	203	2376	84	7	8	○○○	13	Venezuela
32.6	2130	6.0	471	202	191	1700	0.688	52	2533	56	6	9	678	562	Vietnam
○○○	○○○	○○○	○○○	○○○	○○○	○○○	○○○	○○○	○○○	○○○	○○○	○○○	○○○	○○○	Western Sahara
8.3	770	2.3	201	128	216	265	0.470	22	2050	69	33	75	419	101	Yemen
3.3	790	-2.1	619	71	82	795	0.386	7	1885	64	15	29	238	107	Zambia
6.2	2340	0.4	809	119	137	178	0.496	14	2133	85	7	15	661	61	Zimbabwe

Explanation of datasets

Wealth

GNP Gross National Product (GNP) is the total value of goods and services produced in a country plus income from abroad.

Purchasing power Gross Domestic Product (GDP) is the total value of goods and services produced in a country. Purchasing power parity (PPP) is GDP per person, adjusted for the local cost of living

Growth of PP average annual growth (or decline, shown as a negative value in the table) in purchasing power. This figure shows whether people are becoming better or worse off

Energy and trade

Energy consumption consumption of commercial energy per person shown as the equivalent in kilograms of oil

Imports total value of imports per person shown in US dollars

Exports total value of exports per person shown in US dollars

Aid received (given) amount of economic aid a country has received. Negative values indicate that the repayment of loans exceeds the amount of aid received. Figures in brackets show aid given

Quality of life

HDI Human Development Index (HDI) measures the relative social and economic progress of a country. It combines life expectancy, adult literacy, average number of years of schooling, and purchasing power. Economically more developed countries have an HDI approaching 1.0. Economically less developed countries have an HDI approaching 0.

Health care number of doctors in each country per 100 000 people

Food consumption average number of calories consumed by each person each day

Safe water percentage of the population with access to safe drinking water

Illiteracy percentage of men and women who are unable to read and write

Higher education number of students in higher education per 100 000 people

Cars the number of people for every car

How to use the index

To find a place on an atlas map use either the grid code or latitude and longitude.

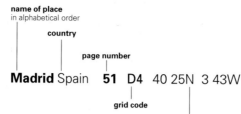

name of place
in alphabetical order

country

page number

Madrid Spain   **51**   D4   40 25N   3 43W

grid code

latitude and longitude

Grid code

Madrid Spain   **51**   D4   40 25N   3 43W

Madrid is in grid square D4

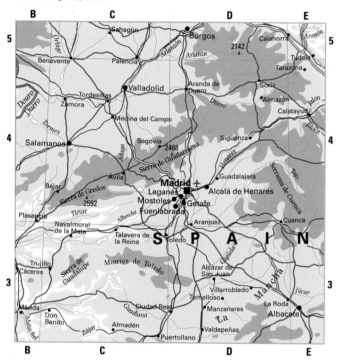

Latitude and longitude

Madrid Spain   **51**   D4   40 25N   3 43W

Madrid is at latitude 40 degrees, 25 minutes north and 3 degrees, 43 minutes west

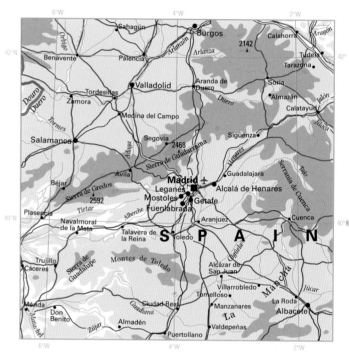

Geographical abbreviations

admin	administrative area
Arch.	Archipelago
b.	bay or harbour
c.	cape, point, or headland
can.	canal
co.	county
d.	desert
fj.	fjord
G.	Gunung; Gebel
g.	gulf
geog. reg.	geographical region
i.	island
is.	islands
Kep.	Kepulauan
l.	lake, lakes, lagoon
mt.	mountain, peak, or spot height
mts.	mountains
NP	National Park
P.	Pulau
p; pen	peninsula
Peg	Pegunungan
plat.	plateau
prov.	province
Pt.	Point
Pta.	Punta
Pte.	Pointe
Pto.	Porto; Puerto
r.	river
Ra.	Range
res.	reservoir
salt l.	salt lake
sd.	sound, strait, or channel
St.	Saint
Ste.	Sainte
Str.	Strait
sum.	summit
tn.	town or other populated place
v.	valley
vol.	volcano

Political abbreviations

Aust.	Australia
Bahamas	The Bahamas
CAR	Central African Republic
Col.	Columbia
CDR	Congo Democratic Republic
Czech Rep.	Czech Republic
Dom. Rep.	Dominican Republic
Eq. Guinea	Equatorial Guinea
Fr.	France
Med. Sea	Mediterranean Sea
Neths	Netherlands
NI	Northern Ireland
NZ	New Zealand
Philippines	The Philippines
PNG	Papua New Guinea
Port.	Portugal
RoI	Republic of Ireland
RSA	Republic of South Africa
Sp.	Spain
Switz.	Switzerland
UAE	United Arab Emirates
UK	United Kingom
USA	United States of America
W. Indies	West Indies
Yemen	Yemen Republic

A

Place	Page	Grid	Lat	Long
Aachen Germany	52	C5	50 46N	6 06E
Aalten Belgium	48	B4	51 56N	6 35E
Abādān Iran	65	C5	30 20N	48 15E
Abbeville France	50	E6	50 06N	1 51E
Abbey RoI	21	B3	53 06N	8 24W
Abbeyfeale RoI	21	B2	52 24N	9 18W
Abbeyleix RoI	21	D2	52 55N	7 20W
Abbeytown England	12	C3	54 51N	3 17W
Abbotsbury England	19	E2	50 40N	2 36W
Aberaeron Wales	14	B2	52 49N	44 43W
Abercarn Wales	14	C1	51 39N	3 08W
Aberchirder Scotland	9	G2	57 33N	2 38W
Aberdare Wales	14	C1	51 43N	3 27W
Aberdaron Wales	14	B2	52 49N	44 43W
Aberdeen Scotland	9	G2	57 10N	2 04W
Aberdeen USA	91	G6	45 28N	98 30W
Aberdeen City u.a. Scotland	9	G2	57 10N	2 00W
Aberdeenshire u.a. Scotland	9	G2	57 10N	2 50W
Aberdyfi Wales	14	B2	52 33N	4 02W
Aberfeldy Scotland	9	F1	56 37N	3 54W
Aberffraw Wales	14	B3	53 12N	4 28W
Aberfoyle Scotland	11	E3	56 11N	4 23W
Abergavenny Wales	14	C1	51 50N	3 00W
Abergele Wales	14	C3	53 17N	3 34W
Aberlady Scotland	11	G3	56 01N	2 51W
Aberporth Wales	14	B2	52 07N	4 34W
Abersoch Wales	14	B2	52 50N	4 31W
Abertillery Wales	14	C1	51 45N	3 09W
Aberystwyth Wales	14	B2	52 25N	4 05W
Abidjan Côte d'Ivoire	80	D3	5 19N	4 01W
Abilene USA	90	G3	32 27N	99 45W
Abingdon England	16	B2	51 41N	1 17W
Abington Scotland	11	F2	55 29N	3 42W
Aboyne Scotland	9	G2	57 05N	2 50W
Abu Dhabi UAE	65	F3	24 28N	54 25E
Abuja Nigeria	80	F2	9 10N	7 11E
Acapulco Mexico	94	E3	16 51N	99 56W
Accra Ghana	80	D3	5 33N	0 15W
Accrington England	12	D2	53 46N	2 21W
Achill Head RoI	20	A3	53 59N	10 13W
Achill Island RoI	20	A3	53 55N	10 05W
Achill Sound tn. RoI	20	B3	53 56N	9 54W
Achnacroish Scotland	8	D1	56 32N	5 30W
Achnasheen Scotland	9	D2	57 35N	5 06W
Ackworth Moor Top England	13	E2	53 39N	1 20W
Aclare RoI	20	C4	54 02N	8 54W
Acle England	17	E3	52 38N	1 33E
Adana Turkey	57	E2	37 00N	35 19E
Adare RoI	21	C2	52 34N	8 48W
Ad Dammām Saudi Arabia	65	F4	26 25N	50 06E
Addis Ababa Ethiopia	81	N3	9 03N	38 42E
Addlestone England	16	C2	51 22N	0 31W
Adelaide Australia	73	G4	34 56S	138 36E
Aden Yemen	64	E1	12 50N	45 03E
Aden, Gulf of Indian Ocean	65	E1	12 30N	47 30E
Adriatic Sea Med. Sea	54	F5	43 00N	15 00E
Adrigole RoI	21	B1	51 44N	9 42W
Adur r. England	16	C1	50 55N	0 20W
Adwick le Street England	13	E2	53 34N	1 11W
Aegean Sea Med. Sea	55	L3	39 00N	24 00E
AFGHANISTAN	66	A6/B6		
Agen France	50	E3	44 12N	0 38E
Aghaville RoI	21	B1	51 39N	9 21W
Agra India	66	D5	27 09N	78 00E
Ağri Daği mt. Turkey	57		39 44N	44 15E
Agropoli Italy	54	F4	40 21N	14 59E
Ahascragh RoI	20	C3	53 24N	8 20W
Ahmadabad India	66	C4	23 03N	72 40E
Ahoghill NI	10	C1	54 51N	6 22W
Ailsa Craig i. Scotland	10	D2	55 16N	5 07W
Airdrie Scotland	11	F2	55 52N	3 59W
Aire r. England	13	E2	53 40N	1 00W
Aire-sur-l'Adour France	50	D2	43 42N	0 15W
Aix-en-Provence France	50	G2	43 31N	5 27E
Aix-les-Bains France	50	G3	45 41N	5 55E
Ajaccio France	50	J1	41 55N	8 43E
Ajmer India	66	C5	26 29N	74 40E
Akron USA	91	K5	41 04N	81 31W
Alabama state USA	91	J3	32 00N	87 00W
Åland is. Finland	49	E3	60 15N	20 00E
Alaska state USA	88	D6/F6	63 10N	157 30W
Alaska, Gulf of USA	88	F5/G6	58 00N	147 00W
Alaska Range USA	88	E6/G6	62 30N	152 30W
Albacete Spain	51	E3	39 00N	1 52W
ALBANIA	55	H4/J4		
Al Başrah Iraq	65	E5	30 30N	47 50E
Albert France	50	F6	50 00N	2 40E
Alberta prov. Canada	88	M4/N4	54 00N	117 30W
Albertville France	50	H3	45 40N	6 24E
Albi France	50	F2	43 56N	2 08E
Ålborg Denmark	49	C2	57 05N	9 50E
Albrighton England	15	D2	52 38N	2 16W
Albuquerque USA	90	E4	35 05N	106 38W
Alcalá de Henares Spain	51	D4	40 28N	3 22W
Alcantarilla Spain	51	E2	37 59N	1 12W
Alcázar de San Juan Spain	51	D3	39 24N	3 12W
Alcester England	15	E2	52 13N	1 52W
Alcira Spain	51	E3	39 10N	0 27W
Aldbourne England	16	B2	51 30N	1 37W
Aldbrough England	13	F2	53 50N	0 06W
Alde r. England	17	E3	52 10N	1 30E
Aldeburgh England	17	E3	52 09N	1 35E
Alderley Edge tn. England	12	D2	53 18N	2 15W
Alderney i. Channel Islands	19	E1	49 43N	2 12W
Aldershot England	16	C2	51 15N	0 47W
Aldridge England	15	E2	52 36N	1 55W
Aldsworth England	15	E1	51 48N	1 46W
Alençon France	50	E5	48 25N	0 05E
Aleppo Syria	64	C6	36 14N	37 10E
Alès France	50	G3	44 08N	4 05E
Alessándria Italy	54	C6	44 55N	8 37E
Ålesund Norway	49	C3	62 28N	6 11E
Aleutian Range USA	88	D5	56 30N	159 00W
Alexandria Egypt	81	L8	31 13N	29 55E
Alexandria Scotland	11	E2	55 59N	4 36W
Alexandroúpoli Greece	55	L4	40 51N	25 53E
Alford England	13	G2	53 17N	0 11E
Alford Scotland	9	G2	57 13N	2 42W
Alfreton England	13	E2	53 06N	1 23W
Algeciras Spain	51	C2	36 08N	5 27W
ALGERIA	80	D7/F7		
Algiers Algeria	80	E6	36 50N	3 00E
Alicante Spain	51	E3	38 21N	0 29W
Alice USA	91	G2	27 45N	98 06W
Alice Springs tn. Australia	72	F6	23 42S	133 52E
Alkmaar Neths	48	C5	52 38N	4 44E
Allahabad India	66	E5	25 27N	81 50E
Allegheny Mountains USA	93	E1/2	40 00N	79 00W
Allen r. England	12	D3	54 50N	2 20W
Allendale Town England	12	D3	54 54N	2 15W
Allentown USA	91	L5	40 37N	75 30W
Alloa Scotland	11	F3	56 07N	3 49W
Alma USA	93	D2	43 23N	84 40W
Almadén Spain	51	C3	38 47N	4 50W
Almansa Spain	51	E3	38 52N	1 06W
Almaty Kazakhstan	62	K5	43 19N	76 55E
Almería Spain	51	D2	36 50N	2 26W
Älmhult Sweden	49	D2	56 32N	14 10E
Aln r. England	11	H2	55 25N	1 45W
Alness Scotland	9	E2	57 41N	4 15W
Alnwick England	11	H2	55 25N	1 42W
Alpes Maritimes mts. France/Italy	50	H2	44 15N	6 45E
Alpi Dolomitiche mts. Italy	54	D7	46 00N	12 00E
Alpi Pennine mts. Italy/Switz.	52	C3	45 55N	7 30E
Alps mts. Europe	52	D3	46 00N	7 30E
Alsager England	12	D2	53 06N	2 19W
Alston England	12	D3	54 49N	2 26W
Altai mts. Mongolia	68	F7	47 00N	92 30E
Altamira Brazil	96	G13	3 13S	52 15W
Altnaharra Scotland	9	E3	58 16N	4 27W
Alton England	16	C2	51 09N	0 59W
Altrincham England	12	D2	53 24N	2 21W
Alyth Scotland	9	F1	56 37N	3 13W
Amarillo USA	90	F4	35 14N	101 50W
Amazonas r. Brazil	96	G13	2 00S	53 00W
Amble England	11	H2	55 20N	1 34W
Ambleside England	12	D3	54 26N	2 58W
Ambon Indonesia	71	H3	3 41S	128 10E
Amersfoort Neths	48	D5	52 09N	5 23E
Amersham England	16	C2	51 40N	0 38W
Amesbury England	16	B2	51 10N	1 47W
Amfípoli Greece	55	K4	40 48N	23 52E
Amiens France	50	F5	49 54N	2 18E
Amlwch Wales	14	B3	53 25N	4 20W
Amman Jordan	64	C5	31 04N	46 17E
Ammanford Wales	14	B1	51 48N	3 58W
Ampthill England	16	C3	52 02N	0 30W
Amritsar India	66	C6	31 35N	74 56E
Amsterdam Neths	48	C5	52 22N	4 54E
Amstetten Austria	52	G4	48 08N	14 52E
Amur r. Asia	69	N8	52 30N	126 30E
Anacscaul RoI	21	A2	52 09N	10 04W
Anchorage USA	88	F6	61 10N	150 00W
Ancona Italy	54	E5	43 37N	13 31E
Ancroft England	11	G2	55 42N	2 00W
Andalsnes Norway	49	C3	62 33N	7 43E
Andaman Islands India	67	G2	12 00N	94 00E
Anderlecht Belgium	48	C2	50 50N	4 20E
Andermatt Switz.	52	D3	46 38N	8 36E
Andes mts. S. America	96/97	B14/C6	10 00S	77 00W
ANDORRA	50	E2		
Andorra la Vella Andorra	50	E2	42 30N	1 30E
Andover England	16	B2	51 13N	1 28W
Andreas Isle of Man	12	B3	54 22N	4 26W
Ándros i. Greece	55	L2	37 49N	24 54E
Andújar Spain	51	C3	38 02N	4 03W
Angara r. Russia	63	M8	58 00N	97 30E
Angers France	50	D4	47 29N	0 32W
Angle Wales	14	A1	51 41N	5 06W
Anglesey i. Wales	14	B3	53 18N	4 25W
Anglesey, Isle of u.a. Wales	14	B3	53 18N	4 25W
ANGOLA	82	C5		
Angoulême France	50	E3	45 40N	0 10E
Anguilla i. Leeward Islands	94	P10	18 14N	63 05W
Angus u.a. Scotland	9	G1	56 45N	3 00W
'Annaba Algeria	80	F9	36 55N	7 47E
Annalong NI	10	D1	54 06N	5 55W
Annan r. Scotland	11	F2	55 05N	3 20W
Annan Scotland	11	F2	54 59N	3 16W
Annapolis USA	91	L4	38 59N	76 30W
Annapurna mt. Nepal	66	E5	28 34N	83 50E
Annbank England	11	E2	55 28N	4 30W
Annecy France	50	H3	45 54N	6 07E
Annfield Plain England	13	E3	54 52N	1 45W
Ansbach Germany	52	E4	49 18N	10 36E
Anshan China	69	M6	41 05N	122 58E
Anstey England	15	E2	52 40N	1 10W
Anston England	13	E2	53 22N	1 13W
Anstruther Scotland	11	G3	56 14N	2 42W
Antalya Turkey	57	D2	36 53N	30 42E
Antananarivo Madagascar	82	J4	18 52S	47 30E
Antarctica	101			
Antequera Spain	51	C2	37 01N	4 34W
Antibes France	50	H2	43 35N	7 07E
ANTIGUA & BARBUDA	94	Q9		
Antrim NI	10	C1	54 43N	6 13W
Antrim district NI	10	C1	54 40N	6 10W
Antrim Mountains NI	10	C2	55 00N	6 10W
Antwerpen Belgium	48	C4	51 13N	4 25W
Aosta Italy	54	B6	45 43N	7 19E
Apeldoorn Neths	48	D5	52 13N	5 57E
Appalachian Mountains USA	91	K4	37 00N	82 00W
Appennini mts. Italy	54	C6/F4	43 00N	12 30E
Appleby-in-Westmorland England	12	D3	53 36N	2 29W
Appledore England	18	C3	51 03N	4 12W
Appleton USA	91	J5	44 17N	88 24W
'Aqaba, Gulf of Middle East	64	D4	28 40N	34 40E
Arabian Sea Indian Ocean	65	H3	22 00N	63 00E
Aral Sea Asia	62	H5/J6	45 00N	60 00E
Aranda de Duero Spain	51	D4	41 40N	3 41W
Aran Fawddwy mt. Wales	14	C2	52 47N	3 41W
Aran Island RoI	20	C4	55 00N	8 40W
Aran Islands RoI	21	B3	53 10N	9 50W
Aranjuez Spain	51	D4	40 02N	3 37W
Arbil Iraq	64	D6	36 12N	44 01E
Arbroath Scotland	9	G1	56 34N	2 35W
Arcachon France	50	D3	44 40N	1 11W
Arctic Ocean	101			
Ardara RoI	20	C4	54 46N	8 25W
Ardbeg Scotland	10	C2	55 39N	6 05W
Ardee RoI	20	E3	53 52N	6 33W
Ardennes mts. Belgium	48	D3	50 10N	5 45E
Ardfert RoI	21	B2	52 20N	9 47W
Ardglass NI	10	D1	54 16N	5 37W
Ardle r. Scotland	9	F1	56 40N	3 30W
Ardminish Scotland	10	D2	55 42N	5 44W
Ardmore RoI	21	D1	51 57N	7 43W
Ardmore Point Scotland	10	D2	55 41N	6 01W
Ardnamurchan, Point of Scotland	8	C1	56 44N	6 14W
Ardrossan Scotland	11	E2	55 39N	4 49W
Ards district NI	10	D1	54 35N	5 35W
Ards Peninsula NI	10	D1	54 25N	5 30W
Ardvasar Scotland	8	D2	57 03N	5 55W
Arendal Norway	49	C2	58 27N	8 56E
Arezzo Italy	54	D5	43 28N	11 53E
Argentan France	50	D5	48 45N	0 01W
ARGENTINA	97	D5		
Argyll and Bute u.a. Scotland	10	D3	56 10N	5 00W
Århus Denmark	49	D2	56 15N	10 10E
Arinagour Scotland	8	C1	56 37N	6 31W
Arisaig Scotland	8	D1	56 51N	5 51W
Arisaig, Sound of Scotland	8	D1	56 50N	5 50W
Arizona state USA	90	D3	34 00N	112 00W
Arkansas state USA	91	H3	34 00N	93 00W
Arkansas r. USA	90	G4	36 00N	97 00W
Arkansas City USA	91	G4	37 03N	97 02W
Arkhangel'sk Russia	62	G9	64 32N	40 40E
Arklow RoI	21	E2	52 48N	6 09W
Arles France	50	G2	43 41N	4 38E
Arlon Belgium	48	D2	49 41N	5 49E
Armadale Highland Scotland	8	D2	57 05N	5 54W
Armadale West Lothian Scotland	11	F2	55 54N	3 41W
Armagh NI	10	C1	54 21N	6 39W
Armagh district NI	10	C1	54 20N	6 40W
ARMENIA	57	F3		
Armentières France	50	F6	50 41N	2 53E
Armthorpe England	13	E2	53 32N	1 03W
Arnhem Neths	48	D4	51 59N	5 53E
Arnold England	15	E2	53 00N	1 09W
Arran i. Scotland	10	D2	55 35N	5 15W
Arras France	50	F6	50 17N	2 46E
Artane RoI	20	E3	53 23N	6 12W
Arthur's Seat sum. Scotland	11	F2	55 57N	3 11W
Arthurstown RoI	21	E2	52 15N	6 57W
Aruba i. Neths	96	C16		
Arun r. England	16	C2	51 00N	0 30W
Arundel England	16	C1	50 51N	0 34W
Arvika Sweden	49	D2	59 41N	12 38E
Ascoli Piceno Italy	54	E5	42 52N	13 35E
Ascot England	16	C2	51 25N	0 41W
Ash England	17	E2	51 17N	1 16E
Ashbourne England	13	E2	53 01N	1 43W
Ashbourne RoI	20	E3	53 31N	6 24W
Ashburton England	18	D2	50 31N	3 45W
Ashby-de-la-Zouch England	15	E2	52 46N	1 28W
Ashford England	17	D2	51 09N	0 53E
Ash Fork USA	90	D4	35 13N	112 29W
Ashgabat Turkmenistan	62	H4	37 58N	58 24E
Ashington England	13	E4	55 11N	1 34W
Ashkirk Scotland	11	G2	55 29N	2 50W
Ashton-in-Makerfield England	12	D2	53 29N	2 39W
Ashton-under-Lyne England	12	D2	53 29N	2 06W
Ashwell England	16	C3	52 03N	0 09W
Askeaton RoI	21	C2	52 36N	8 58W
Askern England	13	E2	53 37N	1 09W
Askrigg England	12	D3	54 19N	2 04W
Asmara Eritrea	81	N5	15 20N	38 58E
Aspatria England	12	C3	54 46N	3 20W
Assisi Italy	54	E5	43 04N	12 37E
Astana Kazakhstan	62	K7	51 10N	71 28E
Astee RoI	21	B2	52 33N	9 34W
Asti Italy	54	C6	44 54N	8 13E
Astorga Spain	51	B5	42 27N	6 04W
Astoria USA	90	B6	46 12N	123 50W
Astrakhan' Russia	62	G6	46 22N	48 04E
Asunción Paraguay	96	F7	25 15S	57 40W
Aswân Egypt	81	M6	24 05N	32 56E
Athabasca Canada	88	N4	54 44N	113 15W
Athabasca, Lake Canada	88	P5	59 10N	109 30W
Athboy RoI	20	E3	53 37N	6 55W
Athenry RoI	20	C3	53 18N	8 45W
Athens Greece	55	K2	38 00N	23 44E
Atherstone England	15	E2	52 35N	1 31W
Athleague RoI	20	C3	53 34N	8 15W
Athlone RoI	20	D3	53 25N	7 56W
Áthos mt. Greece	55	L4	40 10N	24 19E
Athy RoI	21	E2	52 59N	6 59W
Atlanta USA	91	K3	33 45N	84 23W
Atlantic City USA	91	M4	39 23N	74 27W
Atlantic Ocean	104			
Attleborough England	17	E3	52 31N	1 01E
Attymass RoI	20	B4	54 03N	9 04W
Aubagne France	50	G2	43 17N	5 35E
Aubenas France	50	G3	44 37N	4 24E
Auch France	50	E2	43 40N	0 36E
Auchencairn Scotland	11	F1	54 51N	3 53W
Auchterarder Scotland	11	F3	56 18N	3 43W
Auchtermuchty Scotland	11	F3	56 17N	3 15W
Auckland NZ	73	P3	36 51S	174 46E
Audley England	12	D2	53 03N	2 20W
Augher NI	10	B1	54 26N	7 08W
Aughnacloy NI	10	C1	54 25N	6 59W
Aughrim RoI	21	E2	52 52N	6 20W
Aughton England	13	E2	53 22N	1 19W
Augsburg Germany	52	E4	48 21N	10 54E
Augusta USA	91	K3	33 29N	82 00W
Auldgirth Scotland	11	F2	55 12N	3 43W
Aurillac France	50	F3	44 56N	2 26E
Austin USA	91	G3	30 18N	97 47W
AUSTRALIA	72/73			
AUSTRIA	52	E3/G3		
Autun France	50	G4	46 58N	4 18E
Auxerre France	50	F4	47 48N	3 35E
Avallon France	50	F4	47 30N	3 54E
Avebury England	16	B2	51 25N	1 51W
Aveiro Portugal	51	A4	40 38N	8 40W
Aveley England	17	D2	51 30N	0 15E
Avesta Sweden	49	E3	60 09N	16 10E
Avezzano Italy	54	E5	42 02N	13 26E
Aviemore Scotland	9	F2	57 12N	3 50W
Avignon France	50	G2	43 56N	4 48E
Ávila Spain	51	C4	40 39N	4 42W
Avoca RoI	21	E2	52 52N	6 13W
Avon r. Warwickshire England	15	E2	52 10N	1 55W
Avon r. Hampshire England	16	B1	51 05N	1 55W
Avon r. Wiltshire England	16	A2	51 25N	2 05W
Avon r. Devon England	18	D2	50 20N	3 48W
Avon r. Scotland	9	F2	51 27N	1 40W
Avonmouth England	19	E3	51 31N	2 42W
Avranches France	50	D5	48 42N	1 21W
Axbridge England	19	E3	51 18N	2 49W
Axe r. Somerset England	19	E3	51 11N	2 43W
Axe r. Dorset England	19	E2	50 50N	2 50W
Axminster England	19	E2	50 47N	3 00W
Ayamonte Spain	51	B2	37 13N	7 24W
Ayers Rock mt. Australia	72	F5	25 18S	131 18E
Aylesbury England	16	C2	51 50N	0 50W
Aylesford England	17	D2	51 18N	0 30E
Aylesham England	17	E2	51 12N	1 11E

Aylsham England 17 E3 52 49N 1 15E
Ayr r. Scotland 11 E2 55 30N 4 10W
Ayr Scotland 11 E2 55 28N 4 38W
Ayre, Point of
Isle of Man 12 B3 54 25N 4 22W
Aysgarth England 12 E3 54 17N 2 00W
AZERBAIJAN 57 G3
Azov, Sea of Asia 57 E4 46 00N 36 00E
Azuaga Spain 51 C3 38 16N 5 40W

B

Babbacombe Bay
England 18 D2 50 30N 3 30W
Bacup England 12 D2 53 42N 2 12W
Badajoz Spain 51 B3 38 53N 6 58W
Badalona Spain 51 G4 41 27N 2 15E
Baden Switz. 52 D3 47 28N 8 19E
Bad Ischl Austria 52 F3 47 43N 13 38E
Baffin Bay Canada/
Greenland 89 X8/Z8 72 00N 65 00W
Baffin Island Canada 89 U8/W7 68 30N 70 00W
Baggy Point England 18 C3 51 09N 4 16W
Baghdad Iraq 64 D5 33 20N 44 26E
BAHAMAS, THE 95 J4
Bahía Blanca Argentina 97 E6 38 45S 62 15W
Bahia de Campeche
Mexico 94 E4/F4 20 00N 95 00W
BAHRAIN 65 F4
Bahrain, Gulf of
The Gulf 65 F4 25 55N 50 30E
Bahr el Abiad r. Sudan 81 M4 14 00N 32 20E
Bahr el Azraq r. Sudan 81 M4 13 30N 33 45E
Baia Mare Romania 53 L3 47 39N 23 36E
Baie de la Seine France 50 D5 49 40N 0 30W
Baildon England 13 E2 53 52N 1 46W
Bailieborough Rol 20 E3 53 54N 6 59W
Baja California p.
Mexico 94 B5 27 30N 113 00W
Bakersfield USA 90 C4 35 25N 119 00W
Bakewell England 13 E2 53 13N 1 40W
Baku Azerbaijan 57 G3 40 22N 49 53E
Bala Wales 14 C2 52 54N 3 35W
Balaton l. Hungary 53 H3 47 00N 17 30E
Balbriggan Rol 20 E3 53 37N 6 11W
Balcombe England 16 C2 51 04N 0 08W
Baldock England 16 C2 51 59N 0 12W
Balearic Islands
Med. Sea 51 F3/H3 40 00N 2 00E
Baleshare i. Scotland 8 B2 57 32N 7 22W
Bali i. Indonesia 71 E2/F2 8 30S 115 00E
Ballachulish Scotland 8 D1 56 40N 5 10W
Ballagan Point Rol 20 E4 54 00N 6 06W
Ballaghaderreen Rol 20 C3 53 55N 8 36W
Ballantrae Scotland 10 D2 55 06N 5 00W
Ballater Scotland 9 F2 57 03N 3 03W
Ballaugh Isle of Man 12 B3 54 18N 4 32W
Ballina Rol 20 B4 54 07N 9 09W
Ballinafad Rol 20 C4 54 02N 8 20W
Ballinagleragh Rol 20 C4 54 09N 8 01W
Ballinalack Rol 20 D3 53 38N 7 28W
Ballinalee Rol 20 D3 53 46N 7 39W
Ballinamore Rol 20 D4 54 03N 7 47W
Ballinasloe Rol 20 C3 53 20N 8 13W
Ballincollig Rol 21 C1 51 54N 8 35W
Ballindine Rol 20 C3 53 40N 8 57W
Ballingry Scotland 11 F3 56 11N 3 20W
Ballinhassig Rol 21 C1 51 49N 8 32W
Ballinrobe Rol 20 B3 53 37N 9 13W
Ballintra Rol 20 C4 54 35N 8 07W
Ballon Rol 21 E2 52 44N 6 46W
Ballybay Rol 20 E4 54 08N 6 54W
Ballybofey Rol 20 D4 54 48N 7 47W
Ballybunnion Rol 21 B2 52 31N 9 40W
Ballycanew Rol 21 E2 52 36N 6 18W
Ballycastle NI 10 C2 55 12N 6 15W
Ballycastle Rol 20 B4 54 17N 9 22W
Ballyclare NI 10 C1 54 45N 6 00W
Ballycolla Rol 21 D2 52 52N 7 26W
Ballyconnell Rol 20 D4 54 07N 7 35W
Ballycotton Rol 21 C1 51 50N 8 01W
Ballycotton Bay Rol 21 D1 51 51N 7 57W
Ballycroy Rol 20 B4 54 02N 9 49W
Ballydavid Head Rol 21 A2 52 14N 10 21W
Ballydehob Rol 21 B1 51 34N 9 28W
Ballydesmond Rol 21 B2 52 10N 9 13W
Ballydonegan Rol 21 A1 51 37N 10 12W
Ballydonegan Bay Rol 21 A1 51 29N 10 09W
Ballygalley Head NI 10 D1 54 54N 5 51W
Ballygowan NI 10 D1 54 30N 5 47W
Ballyhaunis Rol 20 C3 53 46N 8 46W
Ballyheige Rol 21 B2 52 24N 9 50W
Ballyheige Bay Rol 21 B2 52 23N 9 52W
Ballyhoura Mountains
Rol 21 C2 52 17N 8 33W
Ballyjamesduff Rol 20 D3 53 52N 7 12W
Ballykinler NI 10 D1 54 17N 5 47W
Ballylanders Rol 21 C2 52 23N 8 21W
Ballylongford Rol 21 B2 52 33N 9 28W
Ballymacarbry Rol 21 D2 52 16N 7 12W
Ballymahon Rol 20 D3 53 34N 7 45W
Ballymena NI 10 C1 54 52N 6 17W
Ballymena district NI 10 C1 54 55N 6 20W
Ballymoe Rol 20 C3 53 42N 8 28W
Ballymoney NI 10 C2 55 04N 6 31W
Ballymoney district NI 10 C2 55 00N 6 30W

Ballymore Donegal Rol 20 D5 55 09N 7 56W
Ballymore
Westmeath Rol 20 D3 53 29N 7 40W
Ballymote Rol 20 C4 54 06N 8 31W
Ballynahinch NI 10 D1 54 24N 5 54W
Ballynamona Rol 21 C2 52 05N 8 39W
Ballynamult Rol 21 D2 52 13N 7 40W
Ballyquintin Point NI 10 D1 54 19N 5 30W
Ballyragget Rol 21 D2 52 47N 7 20W
Ballyshannon Rol 20 C4 54 30N 8 11W
Ballyteige Bay Rol 21 E2 52 12N 6 45W
Ballyvaghan Rol 21 B3 53 07N 9 09W
Ballyvourney Rol 21 B1 51 56N 9 10W
Ballywalter NI 10 D1 54 33N 5 30W
Balmaclellan Scotland 11 E2 55 05N 4 07W
Balmoral Scotland 9 F2 57 02N 3 13W
Balrath Rol 20 E3 53 37N 6 29W
Baltic Sea Europe 49 E2/F2 55 15N 17 00E
Baltimore Rol 21 B1 51 29N 9 22W
Baltimore USA 91 L4 39 18N 76 38W
Baltinglass Rol 21 E2 52 55N 6 41W
Baltray Rol 20 E3 53 44N 6 16W
Bamako Mali 80 C4 12 40N 7 59W
Bamberg Germany 52 E4 49 54N 10 54E
Bamburgh England 11 H2 55 36N 1 42W
Bampton England 18 D2 51 00N 3 29W
Banagher Rol 21 D3 53 11N 7 59W
Banbridge NI 10 C1 54 21N 6 16W
Banbridge district NI 10 C1 54 15N 6 20W
Banbury England 16 B3 52 04N 1 20W
Banchory Scotland 9 G2 57 30N 2 30W
Bandar Seri Begawan
Brunei 71 F4 4 53N 115 00E
Bandon Rol 21 C1 51 45N 8 45W
Bandung Indonesia 71 D2 6 57S 107 34E
Banff Canada 88 M4 51 10N 115 34W
Banff Scotland 9 G2 57 40N 2 33W
Bangalore India 66 D2 12 58N 77 35E
Bangkok Thailand 71 C6 13 44N 100 30E
BANGLADESH 67 F4/G4
Bangor NI 10 D1 54 40N 5 40W
Bangor Rol 20 B4 54 09N 9 44W
Bangor Wales 14 B3 53 13N 4 08W
Bangui CAR 81 J2 4 23N 18 37E
Banja Luka
Bosnia-Herzegovina 55 G6 44 47N 17 11E
Banjul The Gambia 80 A4 13 28N 16 39W
Bann r. Coleraine NI 10 C2 55 05N 6 40W
Bann r. Banbridge NI 10 C1 54 20N 6 11W
Bann r. Rol 21 E2 52 39N 6 24W
Bannockburn Scotland 11 F3 56 05N 3 56W
Bannow Bay Rol 21 E2 52 13N 6 48W
Bansha Rol 21 C2 52 28N 8 04W
Banstead England 16 C2 51 19N 0 12W
Banteer Rol 21 C2 52 08N 8 54W
Bantry Rol 21 B1 51 41N 9 27W
Bantry Bay Rol 21 B1 51 35N 9 40W
Baotou China 69 J6 40 38N 109 59E
Baracaldo Spain 51 D5 43 17N 2 59W
Baranavichy Belarus 53 N6 53 09N 26 00E
BARBADOS 94 S11
Barbastro Spain 51 F5 42 02N 0 07E
Barcelona Spain 51 G4 41 25N 2 10E
Barcs Hungary 53 H2 45 58N 17 30E
Bardsey Island Wales 14 B2 52 46N 4 48W
Barents Sea
Arctic Ocean 101 75 00N 40 00E
Bargoed Wales 14 C1 51 43N 3 15W
Bari Italy 55 G4 41 07N 16 52E
Barisal Bangladesh 67 G4 22 41N 90 20E
Barking England 17 D2 51 33N 0 06E
Barle r. England 18 D2 51 05N 3 36W
Bar-le-Duc France 50 G5 48 46N 5 10E
Barletta Italy 54 G4 41 20N 16 17E
Barmouth Wales 14 B2 52 43N 4 03W
Barnard Castle England 13 E3 54 33N 1 55W
Barnatra Rol 20 B4 54 13N 9 50W
Barnet England 16 C2 51 39N 0 12W
Barnoldswick England 12 D2 53 56N 2 16W
Barnsley England 13 E2 53 34N 1 28W
Barnstaple England 18 C3 51 05N 4 04W
Barnstaple or Bideford
Bay England 18 C3 51 05N 4 25W
Barquisimeto
Venezuela 96 D16 10 03N 69 18W
Barra i. Scotland 8 B1/B2 57 00N 7 25W
Barra Head Scotland 8 B1 56 47N 7 36W
Barranquilla Colombia 96 C16 11 10N 74 50W
Barra, Sound of
Scotland 8 B2 57 06N 7 22W
Barre USA 91 M5 44 13N 72 31W
Barreiro Portugal 51 A3 38 40N 9 05W
Barrhead Scotland 11 E2 55 48N 4 24W
Barrow r. Rol 21 E2 52 38N 6 58W
Barrow-in-Furness
England 12 C3 54 07N 3 14W
Barry Wales 14 C1 51 24N 3 18W
Barton-upon-Humber
England 13 F2 53 41N 0 27W
Barvas Scotland 8 C3 58 22N 6 32W
Barysaw Belarus 53 P7 54 09N 28 30E
Basel Switz. 52 C3 47 33N 7 36E
Basildon England 17 D2 51 34N 0 25E
Basingstoke England 16 B2 51 16N 1 05W
Bassenthwaite Lake
England 12 C3 54 40N 3 13W
Bastia France 50 J2 42 14N 9 26E

Bastogne Belgium 48 D3 50 00N 5 43E
Bath England 19 E3 51 23N 2 22W
Bath and North East
Somerset u.a. England 19 E3 51 25N 2 30W
Bathgate Scotland 11 F2 55 55N 3 39W
Bathurst Canada 89 X3 47 37N 65 40W
Batley England 13 E2 53 44N 1 37W
Baton Rouge USA 91 H3 30 30N 91 10W
Battle England 17 D1 50 55N 0 29E
Bat Yam Israel 64 N10 31 59N 34 45E
Bawdsey England 17 E3 52 01N 1 25E
Bawtry England 13 E2 53 26N 1 01W
Bayeux France 50 D5 49 16N 0 42W
Bayonne France 50 D2 43 30N 1 28W
Bayreuth Germany 52 E4 49 27N 11 35E
Bayston Hill tn.
England 14 D2 52 40N 2 48W
Beachy Head England 17 D1 50 44N 0 16E
Beaconsfield England 16 C2 51 37N 0 39W
Beadnell Bay England 11 H2 55 32N 1 30W
Beaminster England 19 E2 50 49N 2 45W
Bear Island Rol 21 B1 51 40N 9 48W
Bearsden Scotland 11 E2 55 56N 4 20W
Bearsted England 17 D2 51 17N 0 35E
Beatrice USA 91 G5 40 17N 96 45W
Beaulieu England 16 B1 50 49N 1 27W
Beauly Scotland 9 E2 57 29N 4 29W
Beauly r. Scotland 9 E2 57 25N 4 33W
Beauly Firth Scotland 9 E2 57 30N 4 20W
Beaumaris Wales 14 B3 53 16N 4 05W
Beaune France 50 G4 47 02N 4 50E
Beauvais France 50 F5 49 26N 2 05E
Bebington England 12 D2 53 20N 2 59W
Beccles England 17 E3 52 28N 1 34E
Bedale England 13 E3 54 17N 1 35W
Bedford England 16 C3 52 08N 0 29W
Bedfordshire co.
England 16 C2 52 08N 0 29W
Bedlington England 13 E4 55 08N 1 25W
Bedwas Wales 14 C1 51 35N 3 12W
Bedworth England 15 E2 52 29N 1 28W
Beeston England 15 E2 52 56N 1 12W
Beighton England 13 E2 53 21N 1 21W
Beijing China 69 L5 39 55N 116 26E
Beinn Dearg mt.
Scotland 9 E2 57 47N 4 56W
Beira Mozambique 82 F4 19 49S 34 52E
Beirut Lebanon 64 C5 33 52N 35 30E
Beith Scotland 11 E2 55 45N 4 38W
Beja Portugal 51 B3 38 01N 7 52W
Bejaïa Algeria 80 F9 36 49N 5 03E
Béjar Spain 51 C4 40 24N 5 45W
BELARUS 56 B5/6
Belderg Rol 20 B4 54 18N 9 33W
Belém Brazil 96 H12 1 27S 48 29W
Belfast NI 10 D1 54 35N 5 55W
Belfast district NI 10 C1/D1 54 40N 6 05W
Belfast Lough est. NI 10 D1 54 40N 5 50W
Belford England 11 H2 55 36N 1 49W
Belfort France 50 H4 47 38N 6 52E
BELGIUM 48 B3/D3
Belgrade
Serbia & Montenegro 55 J6 44 50N 20 30E
BELIZE 94 G3
Bellac France 50 E4 46 07N 1 04E
Bellacorick Rol 20 B4 54 07N 9 34W
Bellanagh Rol 20 D3 53 56N 7 24W
Bellavary Rol 20 B3 53 53N 9 12W
Bellingham England 12 D4 55 09N 2 16W
Bellsbank Scotland 11 E2 55 19N 4 24W
Bellshill Scotland 11 E2 55 49N 4 02W
Belmont Scotland 7 D3 60 41N 0 58W
Belmopan Belize 94 G3 17 13N 88 48W
Belmullet Rol 20 B4 54 14N 10 00W
Belo Horizonte Brazil 96 J10 19 54S 43 54W
Belper England 13 E2 53 01N 1 29W
Belton England 17 E3 52 34N 1 40E
Beltra Lough Rol 20 B3 53 55N 9 25W
Belturbet Rol 20 D4 54 06N 7 28W
Belvoir, Vale of
England 15 F2 52 58N 0 55W
Bembridge England 16 B1 50 41N 1 05W
Ben Alder mt. Scotland 9 E1 56 49N 4 28W
Benavente Spain 51 C4 42 00N 5 40W
Benbane Head NI 10 C2 55 14N 6 29W
Benbecula i. Scotland 8 B2 57 25N 7 20W
Ben Cleuch mt.
Scotland 11 F3 56 11N 3 47W
Ben Cruachan mt.
Scotland 8 D1 56 26N 5 09W
Benevento Italy 54 F4 41 08N 14 46E
Bengal, Bay of
Indian Ocean 67 F3 17 00N 88 00E
Benghazi Libya 81 K8 32 07N 20 04E
Ben Hope mt. Scotland 9 E3 58 24N 4 37W
Benicarló Spain 51 F4 40 25N 0 25E
Benidorm Spain 51 E3 38 33N 0 09W
BENIN 80 E4
Benin City Nigeria 80 E4 6 19N 5 41E
Ben Klibreck mt.
Scotland 9 E3 58 14N 4 22W
Ben Lawers mt.
Scotland 11 E3 56 33N 4 15W
Benllech Wales 14 B3 53 19N 4 15W
Ben Lomond mt.
Scotland 11 E3 56 12N 4 38W
Ben Loyal mt. Scotland 9 E3 58 24N 4 26W

Ben Macdui mt.
Scotland 9 F2 57 04N 3 40W
Ben More mt.
Highland Scotland 8 C1 56 25N 6 02W
Ben More mt.
Stirling Scotland 9 E1 56 23N 4 31W
Ben More Assynt mt.
Scotland 9 E3 58 07N 4 52W
Bennettsbridge Rol 21 D2 52 35N 7 10W
Ben Nevis mt. Scotland 9 E1 56 40N 5 00W
Benson USA 90 D3 31 58N 110 19W
Bentley England 13 E2 53 33N 1 09W
Benwee Head Rol 20 B4 54 21N 9 48W
Ben Wyvis mt. Scotland 9 E2 57 40N 4 35W
Beppu Japan 70 B1 33 18N 131 30E
Bérgamo Italy 54 C6 45 42N 9 40E
Bergen Norway 49 C3 60 23N 5 20E
Bergerac France 50 E3 44 50N 0 29E
Bergisch Gladbach
Germany 52 C5 50 59N 7 10E
Bering Sea
Pacific Ocean 100 H12/J13 60 00N 175 00W
Bering Strait
Russia/USA 88 B7 69 00N 169 00W
Berkeley USA 15 D1 51 42N 2 27W
Berkhamsted England 16 C2 51 46N 0 35W
Berkshire Downs
England 16 B2 51 30N 1 25W
Berlin Germany 52 F6 52 32N 13 25E
Bern Switz. 52 C3 46 57N 7 26E
Bernalda Italy 55 G4 40 24N 16 443
Berner Alpen mts.
Switz. 52 C3/D3 46 25N 7 30E
Berneray i. Scotland 8 B2 57 45N 7 10W
Bernina Pass Switz. 52 E3 46 25N 10 02E
Berriedale Scotland 9 F3 58 11N 3 33W
Berry Head England 18 D2 50 24N 3 29W
Berwick-upon-Tweed
England 11 G2 55 46N 2 00W
Besançon France 50 G4 47 14N 6 02E
Bessacarr England 13 E2 53 30N 1 05W
Bessbrook NI 10 C1 54 12N 6 24W
Betanzos Spain 51 A5 43 17N 8 13W
Bethersden England 17 D2 51 07N 0 45W
Bethesda Wales 14 B3 53 11N 4 03W
Bethlehem Middle East 64 C5 31 42N 35 12E
Béthune France 50 F6 50 32N 2 38E
Bettyhill Scotland 9 E3 58 32N 4 14W
Betws-y-Coed Wales 14 C3 53 05N 3 48W
Beverley England 13 F2 53 51N 0 26W
Bewdley England 15 D2 52 22N 2 19W
Bewl Water l. England 17 D2 51 02N 0 23E
Bexhill England 17 D1 50 50N 0 29E
Bexley England 17 D2 51 27N 0 09E
Béziers France 50 F2 43 21N 3 13E
Bharatpur India 66 D5 27 14N 77 29E
Bhopal India 66 D4 23 17N 77 28E
Bhubaneshwar India 67 F4 20 13N 85 50E
BHUTAN 67 G5
Białystok Poland 53 L6 53 09N 23 10E
Biarritz France 50 D2 43 29N 1 33W
Bicester England 16 B2 51 54N 1 09W
Biddeford USA 91 M5 43 29N 70 27W
Biddulph England 12 D2 53 08N 2 10W
Bideford England 18 C3 51 01N 4 13W
Biel Switz. 52 C3 46 27N 8 13E
Bielefeld Germany 52 D6 52 02N 8 32E
Bielsko-Biała Poland 53 J4 49 50N 19 00E
Bigbury Bay England 18 D2 50 17N 4 00W
Biggar Scotland 11 F2 55 38N 3 32W
Biggleswade England 16 C3 52 05N 0 17W
Bihać
Bosnia-Herzegovina 54 F6 44 49N 15 53E
Bikaner India 66 C5 28 01N 73 22E
Bila Tserkva Ukraine 53 Q4 49 49N 30 10E
Bilbao Spain 51 D5 43 15N 2 56W
Billericay England 17 D2 51 38N 0 25E
Billinge England 12 D2 53 30N 2 42W
Billingham England 13 E3 54 36N 1 17W
Billingshurst England 16 C2 51 01N 0 28W
Bill of Portland c.
England 19 E2 50 31N 2 27W
Bingham England 15 F2 52 57N 0 57W
Bingley England 13 E2 53 51N 1 50W
Birchwood tn. England 13 E2 53 14N 0 33W
Birkenhead England 12 C2 53 24N 3 02W
Birmingham England 15 E2 52 30N 1 50W
Birmingham USA 91 J3 33 30N 86 55W
Birr Rol 21 D3 53 05N 7 54W
Birstall England 15 E2 52 40N 1 08W
Biscay, Bay of
Atlantic Ocean 50 C3 45 30N 2 50W
Bishkek Kyrgyzstan 62 K5 42 53N 74 46E
Bishop Auckland
England 13 E3 54 40N 1 40W
Bishopbriggs Scotland 11 E2 55 54N 4 14W
Bishop's Castle tn.
England 14 C2 52 29N 3 00W
Bishop's Cleeve
England 15 D1 51 57N 2 04W
Bishop's Lydeard
England 18 D3 51 04N 3 12W
Bishop's Stortford
England 17 D2 51 53N 0 09E
Bishopston Wales 14 B1 51 35N 4 03W
Bishop's Waltham
England 16 B1 50 58N 1 12W

Bishopton Scotland 11 E2 55 54N 4 31W
Bissau Guinea-Bissau 80 A4 11 52N 15 39W
Blaby England 15 E2 52 35N
Black r. Rol 20 D3 53 55N 7 42W
Blackburn England 12 D2 53 45N 2 29W
Blackdown Hills
 England 19 D2 50 55N 3 10W
Blackhall Colliery tn.
 England 13 E3 54 43N 1 20W
Black Head Rol 21 B3 53 09N 9 16W
Blackhope Scar mt.
 Scotland 11 F2 55 58N 3 07W
Black Isle Scotland 9 E2 57 35N 4 15W
Blackmoor Vale
 England 19 E2 50 56N 2 19W
Black Mountains Wales14 C1 51 55N 3 10W
Black Mountain Wales 14 C1 51 50N 3 55W
Blackpool England 12 D2 53 50N 3 03W
Black Sea Europe 57 D3/E3 43 00N 35 00E
Blacksod Bay Rol 20 A3/A4 54 05N 10 00W
Blackstairs Mountains
 Rol 21 E2 52 33N 6 49W
Blackwater r.
 Hampshire England 16 C2 51 22N 0 54W
Blackwater r.
 Essex England 17 D2 51 45N 0 50E
Blackwater r.
 Waterford Rol 21 D2 52 02N 7 51W
Blackwater r.
 Meath Rol 20 E3 53 41N 6 44W
Blackwaterfoot
 Scotland 10 D2 55 30N 5 19W
Blackwater r. NI 10 C1 54 20N 6 50W
Blackwood Wales 14 C1 51 41N 3 13W
Blaenau Ffestiniog
 Wales 14 C2 52 59N 3 56W
Blaenau Gwent u.a.
 Wales 14 C1 51 45N 3 10W
Blaenavon Wales 14 C1 51 48N 3 05W
Blagoveshchensk
 Russia 63 Q7 50 19N 127 30E
Blaina Wales 14 C1 51 48N 3 11W
Blair Atholl Scotland 9 F1 56 46N 3 51W
Blairgowrie Scotland 9 F1 56 36N 3 21W
Blakeney Point England17 E3 52 58N 1 00E
Blandford Forum
 England 19 E2 50 52N 2 11W
Blantyre Malawi 82 F4 15 46S 35 00E
Blantyre Scotland 11 E2 55 47N 4 06W
Blarney Rol 21 C1 51 56N 8 34W
Blennerville Rol 21 B2 52 15N 9 43W
Blessington Rol 21 E3 53 10N 6 32W
Bletchley England 16 C3 52 00N 0 46W
Blidworth England 13 E2 53 09N 1 11W
Blithe r. England 15 E2 52 45N 1 50W
Blois France 50 E4 47 36N 1 20E
Bloody Foreland Rol 20 C5 55 10N 8 15W
Bludenz Austria 52 D3 47 10N 9 50E
Blue Stack Mountains
 Rol 20 C4 54 44N 8 03W
Blyth Nottinghamshire
 England 13 E2 53 23N 1 03W
Blyth Northumberland
 England 13 E4 55 07N 1 30W
Blyth r. England 13 E4 55 08N 1 45W
Blyth r. England 17 E3 52 28N 1 45E
Boa Vista Brazil 96 E14 3 23S 55 30W
Bocholt Germany 52 C5 51 49N 6 37E
Bochum Germany 52 C5 51 28N 7 11E
Boddam Scotland 9 H2 57 28N 1 48W
Boden Sweden 49 F4 65 50N 21 44E
Bodensee l. Switz. 52 D3 47 40N 9 30E
Bodmin England 18 C2 50 29N 4 43W
Bodmin Moor England 18 C2 50 35N 4 40W
Boggeragh Mountains
 Rol 21 B2/C2 52 00N 8 50W
Bogie r. Scotland 9 G2 57 25N 2 50W
Bognor Regis England 16 C1 50 47N 0 41W
Bogotá Colombia 96 C14 4 38N 74 05W
Böhmer Wald mts.
 Germany 52 F4 49 00N 13 00E
Boise City USA 90 F4 36 44N 102 31W
Boldon England 13 E3 54 57N 1 27W
BOLIVIA 96D10/E10
Bollington England 12 D2 53 18N 2 06W
Bologna Italy 54 E6 44 30N 11 20E
Bolsover England 13 E2 53 15N 2 26W
Bolton England 12 D2 53 35N 2 26W
Bolus Head Rol 21 A1 51 45N 10 10W
Bolzano Italy 54 D7 46 30N 11 22E
Bonar Bridge tn.
 Scotland 9 E2 57 53N 4 21W
Bo'ness Scotland 11 F3 56 01N 3 37W
Bonifacio France 50 J1 41 23N 9 10E
Bonifacio, Strait of
 France/Italy 50 J1 41 20N 8 45E
Bonn Germany 52 C5 50 44N 7 06E
Bonnybridge Scotland 11 F2 55 59N 3 54W
Bonnyrigg Scotland 11 F2 55 52N 3 08W
Boolakennedy Rol 21 C2 52 20N 8 03W
Bootle Cumbira England12 C3 54 17N 3 23W
Bootle
 Merseyside England 12 C2 53 28N 3 00W
Bordeaux France 50 D3 44 50N 0 34W
Bordon Camp England 16 C2 51 07N 0 53W
Borneo
 Indonesia/Malaysia 71 D3/F5 1 00N 113 00E

Bornholm i. Denmark 49 D2 55 02N 15 00E
Boroughbridge
 England 13 E3 54 05N 1 24W
Borris in Ossory Rol 21 D2 52 57N 7 37W
Borrisokane Rol 21 C2 53 00N 8 08W
Borrisoleigh Rol 21 D2 52 45N 8 00W
Borrowash England 15 E2 52 55N 1 24W
Borth Wales 14 B2 52 29N 4 03W
Boscastle England 18 C2 50 41N 4 42W
BOSNIA-
 HERZEGOVINA 55 G6/H6
Boston England 13 F1 52 59N 0 01W
Boston USA 91 M5 42 20N 71 05W
Boston Spa England 13 E2 53 54N 1 21W
Bothnia, Gulf of
 Finland/Sweden 49 E3/F3 61 00N 19 10E
BOTSWANA 82 D3/E3
Bottrop Germany 52 C5 51 31N 6 55E
Boulder USA 90 E5 40 02N 105 16W
Boulogne-sur-Mer
 France 50 E6 50 43N 1 37E
Bourg-en-Bresse
 France 50 G4 46 12N 5 13E
Bourges France 50 F4 47 05N 2 23E
Bourne England 15 F2 52 46N 0 23W
Bourne End England 16 C2 51 34N 0 42W
Bournemouth England 19 F2 50 43N 1 54W
Bournemouth u.a.
 England 19 F2 50 43N 1 54W
Bourton-on-the-Water
 England 15 E1 51 53N 1 46W
Bovey r. England 18 D2 50 40N 3 50W
Bovey Tracey England 18 D2 50 36N 3 40W
Bowes England 12 D3 54 30N 2 01W
Bowland, Forest of
 England 12 D2/D3 54 00N 2 40W
Bowmore Scotland 10 C2 55 45N 6 17W
Bowness-on-
 Windermere England 12 D3 54 22N 2 55W
Boxtel Neths 48 D4 51 36N 5 20E
Boyle Rol 20 C3 53 58N 8 18W
Boyne r. Rol 20 E3 53 45N 6 25W
Bozeman USA 90 D6 45 40N 111 00W
Brabourne Lees
 England 17 D2 51 08N 1 00E
Brackley England 15 E2 52 02N 1 09W
Bracknell England 16 C2 51 26N 0 46W
Bracknell Forest u.a.
 England 16 C1 50 25N 0 50W
Bradford England 13 E2 53 48N 1 45W
Bradford-on-Avon
 England 16 A2 51 22N 2 15W
Bradwell-on-Sea
 England 17 D2 51 44N 0 54E
Bradworthy England 18 C2 50 54N 4 24W
Braemar Scotland 9 F2 57 01N 3 23W
Braga Portugal 51 A4 41 32N 8 26W
Bragança Portugal 51 B4 41 47N 6 46W
Brahmaputra r.
 India/Bangladesh 67 G5 26 40N 93 00E
Brăila Romania 53 N2 45 17N 27 58E
Brailsford England 15 E2 52 59N 1 36W
Braintree England 17 D2 51 53N 0 32E
Brampton England 12 D3 54 57N 2 43W
Brandenburg Germany 52 F6 52 25N 12 34E
Brandon
 Durham England 13 E3 54 46N 1 38W
Brandon
 Suffolk England 17 D3 52 27N 0 37E
Brandon Bay Rol 21 A2 52 15N 10 05W
Brandon Mountain Rol 21 A2 52 10N 10 10W
Brandon Point Rol 21 A2 52 15N 10 05W
Brant r. England 13 F2 53 05N 0 35W
Brasília Brazil 96 H10 15 45S 47 57W
Braşov Romania 53 M2 45 39N 25 35E
Bratislava Slovakia 53 H4 48 10N 17 10E
Braunau Austria 52 F4 48 16N 13 03E
Braunschweig
 Germany 52 E6 52 15N 10 30E
Braunton England 18 C3 51 07N 4 10W
Bray Rol 20 E3 53 12N 6 06W
Bray Head Rol 21 A1 53 12N 6 05W
BRAZIL 96F11/H11
Brazzaville Congo 82 C7 4 14S 15 14E
Breaston England 15 E2 52 56N 1 12W
Brechin Scotland 9 G1 56 44N 2 40W
Brecon Wales 14 C1 51 57N 3 24W
Breda Neths 48 C4 51 35N 4 46E
Bregenz Austria 52 D3 47 31N 9 46E
Bremen Germany 52 D6 53 05N 8 48E
Bremerhaven Germany 52 D6 53 33N 8 35E
Brent England 16 C2 51 34N 0 17W
Brentwood England 17 D2 51 38N 0 18E
Brescia Italy 54 D6 45 33N 10 13E
Bressay i. Scotland 7 C3 60 08N 1 05W
Brest Belarus 56 B5 52 08N 23 40E
Brest France 50 B5 48 23N 4 30W
Briançon France 50 H3 44 53N 6 39E
Bridgend Wales 14 C1 51 31N 3 35W
Bridgend u.a. Wales 14 C1 51 32N 3 35W
Bridge of Dee tn.
 Scotland 9 F1 56 59N 3 20W
Bridge of Don tn.
 Scotland 9 G2 57 11N 2 05W
Bridge of Ericht tn.
 Scotland 9 E1 56 44N 4 23W

Bridge of Orchy tn.
 Scotland 9 E1 56 30N 4 46W
Bridge of Weir tn.
 Scotland 11 E2 55 52N 4 35W
Bridgeport USA 91 M5 41 12N 73 12W
Bridgetown Rol 21 E2 52 14N 6 33W
Bridgnorth England 15 D2 52 33N 2 25W
Bridgwater England 19 D3 51 08N 3 00W
Bridgwater Bay
 England 19 D3 51 15N 3 20W
Bridlington England 13 F3 54 05N 0 12W
Bridlington Bay
 England 13 F3 54 03N 0 10W
Bridport England 19 E2 50 44N 2 46W
Brierfield England 12 D2 53 50N 2 14W
Brig Switz. 52 C3 46 19N 8 00E
Brigg England 13 F2 53 34N 0 30W
Brighouse England 13 E2 53 42N 1 47W
Brightlingsea England 17 D2 51 49N 1 02E
Brighton England 16 C1 50 50N 0 10W
Brighton and Hove u.a.
 England 16 C1 50 51N 0 09W
Brignoles France 50 H2 43 25N 6 03E
Brindisi Italy 55 G4 40 37N 17 57E
Brisbane Australia 73 K5 27 30S 153 00E
Bristol England 19 E3 51 27N 2 35W
Bristol u.a. England 19 E3 51 30N 2 38W
Bristol Channel UK 18 C1/D1 51 20N 4 00W
British Columbia prov.
 Canada 88 K4/K5 56 50N 125 30W
British Isles Europe 6
Briton Ferry tn. Wales 14 C1 51 38N 3 49W
Brittas Rol 20 E3 53 14N 6 27W
Brive-la-Gaillarde
 France 50 E3 45 09N 1 32E
Brixham England 18 D2 50 23N 3 30W
Brno Czech Rep. 53 H4 49 13N 16 40E
Broad Bay Scotland 8 C3 58 15N 6 10W
Broadford Rol 21 C2 52 48N 8 38W
Broadford Scotland 8 D2 57 14N 5 54W
Broad Haven b. Rol 20 B4 54 18N 9 55W
Broadstairs England 17 E2 51 22N 1 27E
Broadstone England 19 E2 50 45N 2 00W
Broadway England 15 E2 52 02N 1 50W
Brockenhurst England 16 B1 50 49N 1 34W
Brodick Scotland 10 D2 55 35N 5 09W
Bromley England 16 D2 51 31N 0 01E
Bromsgrove England 15 D2 52 20N 2 03W
Bromyard England 15 D2 52 11N 2 30W
Brora Scotland 9 F3 58 01N 3 51W
Brora r. Scotland 9 E3 58 05N 4 00W
Broseley England 15 D2 52 37N 2 29W
Brotton England 13 F3 54 34N 0 56W
Brough East Riding of
 Yorkshire England 13 F2 53 44N 0 35W
Brough
 Cumbria England 12 D3 54 32N 2 19W
Brough Head Scotland 7 A2 59 09N 3 19W
Broughshane NI 10 C1 54 54N 6 12W
Broughton Wales 14 D3 53 10N 3 00W
Broughton in Furness
 England 12 C3 54 17N 3 13W
Broughty Ferry tn.
 Scotland 9 G1 56 28N 2 53W
Brownhills tn. England 15 E2 52 39N 1 55W
Broxburn Scotland 11 F2 55 57N 3 29W
Bruay-en-Artois France 50 F6 50 29N 2 33E
Brue r. England 19 E3 51 10N 2 50W
Brugg Switz. 52 D3 47 29N 8 13E
Brugge Belgium 48 B4 51 13N 3 14E
BRUNEI 71 E4/F4
Brunico Italy 54 D7 46 47N 11 57E
Brunswick USA 91 K3 31 09N 81 30W
Brussels Belgium 48 C3 50 50N 4 21E
Bruton England 19 E3 51 07N 2 27W
Bryher i. England 18 A1 49 57N 6 21W
Brymbo Wales 14 C3 53 05N 3 03W
Brynamman Wales 14 C1 51 49N 3 52W
Brynmawr Wales 14 C1 51 49N 3 11W
Bucharest Romania 53 N2 44 25N 26 07E
Buchan Ness Scotland 9 H2 57 28N 1 47W
Buckfastleigh England 18 D2 50 29N 3 46W
Buckhaven Scotland 11 F3 56 11N 3 03W
Buckie Scotland 9 G2 57 40N 2 58W
Buckingham England 16 C2 52 00N 1 00W
Buckinghamshire co.
 England 16 C2 51 50N 0 50W
Buckley Wales 14 C3 53 10N 3 05W
Budapest Hungary 53 J3 47 30N 19 03E
Buddon Ness Scotland 9 G1 56 28N 2 45W
Bude England 18 C2 50 50N 4 33W
Bude Bay England 18 C2 50 50N 4 40W
Budleigh Salterton
 England 19 D2 50 38N 3 20W
Buenaventura
 Colombia 96 B14 3 54N 77 02W
Buenos Aires Argentina97 F7 34 40S 58 30W
Buffalo USA 91 L5 42 52N 78 55W
Builth Wells Wales 14 C2 52 09N 3 24W
Bujumbura Burundi 83 A3 3 22S 29 19E
Bulford England 16 B2 51 12N 1 46W
BULGARIA 55 K5/M5
Bulkington England 15 E2 52 29N 1 25W
Bull Point NI 10 C2 55 18N 6 16W
Bunclody Rol 21 E2 52 39N 6 40W
Buncrana Rol 20 D5 55 08N 7 27W
Bundoran Rol 20 C4 54 28N 8 17W

Bungay England 17 E3 52 28N 1 26E
Bunmahon Rol 21 D2 52 08N 7 23W
Bunnahown Rol 20 B3 53 24N 9 47W
Bunnyconnellan Rol 20 B4 54 06N 9 01W
Buraydah Saudi Arabia 64 D4 26 20N 43 59E
Bure r. England 17 E3 52 47N 1 20E
Burgas Bulgaria 55 M5 42 30N 27 29E
Burgess Hill tn.
 England 16 C1 50 58N 0 08W
Burghead tn. Scotland 9 F2 57 42N 3 30W
Burghead Bay Scotland 9 F2 57 41N 3 31W
Burgh le Marsh
 England 13 G2 53 10N 0 15E
Burgos Spain 51 D5 42 21N 3 41W
BURKINA 80 D4
Burley-in-Wharfedale
 England 13 E2 53 55N 1 45W
Burnham Market
 England 17 D3 52 57N 0 44E
Burnham-on-Crouch
 England 17 D2 51 38N 0 49E
Burnham-on-Sea
 England 19 D3 51 15N 3 00W
Burnley England 12 D2 53 48N 2 14W
Burnmouth Scotland 11 G2 55 50N 2 04W
Burnsall England 12 E3 54 03N 1 57W
Burntisland tn.
 Scotland 11 F3 56 03N 3 15W
Burntwood England 15 E2 52 40N 1 56W
Burray i. Scotland 7 B1 58 51N 2 54W
Burrow Head Scotland 11 E1 54 41N 4 24W
Burry Port Wales 14 B1 51 42N 4 15W
Bursa Turkey 57 C3 40 12N 29 04E
Burscough Bridge tn.
 England 12 D2 53 37N 2 51W
Burton Agnes England 13 F3 54 03N 0 19W
Burton Latimer
 England 15 F2 52 22N 0 40W
Burton upon Trent
 England 15 E2 52 48N 1 36W
BURUNDI 83 A3/B3
Burwell England 17 D3 52 16N 0 19E
Bury England 12 D2 53 36N 2 17W
Bury St. Edmunds
 England 17 D3 52 15N 0 43E
Bush r. NI 10 C2 55 10N 6 30W
Bushey England 16 C2 51 39N 0 22W
Bushmills NI 10 C2 55 12N 6 32W
Bute i. Scotland 10 D2 55 50N 5 05W
Bute, Sound of
 Scotland 10 D2 55 45N 5 10W
Butler's Bridge Rol 20 D4 54 03N 7 22W
Buttermere l. England 12 C3 54 32N 3 16W
Buttevant Rol 21 C2 52 14N 8 40W
Butt of Lewis c.
 Scotland 8 C3 58 30N 6 20W
Buxton England 13 E2 53 15N 1 55W
Bydgoszcz Poland 53 H6 53 16N 18 00E
Byfield England 15 E2 52 11N 1 14W
Bytom Poland 53 J5 50 21N 18 51E

C

Cabo de Hornos Chile 97 D2 56 00S 67 15W
Cabo Finisterre Spain 51 A5 42 52N 9 16W
Cabrera i. Spain 51 G3 39 00N 2 59E
Cáceres Spain 51 B3 39 29N 6 23W
Cadair Idris mt. Wales 14 C2 52 42N 3 54W
Cádiz Spain 51 B2 36 32N 6 18W
Cádiz, Gulf of Spain 51 B2 36 30N 7 15W
Caen France 50 D5 49 11N 0 22W
Caerleon Wales 14 D1 51 37N 2 57W
Caernarfon Wales 14 B3 53 08N 4 16W
Caernarfon Bay Wales 14 B3 53 05N 4 30W
Caerphilly Wales 14 C1 51 35N 3 14W
Caerphilly u.a. Wales 14 C1 51 37N 3 5W
Caersws Wales 14 C2 52 31N 3 26W
Cágliari Italy 54 C3 39 13N 9 08E
Caha Mountains Rol 21 B1 51 40N 9 40W
Caher Rol 21 D2 52 21N 7 56W
Caher Island Rol 20 A3 53 43N 10 01W
Cahersiveen Rol 21 A1 51 57N 10 13W
Cahore Point Rol 21 E2 52 34N 6 11W
Cahors France 50 E3 44 28N 0 26E
Cairn Gorm mt.
 Scotland 9 F2 57 07N 3 40W
Cairngorms mts.
 Scotland 9 F2 57 10N 3 30W
Cairnryan Scotland 10 D2 54 58N 5 02W
Cairns Australia 73 J7 16 51S 145 43E
Cairo Egypt 81 M7 30 00N 31 15E
Caister-on-Sea England17 E3 52 39N 1 44E
Caistor England 13 F2 53 30N 0 20W
Calahorra Spain 51 E5 46 19N 1 58W
Calais France 50 E6 50 57N 1 52E
Calamocha Spain 51 E4 40 54N 1 18W
Calatayud Spain 51 E4 41 21N 1 39W
Caldew r. England 12 C3 54 45N 3 00W
Caldey Island Wales 14 B1 51 38N 4 42W
Caldicot Wales 14 D1 51 36N 2 45W
Caldwell USA 90 C5 43 39N 116 40W
Calgary Canada 88 N4 51 05N 114 05W
Cali Colombia 96 B14 3 24N 76 30W
California state USA 90 C4 35 00N 119 00W
Callan Rol 21 D2 52 33N 7 23W
Callander Scotland 11 E3 56 15N 4 13W
Calligarry Scotland 8 D2 57 02N 5 58E

Callington England 18 C2 50 30N 4 18W
Calne England 16 A2 51 27N 2 00W
Calverton England 13 E2 53 03N 1 05W
Calvi France 50 J2 42 34N 8 44E
Cam r. England 17 D3 52 15N 0 11E
Camberley England 16 C2 51 21N 0 45W
CAMBODIA 71 C6/D6
Camborne England 18 B2 50 12N 5 19W
Cambrai France 50 F6 50 10N 3 14E
Cambrian Mountains
  Wales 14 C2 52 15N 3 45W
Cambridge England 17 D3 52 12N 0 07E
Cambridge USA 91 L4 38 34N 76 04W
Cambridgeshire co.
  England 16 C3 52 30N 0 00
Camel r. England 18 C2 50 31N 4 44W
Camelford England 18 C2C 50 37N 4 41W
CAMEROON 80 G3
Campbeltown Scotland 10 D2 55 26N 5 36W
Campina Grande Brazil 96 K12 7 15S 35 50W
Campinas Brazil 96 H9 22 54S 47 06W
Campobasso Italy 54 F4 41 33N 14 39E
Campsie Fells Scotland 11 E3 56 00N 4 15W
CANADA 88/89
Canadian r. USA 90 F4 35 00N 104 00W
Canary Islands Spain 80 A7/B7 28 30N 15 10W
Canaveral, Cape USA 91 K2 28 28N 80 28W
Canberra Australia 73 J3 35 18S 149 08E
Cancún Mexico 94 G4 21 09N 86 45W
Canisp mt. Scotland 9 D3 58 07N 5 03W
Canna i. Scotland 8 C2 57 05N 6 35W
Canna, Sound of
  Scotland 8 C2 57 00N 6 30W
Cannes France 50 H2 43 33N 7 00E
Cannich Scotland 9 E2 57 12N 4 46W
Cannington England 19 D3 51 09N 3 04E
Cannock England 15 D2 52 42N 2 01W
Cannock Chase
  England 15 D2/E2 52 45N 2 04W
Canonbie Scotland 11 G2 55 05N 2 57W
Canterbury England 17 E2 51 17N 1 05E
Canvey Island England 17 D2 51 32N 0 33E
Cap de la Hague France 50 D5 49 44N 1 56W
Cape Clear RoI 21 B1 51 30N 9 30W
Cape Cornwall England 18 B2 50 07N 5 44W
Capel England 16 C2 51 10N 0 20W
Cape Town RSA 82 C1 33 56S 18 28E
CAPE VERDE 102
Cape York Peninsula
  Australia 73 H8 12 30S 142 30E
Cap Ferret c. France 50 D3 44 42N 1 16W
Cappagh White RoI 21 C2 52 40N 8 10W
Cappamore RoI 21 C2 52 37N 8 20W
Cappoquin RoI 21 D2 52 08N 7 50W
Capri i. Italy 54 F4 40 33N 14 15E
Caracas Venezuela 96 D16 10 35N 66 56W
Carcassonne France 50 F2 43 13N 2 21E
Cardiff Wales 14 C1 51 30N 3 13W
Cardiff u.a. Wales 14 C1 51 32N 3 14W
Cardigan Wales 14 B2 52 06N 4 40W
Cardigan Bay Wales 14 B2 52 30N 4 30W
Cargenbridge Scotland 11 F2 55 05N 3 41W
Caribbean Sea
  Central America 95 J3/L3 15 00N 75 00W
Carlingford RoI 20 E4 54 02N 6 11W
Carlingford Lough
  NI/RoI 10 C1 54 05N 6 10W
Carlisle England 12 D3 54 54N 2 55W
Carlow RoI 21 E2 52 50N 6 55W
Carlow co. RoI 21 E2 52 40N 6 55W
Carloway Scotland 8 C3 58 17N 6 48W
Carlton in Lindrick
  England 13 E2 53 22N 1 06W
Carlton-on-Trent
  England 13 F2 53 10N 0 48W
Carluke Scotland 11 F2 55 45N 3 51W
Carmarthen Wales 14 B1 51 51N 4 20W
Carmarthen Bay Wales 14 B1 51 40N 4 30W
Carmarthenshire u.a.
  Wales 14 B1 51 55N 4 00W
Carmel Head Wales 14 B3 53 24N 4 34W
Carndonagh RoI 20 D5 55 15N 7 15W
Carn Eige mt. Scotland 9 D2 57 22N 5 07W
Carnforth England 12 D3 54 08N 2 46W
Carnlough NI 10 D1 54 59N 5 59W
Carnlough Bay NI 10 D1 54 59N 5 57W
Carnoustie Scotland 9 G1 56 30N 2 44W
Carnsore Point RoI 21 E2 52 10N 6 22W
Carpathians mts.
  Europe 53 J4/M3 49 00N 22 00E
Carpentras France 50 G3 44 03N 5 03E
Carradale Scotland 10 D2 55 35N 5 28E
Carrauntoohil mt. RoI 21 B2 52 00N 9 45W
Carrbridge Scotland 9 F2 57 17N 3 49W
Carrick Scotland 10 C4 54 39N 8 38W
Carrickboy RoI 20 D3 53 37N 7 41W
Carrickfergus NI 10 D1 54 43N 5 49W
Carrickfergus district
  NI 10 D1 54 45N 5 50W
Carrickmacross RoI 20 E3 53 58N 5 49W
Carrick-on-Shannon
  RoI 20 C3 53 57N 8 05W
Carrick-on-Suir RoI 21 D2 52 21N 7 25W
Carrigaline RoI 21 C1 51 48N 8 24W
Carriganimmy RoI 21 B1 51 57N 9 02W
Carrigtohill RoI 21 C2 51 55N 8 16W

Carron r. Scotland 9 E2 57 53N 4 30W
Carronbridge Scotland 11 F2 55 16N 3 48W
Carrutherstown
  Scotland 11 F2 55 04N 3 24W
Carryduff NI 10 D1 54 31N 5 53W
Carsethorn Scotland 11 F1 54 55N 3 35W
Carsphairn Scotland 11 E2 55 13N 4 16W
Cartagena Colombia 96 B16 10 24N 75 33W
Cartagena Spain 51 E2 37 36N 0 59W
Carterton England 16 B2 51 45N 1 35W
Casablanca Morocco 80 C8 33 39N 7 35W
Cascade Range
  N. America 90 B5/6 48 00N 121 00W
Caserta Italy 54 F4 41 04N 14 20E
Cashel RoI 21 D2 52 31N 7 53W
Casper USA 90 E5 42 50N 106 20W
Caspian Sea Asia 57 G3/H3 41 00N 50 00E
Cassino Italy 54 F4 41 29N 13 50E
Castellane France 50 H2 43 50N 6 30E
Castellón de la Plana
  Spain 51 E3 39 59N 0 03W
Castelnaudary France 50 E2 43 18N 1 57E
Castelo Branco
  Portugal 51 B3 39 50N 7 30W
Castelvetrano Italy 54 E2 37 41N 12 47E
Castlebar RoI 20 B3 53 52N 9 17W
Castlebay Scotland 8 B1 56 57N 7 28W
Castleblaney RoI 20 E4 54 07N 6 44W
Castle Cary England 19 E3 51 06N 2 31W
Castlecomer RoI 21 D2 52 48N 7 12W
Castleconnell RoI 21 C2 52 43N 8 30W
Castledawson NI 10 C1 54 47N 6 33W
Castlederg NI 10 B1 54 42N 7 36W
Castledermot RoI 21 E2 52 55N 6 50W
Castle Donington
  England 15 E2 52 51N 1 19W
Castle Douglas
  Scotland 11 F1 54 57N 3 56W
Castlefin RoI 20 D4 54 47N 7 35W
Castleford England 13 E2 53 44N 1 21W
Castleisland RoI 21 B2 52 14N 9 27W
Castle Kennedy
  Scotland 10 E1 54 54N 4 57W
Castlemaine Harbour
  RoI 21 B2 52 08N 9 33W
Castlepollard RoI 20 D3 53 41N 7 17W
Castlerea RoI 20 C3 53 46N 8 29W
Castlereagh district NI 10 D1 54 35N 5 55W
Castletown Isle of Man 12 B3 54 04N 4 38W
Castletown Scotland 9 F3 58 35N 3 23W
Castletown Bearhaven
  RoI 21 B2 51 39N 9 55W
Castletownroche RoI 21 C2 52 10N 8 28W
Castlewellan NI 10 D1 54 16N 5 57W
Castres France 50 F2 43 36N 2 14E
Castrovillari Italy 54 G3 39 48N 16 12E
Catània Italy 54 F2 37 31N 15 06E
Catanzaro Italy 55 G3 38 54N 16 36E
Caterham England 16 C2 51 17N 0 04W
Catlemartyr RoI 21 C1 51 55N 8 03W
Catrine Scotland 11 E2 55 30N 4 20W
Catshill tn. England 15 D2 52 22N 2 03W
Catterick Garrison
  England 13 E3 54 23N 1 40W
Caucasus mts. Asia 57 F3/G3 43 00N 43 00E
Cavan RoI 20 D3 53 58N 7 21W
Cavan co. RoI 20 D3/4 54 02N 7 10W
Cawood England 13 E2 53 50N 1 07W
Caxias Brazil 96 J13 4 53N 43 20W
Cayenne French Guiana 96 G14 4 55N 52 18W
Cedar Rapids tn. USA 91 H5 41 59N 91 39W
Cefalù Italy 54 F3 38 03N 14 03E
Cefn-mawr Wales 14 C2 52 59N 3 02W
Cellar Head Scotland 8 C3 58 25N 6 11W
Celle Germany 52 E6 52 37N 10 05E
Cemaes Wales 14 B3 53 24N 4 27W
Cemaes Head Wales 14 B2 53 10N 4 50W
CENTRAL AFRICAN
  REPUBLIC 81 J3/K3
Ceredigion u.a. Wales 14 B2/C2 52 14N 4 00W
Cergy-Pontoise France 50 F5 49 02N 2 04E
Cerignola Italy 54 F4 41 16N 15 54E
Cerne Abbas England 19 E2 50 49N 2 29W
Cesena Italy 54 E6 44 09N 12 15E
České Budějovice
  Czech Rep. 52 G4 48 58N 14 29E
Ceuta territory Spain 51 C1 35 53N 5 19W
Cévennes mts. France 50 F3 44 20N 3 30E
CHAD 81 J4/K4
Chadderton England 12 D2 53 33N 2 08W
Chad, Lake West Africa 81 G4 13 50N 14 00E
Chagford England 18 D2 50 41N 3 50W
Chalfont St. Giles
  England 16 C2 51 39N 0 35W
Chalkída Greece 55 K3 38 28N 23 36E
Chalkidiki p. Greece 55 K4 40 30N 23 00E
Chalmer r. England 17 D2 51 54N 0 21E
Châlons-sur-Marne
  France 50 G5 48 58N 4 22E
Chalon-sur-Saône
  France 50 G4 46 47N 4 51E
Chambéry France 50 G3 45 34N 5 55E
Chamonix France 50 H3 45 55N 6 52E
Champlain, Lake USA 93 F2 45 00N 73 00W
Chandigarh India 66 D6 30 44N 76 54E
Chang Jiang r. China 69 J4 31 00N 110 00E
Changsha China 69 K3 28 10N 113 00E

Chaniá Greece 55 L1 35 31N 24 01E
Channel Islands
  British Isles 19 E1 49 30N 2 30W
Chapel-en-le-Frith
  England 13 E2 53 20N 1 54W
Chapel St. Leonards
  England 13 G2 53 14N 0 20E
Chapeltown England 13 E2 53 28N 1 27W
Chard England 19 E2 50 53N 2 58W
Charing England 17 D2 51 13N 0 48E
Charlbury England 16 B2 51 53N 1 29W
Charleroi Belgium 48 C3 50 25N 4 27E
Charleston USA 91 K4 38 23N 81 40W
Charlestown RoI 20 C3 53 58N 8 47W
Charlestown of
  Aberlour Scotland 9 F2 57 28N 3 14W
Charleville-Mézières
  France 50 G5 49 46N 4 43E
Charlotte USA 91 K4 35 03N 80 50W
Charlottesville USA 91 L4 38 02N 78 29W
Charlton Kings England 15 D2 51 53N 2 03W
Chartres France 50 E5 48 27N 1 30E
Châteaubriant France 50 D4 47 43N 1 22W
Châteaudun France 50 E5 48 04N 1 20E
Châteauroux France 50 E4 46 49N 1 41E
Château-Thierry
  France 50 F5 49 03N 3 24E
Châtellerault France 50 E4 46 49N 0 33E
Chatham England 17 D2 51 23N 0 32E
Chatham Canada 89 U2 42 24N 82 11W
Châtillon-sur-Seine
  France 50 G4 47 52N 4 35E
Chattanooga USA 91 J4 35 02N 85 18W
Chatteris England 16 D3 52 27N 0 03E
Chaumont France 50 G3 48 07N 5 08E
Cheadle Greater
  Manchester England 12 D2 53 24N 2 13W
Cheadle
  Staffordshire England 15 E2 52 59N 1 59W
Cheddar England 19 E3 51 17N 2 46W
Chelmsford England 17 D2 51 44N 0 28E
Cheltenham England 15 D2 51 54N 2 04W
Chelyabinsk Russia 62 J8 55 12N 61 25E
Chemnitz Germany 52 F5 50 50N 12 55E
Chengdu China 69 H4 30 37N 104 06E
Chennai India 66 E2 13 05N 80 18E
Chepstow Wales 15 D1 51 39N 2 41W
Cherbourg France 50 D5 49 38N 1 37W
Cherkasy Ukraine 56 D4 49 27N 32 04E
Chernivtsi Ukraine 53 M4 48 19N 25 52E
Chertsey England 16 C2 51 23N 0 30W
Cherwell r. England 16 B2 51 55N 1 18W
Chesapeake USA 91 L4 36 45N 76 15W
Chesham England 16 C2 51 43N 0 38W
Cheshire co. England 12 D2 53 30N 2 30W
Cheshire Plain England 12 D2 53 12N 2 50W
Cheshunt England 16 C2 51 43N 0 02W
Chesil Beach England 19 E2 50 38N 2 50W
Chester England 12 D2 53 12N 2 54W
Chesterfield England 13 E2 53 15N 1 25W
Chester-le-Street
  England 13 E3 54 52N 1 34W
Cheviot Hills
  England/Scotland 11 G2 55 25N 2 30W
Cheviot, The mt.
  England 11 G2 55 29N 2 20W
Chew r. England 19 E3 51 21N 2 40W
Chiba Japan 70 D2 35 38N 140 07E
Chicago USA 91 J5 41 50N 87 45W
Chichester England 16 C1 50 50N 0 48W
Chieti Italy 54 F5 42 21N 14 10E
Chigwell England 17 D2 51 37N 0 05E
CHILE 96/97 C5/C8
Chiltern Hills England 16 B2/C2 51 40N 1 00W
Chimborazo mt.
  Ecuador 96 B13 1 29S 78 52W
CHINA 68/69
Chinnor England 16 C2 51 43N 0 56W
Chioggia Italy 54 E6 45 13N 12 17E
Chíos i. Greece 55 E3 38 00N 26 00E
Chippenham England 15 D2 51 28N 2 07W
Chipping Campden
  England 15 E2 52 03N 1 46W
Chipping Norton
  England 16 B2 51 56N 1 32W
Chipping Ongar
  England 17 D2 51 43N 0 15E
Chipping Sodbury
  England 15 D2 51 33N 2 24W
Chirk Wales 14 C2 52 56N 3 03W
Chisinău Moldova 53 P3 47 00N 28 50E
Chita Russia 63 P7 52 03N 113 35E
Chittagong Bangladesh 67 G4 22 20N 91 48E
Chitterne England 19 E3 51 11N 2 02W
Chobham England 16 C2 51 21N 0 37W
Cholet France 50 D4 47 04N 0 53W
Chongqing China 69 J3 29 30N 106 35E
Chorley England 12 D2 53 40N 2 38W
Chorleywood England 16 C2 51 40N 0 29W
Chornobyl Ukraine 53 Q5 51 17N 30 15E
Christchurch England 19 F2 50 44N 1 45W
Christchurch NZ 73 P2 43 32S 172 38E
Chudleigh England 18 D2 50 36N 3 45W
Chudskoye Ozero l.
  Russia/Estonia 49 C6 58 40N 27 30E
Chulmleigh England 18 D2 50 55N 3 52W
Churn r. England 15 D1 51 46N 1 58W

Chur Switz. 52 D3 46 52N 9 32E
Churchill Canada 89 S5 58 45N 94 00W
Church Stoke Wales 14 C2 52 32N 3 05W
Church Stretton
  England 14 D2 52 32N 2 49W
Chute-aux-Outardes
  Canada 93 G3 49 17N 67 57W
Cincinnati USA 91 K4 39 10N 83 30W
Cinderford England 15 D1 51 50N 2 29W
Cirencester England 15 E1 51 44N 1 59W
Citlaltépetl mt. Mexico 94 E3 19 00N 97 18W
City of Edinburgh u.a.
  Scotland 11 F2 55 55N 3 15W
City of Kingston upon
  Hull u.a. England 13 F2 53 45N 0 25W
Ciudad Bolívar
  Venezuela 96 E15 8 06N 63 36W
Ciudadela Spain 51 G3 40 00N 3 50E
Ciudad Guayana
  Venezuela 96 E15 8 22N 62 37W
Ciudad Juárez Mexico 94 C6 31 42N 106 29W
Ciudad Obregón
  Mexico 94 C5 27 28N 109 59W
Ciudad Real Spain 51 D3 38 59N 3 55W
Ciudad Rodrigo Spain 51 B4 40 36N 6 33W
Civitavecchia Italy 54 D5 42 05N 11 47E
Clachan Scotland 10 D2 55 45N 5 34W
Clackmannan Scotland 11 F3 56 05N 3 46W
Clackmannanshire u.a.
  Scotland 11 F3 56 10N 3 40W
Clacton on Sea
  England 17 E2 51 48N 1 09E
Clane RoI 20 E3 53 18N 6 41W
Claonaig Scotland 10 D2 55 46N 5 22W
Clara RoI 20 D3 53 20N 7 36W
Clare r. RoI 20 C3 53 20N 9 00W
Clare co. RoI 21 B2/C2 52 45N 9 00W
Clarecastle RoI 21 C2 52 49N 8 57W
Claregalway RoI 20 C3 53 21N 8 57W
Clare Island RoI 20 A3/B3 53 49N 10 00W
Claremorris RoI 20 C3 53 44N 9 00W
Clarksville USA 91 J4 36 31N 87 21W
Clashmore RoI 21 D2 52 00N 7 49W
Clay Cross England 13 E2 53 10N 1 24W
Claydon England 17 E3 52 06N 1 07E
Clay Head Isle of Man 12 B3 54 11N 4 25W
Clayton-le-Moors
  England 12 D2 53 47N 2 23W
Clayton West England 13 E2 53 36N 1 37W
Clear Island RoI 21 B1 51 26N 9 30W
Clearwater USA 91 K2 27 57N 82 48W
Cleator Moor England 12 C3 54 31N 3 30W
Cleckheaton England 13 E2 53 44N 1 43W
Cleethorpes England 13 F2 53 34N 0 02W
Cleobury Mortimer
  England 15 D2 52 23N 2 29W
Clermont-Ferrand
  France 50 F3 45 47N 3 05E
Clevedon England 19 E3 51 27N 2 51W
Cleveland USA 91 K5 43 15N 75 50W
Cleveland Hills England 13 E3 54 25N 1 15W
Cleveleys England 12 C2 53 53N 3 03W
Clew Bay RoI 20 B3 53 50N 9 50W
Clifden RoI 20 A3 53 29N 10 01W
Clinton USA 91 H5 41 51N 90 12W
Clisham mt. Scotland 8 C2 57 58N 6 50W
Clitheroe England 12 D2 53 53N 2 23W
Cloghan RoI 20 D3 53 13N 7 53W
Clogheen RoI 21 D2 52 17N 8 00W
Clogher NI 10 B1 54 25N 7 10W
Clogherhead RoI 20 E3 53 45N 6 15W
Clogher Head RoI 20 E3 53 48N 6 13W
Cloghjordan RoI 21 C2 52 57N 8 02W
Clonakilty RoI 21 C1 51 37N 8 54W
Clonakilty Bay RoI 21 C1 51 33N 8 50W
Clonaslee RoI 21 D3 53 09N 7 31W
Clondalkin RoI 20 E3 53 19N 6 24W
Clonee RoI 20 E3 53 25N 6 26W
Clones RoI 20 D4 54 11N 7 15W
Clonmany RoI 20 D5 55 16N 7 25W
Clonmel RoI 21 D2 52 21N 7 42W
Clonroche RoI 21 E2 52 27N 6 43W
Clontarf RoI 20 E3 53 22N 6 12W
Cloondara RoI 20 D3 53 43N 7 53W
Cloppenburg Germany 52 D6 52 52N 8 02E
Cloughton England 13 F3 54 20N 0 27W
Clovelly England 18 C2 51 00N 4 24W
Clowne England 13 E2 53 17N 1 15W
Cluj-Napoca Romania 53 L3 46 47N 23 37E
Clwydian Range Wales 14 C3 53 12N 3 20W
Clydach Wales 14 C1 51 42N 3 56W
Clyde r. Scotland 11 F2 55 40N 3 50W
Clydebank Scotland 11 E2 55 54N 4 24W
Clyde River tn. Canada 89 X8 70 30N 68 30W
Coachford RoI 21 C1 51 55N 8 47W
Coalisland NI 10 C1 54 32N 6 42W
Coalville England 15 E2 52 44N 1 20W
Coast Ranges USA 90 B4/6 41 00N 123 00W
Coatbridge Scotland 11 E2 55 52N 4 01W
Coburg Germany 52 E5 50 15N 10 58E
Cochin India 66 D1 9 56N 76 50E
Cockburnspath
  Scotland 11 G2 55 56N 2 21W
Cockenzie Scotland 11 G2 55 58N 2 58W
Cockermouth England 12 C3 54 40N 3 21W
Codsall England 15 D2 52 37N 2 12W

Coggeshall England 17 D2 51 52N 0 41E
Cognac France 50 D3 45 42N 0 19E
Coimbra Portugal 51 A4 40 12N 8 25W
Colchester England 17 D2 51 54N 0 54E
Coldingham Scotland 11 G2 55 53N 2 10W
Coldstream Scotland 11 G2 55 39N 2 15W
Coleford England 15 D1 51 48N 2 37W
Coleraine NI 10 C2 55 08N 6 40W
Coleraine district NI 10 C2 55 00N 6 40W
Coleshill England 15 E2 52 30N 1 42W
Colgrave Sound Scotland 7 D3 60 35N 0 55W
Colintraive Scotland 10 D2 55 56N 5 09W
Coll i. Scotland 8 C1 56 40N 6 35W
Collin Scotland 11 F2 55 04N 3 32W
Collon Rol 20 E3 53 47N 6 29W
Collooney Rol 20 C4 54 11N 8 29W
Colmar France 50 H5 48 05N 7 21E
Colmonell Scotland 10 E2 55 08N 4 55W
Coln r. England 15 E1 51 46N 1 50W
Colne England 12 D2 53 32N 2 09W
Colne r. England 17 D2 51 53N 0 45E
Cologne Germany 52 C5 50 56N 6 57E
COLOMBIA 96 C14
Colombo Sri Lanka 66 D1 6 55N 79 52E
Colonsay i. Scotland 10 C3 56 05N 6 15W
Colorado r. N. America 90 J3 31 00N 114 00W
Colorado state USA 90 E4/F4 39 00N 106 00W
Colorado Springs USA 90 F4 38 50N 104 50W
Colsterworth England 15 F2 52 48N 0 37W
Coltishall England 17 E3 52 44N 1 22E
Columbia r. N. America 90 B6 46 00N 120 00W
Columbus USA 91 K5 39 59N 83 03W
Colwyn Bay tn. Wales 14 C3 53 18N 3 43W
Comacchio Italy 54 E6 44 42N 12 11E
Combe Martin England 18 C3 51 13N 4 02W
Comber NI 10 D1 54 33N 5 45W
Comeragh Mountains Rol 21 D2 52 19N 7 40W
Como Italy 54 C6 45 48N 9 05E
COMOROS 82 H5
Compiègne France 50 F5 49 25N 2 50E
Comrie Scotland 9 F1 56 23N 4 00W
Conakry Guinea 80 B3 9 30N 13 43W
Concordia USA 91 G4 39 35N 97 39W
Condom France 50 E2 43 58N 0 23E
Conflans-Ste. Honorine France 50 F5 49 01N 2 09E
Cong Rol 20 B3 53 33N 9 16W
Congleton England 12 D2 53 10N 2 13W
CONGO 82 C7
Congo r. Congo/CDR 82 J2 2 00S 17 00E
CONGO DEMOCRATIC REPUBLIC 82 D7/E7
Congresbury England 19 E3 51 23N 2 48W
Conisbrough England 13 E2 53 29N 1 13W
Coniston England 12 C3 54 22N 3 05W
Coniston Water England 12 C3 54 20N 3 05W
Connah's Quay Wales 14 C3 53 13N 3 03W
Connecticut state USA 91 M5 41 00N 73 00W
Conon Bridge Scotland 9 E2 57 33N 4 26W
Consett England 13 E3 54 51N 1 49W
Constanța Romania 53 P2 44 12N 28 40E
Conwy Wales 14 C3 53 17N 3 50W
Conwy r. Wales 14 C3 53 10N 3 49W
Conwy u.a. Wales 14 C3 53 10N 3 40W
Cookham England 16 C2 51 34N 0 43W
Cook, Mount NZ 73 P2 43 36S 170 09E
Cookstown district NI 10 C1 54 35N 6 55W
Coolgrange Rol 21 D2 53 38N 7 08W
Cootehill Rol 20 D4 54 04N 7 05W
Copeland Island NI 10 D1 54 40N 5 31W
Copenhagen Denmark 49 D2 55 43N 12 34E
Copper Harbor USA 91 J6 47 28N 87 54W
Coppull England 12 C2 53 37N 2 40W
Coquet r. England 11 G2 55 20N 2 05W
Corbally Rol 20 B4 54 10N 9 03W
Corbeil-Essonnes France 50 F5 48 36N 2 29E
Corbridge England 12 D3 54 58N 2 01W
Corby England 15 F2 52 49N 0 32W
Cordillera Cantabrica mts. Spain 51 B5/C5 43 00N 5 30W
Córdoba Mexico 94 E3 18 55N 96 55W
Córdoba Spain 51 C2 37 53N 4 46W
Corfe Castle England 19 E2 50 38N 2 04W
Corfu Greece 55 H3 39 38N 19 55E
Corinth USA 91 J3 34 58N 88 30W
Cork Rol 21 C1 51 54N 8 28W
Cork co. Rol 21 C1 51 58N 8 40W
Cork Harbour Rol 21 C1 51 50N 8 10W
Corraun Peninsula Rol 20 B3 53 54N 9 51W
Corsewall Point Scotland 10 D2 55 00N 5 10W
Corsham England 15 D2 51 26N 2 11W
Corsica i. France 50 J1/J2 42 00N 9 00E
Corwen Wales 14 C2 52 59N 3 22W
Cosenza Italy 54 G3 39 17N 16 16E
COSTA RICA 95 H1/2
CÔTE D'IVOIRE 80 C3/D3
Cotgrave England 15 E3 52 54N 1 03W
Cotopaxi mt. Ecuador 96 B13 0 40S 78 28W
Cotswold Hills England 15 D1/E1 51 40N 2 10W
Cottbus Germany 52 G5 51 43N 14 21E
Cottenham England 16 D2 52 18N 0 09E
Coulommiers France 50 F5 48 49N 3 05E

Countesthorpe England 15 E2 52 33N 1 09W
Coupar Angus Scotland 9 F1 56 33N 3 17W
Courtown Rol 21 E2 52 38N 6 13W
Cove Bay tn. Scotland 9 G2 57 05N 2 05W
Coventry England 15 E2 52 25N 1 30W
Coverack England 18 B2 50 01N 5 05W
Cowbridge Wales 14 C1 51 28N 3 27W
Cowdenbeath Scotland 11 F3 56 07N 3 21W
Cowes England 16 B1 50 45N 1 18W
Cox's Bazar Bangladesh 67 G4 21 25N 91 59E
Craigavon NI 10 C1 54 28N 6 25W
Craigavon district NI 10 C1 54 30N 6 30W
Craigellachie Scotland 9 F2 57 29N 3 12W
Craighouse Scotland 10 D2 55 51N 5 57W
Craignure Scotland 8 D1 56 28N 5 42W
Crail Scotland 11 G3 56 16N 2 38W
Craiova Romania 53 L2 44 18N 23 47E
Cramlington England 13 E4 55 05N 1 35W
Cranleigh England 16 C2 51 09N 0 30W
Crathie Scotland 9 F2 57 02N 3 12W
Craughwell Rol 20 C3 53 14N 8 44W
Craven Arms England 14 D2 52 26N 2 50W
Crawford Scotland 11 F2 55 28N 3 40W
Crawley England 16 C2 51 07N 0 12W
Credenhill England 15 D2 52 05N 2 48W
Crediton England 18 D2 50 47N 3 39W
Cree r. Scotland 11 E2 55 00N 4 30W
Creeslough Rol 20 D5 55 07N 7 55W
Creetown Scotland 11 E1 54 54N 4 23W
Cregganbaun Rol 20 B3 53 42N 9 51W
Cremona Italy 54 D6 45 08N 10 01E
Creswell England 13 E2 53 16N 1 12W
Créteil France 50 F5 48 47N 2 28E
Crewe England 12 D2 53 05N 2 27W
Crewkerne England 19 E2 50 53N 2 48W
Crianlarich Scotland 9 E1 56 23N 4 37W
Criccieth Wales 14 B2 52 55N 4 14W
Crickhowell Wales 14 C1 51 53N 3 09W
Cricklade England 16 B2 51 39N 1 51W
Crieff Scotland 9 F1 56 23N 3 52W
Crinan Scotland 10 D3 56 06N 5 35W
CROATIA 55 G6
Crofton England 13 E2 53 39N 1 26W
Cromarty Scotland 9 E2 57 40N 4 02W
Cromarty Firth Scotland 9 E2 57 40N 4 20W
Cromer England 17 E3 52 56N 1 18E
Crook England 13 E3 54 43N 1 44W
Crookhaven Rol 21 B1 51 28N 9 43W
Crookstown Rol 21 C1 51 50N 8 50W
Croom Rol 21 C2 52 31N 8 43W
Crosby England 12 C2 53 30N 3 02W
Cross Fell mt. England 12 D3 54 43N 2 29W
Crossgar NI 10 D1 54 24N 5 45W
Cross Hands Wales 14 B1 51 48N 4 05W
Crosshaven Rol 21 C1 51 48N 8 17W
Crossmaglen NI 10 C1 54 05N 6 37W
Crossmolina Rol 20 B4 54 06N 9 20W
Crouch r. England 17 D2 51 38N 0 42E
Crowborough England 17 D2 51 03N 0 09E
Crowland England 16 C3 52 41N 0 11W
Crowle England 13 F2 53 37N 0 49W
Crowthorne England 16 C2 51 23N 0 49W
Croyde England 18 C3 51 08N 4 15W
Croydon England 16 C2 51 23N 0 06W
Crumlin NI 10 C1 54 37N 6 14W
Crummock Water England 12 C3 54 34N 3 18W
Crusheen Rol 21 C2 52 56N 8 53W
Crymych Wales 14 B1 51 59N 4 40W
CUBA 95 J4
Cuckfield England 16 C2 51 00N 0 09W
Cudworth England 13 E2 53 35N 1 25W
Cuenca Spain 51 D4 40 04N 2 07W
Cuiabá Brazil 96 F10 15 32S 56 05W
Cuillin Hills Scotland 8 C2 57 15N 6 15W
Culdaff Rol 20 D5 55 17N 7 10W
Cullen Scotland 9 G2 57 41N 2 49W
Cullompton England 18 D2 50 52N 3 24W
Cullybackey NI 10 C1 54 53N 6 21W
Culm r. England 19 D2 50 55N 3 13W
Culross Scotland 11 F3 56 03N 3 35W
Cumbernauld Scotland 11 F3 55 57N 4 00W
Cumbria co. England 12 C3/D3 54 35N 3 00W
Cumbrian Mountains England 12 C3/D3 54 30N 3 00W
Cumnock Scotland 11 E2 55 27N 4 16W
Cuneo Italy 54 B6 44 24N 7 33E
Cupar Scotland 9 F1 56 19N 3 01W
Curitiba Brazil 96 H8 25 25S 49 25W
Cushendall NI 10 C2 55 04N 6 04W
Cushendun NI 10 C2 55 08N 6 03W
Cuxhaven Germany 52 D6 53 52N 8 42E
Cuzco Peru 96 C11 13 32S 71 57W
Cwmbran Wales 14 C1 51 39N 3 00W
CYPRUS 57 D1/D2
CZECH REPUBLIC 52/53 G4/H4
Częstochowa Poland 53 J5 50 49N 19 07E

D
Dachau Germany 52 E4 48 15N 11 26E
Daingean Rol 20 D3 53 17N 7 17W
Dakar Senegal 80 A4 14 38N 17 27W
Dalbeattie Scotland 11 F1 54 56N 3 49W
Dalby Isle of Man 12 B3 54 10N 4 44W

Dalgety Bay tn. Scotland 11 F3 56 03N 3 18W
Dalian China 69 M5 38 53N 121 37E
Dalkeith Scotland 11 F2 55 51N 3 04W
Dallas USA 91 G3 32 47N 96 48W
Dalmally Scotland 9 E1 56 24N 4 58W
Dalmellington Scotland 11 E2 55 19N 4 24W
Dalry Scotland 11 E2 55 43N 4 44W
Dalton USA 91 K3 34 46N 84 59W
Dalton-in-Furness England 12 C3 54 09N 3 11W
Dalwhinnie Scotland 9 E1 56 56N 4 14W
Damascus Syria 64 C5 33 30N 36 19E
Danbury England 17 E2 51 44N 0 33E
Danville USA 91 J5 40 09N 87 37W
Dardanelles sd. Turkey 57 C3 40 08N 26 10E
Dar es Salaam Tanzania 83 F1 6 51S 39 18E
Darfield England 13 E2 53 34N 1 22W
Darjiling India 67 F5 27 02N 88 20E
Darling r. Australia 73 H4 30 30S 144 00E
Darlington England 13 E3 54 31N 1 34W
Darlington u.a. England 13 E3 54 30N 1 30W
Darmstadt Germany 52 D4 49 52N 8 39E
Dart r. England 18 D2 50 30N 3 50W
Dartford England 17 D2 51 27N 0 13E
Dartmouth England 18 D2 50 21N 3 35W
Darton England 13 E2 53 36N 1 32W
Darvel Scotland 11 E2 55 37N 4 18W
Darwen England 12 D2 53 42N 2 28W
Darwin Australia 72 F8 12 23S 130 44E
Daugava r. Europe 49 F2 56 45N 24 30E
Daugavpils Latvia 49 G2 55 52N 26 31E
Davenport USA 91 H5 41 32N 90 36W
Daventry England 15 E2 52 16N 1 09W
Davis Strait Canada/Greenland 89 Y7/Z6 69 00N 60 00W
Davos Switz. 52 D3 46 47N 9 50E
Dawley England 15 D2 52 40N 2 28W
Dawlish England 18 D2 50 35N 3 28W
Dawros Head Rol 20 C4 54 49N 8 34W
Dead Sea Israel/Jordan 64 C5 31 35N 35 30E
Deal England 17 E2 51 14N 1 24E
Deel r. Rol 21 C2 52 32N 8 57W
Death Valley USA 90 C4 36 00N 117 00W
Deben r. England 17 E2 52 02N 1 25E
Debenham England 17 E3 52 13N 1 11E
Debrecen Hungary 53 K3 47 30N 21 37E
Decatur USA 91 J4 39 51N 88 57W
Deccan plat. India 66 D3 18 00N 78 00E
Deddington England 16 B2 51 59N 1 19W
Dee r. England/Wales 14 C3 53 15N 3 10W
Dee r. Rol 20 E3 53 49N 6 38W
Dee r. Aberdeenshire Scotland 9 G2 57 05N 2 10W
Dee r. Dumfries and Galloway Scotland 11 E1 54 50N 4 00W
Deel r. Rol 20 D3 53 33N 7 07W
Deer Sound Scotland 7 B1 58 57N 2 47W
Delaware state USA 91 L4 39 00N 75 00W
Delft Neths 48 C5 52 00N 4 22E
Delfzijl Neths 48 E6 53 19N 6 56E
Delhi India 66 D5 28 40N 77 14E
Delvin Rol 20 D3 53 37N 7 06W
Denbigh Wales 14 C3 53 11N 3 25W
Denbighshire u.a. Wales 14 C3 53 05N 3 30W
Denby Dale tn. England 13 E2 53 35N 1 38W
Den Helder Neths 48 C5 52 58N 4 46E
Denholme England 13 E2 53 47N 1 53W
Denison USA 91 G3 33 47N 96 34W
Denizli Turkey 57 C3 37 46N 29 05E
DENMARK 49 C2/D2
Denny Scotland 11 F3 56 02N 3 55W
Denpasar Indonesia 71 F2 8 40S 115 14E
Denton England 12 D2 53 27N 2 07W
Denver USA 90 E4 39 45N 105 00W
De Panne Belgium 48 A4 51 06N 2 35E
Derby England 15 E2 52 55N 1 30W
Derby City u.a. England 15 E2 52 50N 1 30W
Derbyshire co. England 13 E2 53 10N 1 30W
Derg r. NI 10 B1 54 45N 7 30W
Derriana Lough Rol 21 A1/B1 51 54N 10 01W
Derrybeg Rol 21 C3 53 04N 8 37W
Dersingham England 17 D3 52 51N 0 30E
Derwent r. North Yorkshire England 13 F3 54 10N 0 35W
Derwent r. Cumbria England 12 C3 54 40N 3 30W
Derwent r. Derbyshire England 13 E2 53 15N 1 40W
Derwent r. Durham England 13 E3 54 50N 2 05W
Derwent Reservoir England 15 E2 53 25N 1 45W
Derwent Water England 12 C3 54 35N 3 09W
Desborough England 15 F2 52 27N 0 49W
Desierto de Atacama Chile 96 C9/D10 22 30S 70 00W
Des Moines USA 91 H5 41 35N 93 35W
Dessau Germany 52 F5 51 51N 12 15E
Detroit USA 91 K5 42 23N 83 05W
Deveron r. Scotland 9 G2 57 35N 2 35W
Devil's Bridge Wales 14 C2 52 23N 3 51W
Devil's Lake tn. USA 91 G6 48 03N 98 57W
Devizes England 16 B2 51 22N 1 59W

Devon co. England 18 D2 50 45N 3 50W
Dewsbury England 13 E2 53 42N 1 37W
Dezfūl Iran 65 E5 32 23N 48 28E
Dhaka Bangladesh 67 G4 23 42N 90 22E
Didcot England 16 B2 51 37N 1 15W
Dieppe France 50 E5 49 55N 1 05E
Digby Canada 89 X2 44 37N 65 47W
Digne-les-Bains France 50 H3 44 05N 6 14E
Dijon France 50 G4 47 20N 5 02E
Dili East Timor 71 H2 8 33S 125 34E
Dinan France 50 C5 48 27N 2 02W
Dinara Planina mts. Europe 55 G5 44 00N 17 00E
Dinard France 50 C5 48 38N 2 03W
Dinas-Mawddwy Wales 14 C2 52 43N 3 41W
Dinas Powys Wales 14 C1 51 25N 3 14W
Dingle Rol 21 A2 52 08N 10 15W
Dingle Bay Rol 21 A2 52 05N 10 15W
Dingle Peninsula Rol 21 A2 52 12N 10 15W
Dingwall Scotland 9 E2 57 35N 4 29W
Dinnington England 13 E2 53 22N 1 12W
Diss England 17 E3 52 23N 1 06W
DJIBOUTI 81 P4
Djibouti Djibouti 81 P4 11 35N 43 11E
Dnestr r. Ukraine 56 C4 48 00N 27 30E
Dnipro r. Ukraine 56 D4 47 30N 33 00E
Dobrich Bulgaria 55 M5 43 34N 27 51E
Dochart r. Scotland 9 E1 56 25N 4 25W
Docking England 17 D3 52 55N 0 38E
Dodekánisos is. Greece 55 M2 37 00N 26 00E
Dodman Point England 18 C2 50 13N 4 48W
Dodoma Tanzania 83 D1 6 10S 35 40E
Doha Qatar 65 F4 25 15N 51 36E
Dôle France 50 G4 47 05N 5 30E
Dolgellau Wales 14 C2 52 44N 3 53W
Dollar Scotland 11 F3 56 09N 3 41W
Dombas Norway 49 C3 62 05N 9 07E
DOMINICA 94 Q8
DOMINICAN REPUBLIC 95 L3
Don r. England 13 E2 53 37N 1 02W
Don r. Russia 62 G7 50 00N 41 00E
Don r. Scotland 9 F2 57 15N 2 40W
Donabate Rol 20 E3 53 30N 6 09W
Donaghadee NI 10 D1 54 39N 5 33W
Donau r. Europe 52 D4 48 00N 16 00E
Doncaster England 13 E2 53 32N 1 07W
Donegal Rol 20 C4 54 39N 8 07W
Donegal co. Rol 20 C4/D4 54 55N 8 00W
Donegal Bay Rol 20 C4 54 30N 8 30W
Donegal Point Rol 21 B2 52 44N 9 38W
Donets'k Ukraine 56 E4 48 00N 37 50E
Donnington England 15 D2 52 43N 2 25W
Donoughmore Rol 21 C1 51 57N 8 45W
Dooagh Rol 20 A3 53 58N 10 07W
Doon r. Scotland 11 E2 55 20N 4 30W
Doonbeg Rol 21 B2 52 44N 9 32W
Dorchester England 19 E2 50 43N 2 26W
Dorchester England 16 B2 51 39N 1 10W
Dordogne r. France 50 E3 44 55N 0 30E
Dordrecht Neths 48 C4 51 48N 4 40E
Dorking England 16 C2 51 14N 0 20W
Dornie Scotland 8 D2 57 17N 5 31W
Dornoch Scotland 9 E2 57 52N 4 02W
Dornoch Firth Scotland 9 E2/F2 57 55N 3 55W
Dorset co. England 19 E2 50 50N 2 20W
Dortmund Germany 52 C5 51 32N 7 27E
Douai France 50 F6 50 22N 3 05E
Douala Cameroon 80 F2 4 04N 9 43E
Douglas Isle of Man 12 B3 54 09N 4 29W
Douglas Scotland 11 F2 55 33N 3 51W
Douglas r. England 12 D2 53 38N 2 48W
Doulus Head Rol 21 A1 51 57N 10 19W
Doune Scotland 11 E3 56 11N 4 04W
Douro r. Portugal/Spain 51 B4 41 00N 8 30W
Dove r. England 13 E2 53 05N 1 55W
Dove Dale v. England 13 E2 53 10N 1 45W
Dover England 17 E2 51 08N 1 19E
Dover USA 91 L4 39 10N 75 32W
Dover, Strait of English Channel 17 E1/E2 51 00N 1 20E
Dovrefjell mts. Norway 49 C3 62 15N 9 10E
Down district NI 10 D1 54 25N 5 55W
Downham Market England 17 D3 52 36N 0 23E
Downpatrick NI 10 D1 54 20N 5 43W
Downpatrick Head Rol 20 B4 54 20N 9 15W
Downton England 16 B1 51 00N 1 44W
Dowra Rol 20 C4 54 11N 8 02W
Draguignan France 50 H2 43 32N 6 28E
Drakensberg mts. RSA 82 E1/2 30 00S 28 00E
Drammen Norway 49 C2 59 45N 10 15E
Draperstown NI 10 C1 54 48N 6 47W
Drava r. Europe 53 H3 46 00N 18 00E
Dreghorn Scotland 11 E2 55 37N 4 37W
Dresden Germany 52 F5 51 03N 13 45E
Drimoleague Rol 21 B1 51 40N 9 15W
Drobeta-Turnu-Severin Romania 53 L2 44 36N 22 39E
Drogheda Rol 20 E3 53 43N 6 21W
Droichead Nua Rol 20 E3 53 11N 6 45W
Droitwich England 15 D2 52 16N 2 09W
Dromcolliher Rol 21 C2 52 20N 8 55W
Dromore NI 10 B1 54 31N 7 28W
Dromore NI 10 C1 54 25N 6 09W

Dromore West RoI 20 C4 54 15N 8 53W
Dronfield England 13 E2 53 19N 1 27W
Drongan Scotland 11 E2 55 29N 4 30W
Drumkeeran RoI 20 C4 54 10N 8 08W
Drummore Scotland 10 E1 54 42N 4 54W
Drumnadrochit Scotland 9 E2 57 20N 4 30W
Drumshanbo RoI 20 C4 54 03N 8 02W
Drumsna RoI 20 D3 53 56N 8 00W
Dryden Canada 89 S3 49 48N 92 48W
Dubai UAE 65 G4 25 14N 55 17E
Dublin RoI 20 E3 53 20N 6 15W
Dublin co. RoI 20 E3 53 25N 6 10W
Dublin USA 91 K3 32 31N 82 54W
Dublin Bay RoI 20 E3 53 20N 6 05W
Dubrovnik Croatia 55 H5 42 40N 18 07E
Duddon r. England 12 C3 54 20N 3 20W
Dudley England 15 D2 52 30N 2 05W
Dudley England 13 E4 55 10N 1 20W
Duero r. Spain/Portugal 51 B4 41 25N 6 30W
Duffield England 15 E2 52 59N 1 29W
Dufftown Scotland 9 F2 57 26N 3 08W
Duisburg Germany 52 C5 51 26N 6 45E
Duleek RoI 20 E3 53 39N 6 25W
Dulnain r. Scotland 9 F2 57 20N 3 57W
Duluth USA 91 H6 46 45N 92 10W
Dulverton England 18 D3 51 03N 3 33W
Dumbarton Scotland 11 E2 55 57N 4 35W
Dumfries Scotland 11 F2 55 04N 3 37W
Dumfries and Galloway u.a. Scotland 11 E2/F2 55 10N 4 10W
Duna r. Hungary 53 J2/J3 46 00N 19 00E
Dunaff Head RoI 20 D5 55 17N 7 31W
Dunany Point RoI 20 E3 53 51N 6 14W
Dunav r. Europe 55 K5 45 00N 20 00E
Dunbar Scotland 11 G2 56 00N 2 31W
Dunbeath Scotland 9 F3 58 15N 3 25W
Dunblane Scotland 11 F3 56 12N 3 59W
Dunboyne RoI 20 E3 53 25N 6 29W
Duncannon RoI 21 E2 51 13N 6 55W
Duncansby Head Scotland 9 F3 58 39N 3 01W
Dunchurch England 15 E2 52 20N 1 16W
Dundalk RoI 20 E4 54 01N 6 25W
Dundalk Bay RoI 20 E3 53 55N 6 15W
Dundee Scotland 9 G1 56 28N 3 00W
Dundee City u.a. Scotland 9 F1/G1 56 30N 2 55W
Dundonald NI 10 D1 54 36N 5 48W
Dundrennan Scotland 11 F1 54 49N 3 57W
Dundrum RoI 20 E3 53 17N 6 15W
Dundrum Bay NI 10 D1 54 13N 5 45W
Dunedin NZ 73 P1 45 53S 170 30E
Dunfermline Scotland 11 F3 56 04N 3 29W
Dungannon NI 10 C1 54 31N 6 46W
Dungannon district NI 10 B1/C1 54 30N 7 05W
Dungarvan RoI 21 D2 52 05N 7 37W
Dungarvan Harbour RoI 21 D2 52 04N 7 35W
Dungeness c. England 17 D1 50 55N 0 58E
Dungiven NI 10 C1 54 56N 6 55W
Dunglow RoI 20 C4 54 57N 8 22W
Dungourney RoI 21 C1 51 58N 8 05W
Dunholme England 13 F2 53 18N 0 29W
Dunkeld Scotland 9 F1 56 34N 3 35W
Dunkerque France 50 F6 51 02N 2 23E
Dunkery Beacon sum. England 18 D3 51 11N 3 35W
Dún Laoghaire RoI 20 E3 53 17N 6 08W
Dunleer RoI 20 E3 53 50N 6 24W
Dunmanus Bay RoI 21 B1 51 30N 9 50W
Dunmanway RoI 21 B1 51 43N 9 06W
Dunmore RoI 20 C3 53 37N 8 44W
Dunnamaggan RoI 21 D2 52 29N 7 17W
Dunnet Scotland 9 F3 58 37N 3 21W
Dunnet Bay Scotland 9 F3 58 36N 3 21W
Dunnett Head Scotland 9 F3 58 40N 3 25W
Dunoon Scotland 10 E2 55 57N 4 56W
Duns Scotland 11 G2 55 47N 2 20W
Dunshaughlin RoI 20 E3 53 31N 6 33W
Dunstable England 16 C2 51 53N 0 32W
Dunvegan Scotland 8 C2 57 26N 6 35W
Dunvegan Head Scotland 8 C2 57 30N 6 42W
Durban RSA 82 F2 29 53S 31 00E
Durham England 13 E3 54 47N 1 34W
Durham USA 91 L4 36 00N 78 54W
Durlston Head England 19 E2 50 35N 1 57W
Durness Scotland 9 E3 58 33N 4 45W
Durrington England 16 B2 51 12N 1 48W
Durrow RoI 21 D2 52 51N 7 23W
Dursey Head RoI 21 A1 51 36N 10 12W
Dursey Island RoI 21 A1 51 36N 10 12W
Dursley England 15 D1 51 42N 2 21W
Dushanbe Tajikistan 62 J4 38 38N 68 51E
Düsseldorf Germany 52 C5 51 13N 6 47E
Dyce Scotland 9 G2 57 12N 2 11W
Dyfi r. Wales 14 C2 52 38N 3 50W
Dyke r. Scotland 9 F3 58 25N 4 00W
Dymchurch England 17 D2 51 02N 1 00E
Dysart Scotland 11 F3 56 08N 3 08W

E

Eaglescliffe England 13 E3 54 31N 1 22W
Eaglesfield Scotland 11 F2 55 04N 3 12W

Ealing England 16 C2 51 31N 0 18W
Earby England 12 D2 53 56N 2 08W
Earls Colne England 17 D2 51 56N 0 42E
Earl Shilton England 15 E2 52 35N 1 18W
Earlston Scotland 11 G2 55 39N 2 40W
Earn r. Scotland 9 F1 56 20N 3 40W
Easington England 13 E3 54 47N 1 21W
Easington England 13 G2 53 40N 0 07E
Easingwold England 13 E3 54 07N 1 11W
Easky RoI 20 C4 54 17N 8 58W
East Ayrshire u.a. Scotland 11 E2 55 30N 4 30W
Eastbourne England 17 D1 50 46N 0 17E
East Burra i. Scotland 7 C3 60 04N 1 19W
East Cowes England 16 B1 50 45N 1 16W
East Dean England 17 D1 50 45N 0 13E
East Dereham England 17 D3 52 41N 0 56E
East Dunbartonshire u.a. Scotland 11 E2 55 55N 4 15W
Eastern Ghats mts. India 66 D2/E3 15 00N 80 00E
Eastfield England 13 F3 54 15N 0 25W
East Grand Forks USA 92 A3 47 56N 96 59W
East Ilsley England 16 B2 51 32N 1 17W
Eastington England 15 D1 51 45N 2 20W
East Kilbride Scotland 11 E2 55 46N 4 10W
East Leake England 15 E2 52 50N 1 11W
Eastleigh England 16 B1 50 58N 1 22W
East Linton Scotland 11 G2 55 59N 2 39W
East Loch Tarbert Scotland 8 C2 57 53N 6 48W
East Lothian u.a. Scotland 11 G2 55 56N 2 42W
Eastmain Canada 89 V4 52 10N 78 30W
East Markham England 13 F2 53 15N 0 54W
Easton England 19 E2 50 32N 2 26W
East Renfrewshire u.a. Scotland 11 E2 55 45N 4 25W
East Riding of Yorkshire u.a. England 13 F2 53 54N 0 40W
Eastriggs Scotland 11 F1 54 59N 3 10W
East Suisnish Scotland 8 C2 57 21N 6 03W
East Sussex co. England 17 D1 50 55N 0 10E
EAST TIMOR 71 H2
East Wittering England 16 C1 50 41N 0 53W
Eastwood England 13 E2 53 01N 1 18W
Eaton Socon England 16 C2 52 13N 0 18W
Ebbw Vale Wales 14 C1 51 47N 3 12W
Ebro r. Spain 51 D5 43 00N 4 30W
Ecclefechan Scotland 11 F2 55 03N 3 17W
Eccles England 12 D2 53 29N 2 21W
Eccleshall England 15 D2 52 52N 2 15W
Eckington England 13 E2 53 19N 1 21W
ECUADOR 96 B13
Eday i. Scotland 7 B2 59 11N 2 47W
Eday Sound Scotland 7 B2 59 10N 2 43W
Ede Neths 48 D5 52 03N 5 40E
Eden r. Cumbria England 12 D3 54 50N 2 45W
Eden r. Kent England 17 D2 51 12N 0 06E
Eden r. Scotland 11 F3 56 20N 3 15W
Eden USA 91 L4 36 30N 79 46W
Edenbridge England 16 C2 51 12N 0 04E
Edenderry RoI 20 D3 53 21N 7 35W
Eden Mouth Scotland 9 G1 56 20N 2 36W
Edessa Greece 55 K4 40 48N 22 03E
Edgeworthstown RoI 20 D3 53 42N 7 36W
Edinburgh Scotland 11 F2 55 57N 3 13W
Edmonton Canada 88 N4 53 34N 113 25W
Eekloo Belgium 48 B4 51 11N 3 34E
Eems r. Neths/Germany 48 E6 53 25N 6 55E
Efyrnwy r. Wales 14 C2 52 40N 3 15W
Egham England 16 C2 51 26N 0 34W
Egilsay i. Scotland 7 B2 59 09N 2 56W
Eglinton NI 10 B2 55 01N 7 11W
Egremont England 12 C3 54 29N 3 33W
EGYPT 81 L7/M7
Eigg i. Scotland 8 C1 56 55N 6 10W
Eindhoven Neths 48 D4 51 26N 5 30E
Elat Israel 64 B4 29 33N 34 57E
Elâzığ Turkey 57 E2 38 41N 39 14E
Elbe est. Europe 52 E6 54 00N 9 00E
Elbeuf France 50 E5 49 17N 1 01E
Elbląg Poland 53 J7 54 10N 19 25E
El'brus mt. Russia 57 F3 43 21N 42 29E
Elburz Mountains Iran 65 F6 36 15N 51 00E
Elche Spain 51 E3 38 16N 0 41W
El Dorado USA 91 H3 33 12N 92 40W
Elgin Scotland 9 F2 57 39N 3 20W
El Giza Egypt 81 M7 30 01N 31 12E
Elgol Scotland 8 C2 57 09N 6 06W
Elie Scotland 11 G3 56 12N 2 50W
Elland England 13 E2 53 41N 1 50W
Ellen r. England 12 C3 54 45N 3 25W
Ellesmere England 14 D2 52 54N 2 54W
Ellesmere Island Canada 89 U9/X10 77 30N 82 30W
Ellesmere Port England 12 D2 53 17N 2 54W
Ellon Scotland 9 G2 57 22N 2 05W
El Minya Egypt 81 M7 28 06N 30 45E
Elmira USA 91 L5 42 06N 76 50W
El Paso USA 90 E3 31 45N 106 30W
EL SALVADOR 94 G2
Ely England 17 D3 52 24N 0 16E
Elyria USA 91 K5 41 22N 82 06W
Embleton England 11 H2 55 30N 1 37W

Emden Germany 52 C6 53 23N 7 13E
Emmeloord Neths 48 D5 52 43N 5 46E
Emmen Neths 48 E5 52 47N 6 55E
Emsworth England 16 C1 50 51N 0 56W
Emyvale RoI 20 E4 54 21N 6 58W
Enard Bay Scotland 8 D3 58 10N 5 25W
Enfield England 16 C2 51 39N 0 05W
England country UK 6 53 00N 2 00W
English Channel UK/France 6 50 00N 2 00W
Enid USA 91 G4 36 24N 97 54W
Ennis RoI 21 C2 52 50N 8 59W
Enniscorthy RoI 21 E2 52 30N 6 34W
Enniskean RoI 21 C1 51 44N 8 56W
Enniskerry RoI 20 E3 53 12N 6 10W
Enniskillen NI 10 B1 54 21N 7 38W
Ennistimon RoI 21 B2 52 57N 9 15W
Enschede Neths 48 E5 52 13N 6 55E
Entebbe Uganda 83 C5 0 04N 32 27E
Épernay France 50 F5 49 02N 3 58E
Épinal France 50 H5 48 10N 6 28E
Epping England 17 D2 51 42N 0 08E
Epsom England 16 C2 51 20N 0 16W
Epworth England 13 F2 53 31N 0 50W
EQUATORIAL GUINEA 80 F2/G2
Erfurt Germany 52 E5 50 58N 11 02E
Erie USA 91 K5 42 07N 80 05W
Erie, Lake Canada/USA 93 D2 42 15N 81 00W
Eriskay i. Scotland 8 B2 57 05N 7 10W
ERITREA 81 P4 14 40N 40 15E
Erlangen Germany 52 E4 49 36N 11 02E
Errigal Mountain RoI 20 C5 55 02N 8 07W
Errill RoI 21 D2 52 52N 7 40W
Erris Head RoI 20 A4 54 20N 10 00W
Erzgebirge mts. Europe 52 F5 50 00N 13 00E
Erzurum Turkey 57 F2 39 57N 41 17E
Esbjerg Denmark 49 C2 55 20N 8 20E
Escondido USA 90 C3 33 07N 117 05W
Eşfahān Iran 65 F5 32 41N 51 41E
Esha Ness c. Scotland 7 C3 60 29N 1 37W
Esher England 16 C2 51 22N 0 22W
Esk r. North Yorkshire England 13 F3 54 25N 0 40W
Esk r. Cumbria England 12 C3 54 25N 3 10W
Esk r. Scotland/England 11 F2 55 10N 3 05W
Eskişehir Turkey 57 D2 39 46N 30 30E
Espoo Finland 49 F3 60 10N 24 40E
Essen Germany 52 C5 51 27N 6 57E
Essex co. England 17 D2 51 46N 0 30E
Eston England 13 E3 54 34N 1 07W
ESTONIA 49 G2
Estremoz Portugal 51 B3 38 50N 7 35W
Étampes France 50 F5 48 26N 2 10E
ETHIOPIA 81 N3/P3
Etna, Mount Italy 54 F2 37 45N 15 00E
Eton England 16 C2 51 31N 0 37W
Ettrick Scotland 11 F2 55 25N 3 05W
Ettrickbridge Scotland 11 G2 55 30N 2 58W
Eugene USA 90 B5 44 03N 123 04W
Euphrates r. Asia 64 D5 34 40N 42 00E
Europoort Neths 48 C4 51 55N 4 10E
Evanton Scotland 9 E2 57 40N 4 20W
Evercreech England 19 E3 51 09N 2 30W
Everest, Mount China/Nepal 67 F5 27 59N 86 56E
Evesham England 15 E2 52 06N 1 56W
Evora Portugal 51 B3 38 46N 7 41W
Evreux France 50 E5 49 03N 1 11E
Evvoia i. Greece 55 L3 38 00N 24 00E
Exe r. England 18 D2 51 08N 3 36
Exeter England 18 D2 50 43N 3 31W
Exmouth England 18 D2 50 37N 3 25W
Eyam England 13 E2 53 24N 1 42W
Eye England 17 E3 52 19N 1 09E
Eyemouth Scotland 11 G2 55 25N 2 06W
Eye Peninsula Scotland 8 C3 58 10N 6 10W
Eyeries RoI 21 B1 51 41N 9 57W
Eynsham England 16 B2 51 46N 1 28W

F

Fairbourne Wales 14 B2 52 41N 4 03W
Fair Head NI 10 C2 55 15N 6 10W
Fair Isle Scotland 7 C2 59 32N 1 38W
Fairlight England 17 D1 50 52N 0 38E
Fairmont USA 91 K4 39 28N 80 08W
Faisalabad Pakistan 66 C6 31 25N 73 09E
Fakenham England 17 D3 52 50N 0 51E
Fal r. England 18 C2 50 16N 4 56W
Falcarragh RoI 20 C5 55 08N 8 06W
Falfurrias USA 91 G2 27 17N 98 10W
Falkirk Scotland 11 F2 55 59N 3 48W
Falkirk u.a. Scotland 11 F2 55 55N 3 45W
Falkland Scotland 11 F3 56 15N 3 13W
Falkland Islands S Atlantic Ocean 97 E2/F2 52 30S 60 00W
Falmouth England 18 B2 50 08N 5 04W
Fanad Head RoI 20 D5 55 17N 7 38W
Fane r. RoI 20 E3 54 00N 6 40W
Fano Italy 54 E5 43 51N 13 01E
Fareham England 16 B1 50 51N 1 10W
Faringdon England 16 B2 51 40N 1 35W
Farnborough England 16 C2 51 17N 0 46W
Farne Islands England 11 H2 55 38N 1 38W
Farnham England 16 C2 51 13N 0 49W

Farnham Royal England 16 C2 51 33N 0 38W
Farnworth England 12 D2 53 33N 2 24W
Faro Portugal 51 B2 37 01N 7 56W
Farranfore RoI 21 B2 52 10N 9 33W
Farrar r. Scotland 9 E2 57 15N 4 41W
Faughan r. NI 10 B1 54 54N 7 09W
Faversham England 17 D2 51 20N 0 53E
Fawley England 16 B1 50 49N 1 20W
Feale r. RoI 21 B2 52 26N 9 22W
Featherstone England 13 E2 53 41N 1 21W
Fécamp France 50 E5 49 45N 0 23E
FEDERATED STATES OF MICRONESIA 100 F8
Feldkirch Austria 52 D3 47 15N 9 38E
Felixstowe England 17 E2 51 58N 1 20E
Felling tn. England 13 E3 54 57N 1 33W
Felton England 11 H2 55 18N 1 42W
Feltwell England 17 D3 52 29N 0 33E
Fens, The England 16 C3/D3 52 45N 0 05E
Feolin Ferry tn. Scotland 10 C2 55 51N 6 06W
Ferbane RoI 20 D3 53 15N 7 49W
Fermanagh district NI 10 B1 54 25N 7 45W
Fermo Italy 54 E5 43 09N 13 44E
Fermoy RoI 21 C2 52 08N 8 16W
Ferndown England 19 F2 50 48N 1 55W
Ferns RoI 21 E2 52 35N 6 30W
Ferrara Italy 54 E6 44 50N 11 38E
Ferryhill tn. England 13 E3 54 41N 1 33W
Fès Morocco 80 C8 34 05N 5 00W
Fethaland, Point of Scotland 7 C3 60 35N 1 18W
Fethard RoI 21 D2 52 27N 7 41W
Fethard RoI 21 E2 52 11N 6 50W
Fetlar i. Scotland 7 D3 60 37N 0 52W
Fettercairn Scotland 9 G1 56 51N 2 34W
Ffestiniog Wales 14 C2 52 58N 3 55W
Fforest Fawr Wales 14 C1 51 50N 3 40W
Ffostrasol Wales 14 B2 52 06N 4 23W
Fiddown RoI 21 D2 52 20N 7 19W
Fife u.a. Scotland 11 G3 56 10N 3 00W
Fife Ness c. Scotland 11 G3 56 17N 2 35W
Figeac France 50 F3 44 32N 2 01E
Figueira da Foz Portugal 51 A4 40 09N 8 51W
Figueres Spain 51 G5 42 16N 2 57E
FIJI 100 H6
Filey England 13 F3 54 12N 0 17W
Filton England 15 D1 51 31N 2 35W
Findhorn r. Scotland 9 F2 57 25N 3 55W
Findhorn Scotland 9 F2 57 39N 3 36W
Findhorn Bay Scotland 9 F2 57 39N 3 36W
Findochty Scotland 9 G2 57 42N 2 55W
Finglas RoI 20 E3 53 24N 6 18W
FINLAND 49 G3
Finland, Gulf of Finland 49 F2/G2 59 40N 23 30E
Finnea RoI 20 D3 53 47N 7 23W
Fintagh Bay RoI 20 C4 54 35N 8 33W
Fintona NI 10 B1 54 30N 7 19W
Fintown RoI 20 C4 54 52N 8 07W
Fionn Loch Scotland 8 D2 57 45N 5 25W
Fionnphort Scotland 8 C1 56 19N 6 23W
Firat r. Asia 57 E2 37 30N 38 00E
Firth of Clyde Scotland 10 D2/E2 55 30N 5 00W
Firth of Forth Scotland 11 F3/G3 56 05N 3 00W
Firth of Lorn Scotland 8 C1 56 15N 6 00W
Firth of Tay Scotland 9 F1 56 25N 3 00W
Fishbourne England 16 B1 50 44N 1 12W
Fishguard Wales 14 B1 51 59N 4 59W
Flagstaff USA 90 D4 35 12N 111 38W
Flamborough England 13 F3 54 07N 0 07W
Flamborough Head England 13 F3 54 06N 0 04W
Fleet England 16 C2 51 16N 0 50W
Fleetwood England 12 C2 53 56N 3 01W
Flekkefjord Norway 49 C2 58 17N 6 40E
Flimby England 12 C3 54 41N 3 31W
Flint Wales 14 C3 53 15N 3 07W
Flintshire u.a. Wales 14 C3 53 15N 3 10W
Flitwick England 16 C2 52 00N 0 29W
Florence Italy 54 D5 43 47N 11 15E
Florida state USA 91 K2 28 00N 82 00W
Florida Keys is. USA 91 K1 25 00N 80 00W
Flotta i. Scotland 7 A1 58 49N 3 07W
Fochabers Scotland 9 F2 57 37N 3 05W
Focşani Romania 55 N2 45 41N 27 12E
Fóggia Italy 55 F4 41 28N 15 33E
Folkestone England 17 E2 51 05N 1 11E
Folkingham England 16 C2 52 54N 0 24W
Fontainebleau France 50 F5 48 24N 2 42E
Fontstown RoI 21 E3 53 03N 6 53W
Fordham England 17 D3 52 19N 0 24E
Fordingbridge England 16 B1 50 56N 1 47W
Foreland p. England 16 B1 50 41N 1 04W
Foreland Point England 18 D3 51 16N 3 47W
Foreness Point England 17 E2 51 25N 1 27E
Forest Channel Islands 19 E1 49 25N 2 35W
Forest Row England 16 C2 51 06N 0 02E
Forfar Scotland 9 G1 56 38N 2 54W
Forlì Italy 54 E6 44 13N 12 02E
Formby England 12 C2 53 34N 3 05W
Formentera i. Spain 51 F3 38 41N 1 30E
FORMER YUGOSLAV REPUBLIC OF MACEDONIA (FYROM) 55 J4/K4
Forres Scotland 9 F2 57 37N 3 38W
Fortaleza Brazil 96 K13 3 45S 38 35W

Fort Augustus Scotland 9 E2 57 09N 4 41W
Fort George Scotland 9 E2 57 35N 4 05W
Forth r. Scotland 11 E3 56 05N 4 05W
Fort Lauderdale USA 91 K2 26 08N 80 08W
Fort Liard Canada 88 L6 60 14N 123 28W
Fortrose Scotland 9 E2 57 34N 4 09W
Fort Saskatchewan Canada 88 N4 53 42N 113 12W
Fortuneswell England 19 E2 50 33N 2 27W
Fort William Scotland 9 D1 56 49N 5 07W
Fort Worth USA 91 G3 32 45N 97 20W
Foula i. Scotland 7 B3 60 08N 2 05W
Foulness Island England 17 D2 51 35N 0 57E
Foulness Point England 17 D2 51 37N 0 57E
Fowey England 18 C2 50 20N 4 38W
Fowey r. England 18 C2 50 27N 4 38W
Foxford RoI 20 B3 53 58N 9 08W
Foyle r. NI/RoI 20 D4 54 55N 7 25W
Foynes RoI 21 B2 52 37N 9 06W
Foz Spain 51 B5 43 34N 7 15W
Framlingham England 17 E3 52 13N 1 21E
Frampton Cotterell England 15 D1 51 32N 2 30W
FRANCE 50
Frankfurt am Main Germany 52 D5 50 06N 8 41E
Frankfurt an der Oder Germany 52 G6 52 20N 14 32E
Fraser r. Canada 88 L4 52 00N 122 00W
Fraserburgh Scotland 9 G2 57 42N 2 00W
Freckleton England 12 D2 53 46N 2 52W
Frederick USA 93 E1 39 25N 77 25W
Fredericksburg USA 91 L4 38 18N 77 30W
Frederikshavn Denmark 49 D2 57 28N 10 33E
Freemount RoI 21 C2 52 17N 8 53W
Freeport Canada 89 X2 44 17N 66 19W
Freetown Sierra Leone 80 B3 8 30N 13 17W
Freiburg im Breisgau Germany 52 C3 48 00N 7 52E
Fréjus France 50 H2 43 26N 6 44E
French Guiana territory France 96 G14 5 00N 53 00W
Frenchpark RoI 20 C3 53 53N 8 24W
Freshwater England 16 B1 50 40N 1 30E
Fresno USA 90 C4 36 41N 119 47W
Fribourg Switz. 52 C3 46 50N 7 10E
Friedrichshafen Germany 52 D3 47 39N 9 29E
Frinton on Sea England 17 E2 51 50N 1 14E
Frodsham England 12 D2 53 18N 2 44W
Frogmore England 16 C2 51 20N 0 50W
Frome England 19 E 51 14N 2 20W
Frome r. Herefordshire England 15 D2 52 05N 2 30W
Frome r. Somerset England 19 E3 51 10N 2 20W
Frome r. Dorset England 19 E2 50 42N 2 16W
Fuday i. Scotland 8 B2 57 05N 7 20W
Fuenlabrada Spain 51 D4 40 16N 3 49W
Fuerteventura i. Spain 80 B7 28 25N 14 00W
Fuji Japan 70 C2 35 10N 138 37E
Fuji-san mt. Japan 70 C2 35 23N 138 42E
Fukuoka Japan 70 B1 33 39N 130 21E
Furnace Scotland 10 D3 56 09N 5 12W
Fürth Germany 52 E4 49 28N 11 00E
Fushun China 69 M6 41 50N 123 54E
Fuzhou China 69 L3 26 09N 119 17E

G
GABON 82 B7
Gaborone Botswana 82 E3 24 45S 25 55E
Gadsden USA 91 J3 34 00N 86 00W
Gaeta Italy 54 E4 41 13N 13 36E
Gainsborough England 13 F2 53 24N 0 48W
Gairloch tn. Scotland 8 D2 57 42N 5 40W
Gairsay i. Scotland 7 B2 59 05N 2 58W
Galashiels Scotland 11 G2 55 37N 2 49W
Galaţi Romania 53 P2 45 27N 28 02E
Gallan Head Scotland 8 B3 58 14N 7 01W
Galley Head RoI 21 C1 51 35N 8 55W
Gallipoli Italy 55 H4 40 03N 17 59E
Gallup USA 90 E4 32 32N 108 46W
Galston Scotland 11 E2 55 36N 4 24W
Galveston USA 91 H2 29 17N 94 48W
Galway co. RoI 20 B3/C3 53 25N 8 45W
Galway RoI 20 B3 53 16N 9 03W
Galway Bay RoI 20 B3 53 15N 9 15W
Gambia r. Senegal/The Gambia 80 B4 13 45N 13 15W
GAMBIA, THE 80 A4
Gandía Spain 51 E3 38 59N 0 11W
Ganga r. India 66 E5 25 00N 83 30E
Gangdisê Shan mts. China 68 D4 31 00N 82 30E
Gap France 50 H3 44 33N 6 05E
Garda Italy 54 D6 45 34N 10 43E
Garden City USA 90 F4 37 57N 100 54W
Gardenstown Scotland 9 G2 57 40N 2 20W
Gare Loch Scotland 11 E3 56 03N 4 39W
Garelochhead Scotland 11 E3 56 05N 4 50W
Garforth England 13 E2 53 48N 1 22W
Garlieston Scotland 11 E1 54 48N 4 22W
Garonne r. France 50 D3 44 45N 0 15E

Garrison NI 10 A1 54 25N 8 05W
Garron Point NI 10 D2 55 05N 6 00W
Garstang England 12 D2 53 55N 2 47W
Garth Wales 14 C2 52 08N 3 32W
Garthorpe England 13 F2 53 40N 0 42W
Garve Scotland 9 E2 57 37N 4 42W
Gaspé Canada 89 Y3 48 50N 64 30W
Gastonia USA 91 K4 35 14N 81 12W
Gatehouse of Fleet Scotland 11 E1 54 53N 4 11W
Gateshead England 13 E3 54 58N 1 35W
Gatty Mountains RoI 21 C2 52 21N 8 11W
Gaydon England 15 E2 52 45N 0 34E
Gaza Middle East 64 N10 31 30N 34 28E
Gaziantep Turkey 57 E2 37 04N 37 21E
Gdańsk Poland 53 J7 54 22N 18 41E
Gdynia Poland 53 J7 54 31N 18 30E
Geleen Neths 48 D3 50 58N 5 45E
Gelligaer Wales 14 C1 51 39N 3 15W
Gelsenkirchen Germany 52 C5 51 30N 7 05E
Geneva Switz. 52 C3 46 13N 6 09E
Genk Belgium 48 D3 50 58N 5 30E
Genova Italy 54 C6 44 24N 8 56E
Gent Belgium 48 B4 51 02N 3 42E
Georgetown Guyana 96 F15 6 46N 58 10W
George Town Malaysia 71 C5 5 25N 100 20E
GEORGIA 57 F3
Georgia state USA 91 K3 33 00N 83 00W
Gera Germany 52 F5 50 51N 12 11E
GERMANY 52
Gerona Spain 51 G4 41 59N 2 49E
Gerrards Cross England 16 C2 51 35N 0 34W
Getafe Spain 51 D4 40 18N 3 44W
GHANA 80 D3
Giant's Causeway NI 10 C2 55 10N 6 30W
Gibraltar territory U.K. 51 C2 36 09N 5 21W
Gigha i. Scotland 10 D2 55 40N 5 45W
Gijón Spain 51 C5 43 32N 5 40W
Gila Bend USA 90 D3 32 56N 112 42W
Gilfach Goch Wales 14 C1 51 38N 3 30W
Gilford NI 10 C1 54 23N 6 22W
Gillingham Medway England 17 D2 51 24N 0 33E
Gillingham Dorset England 19 E3 51 02N 2 17W
Gilsland England 12 D3 55 00N 2 35W
Gironde r. France 50 D3 45 30N 0 45W
Girvan Scotland 10 E2 55 15N 4 51W
Givet Belgium 48 C3 50 08N 4 49E
Glanaman Wales 14 C1 51 47N 3 55W
Glanton England 11 H2 55 26N 1 54W
Glasgow Scotland 11 E2 55 53N 4 15W
Glasgow City u.a. Scotland 11 E2 55 52N 4 16W
Glass r. Scotland 9 E2 57 15N 4 40W
Glassan RoI 20 D3 53 28N 7 52W
Glastonbury England 19 E3 51 09N 2 43W
Glenaffric r. Scotland 8 D2 57 15N 5 15W
Glenbeigh RoI 21 B2 52 03N 9 56W
Glencoe Scotland 9 D1 56 40N 5 04W
Glencolumbkille RoI 20 C4 54 42N 8 44W
Glenfinnan Scotland 8 D1 56 53N 5 27W
Glengad Head RoI 20 D5 55 20N 7 11W
Glengarriff RoI 21 B1 51 45N 9 33W
Glenluce Scotland 11 E1 54 53N 4 49W
Glenamaddy RoI 20 C3 53 37N 8 35W
Glenridding England 12 D3 54 33N 2 58W
Glenrothes Scotland 11 F3 56 12N 3 10W
Glen Shee r. Scotland 9 F1 46 45N 3 25W
Glenties RoI 20 C4 54 47N 8 17W
Glin RoI 21 B2 52 34N 9 17W
Glossop England 13 E2 53 27N 1 57W
Gloucester England 15 D1 51 53N 2 14W
Gloucestershire co. England 15 D1/E1 51 50N 2 20W
Glusburn England 12 D2 53 55N 2 01W
Glydar Fawr mt. Wales 14 B3 53 05N 4 03W
Glyncorrwg Wales 14 C1 51 41N 3 38W
Glyn-neath Wales 14 C1 51 46N 3 38W
Gniezno Poland 53 H6 52 32N 17 32E
Goat Fell mt. Scotland 10 D2 55 39N 5 11W
Gobi Desert Mongolia 68/69 G6/J6 48 30N 100 00E
Godalming England 16 C2 51 11N 0 37W
Godmanchester England 16 C3 52 19N 0 11W
Goiânia Brazil 96 H10 16 43S 49 18W
Goiás Brazil 96 G10 15 57S 50 07W
Golam Head RoI 20 B3 53 14N 9 44W
Golfo de California Mexico 94 B5 27 00N 111 00W
Golfo di Genova Italy 54 C6 44 00N 9 00E
Golfo di Táranto Italy 55 G3/G4 40 00N 17 00E
Golfo di Venézia Italy 54 E6 45 00N 13 00E
Golspie Scotland 9 F2 57 58N 3 58W
Gomera i. Spain 80 A7 28 08N 17 14W
Good Hope, Cape of RSA 82 C1 34 30S 19 00E
Goodland USA 90 F4 39 20N 101 43W
Goodwick Wales 14 B1 52 00N 5 00W
Goole England 13 F2 53 42N 0 52W
Gorebridge Scotland 11 F2 55 51N 3 02W
Gorey RoI 21 E2 52 40N 6 18W
Gorinchem Neths 48 C4 51 50N 4 59E
Goring England 16 B2 51 32N 1 09W

Gorizia Italy 54 E6 45 57N 13 37E
Gorseinon Wales 14 B1 51 41N 4 02W
Gort RoI 21 C3 53 04N 8 50W
Gorteen RoI 20 C3 53 22N 8 35W
Gortmore RoI 20 B3 53 36N 9 36W
Gorumna Island RoI 20 B3 53 15N 9 55W
Gosforth England 13 E4 55 01N 1 37W
Gosport England 16 B1 50 48N 1 08W
Göteborg Sweden 49 D2 57 45N 12 00E
Gotha Germany 52 E5 50 57N 10 43E
Gotland i. Sweden 49 E2 57 30N 18 40E
Göttingen Germany 52 D5 51 32N 9 57E
Gouda Neths 48 C5 52 00N 4 42E
Gourock Scotland 11 E2 55 58N 4 49W
Gower p. Wales 14 B1 51 35N 4 10W
Gowran RoI 21 D2 52 38N 7 04W
Graemsay i. Scotland 7 A1 58 56N 3 17W
Grafham Water England 16 C3 52 18N 0 20W
Graiguenamanagh RoI 21 E2 52 32N 6 56W
Grain England 17 D2 51 28N 0 43E
Grampian Mountains Scotland 9 E1/F1 56 45N 4 00W
Granada Spain 51 D2 37 10N 3 35W
Granard RoI 20 D3 53 47N 7 30W
Gran Canaria i. Spain 80 A7 28 00N 15 35W
Grand Canal RoI 20 D3 53 18N 7 15W
Grand Canyon USA 90 D4 36 04N 112 07W
Grand Cayman i. Caribbean Sea 95 H3 19 20N 81 15W
Grand Rapids tn. USA 91 J5 42 57N 86 40W
Grange RoI 20 C4 54 24N 8 31W
Grangemouth Scotland 11 F3 56 01N 3 44W
Grange-over-Sands tn. England 12 D3 54 33N 3 09W
Grantham England 15 F2 52 55N 0 39W
Grantown-on-Spey Scotland 9 F2 57 20N 3 58W
Granville France 50 D5 48 50N 1 35W
Grasmere England 12 C3 54 28N 3 02W
Grasse France 50 H2 43 40N 5 56E
Grassington England 12 E3 54 04N 1 59W
Gravelines France 48 A3 50 59N 2 08E
Gravesend England 17 D2 51 27N 0 24E
Gray France 50 G4 47 27N 5 35E
Grays England 17 D2 51 29N 0 20E
Graz Austria 52 G3 47 05N 15 22E
Greasby England 12 C2 53 23N 3 10W
Great Bardfield England 17 D2 51 57N 0 26E
Great Bear Lake Canada 88 L7/M7 66 00N 120 00W
Great Broughton England 13 E3 54 27N 1 110W
Great Chesterford England 17 D3 52 04N 0 11E
Great Coates England 13 F2 53 35N 0 08W
Great Cumbrae i. Scotland 10 E2 55 46N 4 55W
Great Dividing Range Australia 73 H8/J3 35 00N 148 00E
Great Driffield England 13 F3 54 01N 0 26E
Great Dunmow England 17 D2 51 53N 0 22E
Great Eccleston England 12 D2 53 51N 2 53W
Greater Antilles is. West Indies 95 H4/L3 19 00N 78 00W
Greater London co. England 17 D2 51 30N 0 10W
Greater Manchester co. England 12 D2 53 30N 2 15W
Great Harwood England 12 D2 53 48N 2 24W
Great Malvern England 15 D2 52 07N 2 19W
Great Missenden England 16 C2 51 43N 0 43W
Great Ormes Head Wales 14 C3 53 21N 3 53W
Great Ouse r. England 17 D3 52 40N 0 20E
Great Salt Lake USA 90 D5 41 10N 112 40W
Great Shelford England 17 D3 52 08N 0 09E
Great Slave Lake Canada 88 N6 62 00N 114 00W
Great Torrington England 18 C2 51 57N 4 09W
Great Victoria Desert Australia 72 E5/F5 28 00S 130 00E
Great Whernside sum. England 12 E3 54 10N 1 59W
Great Wyrley England 15 D2 52 27N 2 02W
Great Yarmouth England 17 E3 52 37N 1 44E
GREECE 55 J3/K3
Greencastle NI 10 C1 54 02N 6 06W
Greenisland tn. NI 10 D1 54 42N 5 52W
GREENLAND 89 BB8/EE8
Greenlaw Scotland 11 G2 55 43N 2 28W
Greenock Scotland 11 E2 55 57N 4 45W
Greenore RoI 20 E4 54 02N 6 08W
Greenore Point RoI 21 E2 52 15N 6 18W
Greenstone Point Scotland 8 D2 57 55N 5 37W
GRENADA 94 R11
Grenoble France 50 G3 45 11N 5 43E
Greta r. England 12 D3 54 10N 2 30W
Gretna Scotland 11 F1 54 59N 3 04W

Gretna Green Scotland 11 F1 55 00N 3 04W
Greystones RoI 21 E3 53 09N 6 04W
Grimethorpe England 13 E2 53 34N 1 23W
Grimsby England 13 F2 53 35N 0 05W
Groningen Neths 48 E6 53 13N 6 35E
Grosseto Italy 54 D5 42 46N 11 07E
Grove England 16 B2 51 37N 1 26W
Groznyy Russia 62 G5 43 21N 45 42E
Gruinard Bay Scotland 8 D2 57 55N 5 30W
Guadalajara Mexico 94 D4 20 40N 103 20W
Guadalajara Spain 51 D4 40 37N 3 10W
Guadalquivir r. Spain 51 C2 37 45N 5 30W
Guadeloupe i. Lesser Antilles 94 Q9 16 30N 61 30W
GUAM 100 E9
Guangzhou China 69 K2 23 08N 113 20E
Guantánamo Cuba 95 J4 20 09N 75 14W
Guarda Portugal 51 B4 40 32N 7 17W
GUATEMALA 94 F3
Guatemala City Guatemala 94 F2 14 38N 90 22W
Guayaquil Ecuador 96 A13 2 13S 79 54W
Guéret France 50 E4 46 10N 1 52E
Guernsey i. Channel Islands 19 E1 46 27N 2 35W
Guide Post England 13 E4 55 10N 1 36W
Guildford England 16 C2 51 14N 0 35W
Guimarães Portugal 51 A4 41 26N 8 19W
GUINEA 80 B4
GUINEA-BISSAU 80 A4/B4
Guisborough England 13 E3 54 32N 1 04W
Guiseley England 13 E2 53 53N 1 42W
Guiyang China 69 J3 26 35N 106 40E
Gujranwala Pakistan 66 C6 32 06N 74 11E
Gulf, The Middle East 65 F4 27 20N 51 00E
Gullane Scotland 11 G3 56 02N 2 50W
Gunnislake England 18 C2 50 31N 4 12W
Gutcher Scotland 7 C3 60 40N 1 00W
Guthrie USA 91 G4 35 54N 97 26W
GUYANA 96 F14
Gweebarra Bay RoI 20 C4 54 55N 8 30W
Gweedore RoI 20 C5 55 03N 8 14W
Gwynedd u.a. Wales 14 C2 52 45N 3 55W
Győr Hungary 53 H3 47 41N 17 40E

H
Haarlem Neths 48 C5 52 23N 4 39E
Hacketstown RoI 21 E2 52 52N 6 33W
Haddington Scotland 11 G2 55 58N 2 47W
Hadleigh England 17 D3 52 02N 0 57E
Hadleigh England 17 D2 51 34N 0 36E
Hadley England 15 D2 52 43N 2 28W
Hagen Germany 52 C5 51 22N 7 27E
Hagley England 15 D2 52 26N 2 08W
Hagondange France 50 H5 49 16N 6 11E
Hags Head RoI 21 B2 52 56N 9 30W
Haguenau France 50 H5 48 49N 7 47E
Haifa Israel 64 B5 32 49N 34 59E
Hailsham England 17 D1 50 52N 0 16E
Hainan Dao i. China 69 J1/K1 18 50N 109 50E
Hai Phong Vietnam 69 J2 20 50N 106 41E
HAITI 95 K3
Hakodate Japan 70 D3 41 46N 140 44E
Hale England 12 D2 53 22N 2 20W
Halesowen England 15 D2 52 26N 2 05W
Halesworth England 17 E3 52 21N 1 30E
Halifax England 13 E2 53 44N 1 52W
Halifax Canada 89 Y2 44 38N 63 35W
Halkirk Scotland 9 F3 58 30N 3 30W
Halladale r. Scotland 9 F3 58 30N 3 55W
Halle Germany 52 E5 51 28N 11 58E
Hallein Austria 52 F3 47 41N 13 06E
Halmstad Sweden 49 D2 56 41N 12 55E
Halstead England 17 D2 51 57N 0 38E
Haltwhistle England 12 D3 54 58N 2 27W
Hamāh Syria 64 C6 35 10N 36 45E
Hamamatsu Japan 70 C1 34 42N 137 42E
Hamble-le-Rice England 16 B1 50 52N 1 19W
Hambleton Hills England 13 E3 54 15N 1 15W
Hamburg Germany 52 E6 53 33N 10 00E
Hämeenlinna Finland 49 F3 61 00N 24 25E
Hamilton Canada 89 U2 43 15N 79 50W
Hamilton NZ 73 Q3 37 47S 175 17E
Hamilton Scotland 11 E2 55 47N 4 03W
Hamm Germany 52 C5 51 40N 7 49E
Hammerfest Norway 49 F5 70 40N 23 44E
Hampshire co. England 16 B2 51 15N 1 10W
Hampshire Downs England 16 B2 51 15N 1 10W
Hamstreet England 17 D2 51 05N 0 52E
Hangzhou China 69 M4 30 18N 120 07E
Hanko Finland 49 F2 59 50N 23 00E
Hanley England 12 D2 53 01N 2 10W
Hannover Germany 52 D6 52 23N 9 44E
Hanoi Vietnam 69 J2 21 01N 105 52E
Harare Zimbabwe 82 F4 17 50S 31 03E
Harbin China 69 N7 45 45N 126 41E
Harlech Wales 14 B2 52 52N 4 07W
Harleston England 17 E3 52 24N 1 18E
Harlingen Neths 48 D6 53 10N 5 25E
Harlow England 17 D2 51 47N 0 08E
Haroldswick Scotland 7 D3 60 47N 0 50W

Harpenden England 16 C2 51 49N 0 22W
Harris i. Scotland 8 C2 57 50N 6 55W
Harris, Sound of
  Scotland 8 B2 57 40N 9 12W
Harrogate England 13 E2 54 00N 1 33W
Harrow England 16 C2 51 34N 0 20W
Hartford USA 91 M5 41 00N 72 00W
Hartington England 13 E2 53 09N 1 48W
Hartland England 18 C2 50 59N 4 29W
Hartland Point England 18 C2 51 02N 4 31W
Hartlepool England 13 E3 54 41N 1 13W
Hartlepool u.a. England13 E3 54 41N 1 13W
Hartshill England 15 E2 52 33N 1 30W
Harwell England 16 B2 51 37N 1 18W
Harwich England 17 E2 51 57N 1 17E
Harworth England 13 E2 53 26N 1 04W
Harz mts. Europe 52 E5 52 00N 10 00E
Hascosay i. Scotland 7 D3 60 36N 1 00W
Haslemere England 16 C2 51 06N 0 43W
Haslingden England 12 D2 53 43N 2 18W
Hasselt Belgium 48 D3 50 56N 5 20E
Hastings England 17 D1 50 51N 0 36E
Hatfield South Yorkshire
  England 13 F2 53 36N 0 59W
Hatfield Hertfordshire
  England 16 C2 51 46N 0 13W
Hatherleigh England 18 C2 50 49N 4 04W
Hathersage England 13 E2 53 19N 1 38W
Hatton Scotland 9 H2 57 25N 1 55W
Haugesund Norway 49 C2 59 25N 5 16E
Haut Atlas mts.
  Morocco 80 C8 30 45N 6 50W
Havana Cuba 95 H4 23 07N 82 25W
Havant England 16 C1 50 51N 0 59W
Haverfordwest Wales 14 B1 51 49N 4 58W
Haverhill England 17 D3 52 05N 0 26E
Havering England 17 D2 51 34N 0 14E
Hawaiian Islands
  Pacific Ocean 100 J10/L9 25 00N 166 00W
Hawarden Wales 14 C3 53 11N 3 02W
Hawes England 12 D3 54 18N 2 12W
Hawick Scotland 11 G2 55 25N 2 47W
Hawkesbury Canada 89 W3 45 36N 74 38W
Hawkhurst England 17 C1 51 02N 0 30E
Haworth England 13 E2 53 50N 1 57W
Haxby England 13 E3 54 01N 1 05W
Haydon Bridge tn.
  England 12 D3 54 58N 21 4W
Hayle England 18 B2 50 10N 5 25W
Hay-on-Wye Wales 14 C2 52 04N 3 07W
Haywards Heath
  England 16 C2 51 00N 0 06W
Hazel Grove England 12 D2 53 23N 2 08W
Hazelmere England 16 C2 51 38N 0 44W
Heacham England 17 D3 52 55N 0 30E
Headford Rol 20 B3 53 28N 9 06W
Heanor England 13 E2 53 01N 1 22W
Heathfield England 17 D1 50 58N 0 15E
Hebden Bridge England12 D2 53 45N 2 00W
Hebi China 69 K5 35 57N 114 08E
Heckington England 15 F2 52 59N 0 18W
Heckmondwike
  England 13 E2 53 43N 1 45W
Hedge End England 16 B1 50 55N 1 18W
Hednesford England 15 E2 52 43N 2 00W
Hedon England 13 F2 53 44N 0 12W
Heerenveen Neths 48 D5 52 57N 5 55E
Heerlen Neths 48 D3 50 53N 5 59E
Hefei China 69 L4 31 55N 117 18E
Heidelberg Germany 52 D4 49 25N 8 42E
Heighington England 13 E2 54 36N 1 37W
Heisker i. Scotland 8 B2 57 30N 7 40W
Hekla mt. Iceland 49 L6 64 00N 19 41W
Helchteren Belgium 48 D4 51 03N 5 23E
Helena USA 90 D6 46 35N 112 00W
Helen's Bay tn. NI 10 D1 54 41N 5 50W
Helensburgh Scotland 11 E3 56 01N 4 44W
Hellifield England 12 D3 54 01N 2 12W
Helmsdale r. Scotland 9 F3 58 10N 3 50W
Helmsdale Scotland 9 F3 58 07N 3 40W
Helmsley England 13 E3 54 14N 1 04W
Helsingborg Sweden 49 D2 56 03N 12 43E
Helston England 18 B2 50 05N 5 16W
Helvellyn mt. England 12 C3 54 32N 3 02W
Hemel Hempstead
  England 16 C2 51 46N 0 28W
Hemsworth England 13 E2 53 38N 1 21W
Henfield England 16 C1 50 56N 0 17W
Hengelo Neths 48 E5 52 16N 6 46E
Henley-in-Arden
  England 15 E2 52 17N 1 46W
Henley-on-Thames
  England 16 C2 51 32N 0 56W
Herbertstown Rol 21 C2 52 32N 8 28W
Hereford England 14 D2 52 04N 2 43W
Herefordshire co.
  England 14/15 D2 52 10N 2 45W
Herentals Belgium 48 C4 51 11N 4 50E
Herm i. Channel Islands 19 E1 49 28N 2 27W
Herne Germany 48 F4 51 32N 7 12E
Herne Bay England 17 E2 51 23N 1 08E
Herning Denmark 49 C2 56 08N 8 59E
Hertfordshire co.
  England 16 C2 51 50N 0 05W
Hessle England 13 F2 53 44N 0 26W

Hetton-le-Hole England 13 E3 54 50N 1 27W
Hexham England 12 D3 54 58N 2 06W
Heysham England 12 D3 54 02N 2 54W
Heywood England 12 D2 53 36N 2 13W
Higham Ferrers
  England 15 F2 52 18N 0 36W
High Bentham England 12 D3 54 08N 2 30W
Higher Walton England 12 D2 53 45N 2 37W
Highland u.a. Scotland8/9 D2/E2 57 00N 5 00W
Highworth England 16 B2 51 38N 1 43W
High Wycombe England16 C2 51 38N 0 46W
Hildesheim Germany 52 D6 52 09N 9 58E
Hinckley England 15 E2 52 33N 1 21W
Hindhead England 16 C2 51 07N 0 44W
Hindley England 12 D2 53 32N 2 35W
Hindu Kush mts.
  Afghanistan 66 B7/C7 35 00N 70 00E
Hiroshima Japan 70 B1 34 23N 132 27E
Hirwaun Wales 14 C1 51 45N 3 30W
Histon England 17 D3 52 15N 0 06E
Hitachi Japan 70 D2 36 35N 140 40E
Hitchin England 16 C2 51 57N 0 17W
Hobart Australia 73 J2 42 54S 147 18E
Hồ Chi Minh Vietnam 71 D6 10 46N 106 43E
Hockley England 17 D2 51 35N 0 39E
Hodder r. England 12 D2 53 55N 2 30W
Hoddesdon England 16 C2 51 46N 0 01W
Hodnet England 15 D2 52 51N 2 35W
Hoek van Holland
  Neths 48 C5 51 59N 4 08E
Hohhot China 69 K6 40 49N 117 37E
Hokkaidō i. Japan 70 D3 43 30N 143 00E
Holbeach England 15 F2 52 49N 0 01E
Holderness p. England 13 F2 53 45N 0 05W
Hollyford Rol 21 C2 52 38N 8 06W
Hollywood Rol 21 E3 53 06N 6 35W
Holmes Chapel tn.
  England 12 D2 53 12N 2 22W
Holme-on-Spalding-Moor
  England 13 F2 53 49N 0 46W
Holmfirth England 13 E2 53 35N 1 46W
Holmhead Scotland 11 E2 55 29N 4 17W
Holsworthy England 18 C2 50 49N 4 21W
Holt England 17 E3 52 55N 1 05E
Holycross Limerick Rol 21 C2 52 38N 7 52W
Holycross Tipperary Rol21 D2 52 38N 7 52W
Holyhead Wales 14 B3 53 19N 4 38W
Holy Island England 11 H2 55 41N 1 48W
Holy Island Wales 14 B3 53 16N 4 39W
Holywell Wales 14 C3 53 17N 3 13W
Holywood NI 10 D1 54 38N 5 50W
Homs Syria 64 C5 34 42N 36 40E
Homyel' Belarus 53 Q6 52 25N 31 00E
Honddu r. Wales 14 C1 51 50N 2 50W
HONDURAS 94 G2
Hong Kong China 69 K2 23 00N 114 00E
Honiton England 19 D2 50 48N 3 13W
Honshū i. Japan 70 C2 37 15N 139 00E
Hoo England 17 D2 51 26N 0 34E
Hoogeveen Neths 48 E5 52 46N 6 29E
Hook England 16 C2 51 17N 0 58W
Hook Head Rol 21 E2 52 10N 6 55W
Hope Wales 14 C3 53 07N 3 03W
Hopton on Sea England17 E3 52 33N 1 43E
Horbury England 13 E2 53 41N 1 33W
Horley England 16 C2 51 11N 0 11W
Horncastle England 13 F2 53 13N 0 07W
Horn Head Rol 20 D5 55 13N 7 59W
Hornsea England 13 F2 53 55N 0 10W
Horsforth England 13 E2 53 51N 1 39W
Horsham England 16 C2 51 04N 0 21W
Horwich England 12 D2 53 37N 2 33W
Hospital Rol 21 C2 52 29N 8 25W
Hospitalet Spain 51 G4 41 21N 2 06E
Houghton-le-Spring
  England 13 E3 54 51N 1 28W
Hounslow England 16 C2 51 28N 0 21W
Houston USA 91 G2 29 45N 95 25W
Hove England 16 C1 50 49N 0 11W
Hovingham England 13 F3 54 10N 0 59W
Howden England 13 F2 53 45N 0 52W
Howth Rol 20 E3 53 23N 6 04W
Hoy i. Scotland 7 A1 58 48N 3 20W
Hoylake England 12 C2 53 23N 3 11W
Hoyland England 13 E2 53 30N 1 27W
Hoy Sound Scotland 7 A1 58 56N 3 20W
Hrodna Belarus 53 L6 53 40N 23 50E
Huang He r. China 69 K5 38 00N 111 00E
Hucknall England 13 E2 53 02N 1 11W
Huddersfield England 13 E2 53 39N 1 47W
Hudson Bay Canada 89 T5/T6 60 00N 89 00W
Huelva Spain 51 C2 37 15N 6 56W
Huesca Spain 51 E5 42 08N 0 25W
Hugh Town England 18 A1 49 55N 6 19W
Hull r. England 13 F2 53 55N 0 20W
Hullbridge England 17 D2 51 37N 0 37E
Humberston England 13 F2 53 32N 0 02W
HUNGARY 53 H3/K3
Hungerford England 16 B2 51 26N 1 30W
Hunmanby England 13 F3 54 11N 0 19W
Hunstanton England 17 D3 52 57N 0 30E
Huntford Scotland 11 G2 55 22N 2 28W
Huntingdon England 15 C3 52 20N 0 12W

Huntington USA 91 K4 38 24N 82 26W
Huntly Scotland 9 G2 57 27N 2 47W
Huntsville USA 91 J3 34 44N 86 35W
Huron, Lake
  Canada/USA 93 D2/3 45 00N 83 00W
Hurstpierpoint England 16 C1 50 56N 0 11W
Husbands Bosworth
  England 15 E2 52 27N 1 03W
Husum Germany 52 D7 54 29N 9 04E
Hutton Cranswick
  England 13 F2 53 57N 0 27W
Hyde England 12 D2 53 27N 2 04W
Hyderabad India 66 D3 17 22N 78 26E
Hyderabad Pakistan 66 B5 25 23N 68 24E
Hythe Hampshire
  England 16 B1 50 51N 1 24W
Hythe Kent England 17 E2 51 05N 1 05E

I
Iaşi Romania 53 N3 47 09N 27 38E
Ibadan Nigeria 80 E2 7 23N 3 56E
Ibiza i. Spain 51 F3 39 00N 1 20E
Ibstock England 15 E2 52 42N 1 23W
ICELAND 49 L7
Idaho state USA 90 D5 44 00N 115 00W
Idrigill Point Scotland 8 C2 57 21N 6 35W
Ieper Belgium 48 A3 50 51N 2 53E
Iglesias Italy 54 C3 39 19N 8 32E
IJsselmeer l. Neths 48 D5 52 50N 5 15E
Ilam England 13 E2 53 04N 1 49W
Ilchester England 19 E2 51 00N 2 41W
Îles Loyauté is.
  Pacific Ocean 73 N6/N7 21 00S 167 00E
Ilfracombe England 18 C2 51 13N 4 08W
Ilhéus Brazil 96 K11 14 50S 39 06W
Ilkeston England 15 E2 52 59N 1 18W
Ilkley England 13 E2 53 55N 1 50W
Illinois state USA 91 J5 40 00N 89 00W
Ilminster England 19 E2 50 56N 2 55W
Immingham England 13 F2 53 36N 0 11W
Imola Italy 54 E6 44 22N 11 43E
Imperia Italy 54 C5 43 53N 8 03E
Imphal India 67 G4 24 47N 93 55E
Inch Island i. Rol 20 D5 55 04N 7 30W
Inchon S. Korea 69 N5 37 30N 126 38E
Independence USA 91 G3 47 13N 95 43W
INDIA 66/67
Indiana state USA 91 J5 40 00N 86 00W
Indianapolis USA 91 J4 39 45N 86 10W
Indian Ocean 105
INDONESIA 71 C3/H3
Indus r. Pakistan 66 B5 28 00N 69 00E
Ingatestone England 17 D2 51 41N 0 22E
Ingleborough sum.
  England 12 D3 54 10N 2 23W
Ingleton England 12 D3 54 10N 2 27W
Ingolstadt Germany 52 E4 48 46N 11 27E
Inishannon Rol 21 C1 51 45N 8 38W
Inishbofin i. Rol 20 A3 53 38N 10 12W
Inishcrone Rol 20 B4 54 13N 9 05W
Inisheer i. Rol 21 B3 53 03N 9 30W
Inishkea North i. Rol 20 A4 54 08N 10 11W
Inishkea South i. Rol 20 A4 54 08N 10 11W
Inishmaan i. Rol 21 B3 53 05N 9 35W
Inishmore i. Rol 21 B3 53 07N 9 45W
Inishmurray i. Rol 20 C4 54 25N 8 35W
Inishowen Peninsula
  Rol 20 D5 55 15N 7 15W
Inishshark i. Rol 20 A3 53 36N 10 16W
Inishturk i. Rol 20 A3 53 43N 10 05W
Inn r. Europe 52 E3 48 00N 12 00E
Inner Hebrides is. Scotland 8 C1/C2 56 45N
  6 45W
Innerleithen Scotland 11 F2 55 38N 3 05W
Inner Sound Scotland 8 D2 57 25N 5 55W
Innfield Rol 20 D3 53 25N 6 50W
Innsbruck Austria 52 E3 47 17N 11 25E
Inny r. Rol 21 A1 51 54N 10 06W
Interlaken Switz. 52 C3 46 42N 7 52E
Inuvik Canada 88 J7 68 16N 133 40W
Inveraray Scotland 10 D3 56 13N 5 05W
Inver Bay Rol 20 C4 54 36N 8 20W
Inverbervie Scotland 9 G1 56 51N 2 17W
Invercargill NZ 73 N1 46 25S 168 22E
Inverclyde u.a. Scotland11 E2 55 50N 4 45W
Invergarry Scotland 9 E2 57 02N 4 47W
Invergordon Scotland 9 E2 57 42N 4 10W
Inverkeithing Scotland 11 F3 56 02N 3 25W
Invermoriston Scotland 9 E2 57 13N 4 38W
Inverness Scotland 9 E2 57 27N 4 15W
Inverquharity Scotland 9 G1 56 44N 2 59W
Inverurie Scotland 9 G2 57 17N 2 23W
Ioánnina Greece 55 J3 39 40N 20 51E
Iona i. Scotland 8 C2 56 19N 6 25W
Iónia Nisiá Greece 55 H3 39 00N 20 00E
Íos i. Greece 55 L2 36 00N 25 00E
Iowa state USA 91 H5 42 00N 94 00W
Iowa City USA 91 H5 41 39N 91 31W
Ipswich England 17 E2 52 04N 1 10E
IRAN 65 F5/G5
IRAQ 64 D5
Irbid Jordan 64 C5 32 33N 35 51E
Irfon r. Wales 14 C2 52 10N 3 25W
Irish Sea British Isles 6 53 30N 5 30W
Irkutsk Russia 63 N7 52 18N 104 15E
Ironbridge England 15 D2 52 38N 2 30W

Irrawaddy r. Myanmar 71 A8 20 00N 95 00E
Irthing r. England 12 D3 55 00N 2 40W
Irthlingborough
  England 15 F2 52 20N 0 37W
Irtysh r. Asia 62 K8 57 30N 72 30E
Irún Spain 51 E5 43 20N 1 48W
Irvine Scotland 11 E2 55 37N 4 40W
Irvinestown NI 10 B1 54 29N 7 38W
Irving USA 91 G3 32 49N 96 57W
Ise r. England 15 F2 52 25N 00 50W
Isernia Italy 54 F4 41 35N 14 14E
Iskenderun Turkey 57 36 37N 36 08E
Isla r. Scotland 9 F1 56 35N 3 10W
Isla d'Elba Italy 54 D5 42 00N 10 00E
Isla Grande de Tierra del Fuego
  Chile/Argentina 97 D2 54 00S 67 30W
Islamabad Pakistan 66 C6 33 40N 73 08E
Island Magee NI 10 D1 54 45N 5 40W
Islay i. Scotland 10 C2 55 48N 6 12W
Isleham England 17 D3 52 21N 0 25E
Isle of Man British Isles 12 B3 54 15N 4 15W
Isle of Portland England19 E2 50 33N 2 27W
Isle of Purbeck England 19 E2 50 38N 2 05W
Isle of Whithorn tn.
  Scotland 11 E1 54 42N 4 22W
Isle of Wight u.a.
  England 16 B1 50 40N 1 20W
ISRAEL 64 B5/C5
Istanbul Turkey 57 C3 41 02N 28 57E
Itabuna Brazil 96 K11 14 48S 39 18W
ITALY 54 D5/E5
Itchen r. England 16 B1 51 05N 1 15W
Ithon r. Wales 14 C2 52 20N 3 25W
Itzehoe Germany 52 D6 53 56N 9 32E
Ivybridge England 18 D2 50 23N 3 56W
Ixworth England 17 D3 52 18N 0 50E
Izhevsk Russia 62 H8 56 49N 53 11E
Izmir Turkey 57 C2 38 25N 27 10E

J
Jackson USA 91 H3 32 20N 90 11W
Jacksonville USA 91 K3 30 20N 81 40W
Jaén Spain 51 D2 37 46N 3 48W
Jaipur India 66 D5 26 53N 75 50E
Jakarta Indonesia 71 D2 6 08S 106 45E
Jakobstad Finland 49 F3 63 40N 22 42E
JAMAICA 95 J3
James Bay Canada 89 U4 53 45N 81 00W
Jamestown USA 91 G6 46 54N 98 42W
Jammu India 66 C6 32 43N 74 54E
JAPAN 70
Jarrow England 13 E3 54 59N 1 29W
Jasper Canada 88 M4 52 55N 118 05W
Jastrowie Poland 53 H6 53 26N 16 50E
Jawa i. Indonesia 71 D2/E2 7 00S 110 00E
Jedburgh Scotland 11 G2 55 29N 2 34W
Jedda Saudi Arabia 64 C3 21 30N 39 10E
Jefferson City USA 91 H4 38 33N 92 10W
Jena Germany 52 E5 50 56N 11 35E
Jerez de la Frontera
  Spain 51 C2 36 41N 6 08W
Jericho Middle East 64 N10 31 51N 35 27E
Jersey i.
  Channel Islands 19 E1 49 13N 2 07W
Jerusalem Israel/Jordan64 C5 31 47N 35 13E
Jilin China 69 N6 43 53N 126 35E
Jinan China 69 L5 36 41N 117 00E
Jinja Uganda 83 C5 0 27N 33 14E
João Pessoa Brazil 96 K12 7 06S 34 53W
Jodhpur India 66 C5 26 18N 73 08E
Joensuu Finland 49 G3 62 35N 29 46E
Johannesburg RSA 82 B2 26 10S 28 02E
John o'Groats Scotland 9 F3 58 38N 3 05W
Johnstone Scotland 11 E2 55 50N 4 31W
Jönköping Sweden 49 D2 57 45N 14 10E
Jonquière Canada 89 W3 48 25N 71 16W
JORDAN 64 C5
Jordan r. Middle East 64 N11 32 15N 32 10E
Joyce Country Rol 20 B3 53 32N 9 33W
Juàzeiro Brazil 96 J12 9 25S 40 30W
Juneau USA 88 J5 58 20N 134 20W
Jungfrau mt. Switz.52 C346 33N 7 58E
Junsele Sweden 49 E3 63 40N 16 55E
Jura mts. France/Switz. 50 G4/H4 46 30N 6 00E
Jura i. Scotland 10 D2/D3 55 55N 6 00W
Jura, Sound of
  Scotland 10 D2 55 45N 5 55W
Jylland p. Denmark 49 C2 55 00N 9 00E
Jyväskylä Finland 49 G3 62 16N 25 50E

K
K2 mt. China/India 68 C5 35 47N 76 30E
Kābul Afghanistan 66 B6 34 30N 69 10E
Kagoshima Japan 70 B1 31 37N 130 32E
Kaiserslautern
  Germany 52 C4 49 27N 7 47E
Kajaani Finland 49 G3 64 14N 27 37E
Kalahari Desert
  Southern Africa 82 D3 23 30S 23 00E
Kalamáta Greece 55 K2 37 02N 22 07E
Kaliavesi i. Finland 49 G3 63 00N 27 20E
Kaliningrad Russia 49 F1 54 40N 20 30E
Kalmar Sweden 49 E2 56 39N 16 20E
Kalmthout Belgium 48 C4 51 23N 4 29E
Kamchatka p. Russia 63 T8 57 30N 160 00E

Kames Scotland	10	D2	55 54N	5 15W
Kamloops Canada	88	L4	50 39N	120 24W
Kampala Uganda	83	C5	0 19N	32 35E
Kankakee USA	91	J5	41 08N	87 52W
Kannapolis USA	91	K4	35 30N	80 36W
Kano Nigeria	80	F4	12 00N	8 31E
Kanpur India	66	E5	26 27N	80 14E
Kansas state USA	90/91	G4	38 00N	98 00W
Kansas City USA	91	H4	39 02N	94 33W
Kanturk Rol	21	C2	52 10N	8 55W
Kaohsiung Taiwan	69	M2	22 36N	120 17E
Kapukasing Canada	89	U3	49 25N	82 26W
Karachi Pakistan	66	B4	24 51N	67 02E
Kara Sea Russia	101		75 00N	70 00E
Karasjok Norway	49	G4	69 27N	25 30E
Karcag Hungary	53	K3	47 19N	20 53E
Karlovac Croatia	54	F6	45 30N	15 34E
Karlskoga Sweden	49	D2	59 19N	14 33E
Karlskrona Sweden	49	E2	56 10N	15 35E
Karlsruhe Germany	52	D4	49 00N	8 24E
Karlstad Sweden	49	D2	59 24N	13 32E
Kaskinen Finland	49	F3	62 23N	21 10E
Kassel Germany	52	D5	51 18N	9 30E
Kathmandu Nepal	67	F5	27 42N	85 19E
Katowice Poland	53	J5	50 15N	18 59E
Katrineholm Sweden	49	E2	58 59N	16 15E
Kattegat sd. Denmark/Sweden	49	D2	57 00N	11 00E
Kaunas Lithuania	49	F1	54 52N	23 55E
Kawasaki Japan	70	C2	35 30N	139 45E
Kayseri Turkey	57	E2	38 42N	35 28E
KAZAKHSTAN	62	H6/J6		
Kazan' Russia	62	G8	55 45N	49 10E
Keady NI	10	C1	54 15N	6 42W
Kealkill Rol	21	B1	51 45N	9 20W
Kecskemét Hungary	53	J3	46 56N	19 43E
Kefallonia i. Greece	55	J3	38 00N	20 00E
Keighley England	13	D2	53 52N	1 54W
Keith Scotland	9	G2	57 32N	2 57W
Kells Rol	20	E3	53 44N	6 53W
Kelowna Canada	88	M3	49 50N	119 29W
Kelso Scotland	11	G2	55 36N	2 25W
Kelvedon England	17	D2	51 51N	0 42E
Kemnay Scotland	9	G2	57 14N	2 27W
Kempston England	16	C3	52 07N	0 30W
Kempten Germany	52	E3	47 44N	10 19E
Kendal England	12	D3	54 20N	2 45W
Kenilworth England	15	E2	52 21N	1 34W
Kenmare Rol	21	B1	51 53N	9 35W
Kennacraig Scotland	10	D2	55 50N	5 27W
Kennet r. England	16	B2	51 30N	1 45W
Kennington England	17	D2	51 09N	0 55E
Kennoway Scotland	11	F3	56 12N	3 03W
Kenora Canada	89	S3	49 47N	94 26W
Kent co. England	17	D2	51 10N	0 45E
Kentford England	17	D3	52 16N	0 30E
Kentucky state USA	91	J4	37 00N	85 00W
KENYA	83	E5/F5		
Kerkrade Neths	48	E3	50 52N	6 04E
Kérkyra i. Greece	55	H3	39 00N	19 00E
Kerpen Germany	48	E3	50 52N	6 42E
Kerrera i. Scotland	8	D1	56 25N	5 34W
Kerry co. Rol	21	B2	52 10N	9 30W
Kerry Head Rol	21	B2	52 25N	9 55W
Kesh NI	10	B1	54 31N	7 43W
Kessingland England	17	E3	52 25N	1 42E
Keswick England	12	C3	54 37N	3 08W
Kettering England	15	F2	52 24N	0 44W
Keynsham England	19	E3	51 26N	2 30W
Key West USA	91	K1	24 34N	81 48W
Keyworth England	15	E2	52 52N	1 05W
Khabarovsk Russia	63	R6	48 32N	135 08E
Khartoum Sudan	81	M5	15 33N	32 35E
Kherson Ukraine	57	D4	46 39N	32 38E
Khmel'nyts'kyy Ukraine	53	N4	49 25N	26 59E
Khulna Bangladesh	67	F4	22 49N	89 34E
Khyber Pass Afghanistan/Pakistan	66	C6	34 06N	71 05E
Kidderminster England	15	D2	52 23N	2 14W
Kidlington England	16	B2	51 50N	1 17W
Kidsgrove England	12	D2	53 05N	2 14W
Kidwelly Wales	14	B1	51 45N	4 18W
Kiel Germany	52	E7	54 20N	10 08E
Kielce Poland	53	K5	50 51N	20 39E
Kielder Water England	12	D4	55 10N	2 30W
Kiev Ukraine	53	Q5	50 25N	30 30E
Kigali Rwanda	83	B4	1 56S	30 04E
Kilbaha Rol	21	B2	52 35N	9 52W
Kilbeggan Rol	20	D3	53 22N	7 30W
Kilberry Rol	20	E3	53 42N	6 41W
Kilbirnie Scotland	11	E2	55 46N	4 41W
Kilbrannan Sound Scotland	10	D2	55 30N	5 30W
Kilcavan Rol	20	D3	53 11N	7 21W
Kilchoan Scotland	8	C1	56 43N	6 06W
Kilcock Rol	20	E3	53 24N	6 40W
Kilcormac Rol	21	D3	53 10N	7 43W
Kilcreggan Scotland	11	E2	56 01N	4 48W
Kilcullen Rol	21	E3	53 08N	6 45W
Kildare Rol	21	E3	53 10N	6 55W
Kildare co. Rol	21	E3	53 10N	6 55W
Kildorrery Rol	21	C2	52 15N	8 20W
Kilfinnane Rol	21	C2	52 22N	8 28W
Kilgetty Wales	14	B1	51 45N	4 44W
Kinglass Lough Rol	20	C3	53 50N	8 01W
Kilimanjaro mt. Tanzania	83	E3	3 04S	37 22E
Kilkeary Rol	21	C2	52 50N	8 07W
Kilkee Rol	21	B2	52 41N	9 38W
Kilkeel NI	10	C1	54 04N	6 00W
Kilkelly Rol	20	C3	53 53N	8 51W
Kilkenny co. Rol	21	D2	52 30N	7 10W
Kilkenny Rol	21	D2	52 39N	7 15W
Kilkhampton England	18	C2	50 53N	4 29W
Kilkieran Bay Rol	20	B3	53 18N	9 41W
Kilkishen Rol	21	C2	52 48N	8 45W
Kill Rol	20	E3	53 15N	6 35W
Killala Rol	20	B4	54 13N	9 13W
Killaloe Rol	21	C2	52 48N	8 27W
Killamarsh England	13	E2	53 20N	1 20W
Killarney Rol	21	B2	52 03N	9 30W
Killary Harbour Rol	20	B3	53 38N	9 55W
Killeigh Rol	20	D3	53 13N	7 27W
Killenaule Rol	21	D2	52 34N	7 40W
Killimer Rol	21	B2	52 37N	9 24W
Killimor Rol	21	C3	53 10N	8 17W
Killin Scotland	9	E1	56 28N	4 19W
Killorglin Rol	21	B2	52 06N	9 47W
Killybegs Rol	20	C4	54 38N	8 27W
Killyleagh NI	10	D1	54 24N	5 39W
Kilmacolm Scotland	11	E2	55 54N	4 38W
Kilmacrenan Rol	20	D5	55 02N	7 47W
Kilmacthomas Rol	21	D2	52 12N	7 25W
Kilmallock Rol	21	C2	52 23N	8 34W
Kilmaluag Scotland	8	C2	57 41N	6 17W
Kilmarnock Scotland	11	E2	55 36N	4 30W
Kilmona Rol	21	C1	51 58N	8 33W
Kilmory Scotland	10	D2	55 55N	5 41W
Kilrea NI	10	C1	54 57N	6 33W
Kilrenny Scotland	11	G3	56 15N	2 41W
Kilrush Rol	21	B2	52 39N	9 30W
Kilsheelan Rol	21	D2	52 22N	7 35W
Kilsyth Scotland	11	E2	55 59N	4 04W
Kiltamagh Rol	20	B3	53 51N	9 00W
Kiltealy Rol	21	E2	52 34N	6 45W
Kiltullagh Rol	20	C3	53 35N	8 35W
Kilwinning Scotland	11	E2	55 40N	4 42W
Kimberley Canada	88	M3	49 40N	115 58W
Kimberley England	15	E2	53 00N	1 17W
Kimbolton England	16	C3	52 18N	0 24W
Kinbrace Scotland	9	F3	58 15N	3 56W
Kineton England	15	E2	52 10N	1 30W
Kingsbridge England	18	D2	50 17N	3 46W
Kingsclere England	16	B2	51 20N	1 14W
Kingscourt Rol	20	E3	53 53N	6 48W
Kingskerswell England	18	D2	50 30N	3 37W
Kings Langley England	16	C2	51 43N	0 28W
King's Lynn England	17	D3	52 45N	0 24E
Kings Muir Scotland	11	F2	55 40N	3 12W
Kingsport USA	91	K4	36 33N	82 34W
Kingsteignton England	18	D2	50 33N	3 35W
Kingston Jamaica	95	U13	17 58N	76 48W
Kingston upon Hull England	13	F2	53 45N	0 20W
Kingston-upon-Thames England	16	C2	51 25N	0 18W
Kingswood England	15	D1	51 28N	2 30W
Kington England	14	C2	52 12N	3 01W
Kingussie Scotland	9	E2	57 05N	4 03W
Kinloch Scotland	8	C2	57 01N	6 17W
Kinlocheil Scotland	8	D1	56 51N	5 20W
Kinlochewe Scotland	8	D2	57 36N	5 20W
Kinlochleven Scotland	8	E1	56 42N	4 58W
Kinloch Rannoch Scotland	9	E1	56 42N	4 11W
Kinloss Scotland	9	F2	57 38N	3 33W
Kinlough Rol	20	C4	54 27N	8 17W
Kinnaird Head Scotland	9	G2	57 40N	2 00W
Kinnegad Rol	20	D3	53 27N	7 05W
Kinnitty Rol	21	D3	53 06N	7 43W
Kinross Scotland	11	F3	56 13N	3 27W
Kinsale Rol	21	C1	51 42N	8 32W
Kinsale Harbour Rol	21	C1	51 41N	8 30W
Kinshasa CDR	82	C7	4 18S	15 18E
Kintore Scotland	9	G2	57 13N	2 21W
Kintyre p. Scotland	10	D2	55 30N	5 35W
Kinvarra Rol	21	C3	53 08N	8 56W
Kippax England	13	E2	53 46N	1 22W
Kippford Scotland	11	F1	54 52N	3 49W
Kirby Muxloe England	15	E2	52 38N	1 14W
Kircubbin NI	10	D1	55 24N	5 28W
KIRIBATI	100	K7		
Kirikkale Turkey	57	D2	39 51N	33 32E
Kirkbean Scotland	11	F1	54 55N	3 36W
Kirkburton England	13	E2	53 37N	1 42W
Kirkby England	12	D2	53 29N	2 54W
Kirkby in Ashfield England	13	E2	53 13N	1 15W
Kirkby Londsale England	12	D3	54 13N	2 36W
Kirkbymoorside England	13	F3	54 16N	0 55W
Kirkby Stephen England	13	D3	54 28N	2 20W
Kirkcaldy Scotland	11	F3	56 07N	3 10W
Kirkcolm Scotland	10	D1	54 58N	5 04W
Kirkconnel Scotland	11	E2	55 23N	4 00W
Kirkcowan Scotland	11	E1	54 55N	4 36W
Kirkcudbright Scotland	11	E1	54 50N	4 03W
Kirkgunzeon Scotland	11	F1	54 58N	3 46W
Kirkham England	12	D2	53 47N	2 53W
Kirkintilloch Scotland	11	E2	55 57N	4 10W
Kirkmuirhill Scotland	11	F2	55 39N	3 55W
Kirkpatrick Durham Scotland	11	F2	55 01N	3 54W
Kirk Sandall England	13	E2	53 34N	1 04W
Kirkwall Scotland	7	B1	58 59N	2 58W
Kirov Russia	62	G8	58 00N	49 38E
Kirovohrad Ukraine	56	D4	48 31N	32 15E
Kirriemuir Scotland	9	F1	56 41N	3 01W
Kirton England	16	C3	52 56N	0 04W
Kisumu Kenya	83	D4	0 08S	34 47E
Kita-Kyūshu Japan	70	B1	33 52N	130 49E
Kitami Japan	70	D3	43 51N	143 54E
Kitchener Canada	89	U2	43 27N	80 30W
Kitimat Canada	88	K4	54 05N	128 38W
Kitzbühel Austria	52	F3	47 27N	12 23E
Klaipėda Lithuania	49	F2	55 43N	21 07E
Klamath Falls tn. USA	90	B5	42 14N	121 47W
Klöfta Norway	49	D3	60 04N	11 06E
Knapdale Scotland	10	D2	55 52N	5 31W
Knaresborough England	13	E3	54 00N	1 27W
Knighton England	14	C2	52 21N	3 03W
Knock Rol	20	C3	53 47N	8 55W
Knockadoon Head Rol	21	D1	51 50N	7 50W
Knockanevin Rol	21	C2	52 17N	8 21W
Knockdrislagh Rol	21	C2	52 03N	8 41W
Knocktopher Rol	21	D2	52 29N	7 13W
Knokke-Heist Belgium	48	B4	51 21N	3 19E
Knottingley England	13	E2	53 43N	1 14W
Knowle England	15	E2	52 23N	1 43W
Knoxville USA	91	K4	36 00N	83 57W
Knutsford England	12	D2	53 18N	2 22W
Kōbe Japan	70	C1	34 40N	135 12E
Koblenz Germany	52	C5	50 21N	7 36E
Kōfu Japan	70	C2	35 42N	138 34E
Kokkola Finland	49	F3	62 45N	30 06E
Kolhapur India	66	C3	16 40N	74 20E
Kolkata India	67	F4	22 30N	88 20E
Komatsu Japan	70	C2	36 25N	136 27E
Komotiní Greece	55	L4	41 06N	25 25E
Kōniz Switz.	52	C3	46 56N	7 25E
Konstanz Germany	52	D3	47 40N	9 10E
Konz Germany	48	E2	49 42N	6 35E
Koper Slovenia	54	E6	45 31N	13 44E
Korbach Germany	52	D5	51 16N	8 53E
Korinthiakós Kólpos g. Greece	55	K3	38 00N	22 00E
Kórinthos Greece	55	K2	37 56N	22 55E
Kortrijk Belgium	48	B3	50 50N	3 17E
Kós i. Greece	55	M2	36 45N	27 10E
Košice Slovakia	53	K4	48 44N	21 15E
Koszalin Poland	53	H7	54 10N	16 10E
Kotka Finland	49	G3	60 26N	26 55E
Kovrov Russia	56	F6	56 23N	41 21E
Kozáni Greece	55	J4	40 18N	21 48E
Kragujevac Serbia & Montenegro	55	J5	44 01N	20 55E
Kraków Poland	53	J5	50 03N	19 55E
Kranj Slovenia	54	F6	46 15N	14 20E
Krefeld Germany	52	C5	51 20N	6 32E
Krems Austria	52	G4	48 25N	15 36E
Kristiansand Norway	49	C2	58 08N	8 01E
Kristianstad Sweden	49	D2	56 02N	14 10E
Kriti i. Greece	55	L1	35 00N	25 00E
Kryvyy Roh Ukraine	56	D4	47 55N	33 24E
Kuala Lumpur Malaysia	71	C4	3 09N	101 42E
Kuching Malaysia	71	E4	1 35N	110 21E
Kufstein Austria	52	F3	47 36N	12 11E
Kumamoto Japan	70	B1	32 50N	130 42E
Kunlun Shan mts. China	68	D5/E5	36 30N	85 00E
Kunming China	69	H3	25 04N	102 41E
Kurashiki Japan	70	B1	34 36N	133 43E
Kurgan Russia	62	J8	55 30N	65 20E
Kuril Islands Russia	63	T6	50 00N	155 00E
Kursk Russia	62	F7	51 45N	36 14E
Kushiro Japan	70	D3	42 58N	144 24E
KUWAIT	65	E4		
Kuwait Kuwait	65	E4	29 20N	48 00E
Kuytun China	68	D6	44 30N	85 00E
Kwangju S. Korea	69	N5	35 07N	126 52E
Kyleakin Scotland	8	D2	57 16N	5 44W
Kyle of Lochalsh Scotland	8	D2	57 17N	5 43W
Kyles of Bute Scotland	10	D2	55 52N	5 13W
Kylestrome Scotland	8	D3	58 16N	5 02W
Kyōto Japan	70	C2	35 02N	135 45E
KYRGYZSTAN	62	K5		
Kythira i. Greece	55	K2	36 00N	23 00E
Kythnos i. Greece	55	L2	37 25N	24 25E
Kyūshū i. Japan	70	B1	32 20N	131 00E

L

Laâyoune Western Sahara	80	B7	27 10N	13 11W
Labrador geog. reg. Canada	89	Y4	54 00N	63 00W
la Chaux-de-Fonds Switz.	52	C3	47 07N	6 51E
la Ciotat France	50	G2	43 10N	5 36E
Lac Léman Switzerland	52	C3	46 20N	6 30E
La Coruña Spain	51	A5	43 22N	8 24W
La Crosse USA	91	H5	43 48N	91 04W
Lacul Razim l. Romania	53	P2	45 00N	29 00E
Ladozhskoye Ozero l. Russia	62	F9	61 00N	30 00E
Ladybank Scotland	11	F3	56 17N	3 08W
Lagan r. NI	10	C1	54 30N	6 05W
Laggan Bay b. Scotland	10	C2	55 38N	6 17W
Lago di Como l. Italy	54	C6	46 00N	9 00E
Lago di Garda l. Italy	54	D6	45 00N	10 00E
Lago Maggiore l. Italy	54	C6	46 00N	8 00E
Lagos Nigeria	80	E3	6 27N	3 28E
Lagos Portugal	51	A2	37 05N	8 40W
Lago Titicaca l. Peru/Bolivia	96	C10/D10	16 00S	69 30W
La Grande France	90	C6	45 21N	118 05W
La Grande Rivière Canada	89	W4	54 00N	74 00W
Lahore Pakistan	66	C6	31 34N	74 22E
Lahti Finland	49	G3	61 00N	25 40E
Lairg Scotland	9	E3	58 01N	4 25W
Lakenheath England	17	D3	52 25N	0 31E
La Línea de la Concepción Spain	51	C2	36 10N	5 21W
La Maddalena Italy	54	C4	41 13N	9 25E
Lamar USA	90	F4	38 04N	102 37W
Lambay Island Rol	20	E3	53 29N	6 01W
Lambourn England	16	B2	51 31N	1 31W
Lambourn r. England	16	B2	51 27N	1 28W
Lamego Portugal	51	B4	41 05N	7 49W
Lamia Greece	55	K3	38 55N	22 26E
Lamlash Scotland	10	D2	55 32N	5 08W
Lammermuir Hills Scotland	11	G2	55 50N	2 45W
Lampeter Wales	14	B2	52 07N	4 05W
Lanark Scotland	11	F2	55 41N	3 48W
Lancashire co. England	12	D2	53 50N	2 30W
Lancaster England	12	D3	54 03N	2 48W
Lanchester England	13	E3	54 50N	1 44W
Lancing England	16	C1	51 50N	0 19W
Landerneau France	50	B5	48 27N	4 16W
Land's End c. England	18	B2	50 03N	5 44W
Landshut Germany	52	F4	48 31N	12 10E
Landskrona Sweden	49	D2	55 53N	12 50E
Langdon USA	92	A3	48 46N	98 21W
Langholm Scotland	11	F2	55 09N	3 00W
Langport England	19	E3	51 02N	2 50W
Langres France	50	G4	47 53N	5 20E
Lannion France	50	C5	48 44N	3 27W
L'Anse USA	92	C5	46 45N	88 27W
Lansing USA	91	K5	42 44N	85 34W
Lanzarote i. Spain	80	B7	29 00N	13 38W
Lanzhou China	69	H5	36 01N	103 45E
Laois co. Rol	21	D2	52 59N	7 25W
Laon France	50	F5	49 34N	3 37E
LAOS	71	C7/D7		
La Paz Bolivia	96	D10	16 30S	68 10W
Lapford England	18	D2	50 52N	3 47W
Lappland geog. reg. Finland/Sweden	49	F4/G4	67 30N	20 05E
Lapua Finland	49	F3	62 57N	23 00E
L'Aquila Italy	54	E5	42 22N	13 24E
Laragh Rol	21	E3	53 00N	6 18W
Laredo USA	90	G2	27 32N	99 22W
Largs Scotland	10	E2	55 48N	4 52W
Lárisa Greece	55	K3	39 38N	22 25E
Larkhall Scotland	11	F2	55 45N	3 59W
Larne NI	10	D1	54 51N	5 49W
Larne district NI	10	D1	54 50N	6 00W
Larne Lough b. NI	10	D1	54 49N	5 49W
la Rochelle France	50	D4	46 10N	1 10W
la Roche-sur-Yon France	50	D4	46 40N	1 25W
La Roda Spain	51	D3	39 13N	2 15W
La See d'Urgel Spain	51	F5	42 22N	1 27E
la Seyne-sur-Mer France	50	G2	43 06N	5 53E
Las Palmas Spain	80	A7	28 08N	15 27W
La Spézia Italy	54	C6	44 07N	9 48E
Las Vegas USA	90	C4	36 10N	115 10W
Latakia Syria	64	C6	35 31N	35 47E
Latheron Scotland	9	F3	58 17N	3 22W
Latina Italy	54	E4	41 28N	12 53E
LATVIA	49	G2		
Lauder Scotland	11	G2	55 43N	2 45W
Laugharne Wales	14	B1	51 47N	4 28W
Launceston Australia	73	J2	41 25S	147 07E
Launceston England	18	C2	50 38N	4 21W
Lauragh Rol	21	B1	51 45N	9 46W
Laurel USA	91	J3	31 41N	89 09W
Laurencekirk Scotland	9	G1	56 50N	2 29W
Laurencetown Rol	20	C3	53 14N	8 10W
Lauria Italy	54	F4	40 03N	15 50E
Laurieston Scotland	11	E1	54 57N	4 03W
Laurieston Scotland	11	F2	55 59N	3 45W
Lausanne Switz.	52	C3	46 32N	6 39E
Laval France	50	D5	48 04N	0 45W
Lavenham England	17	D3	52 06N	0 47E
Lawrence USA	91	G4	38 58N	95 15W
Lawton USA	91	G3	34 36N	98 25W
Laxey Isle of Man	12	B3	54 14N	4 24W
Laxford Bridge tn. Scotland	8	D3	58 22N	5 01W
Lay r. France	50	D4	46 32N	1 15W
Lazonby England	12	D3	54 46N	2 41W
Lea r. England	16	C2	51 47N	0 17W
Leach r. England	15	E1	51 46N	1 44W
Leadhills Scotland	11	F2	55 25N	3 47W
Leadon r. England	15	D1	51 55N	2 21W
Leatherhead England	16	C2	51 18N	0 20W
LEBANON	64	C5		
Lebanon USA	91	H4	37 40N	92 40W
le Blanc France	50	E4	46 38N	1 04E

Lebrija Spain 51 B2 36 55N 6 10W
Lecarrow RoI 20 C3 53 33N 8 02W
Lecce Italy 55 H4 40 21N 18 11E
Lechlade England 15 E1 51 43N 1 41W
le Creusot France 50 G4 46 48N 4 27E
Ledbury England 15 D2 52 02N 2 25W
Ledmore Scotland 9 E3 58 03N 4 58W
Leeds England 13 E2 53 50N 1 35W
Leek England 12 D2 53 06N 2 01W
Leenaun RoI 20 B3 53 36N 9 41W
Leeuwarden Neths 48 D6 53 12N 5 48E
Leeward Islands
  Lesser Antilles 95 M3 17 30N 64 00W
Lefkáda i. Greece 55 J3 38 45N 20 40E
Leganés Spain 51 D4 40 20N 3 46WE
Legnica Poland 53 H5 51 12N 16 10E
le Havre France 50 E5 49 30N 0 06E
Leicester England 15 E2 52 38N 1 05W
Leicester City u.a.
  England 15 E2 52 38N 1 05W
Leicestershire co.
  England 15 E2 52 40N 1 20W
Leiden Neths 48 C5 52 10N 4 30E
Leigh England 12 D2 53 30N 2 33W
Leighton Buzzard
  England 16 C2 51 55N 0 41W
Leipzig Germany 52 F5 51 20N 12 25E
Leiria Portugal 51 A3 39 45N 8 49W
Leiston England 17 E3 52 13N 1 34E
Leith Hill tn. England 16 C2 51 11N 0 23W
Leitrim co. RoI 20 C4 54 05N 8 00W
Leivadiá Greece 55 K3 38 26N 22 53E
Leixlip RoI 20 E3 53 22N 6 30W
le Mans France 50 E4 48 00N 0 12E
Lemybrien RoI 21 D2 52 10N 7 31W
Lena r. Russia 63 Q10 70 00N 125 00E
Lens France 50 F6 50 26N 2 50E
Leoben Austria 52 G3 47 23N 15 06E
Leominster England 14 D2 52 14N 2 45W
León Mexico 94 D4 21 10N 101 42W
León Spain 51 C5 42 35N 5 34W
Leonding Austria 52 G4 48 19N 14 17E
le Puy France 50 F3 45 03N 3 53E
Lerwick Scotland 7 C3 60 09N 1 09W
Lesmahagow Scotland 11 F2 55 38N 3 54W
LESOTHO 52 E2
les Sables-d'Olonne
  France 50 D4 46 30N 1 47W
Lesser Antilles is.
  W. Indies 95 M2/M3 18 00N 65 00W
Lesser Slave Lake
  Canada 88 M5 55 25N 115 30W
Lésvos i. Greece 55 M3 39 00N 26 00E
Leswalt Scotland 10 D1 54 46N 5 05W
Letchworth England 16 C2 51 58N 0 14W
le Touquet-Paris-Plage
  France 50 E6 50 13N 1 36E
le Tréport France 50 E6 50 04N 1 22E
Letterfrack RoI 20 B3 53 33N 9 57W
Letterkenny RoI 20 D4 54 57N 7 44W
Leuchars Scotland 9 G1 56 23N 2 53W
Levanto Italy 54 C6 44 10N 9 37E
Leven England 13 F2 53 54N 0 19W
Leven Scotland 11 G3 56 11N 3 00W
Leverburgh Scotland 8 B2 57 45N 7 00W
Leverkusen Germany 52 C5 51 02N 6 59E
Lewes England 16 D1 50 52N 0 01E
Lewis i. Scotland 8 C3 58 15N 6 30W
Lexington USA 91 K4 38 03N 84 30W
Lexington USA 93 E1 37 47N 79 27W
Leyburn England 13 E3 54 19N 1 49W
Leyland England 12 D2 53 42N 2 42W
Leysdown on Sea
  England 17 D2 51 24N 0 55E
Lhasa China 68 F3 29 41N 91 10E
LIBERIA 80 B3/C3
Libourne France 50 D3 44 55N 0 14W
Libreville Gabon 80 F2 0 30N 9 25E
LIBYA 81 G7/K7
Libyan Desert
  North Africa 81 K7/L6 25 00N 25 00E
Lichfield England 15 E2 52 42N 1 48W
LIECHTENSTEIN 52 D3
Liège Belgium 48 D3 50 38N 5 35E
Lienz Austria 52 F3 46 51N 12 50E
Liepāja Latvia 49 F2 56 30N 21 00E
Liffey r. RoI 20 E3 53 16N 6 37W
Lifford RoI 20 D4 54 50N 7 29W
Lille France 50 F6 50 39N 3 05E
Lillehammer Norway 49 D3 61 06N 10 27E
Lilongwe Malawi 82 F5 13 58S 33 49E
Lima Peru 96 B11 12 06S 8 40W
Limavady NI 10 C2 55 03N 6 57W
Limavady district NI 10 B1/C1 54 55N 7 00W
Limburg Germany 52 D5 50 23N 8 04E
Limerick RoI 21 C2 52 04N 8 38W
Limerick co. RoI 21 C2 52 30N 8 40W
Limoges France 50 E3 45 50N 1 15E
Limoux France 50 F2 43 03N 2 13E
Limpopo r.
  Southern Africa 82 F3 22 30S 32 00E
Linares Spain 51 D3 38 05N 3 38W
Lincoln England 13 F2 53 14N 0 33W
Lincoln USA 91 G5 40 49N 96 41W
Lincolnshire co.
  England 13 F2 53 10N 0 20W
Lincoln Wolds England 13 F2 53 25N 0 05W

Lingen Germany 52 C6 52 32N 7 19E
Lingfield England 16 C2 51 11N 0 01W
Linköping Sweden 49 E2 58 25N 15 35E
Linlithgow Scotland 11 F2 55 59N 3 37W
Linslade England 16 C2 51 55N 0 42W
Linton England 17 D3 52 06N 0 17E
Linz Austria 52 G4 48 19N 14 18E
Liphook England 16 C1 51 05N 0 49W
Lippstadt Germany 52 D5 51 41N 8 20E
Lisbellaw NI 10 B1 54 19N 7 32W
Lisbon Portugal 51 A3 38 44N 9 08W
Lisburn NI 10 C1 54 31N 6 03W
Lisburn co. NI 10 C1 54 35N 6 10W
Liscannor Bay RoI 21 B2 52 55N 9 30W
Lisdoonvarna RoI 21 B3 53 02N 9 17W
Lisieux France 50 E5 49 09N 0 14E
Liskeard England 18 C2 50 28N 4 28W
Lismore RoI 21 D2 52 08N 7 55W
Lismore i. Scotland 8 D1 56 30N 5 30W
Lisnaskea NI 10 B1 54 15N 7 27W
Liss England 16 C2 51 03N 0 55W
Lisse Neths 48 C5 52 16N 4 34E
Lissycasey RoI 21 B2 52 44N 9 12W
Listowel RoI 21 B2 52 27N 9 29W
Litherland England 12 C2 53 28N 2 59W
LITHUANIA 49 F2
Littleborough England 12 D2 53 39N 2 05W
Littlehampton England 16 C1 50 48N 0 33W
Little Minch sd. Scotland 8 C2 57 45N 6 30W
Little Ouse r. England 17 D3 52 30N 0 30E
Littleport England 17 D3 52 28N 0 19E
Liverpool England 12 C2 53 25N 2 55W
Liverpool Bay England 12 C2 53 28N 3 15W
Liversedge England 13 E2 53 43N 1 41W
Livingston Scotland 11 F2 55 53N 3 32W
Livorno Italy 54 D5 43 33N 10 18E
Lizard England 18 B1 49 57N 5 13W
Lizard Point England 18 B1 49 56N 5 13W
Ljubljana Slovenia 54 F7 46 04N 14 30E
Ljusdal Sweden 49 E3 61 57N 16 05E
Llanberis Wales 14 C3 53 07N 4 06W
Llanbister Wales 14 C2 52 21N 3 19W
Llandeilo Wales 14 C1 51 53N 3 59W
Llandovery Wales 14 C1 51 59N 3 48W
Llandrindod Wells
  Wales 14 C2 52 15N 3 23W
Llandudno Wales 14 C3 53 19N 3 49W
Llandysul Wales 14 B2 52 02N 4 19W
Llanelli Wales 14 B1 51 42N 4 10W
Llanerchymedd Wales 14 B3 53 20N 4 22W
Llanes Spain 51 C3 43 25N 4 45W
Llanfair Caereinion
  Wales 14 C2 52 39N 3 20W
Llanfairfechan Wales 14 C3 53 15N 3 58W
Llanfyllin Wales 14 C2 52 46N 3 17W
Llangadfan Wales 14 C2 52 41N 3 28W
Llangadog Wales 14 C1 51 57N 3 53W
Llangefni Wales 14 B3 53 16N 4 19W
Llangollen Wales 14 C2 52 58N 3 10W
Llangurig Wales 14 C2 52 25N 3 36W
Llangynog Wales 14 C2 52 50N 3 25W
Llanharan Wales 14 C1 51 32N 3 28W
Llanidloes Wales 14 C2 52 27N 3 32W
Llanrhystud Wales 14 B2 52 18N 4 09W
Llanrwst Wales 14 C3 53 08N 3 48W
Llantrisant Wales 14 C1 51 33N 3 23W
Llantwit Major Wales 14 C1 51 25N 3 30W
Llanuwchllyn Wales 14 C2 52 52N 3 41W
Llanwrtyd Wells Wales 14 C2 52 07N 3 38W
Llanybydder Wales 14 B2 52 04N 4 09W
Lleida Spain 51 F4 41 37N 0 38E
Lleyn Peninsula Wales 14 B2 52 53N 4 30W
Llyn Brianne Resevoir
  Wales 14 C2 52 09N 3 43W
Llyn Celyn Wales 14 C2 53 04N 4 10W
Llyn Efyrnwy Wales 14 C2 52 50N 3 30W
Llyn Tegid Wales 14 C2 52 53N 3 38W
Loanhead Scotland 11 F2 55 53N 3 09W
Loch Affric Scotland 8 D2 57 15N 5 02W
Lochailort tn. Scotland 8 D1 56 53N 5 40W
Lochaline tn. Scotland 8 D1 56 32N 5 47W
Loch Alsh Scotland 8 D2 57 15N 5 35W
Locharbriggs Scotland 11 F2 55 06N 3 35W
Loch Assynt Scotland 9 D3/E3 58 05N 5 00W
Loch Awe Scotland 10 D3 56 15N 5 17W
Loch Bracadale Scotland 8 C2 57 20N 6 30W
Loch Broom Scotland 8 D2 57 52N 5 08W
Loch Caolisport
  Scotland 10 D2 55 53N 5 38W
Lochcarron tn. Scotland 8 D2 57 24N 5 30W
Loch Carron Scotland 8 D2 57 40N 5 45W
Loch Chroisg Scotland 8 D2 57 30N 5 30W
Loch Craignish
  Scotland 10 D3 56 05N 5 30W
Loch Creran Scotland 8 D1 56 30N 5 20W
Lochdon tn. Scotland 8 D1 56 25N 5 35W
Loch Duich Scotland 8 D2 57 15N 5 30W
Loch Earn Scotland 9 E1 56 25N 4 10W
Lochearnhead Scotland 9 E1 56 23N 4 18W
Loch Eil Scotland 8 D1 56 50N 5 25W
Loch Eishort Scotland 8 C2/D2 57 08N 6 00W
Loch Ericht Scotland 9 E1 56 48N 4 25W
Loch Erisort Scotland 8 C3 58 05N 6 30W
Loches France 50 E4 47 08N 1 00E

Loch Etive Scotland 8 D1 56 30N 5 10W
Loch Ewe Scotland 8 D2 57 50N 5 40W
Loch Eynort Scotland 8 B2 57 10N 7 15W
Loch Fannich Scotland 8 E2 57 40N 5 00W
Loch Fyne Scotland 10 D3 56 00N 5 20W
Loch Gairloch Scotland 8 D2 57 45N 5 45W
Loch Garry Scotland 9 D2 57 05N 5 00W
Lochgelly Scotland 11 F3 56 08N 3 19W
Lochgilphead Scotland 10 D3 56 03N 5 26W
Loch Glass Scotland 9 E2 57 40N 4 30W
Loch Goll Scotland 10 E3 56 05N 4 55W
Loch Gorm Scotland 10 C2 55 49N 6 24W
Loch Gruinart Scotland 10 C2 55 51N 6 21W
Loch Hope Scotland 9 E3 58 25N 4 37W
Loch Indaal Scotland 10 C2 55 45N 6 21W
Lochinver Scotland 8 D3 58 09N 5 15W
Loch Katrine Scotland 11 E3 56 16N 4 30W
Loch Ken Scotland 11 E2 55 02N 4 07W
Loch Laggan Scotland 9 E1 56 53N 4 30W
Loch Langavet Scotland 8 C3 58 05N 6 50W
Loch Leven Scotland 9 D1/E1 56 45N 5 05W
Loch Leven Scotland 11 D1 56 15N 3 23W
Loch Leven Scotland 11 F3 56 15N 3 23W
Loch Linnhe Scotland 8 D1 56 35N 5 25W
Loch Lochy Scotland 9 E1 56 58N 4 55W
Loch Lomond Scotland 11 E3 56 10N 4 35W
Loch Long Scotland 10 E3 56 05N 4 55W
Loch Lyon Scotland 9 E1 56 30N 4 35W
Lochmaben Scotland 11 F2 55 08N 3 27W
Lochmaddy Scotland 8 B2 57 36N 7 08W
Loch Maree Scotland 8 E2 57 40N 5 30W
Loch Meig Scotland 9 E2 57 05N 4 45W
Loch Melfort Scotland 10 D3 56 10N 5 30W
Loch Monar Scotland 9 D2 57 25N 5 02W
Loch Morar Scotland 9 D1 57 55N 5 45W
Loch More Scotland 9 E3 58 15N 4 55W
Loch Mullardoch
  Scotland 9 D2 57 27N 4 58W
Lochnagar mt. Scotland 9 F1 56 57N 3 16W
Loch Nan Clar Scotland 9 E3 58 15N 4 05W
Loch Ness Scotland 9 E2 57 02N 4 30W
Loch Nevis Scotland 8 D1/D2 57 00N 5 40W
Loch of Harray Scotland 7 A2 59 02N 3 14W
Loch Rannoch Scotland 9 E1 56 41N 4 18W
Lochranza tn. Scotland 10 D2 55 42N 5 18W
Loch Roag Scotland 8 C3 58 10N 6 50W
Loch Ryan Scotland 10 D2 55 05N 5 05W
Loch Scridain Scotland 8 C1 56 20N 6 05W
Loch Seaforth Scotland 8 C2 58 00N 6 40W
Loch Shell Scotland 8 C2 58 00N 6 25W
Loch Shiel Scotland 8 D1 56 45N 5 35W
Loch Shin Scotland 8 E3 58 05N 4 30W
Loch Snizort Scotland 8 C2 57 30N 6 30W
Loch Striven Scotland 10 D2 55 58N 5 07W
Loch Sunart Scotland 8 D1 56 40N 5 45W
Loch Sween Scotland 10 D2 55 58N 5 38W
Loch Tarbert Scotland 10 D2 55 57N 5 55W
Loch Tay Scotland 9 E1 56 31N 4 10W
Loch Torridon Scotland 8 D2 57 35N 5 46W
Lockerbie Scotland 11 F2 55 07N 3 22W
Lockhart USA 91 G2 29 54N 97 14W
Locks Heath England 16 B1 50 52N 1 17W
Loddon England 17 E3 52 32N 1 29E
Łódż Poland 53 J5 51 49N 19 28E
Lofoten Islands
  Norway 49 D4 68 30N 15 00E
Lofthouse Gate
  England 13 E2 53 44N 1 30W
Loftus England 13 F3 54 33N 0 53W
Logan, Mount Canada 88 G6 60 34N 140 25W
Logroño Spain 51 D5 42 28N 2 26W
Loire r. France 50 D4 47 20N 1 20W
Loja Spain 51 C2 37 10N 4 09W
Lolland i. Denmark 49 D1 54 45N 12 20E
Lomé Togo 80 E3 6 10N 1 21E
London Canada 89 U2 42 58N 81 15W
London England 16 C2 51 30N 0 10W
Londonderry NI 10 B1 54 59N 7 19W
Londonderry district NI 10 B1 54 55N 7 20W
Londrina Brazil 96 G9 23 18S 51 13W
Long Beach tn. USA 90 C3 33 47N 118 15W
Longbenton England 13 E4 55 02N 1 35W
Long Crendon England 16 C2 51 47N 0 59W
Long Eaton England 15 E2 52 54N 1 15W
Longford RoI 20 D3 53 44N 7 47W
Longford co. RoI 20 D3 53 40N 7 50W
Longhorsley England 13 E4 55 15N 1 46W
Longhoughton England 11 H2 55 26N 1 36W
Long Melford England 17 D3 52 05N 0 43E
Longridge England 12 D2 53 51N 2 36W
Long Sutton England 13 D2 52 47N 0 08E
Longuyon France 50 G5 49 27N 5 36E
Longwy France 50 G5 49 32N 5 46E
Lons-le-Saunier France 50 G4 46 41N 5 33E
Looe England 18 C2 51 21N 4 27W
Loop Head RoI 21 B2 52 30N 9 55W
Lora del Rio Spain 51 C2 37 39N 5 32W
Lorca Spain 51 D2 37 40N 1 41W
Loreto Italy 54 E5 43 36N 13 36E
Lorient France 50 C4 47 45N 3 21W
Los Angeles USA 90 C3 34 00N 118 15W
Lossiemouth Scotland 9 F2 57 43N 3 18W
Lostwithiel England 18 C2 50 25N 4 40W
Loudéac France 50 C5 48 11N 2 45W
Lough Allen RoI 20 C4/D4 54 15N 8 00W
Lough Arrow RoI 20 C4 54 05N 8 15W
Lough Beg NI 10 C1 54 48N 6 30W

Loughborough England 15 E2 52 47N 1 11W
Lough Carra RoI 20 B3 53 40N 9 15W
Lough Conn RoI 20 B4 54 05N 9 10W
Lough Corrib RoI 20 B3 53 10N 9 10W
Lough Cullin RoI 20 B3 53 58N 9 10W
Lough Dan RoI 21 E3 53 05N 6 17W
Lough Derg Donegal
  RoI 20 D4 54 35N 7 55W
Lough Derg Tipperary
  RoI 21 C2 52 55N 8 15W
Lough Derravaragh RoI 20 D3 53 40N 7 22W
Lough Ennell RoI 20 D3 53 28N 7 24W
Lough Eske RoI 20 C4 54 41N 8 05W
Lough Feeagh RoI 20 B3 53 57N 9 35W
Lough Finn RoI 20 C4 54 51N 8 08W
Lough Graney RoI 21 C2 52 59N 8 40W
Lough Kinale RoI 20 D3 53 46N 7 25W
Lough Leane RoI 21 B2 52 03N 9 33W
Lough Macnean Lower
  NI 10 B1 54 17N 7 50W
Lough Macnean Upper
  NI/RoI 10 B1 54 18N 7 55W
Lough Mask RoI 20 B3 53 40N 9 30W
Lough Melvin RoI/NI 20 C4 54 26N 8 05W
Lough Neagh NI 10 C1 54 35N 6 30W
Lough Oughter RoI 20 D4 54 00N 7 30W
Loughrea tn. RoI 20 C3 53 12N 8 34W
Lough Rea RoI 20 C3 53 11N 8 35W
Lough Ree RoI 20 D3 53 30N 8 00W
Lough Sheelin RoI 20 D3 53 48N 7 20W
Lough Swilly RoI 20 D5 55 20N 7 35W
Loughton England 16 D2 51 39N 0 03E
Louisburgh RoI 20 B3 53 46N 9 48W
Louisiana state USA 91 H3 32 00N 92 00W
Louisville USA 91 J4 38 13N 85 48W
Lourdes France 50 D2 43 06N 0 02W
Louth England 13 F2 53 22N 0 01W
Louth RoI 20 E3 53 57N 6 33W
Louth co. RoI 20 E3 53 55N 6 25W
Louviers France 50 E5 49 13N 1 11E
Lower Lough Erne NI 10 B1 54 30N 7 45W
Lowestoft England 17 E3 52 29N 1 45E
Lowick England 11 H2 55 39N 1 58W
Lowther Hills Scotland 11 F2 55 25N 3 45W
Luanda Angola 82 B6 8 50S 13 15E
Luarca Spain 51 B5 43 33N 6 31W
Lubbock USA 90 F3 33 35N 101 53W
Lübeck Germany 52 E6 53 52N 10 40E
Lublin Poland 53 L5 51 18N 22 31E
Lubumbashi CDR 82 E5 11 41S 27 29E
Lucan RoI 20 E3 53 22N 6 27W
Lucca Italy 54 D5 43 50N 10 30E
Luce Bay Scotland 11 E1 54 47N 4 50W
Lucena Spain 51 C2 37 25N 4 29W
Luckenwalde Germany 52 F6 52 05N 13 10E
Lucknow India 66 E5 26 50N 80 54E
Ludgershall England 16 B2 51 16N 1 37W
Ludlow England 14 D2 52 22N 2 43W
Ludwigshafen
  Germany 52 D4 49 29N 8 27E
Ludwigslust Germany 52 E6 53 20N 11 30E
Lugano Switz. 52 D3 46 01N 8 57E
Lugnaquillia mt. RoI 21 E2 52 58N 6 27W
Lugo Spain 51 B5 43 00N 7 34W
Luhans'k Ukraine 56 E4 48 35N 39 20E
Luleå Sweden 49 F4 65 35N 22 10E
Lundy i. England 18 C3 51 11N 4 40W
Lüneburg Germany 52 E6 53 15N 10 24E
Lüneville France 50 H5 48 35N 6 30E
Lurgan NI 10 C1 54 28N 6 20W
Lusaka Zambia 82 E4 15 26S 28 20E
Lusk RoI 20 E3 53 32N 6 10W
Lustenau Austria 52 D3 47 26N 9 42E
Luton England 16 C2 51 53N 0 25W
Luton u.a. England 16 C2 51 53N 0 25W
LUXEMBOURG 48 D2/E2
Luxembourg
  Luxembourg 48 E2 49 37N 6 08E
Luxor Egypt 81 M7 25 41N 32 24E
Luzern Switz. 52 D3 47 03N 8 17E
Luzhou China 69 J3 28 55N 105 25E
Luzon i. Philippines 71 G7 15 00N 122 00E
L'viv Ukraine 53 M4 49 50N 24 00E
Lybster Scotland 9 F3 58 18N 3 13W
Lydd England 17 D1 50 57N 0 55E
Lydham England 14 D2 52 31N 2 59W
Lydney England 15 D1 51 43N 2 32W
Lyme Bay England 19 E2 50 40N 2 55W
Lyme Regis England 19 E2 50 44N 2 57W
Lyminge England 17 D2 51 08N 1 05E
Lymington England 16 B1 50 46N 1 33W
Lymm England 12 D2 53 23N 2 28W
Lyndhurst England 16 B1 50 53N 1 34W
Lynher r. England 18 C2 50 33N 4 25W
Lynmouth England 18 D3 51 15N 3 50W
Lynn Lake tn. Canada 89 Q5 56 51N 101 01W
Lynton England 18 D3 51 15N 3 50W
Lyon France 50 G3 45 46N 4 50E
Lytham St. Anne's
  England 12 C2 53 45N 3 01W

M

Maam Cross RoI 20 B3 53 27N 9 33W
Maas r. Neths 48 E4 51 50N 5 32E
Maastricht Neths 48 D3 50 51N 5 42E

Mablethorpe England 13 G2 53 21N 0 15E
Macao China 69 K2 22 10N 113 40E
Macapá Brazil 96 G14 0 04N 51 04W
Macarata Italy 54 E5 43 18N 13 27E
Macclesfield England 12 D2 53 16N 2 07W
Macdonnell Ranges Australia 72 F6 24 00S 132 30E
Macduff Scotland 9 G2 57 40N 2 29W
Maceió Brazil 96 K12 9 40S 35 44W
Macgillycuddy's Reeks mts. Rol 21 B2 52 00N 9 27W
The Machars Scotland 11 E1 54 49N 4 31W
Machrihanish Scotland 10 D2 55 26N 5 44W
Machynlleth Wales 14 C2 52 35N 3 51W
Mackenzie r. Canada 88 J7 67 00N 132 00W
Mackenzie Mountains Canada 88 J7/L6 66 00N 130 00W
McKinley, Mount USA 88 E6 62 02N 151 01W
McKinney USA 91 G3 33 14N 96 37W
Mâcon France 50 G4 46 18N 4 50E
Macon USA 91 K3 32 49N 83 37W
Macroom Rol 21 C1 51 54N 8 57W
MADAGASCAR 82 H2/J5
Madeira r. Brazil 96 E12 6 00S 61 30W
Madeira Islands Atlantic Ocean 80 A8 32 45N 17 00W
Madison USA 91 J5 43 04N 89 22W
Madrid Spain 51 D4 40 25N 3 43W
Maesteg Wales 14 C1 51 37N 3 40W
Magadan Russia 63 T8 59 38N 150 50E
Magdeburg Germany 52 E6 52 08N 11 37E
Maghera NI 10 C1 54 51N 6 40W
Magherafelt NI 10 C1 54 45N 6 36W
Magherafelt district NI 10 C1 54 45N 6 30W
Maghull England 12 D2 55 32N 2 57W
Mahilyow Belarus 53 Q6 53 54N 30 20E
Mahón Spain 51 H3 39 54N 4 15E
Maidenhead England 16 C2 51 32N 0 44W
Maiden Newton England 19 E2 50 46N 2 35W
Maidstone England 17 D2 51 17N 0 32E
Main r. NI 10 C1 54 50N 6 25W
Maine state USA 91 N6 45 00N 70 00W
Mainz Germany 52 D4 50 00N 8 16E
Málaga Spain 51 C2 36 43N 4 25W
Malahide Rol 20 E3 53 27N 6 09W
Malatya Turkey 57 E2 38 22N 38 18E
MALAWI 82 F5
MALAYSIA 71 C5/E5
Mal Bay Rol 21 B2 52 40N 9 30W
MALDIVES 103
Maldon England 17 D2 51 45N 0 40E
MALI 80 C4/D5
Malin Head Rol 20 D5 55 30N 7 20W
Malin More Rol 20 C4 54 41N 8 46W
Mallaig Scotland 8 D3 57 00N 5 50W
Mallorca i. Spain 51 G3 39 50N 2 30E
Mallow Rol 21 C2 52 08N 8 39W
Malmesbury England 16 A2 51 36N 2 06W
Malmö Sweden 49 D2 55 35N 13 00E
Malpas England 12 D2 53 01N 2 46W
MALTA 54 F1
Maltby England 13 E2 53 26N 1 11W
Malton England 13 F3 54 08N 0 48W
Malvern Hills England 15 D2 52 05N 2 22W
Manacor Spain 51 G3 39 35N 3 12E
Managua Nicaragua 94 G2 12 06N 86 18W
Manama Bahrain 65 F4 26 12N 50 38E
Manaus Brazil 96 F13 3 06S 60 00W
Manchester England 12 D2 53 30N 2 15W
Manfredonia Italy 54 F4 41 37N 15 55E
Mangotsfield England 15 D1 51 29N 2 31W
Manhattan USA 93 F2 40 48N 73 58W
Manila Philippines 71 G6 14 37N 120 58E
Manitoba prov. Canada 89 R5 55 15N 100 00W
Manitoba, Lake Canada 89 R4 50 30N 98 15W
Mannheim Germany 52 D4 49 30N 8 28E
Manningtree England 17 E2 51 57N 1 04E
Manorhamilton Rol 20 C4 54 18N 8 10W
Manresa Spain 51 F4 41 43N 1 50E
Mansfield England 13 E2 53 09N 1 11W
Mansfield Woodhouse England 13 E2 53 10N 1 11W
Mantes-la-Jolie France 50 E5 48 59N 1 43E
Manuta Italy 54 D6 45 10N 10 47E
Manzanares Spain 51 D3 39 00N 3 23W
Maputo Mozambique 82 F2 25 58S 32 35E
Marabá Brazil 96 H12 5 23S 49 07W
Maracaibo Venezuela 96 C16 10 44N 71 37W
Marbella Spain 51 C2 36 31N 4 53W
Marburg Germany 52 D5 50 49N 8 36E
March England 17 D3 52 33N 0 06E
Mar del Plata Argentina 97 F6 38 00S 57 32W
Marden England 17 D2 51 11N 0 30E
Maresfield England 17 D2 51 00N 0 05E
Margam Wales 14 C1 51 34N 3 44W
Margate England 17 E2 51 24N 1 24E
Maribor Slovenia 54 F7 46 34N 15 38E
Marignane France 50 G2 43 25N 5 12E
Mariupol' Ukraine 57 E4 47 05N 37 34E
Market Deeping England 15 F2 52 41N 0 19W
Market Drayton England 15 D2 52 54N 2 29W
Market Harborough England 15 F2 52 29N 0 55W
Markethill NI 10 C1 54 18N 6 31W

Market Rasen England 13 F2 53 24N 0 21W
Market Weighton England 13 F2 53 52N 0 40W
Markinch Scotland 11 F3 56 12N 3 09W
Marlborough England 16 B2 51 26N 1 43W
Marlborough Downs England 16 B2 51 28N 1 50W
Marlow England 16 C2 51 35N 0 48W
Marple England 12 D2 53 24N 2 03W
Marmande France 50 E3 44 30N 0 10E
Marrakesh Morocco 80 C8 31 49N 8 00W
Marsala Italy 54 E2 37 48N 12 27E
Marsden West Yorkshire England 13 E2 53 36N 1 55W
Marsden Tyne and Wear England 13 E3 54 58N 1 21W
Marseille France 50 G2 43 18N 5 22E
MARSHALL ISLANDS 100 G9/H8
Marshfield England 15 D1 51 28N 2 19W
Marske-by-the-Sea England 13 E3 54 36N 1 01W
Martigny Switz. 52 C3 46 07N 7 05E
Martigues France 50 G2 43 24N 5 03E
Martinique i. Lesser Antilles 94 R12 14 30N 61 00W
Martos Spain 51 C2 37 44N 3 58W
Maryland state USA 91 L4 39 00N 77 00W
Maryport England 12 C3 54 43N 3 30W
Maryport Scotland 10 E1 54 43N 3 30W
Maseru Lesotho 82 E2 29 19S 27 29E
Masham England 13 E3 54 13N 1 40W
Mashhad Iran 65 G6 36 16N 59 34E
Massa Italy 54 D5 44 02N 10 09E
Massachusetts state USA 91 M5 42 00N 72 00W
Massif Central France 50 F3 45 00N 3 30E
Massif de la Vanoise France 50 H3 45 20N 6 20E
Mataró Spain 51 G4 41 32N 2 27E
Matera Italy 55 G4 40 40N 16 37E
Matlock England 13 E2 53 08N 1 32W
Matterhorn mt. Switz. 52 C2 45 59N 7 39E
Maubeuge France 50 F6 50 17N 3 58E
Mauchline Scotland 11 E2 55 31N 4 24W
MAURITANIA 80 B5/C6C
MAURITIUS 103
Maybole Scotland 11 E2 55 21N 4 41W
Mayenne France 50 D5 48 18N 0 37W
Maykop Russia 62 G5 44 37N 40 48E
Maynooth Rol 20 E3 53 23N 6 35W
Mayo Rol 20 B3 54 35N 9 07W
Mayo co. Rol 20 B3 53 55N 9 20W
Mazamet France 50 F2 43 29N 2 22E
Mazara del Vallo Italy 54 E2 37 40N 12 34E
Mazarrón Spain 51 E2 37 36N 1 19W
Mazatlán Mexico 94 C4 23 11N 106 25W
Mazirbe Latvia 49 F2 57 40N 22 21E
Meath co. Rol 20 E3 53 35N 6 30W
Meaux France 50 F5 48 58N 2 54E
Mecca Saudi Arabia 64 C3 21 26N 39 49E
Medan Indonesia 71 B4 3 35N 98 39E
Medellín Colombia 96 B15 6 15N 75 36W
Mediterranean Sea 54 B2/E2 35 00N 15 00E
Medway r. England 17 D2 51 24N 0 40E
Medway u.a. England 17 D2 51 25N 0 35E
Meig r. Scotland 9 E2 57 35N 4 50W
Mekong r. Asia 71 C8 16 00N 105 00E
Melbourn England 16 D3 52 05N 0 01E
Melbourne Australia 73 H3 37 45S 144 58E
Melbourne England 15 E2 52 49N 1 25W
Melilla territory Spain 51 D1 35 17N 2 57W
Melitopol' Ukraine 57 E4 46 51N 35 22E
Melksham England 16 A2 51 23N 2 09W
Melrose Scotland 11 G2 55 36N 2 44W
Meltham England 13 E2 53 36N 1 52W
Melton Mowbray England 15 F2 52 46N 0 53W
Melun France 50 F5 48 32N 2 40E
Melvich Scotland 9 F3 58 33N 3 55W
Memmingen Germany 52 E3 47 59N 10 11E
Memphis USA 91 J4 35 10N 90 00W
Menai Bridge tn. Wales 14 B3 53 14N 4 10W
Menai Strait Wales 14 B3 53 14N 4 10W
Mende France 50 F3 44 32N 3 30E
Mendip Hills England 19 E3 51 18N 2 45W
Menorca i. Spain 51 G4/H3 39 45N 4 15E
Menton France 50 H2 43 47N 7 30E
Meppel Neths 48 E5 52 42N 6 12E
Merano Italy 54 D7 46 41N 11 10E
Mere England 16 A2 51 06N 2 16W
Mérida Mexico 94 G3 20 59N 89 39W
Mérida Spain 51 B3 38 55N 6 20W
Mérignac France 50 E3 44 50N 0 36W
Merrick mt. Scotland 11 E2 55 08N 4 29W
Merriott England 19 E2 50 55N 2 49W
Mersea Island England 17 E2 51 46N 0 57
Mersey r. England 12 D2 53 20N 2 53W
Merseyside co. England 12 D2 53 30N 3 00W
Merthyr Tydfil Wales 14 C1 51 46N 3 23W
Merthyr Tydfil u.a. Wales 14 C1 51 48N 3 20W
Merton England 16 C2 51 25N 0 12W
Messina Italy 54 F3 38 13N 15 33E
Metheringham England 13 F2 53 08N 0 25W
Methil Scotland 11 F3 56 11N 3 01W
Methwold England 17 D3 52 30N 0 33E
Metz France 50 H5 49 07N 6 11E

Meuse r. Belgium/France 48 D3 50 03N 4 40E
Mevagissey England 18 C2 50 16N 4 48W
Mexborough England 13 E2 53 30N 1 17W
MEXICO 94 C5/E3
Mexico City Mexico 94 E3 19 25N 99 10W
Mexico, Gulf of Mexico 94 F4/G4 25 00N 90 00W
Miami USA 91 K2 25 45N 80 15W
Michigan state USA 91 J5/K5 45 00N 85 00W
Michigan, Lake Canada/USA 92 C2/C3 45 00N 87 00W
Middlesbrough England 13 E3 54 35N 1 14W
Middlesbrough u.a. England 13 E3 54 33N 1 04W
Middleton England 12 D2 53 33N 2 12W
Middleton-in-Teesdale England 13 D3 54 38N 2 04W
Middleton-on-the-Wolds England 13 F2 53 56N 0 33W
Middlewich England 12 D2 53 11N 2 27W
Midhurst England 16 C1 50 59N 0 45W
Midleton Rol 21 C1 51 55N 8 10W
Midlothian u.a. Scotland 11 F2 55 50N 3 05W
Midsomer Norton England 19 E3 51 17N 2 30W
Mieres Spain 51 C5 43 15N 5 46W
Mikkeli Finland 49 G3 61 44N 27 15E
Milano Italy 54 C6 45 28N 9 12E
Milborne Port England 19 E2 50 58N 2 29W
Mildenhall England 17 D3 52 21N 0 30E
Milestone Rol 21 C2 52 40N 8 05W
Milford Rol 20 D5 55 07N 7 43W
Milford Haven Wales 14 A1 51 44N 5 02W
Millau France 50 F3 44 06N 3 05E
Millisle NI 10 D1 54 37N 5 30W
Millom England 12 C3 54 13N 3 18W
Millport Scotland 10 E2 55 46N 4 55W
Millstreet Rol 21 B2 52 03N 9 04W
Milltown Malbay Rol 21 B2 52 52N 9 23W
Milngavie Scotland 11 E2 55 57N 4 19W
Milnthorpe England 12 D3 54 14N 2 46W
Milton Keynes England 16 C3 52 02N 0 42W
Milton Keynes u.a. England 16 C3 52 02N 0 42W
Milverton England 19 D3 51 02N 3 16W
Milwaukee USA 91 J5 43 03N 87 56W
Mimizan France 50 D3 44 12N 1 14W
Minch, The sd. Scotland 8 C3/D3 58 00N 6 00W
Mindanao i. Philippines 71 G5/H5 8 00N 125 00E
Minden Germany 52 D6 52 18N 8 54E
Mindoro i. Philippines 71 G6 13 00N 121 00E
Minehead England 19 D3 51 13N 3 29W
Mine Head Rol 21 D1 52 00N 7 35W
Mingulay i. Scotland 8 B1 56 49N 7 38W
Minneapolis USA 91 H5 45 00N 93 15W
Minnedosa Canada 89 R4 50 14N 99 50W
Minnesota state USA 91 H6 47 00N 95 00W
Minsk Belarus 56 C5 53 51N 27 30E
Minster England 17 D2 51 26N 0 49E
Minster England 17 E2 51 20N 1 19E
Minsterley England 14 D2 52 39N 2 55W
Mintlaw Scotland 9 G2 57 31N 2 00W
Mirfield England 13 E2 53 41N 1 42W
Miskolc Hungary 53 K4 48 07N 20 47E
Mississippi r. USA 91 H3 35 00N 90 00W
Mississippi state USA 91 H3/J3 32 00N 90 00W
Missouri r. USA 91 H4 39 00N 93 00W
Missouri state USA 91 H4 38 00N 93 00W
Mitchelstown Rol 21 C2 52 16N 8 16W
Mito Japan 70 D2 36 22N 140 29E
Mizen Head Rol 21 B1 51 30N 9 50W
Moate Rol 20 D3 53 24N 7 58W
Mobile USA 91 J3 30 40N 88 05W
Modbury England 18 D2 50 21N 3 53W
Módena Italy 54 D6 44 39N 10 55E
Modesto USA 90 B4 37 37N 121 00W
Mödling Austria 53 H4 48 06N 16 18E
Moelfre Wales 14 B3 53 21N 4 14W
Moffat Scotland 11 F2 55 20N 3 27W
Mogadishu Somalia 81 Q2 2 02N 45 21E
Mohill Rol 20 D4 53 54N 7 52W
Mo-i-Rana Norway 49 D4 66 18N 14 00E
Mold Wales 14 C3 53 10N 3 08W
MOLDOVA 53 P3
Mole r. England 16 C2 51 15N 0 20V
Molfetta Italy 55 G4 41 12N 16 36E
Mölndal Sweden 49 D2 57 40N 12 00E
Mombasa Kenya 83 F2 4 04S 39 40E
MONACO 50 H2
Monadhliath Mountains Scotland 9 E2 57 10N 4 00W
Monaghan Rol 20 E4 54 15N 6 58W
Monaghan co. Rol 20 D4/E4 54 10N 7 00W
Monasterevin Rol 21 D3 53 07N 7 02W
Mönchengladbach Germany 52 C5 51 12N 6 25E
Moncton Canada 89 Y3 46 04N 64 50W
Mondovi Italy 54 B6 44 23N 7 49E
Moneen Rol 20 C3 53 26N 8 54W
Moneymore NI 10 C1 54 42N 6 40W
Monfalcone Italy 54 E6 45 49N 13 32E
MONGOLIA 68/69 G7/K7
Moniaive Scotland 11 F2 55 12N 3 55W
Monifieth Scotland 9 G1 56 29N 2 49W
Monmouth Wales 14 D1 51 50N 2 43W

Monmouthshire u.a. Wales 14 D1 51 47N 2 55W
Monopoli Italy 55 G4 40 57N 17 18E
Monrovia Liberia 80 B3 6 20N 10 46W
Montana Bulgaria 55 K5 43 25N 23 11E
Montana state USA 90 E6 47 00N 111 00W
Montargis France 50 F4 48 00N 2 44E
Montauban France 50 E3 44 01N 1 20E
Montbéliard France 50 H4 47 31N 6 48E
Mont Blanc France/Italy 50 H3 45 50N 6 52E
Montceau-les-Mines France 50 G4 46 40N 4 23E
Mont-de-Marsan France 50 D2 43 54N 0 30W
Montdidier France 50 F5 49 39N 2 35E
Monte Carlo Monaco 50 H2 43 44N 7 25E
Montélimar France 50 G3 44 33N 4 45E
Montepulciano Italy 54 D5 43 05N 11 46E
Monterrey Mexico 94 D5 25 40N 100 20W
Montevideo Uruguay 97 F6 34 55S 56 10W
Montgomery USA 91 J3 32 22N 86 20W
Montgomery Wales 14 C2 52 34N 3 10W
Montluçon France 50 F4 46 20N 2 36E
Montmirail France 50 F5 48 52N 3 34E
Montmorilon France 50 E4 46 26N 0 52E
Montoro Spain 51 C3 38 02N 4 23W
Montpelier Rol 21 C2 52 45N 8 30W
Montpellier France 50 F2 43 36N 3 53E
Montréal Canada 89 W3 45 32N 73 36W
Montreux Switz. 52 C3 46 27N 6 55E
Montrose Scotland 9 G2 56 43N 2 29W
Montserrat i. Lesser Antilles 94 P9 16 45N 62 14W
Monza Italy 54 C6 45 35N 9 16E
Mooncoin Rol 21 D2 52 17N 7 15W
Moone Rol 21 D2 52 58N 6 49W
Moorfoot Hills Scotland 11 F2/G2 55 50N 3 00W
Moosonee Canada 89 U4 51 18N 80 39W
Mora Sweden 49 D3 61 00N 14 30E
Moray u.a. Scotland 9 F2 57 20N 3 10W
Moray Firth Scotland 9 F2 57 45N 3 45W
Morcenx France 50 D3 44 02N 0 55W
Morecambe England 12 D3 54 04N 2 53W
Morecambe Bay England 12 D3 54 10N 2 55W
Morelia Mexico 94 D3 19 40N 101 11W
Moreton England 12 C2 53 24N 3 07W
Moretonhampstead England 18 D2 50 40N 3 45W
Moreton-in-Marsh England 15 E1 51 59N 1 42W
Morlaix France 50 C5 48 35N 3 50W
Morley England 13 E2 53 46N 1 36W
MOROCCO 80 C8/D8
Morón de la Frontera Spain 51 C2 37 07N 5 27W
Morpeth England 13 E4 55 10N 1 41W
Morte Point England 18 C3 51 10N 4 15W
Mosborough England 13 E2 53 19N 1 22W
Moscow Russia 62 F8 55 45N 37 42E
Mosel r. Germany/France 52 C4 50 00N 7 00E
Mossley NI 10 D1 54 42N 5 57W
Mossoró Brazil 96 K12 5 10S 37 18W
Mostar Bosnia-Herzegovina 55 G5 43 20N 17 50E
Móstoles Spain 51 D4 40 19N 3 53W
Mosul Iraq 64 D6 36 21N 43 08E
Motherwell Scotland 11 F2 55 48N 3 59W
Motril Spain 51 D2 36 45N 3 31W
Moulins France 50 F4 47 00N 3 48E
Mountain Ash Wales 14 C1 51 42N 3 24W
Mount Bellew Rol 20 C3 53 28N 8 30W
Mount Leinster Rol 21 E2 52 36N 6 42W
Mountmellick tn. Rol 21 D3 53 07N 7 20W
Mountrath Rol 21 D3 53 00N 7 27W
Mounts Bay England 18 B2 50 05N 5 30W
Mountshannon Rol 21 C2 52 56N 8 26W
Mountsorrel England 15 E2 52 44N 1 07W
Moura Portugal 51 B3 38 08N 7 27W
Mourne Mountains NI 10 C1 54 05N 6 05W
Mousehole England 18 B2 50 04N 5 34W
Moville Rol 20 D5 55 11N 7 03W
Moy NI 10 C1 54 27N 6 42W
Moycullen Rol 20 B3 53 20N 9 10W
Moygashel NI 10 C1 54 31N 6 46W
Moyle district NI 10 C1 54 10N 6 10W
Moyvore Rol 20 D3 53 22N 7 37W
MOZAMBIQUE 82 F3/G5
Much Wenlock England 15 D2 52 36N 2 34W
Muck i. Scotland 8 C1 56 50N 6 15W
Muckross Rol 21 B2 52 00N 9 29W
Muff Rol 20 D5 55 04N 7 16W
Muine Bheag Rol 21 E2 52 41N 6 58W
Muirkirk Scotland 11 E2 55 31N 4 04W
Muir of Ord Scotland 9 E2 57 31N 4 27W
Mulhacén mt. Spain 51 D2 37 04N 3 19W
Mülheim an der Ruhr Germany 48 E4 51 25N 6 50E
Mulhouse France 50 H4 47 45N 7 21E
Mulhuddart Rol 20 E3 53 24N 6 24W
Mulkear r. Rol 21 C2 52 38N 8 24W
Mull i. Scotland 8 D1 56 25N 6 00W
Mullet Peninsula Rol 20 A4 54 07N 10 05W
Mull Head Scotland 7 B2 59 20N 2 58W
Mullinahone Rol 21 D2 52 30N 7 30W

Mullinavat Rol 21 D2 52 22N 7 10W
Mullingar Rol 20 D3 53 32N 7 20W
Mullion England 18 B2 50 01N 5 14W
Mull of Galloway
  Scotland 10 E1 54 38N 4 55W
Mull of Kintyre Scotland 10 D2 55 17N 5 55W
Mull of Oa Scotland 10 C2 55 35N 6 20W
Mull, Sound of Scotland 8 D1 56 30N 6 00W
Multan Pakistan 66 C6 30 10N 71 36E
Mumbai India 66 C3 18 56N 72 51E
Mundesley England 17 E3 52 53N 1 26E
Munich Germany 52 E4 48 08N 11 35E
Münster Germany 52 C5 51 58N 7 37E
Murcia Spain 51 E2 37 59N 1 08W
Murmansk Russia 62 F10 68 59N 33 08E
Murray r. Australia 73 H3 35 30S 144 00E
Murray Bridge Australia 73 G3 35 10S 139 17E
Murton England 13 E4 54 49N 1 23W
Muş Turkey 57 F2 38 45N 41 30E
Muscat Oman 65 G3 23 37N 58 38E
Mushin Nigeria 80 E3 6 30N 3 15E
Musselburgh Scotland 11 F2 55 57N 3 04W
Mutare Zimbabwe 82 F4 18 58N 32 40E
Mutton Island i. Rol 21 B2 52 49N 9 31W
MYANMAR 71 B7
Mybster Scotland 9 F3 58 27N 3 25W
Mykolayiv Ukraine 57 D4 46 57N 32 00E
Mynydd Eppynt Wales 14 C2 52 02N 3 35W
Mynydd Preseli Wales 14 B1 51 58N 4 45W
Mytilini Greece 55 M3 39 06N 26 34E
Mytishchi Russia 56 E6 55 54N 37 47E

N

Naas Rol 20 E3 53 13N 6 39W
Naestved Denmark 49 D2 55 14N 11 47E
Náfplio Greece 55 K2 37 34N 22 48E
Nagano Japan 70 C2 36 39N 138 10E
Nagasaki Japan 70 A1 32 45N 129 52E
Nagles Mountains Rol 21 C2 52 10N 8 25W
Nagoya Japan 70 C2 35 08N 136 53E
Nagpur India 66 D4 21 10N 79 12E
Nailsea England 19 E3 51 26N 2 46W
Nailsworth England 15 D1 51 42N 2 14W
Nairn Scotland 9 F2 57 35N 3 53W
Nairobi Kenya 83 E4 1 17S 36 50E
Namib Desert Namibia 82 B3/C2 22 00S 14 00E
NAMIBIA 82 C3
Namur Belgium 48 C3 50 28N 4 52E
Nanchang China 69 L3 28 33N 115 58E
Nancy France 50 H5 48 42N 6 12E
Nanjing China 69 L4 32 03N 118 47E
Nantes France 50 D4 47 14N 1 35W
Nantwich England 12 D2 53 04N 2 32W
Naples Italy 54 F4 40 50N 14 15E
Naples USA 91 K2 26 09N 81 48W
Narberth Wales 14 B1 51 48N 4 45W
Narbonne France 50 F2 43 11N 3 00E
Narborough England 15 E2 52 35N 1 11W
Narvik Norway 49 E4 68 26N 17 25E
Naseby England 15 F2 52 23N 0 59W
Nashville USA 91 J4 36 10N 86 50W
Nassau Bahamas 95 J5 25 05N 77 20W
Nasser, Lake Egypt 81 M6 22 35N 31 40E
Nässjö Sweden 49 D2 57 40N 14 40E
Natal Brazil 96 K12 5 46S 35 15W
Natchez USA 91 H3 31 32N 91 24W
Naul Rol 20 E3 53 35N 6 17W
NAURU 100 G7
Navan Rol 20 E3 53 39N 6 41W
Navenby England 13 F2 53 06N 0 32W
Naver r. Scotland 9 E3 58 30N 4 10W
Ndjamena Chad 81 J4 12 10N 14 59E
Néapoli Greece 55 K2 36 31N 23 03E
Neath Wales 14 C1 51 40N 3 48W
Neath Port Talbot u.a.
  Wales 14 C1 51 37N 3 43W
Nebraska state USA 90 F5 42 00N 102 00W
Needham Market
  England 17 E3 52 09N 1 03E
Needles, The England 16 B1 50 39N 1 35W
Nefyn Wales 14 B2 52 56N 4 32W
Negro r. Brazil 96 D13 0 05S 67 00W
Nelson England 12 D2 53 51N 2 13W
Neman r.
  Lithuania/Russia 56 C5 55 00N 22 00E
Nenagh Rol 21 C2 52 52N 8 12W
Nene r. England 15 F2 52 25N 0 30W
Nene r. England 17 D3 52 45N 0 10E
NEPAL 66/67 E5/F5
Nephin mt. Rol 20 B4 54 01N 9 22W
Nephin Beg Range Rol 20 B3/B4 54 00N 9 34W
Nerva Spain 51 B2 37 41N 6 33W
Neston England 12 C2 53 18N 3 03W
NETHERLANDS 48 D5/E5
Nether Stowey
  England 19 D3 51 09N 3 10W
Netzahualcóyotl
  Mexico 94 E3 19 24N 99 02W
Neubrandenburg
  Germany 52 F6 53 33N 13 16E
Neuchâtel Switz. 52 C3 46 55N 6 56E
Neufchâteau France 50 G5 48 21N 5 42E
Neufchâtel-en-Bray
  France 48 E5 49 44N 1 26E
Neumünster Germany 52 D7 54 05N 9 59E
Neuruppin Germany 52 F6 52 56N 12 49E

Neuss Germany 52 C5 51 12N 6 42E
Neustrelitz Germany 52 F6 53 22N 13 05E
Nevada state USA 90 C4 39 00N 118 00W
Nevers France 50 F4 47 00N 3 09E
New Abbey Scotland 11 F1 54 59N 3 38W
New Alresford England 16 B2 51 06N 1 10W
Newark USA 91 M5 40 44N 74 24W
Newark-on-Trent
  England 13 F2 53 05N 0 49W
New Ash Green
  England 17 D2 51 21N 0 18E
Newbiggin-by-the-Sea
  England 13 E4 55 11N 1 30W
Newbridge Wales 14 C1 51 41N 3 09W
Newbridge-on-Wye
  Wales 14 C2 52 13N 3 27W
New Brunswick prov.
  Canada 89 X3 47 30N 66 00W
New Buildings NI 10 B1 54 56N 7 21W
Newburgh Scotland 9 F1 56 21N 3 15W
Newburn England 13 E3 54 59N 1 43W
Newbury England 16 B2 51 25N 1 20W
New Caledonia i.
  Pacific Ocean 73 M6/N6 22 00S 165 00E
Newcastle NI 10 D1 54 12N 5 54W
Newcastle Emlyn
  Wales 14 B2 52 02N 4 28W
Newcastle-under-Lyme
  England 12 D2 53 00N 2 14W
Newcastle upon Tyne
  England 13 E3 54 59N 1 35W
Newcastle West Rol 21 B2 52 27N 9 03W
New Cumnock
  Scotland 11 E2 55 24N 4 12W
New Deer Scotland 9 G2 57 30N 2 12W
New Delhi India 66 D5 28 37N 77 14E
Newfoundland i.
  Canada 89 Z3 48 15N 57 00W
Newfoundland prov.
  Canada 89 Y5/AA3 52 30N 62 30W
New Galloway
  Scotland 11 E2 55 05N 4 10W
New Guinea i.
  Pacific Ocean 72/73 F10/J9 5 00S 141 00E
New Hampshire state
  USA 91 M5 43 00N 72 00W
New Haven USA 91 M5 41 18N 72 55W
New Holland England 13 F2 53 42N 0 22W
Newick England 16 D1 50 58N 0 01E
Newinn Rol 21 D2 52 26N 7 53W
New Jersey state USA 91 M4 40 00N 75 00W
New Liskeard Canada 89 V3 47 31N 79 41W
Newlyn England 18 B2 50 06N 5 34W
Newmachar Scotland 9 G2 57 16N 2 10W
Newmains Scotland 11 F2 55 47N 3 53W
Newmarket England 17 D3 52 15N 0 25E
Newmarket Rol 21 C2 52 13N 9 00W
Newmarket-on-Fergus
  Rol 21 C2 52 45N 8 53W
New Mexico state USA 91 E3 35 00N 107 00W
New Milton England 16 B1 50 46N 1 40W
New Orleans USA 91 H2 30 00N 90 03W
Newport Telford and Wrekin
  England 15 D2 52 47N 2 22W
Newport Isle of Wight
  England 16 B1 50 42N 1 18W
Newport Essex England 17 D2 51 58N 0 13E
Newport Mayo Rol 20 B3 53 53N 9 32W
Newport Tipperary Rol 21 C2 52 43N 8 25W
Newport Pembrokeshire
  Wales 14 B2 52 01N 4 50W
Newport Newport
  Wales 14 C1 51 35N 3 00W
Newport u.a. Wales 14 C1/D1 51 33N 3 00W
Newport Bay Rol 20 B3 53 51N 9 41W
Newport News USA 91 L4 36 59N 76 26W
Newport-on-Tay
  Scotland 9 G1 56 27N 2 56W
Newport Pagnell
  England 16 C3 52 05N 0 44W
Newquay England 18 B2 50 25N 5 05W
New Quay Wales 14 B2 52 13N 4 22W
New Radnor Wales 14 C2 52 15N 3 10W
New Romney England 17 D1 50 59N 0 57E
New Ross Rol 21 E2 52 24N 6 56W
New Rossington
  England 13 F2 53 29N 1 04W
Newry NI 10 C1 54 11N 6 20W
Newry and Mourne
  district NI 10 C1 54 10N 6 35W
New Sauchie Scotland 11 F3 56 08N 3 41W
New Scone Scotland 9 F1 56 25N 3 25W
Newton Abbot
  England 18 D2 50 32N 3 36W
Newton Aycliffe
  England 13 E3 54 37N 1 34W
Newton Mearns
  Scotland 11 E2 55 45N 4 18W
Newtonmore Scotland 9 E2 57 04N 4 08W
Newton Stewart
  Scotland 11 E1 54 57N 4 29W
Newtown Rol 21 D2 52 52N 7 07W
Newtown Wales 14 C2 52 32N 3 19W
Newtownabbey NI 10 D1 54 40N 5 54W
Newtownabbey
  district NI 10 C1/D1 54 40N 6 05W
Newtownards NI 10 D1 54 36N 5 41W

Newtown Cunningham
  Rol 20 D4 54 59N 7 31W
Newtownhamilton NI 10 C1 54 12N 6 35W
Newtownmountkennedy
  Rol 21 E3 53 06N 6 07W
Newtown St. Boswells
  Scotland 11 G2 55 34N 2 40W
Newtownstewart NI 10 B1 54 43N 7 24W
New Tredegar Wales 14 C1 51 44N 3 15W
New York USA 91 M5 40 40N 73 50W
New York state USA 91 L5 43 00N 76 00W
NEW ZEALAND 73
Neyland Wales 14 B1 51 43N 4 57W
Niagara Falls tn.
  Canada 93 E2 43 05N 79 06W
Niamey Niger 80 E4 13 32N 2 05E
NICARAGUA 95 G2
Nice France 50 H2 43 42N 7 16E
Nicobar Islands India 67 G1 8 30N 94 00E
Nicosia Cyprus 57 D2 35 11N 33 23E
Nienburg Germany 52 D6 52 38N 9 13E
NIGER 80 E5/G5
Niger r. West Africa 80 F3 5 30N 6 15E
NIGERIA 80 F4/G4
Nigg Scotland 9 G2 57 08N 2 03W
Nigg Bay Highland
  Scotland 9 E2 57 42N 4 01W
Nigg Bay Aberdeenshire
  Scotland 9 G2 57 08N 2 03W
Nijmegen Neths 48 D4 51 50N 5 52E
Nikopol' Ukraine 56 D4 45 34N 34 25E
Nile r. Sudan/Egypt 81 M7 30 30N 31 40E
Nîmes France 50 G2 43 50N 4 21E
Niort France 50 D4 46 19N 0 27W
Nith r. Scotland 11 F2 55 20N 3 50W
Nizhniy Novgorod
  Russia 62 G8 56 20N 44 00E
Nordhausen Germany 52 E5 51 31N 10 48E
North Cape Norway 49 F5 71 11N 25 40E
Norfolk co. England 17 D3 52 45N 1 00E
Norfolk USA 91 L4 36 54N 76 18W
Norham England 11 G2 55 43N 2 10W
Normanton England 13 E2 53 42N 1 25W
Norrköping Sweden 49 E2 58 35N 16 10E
Northallerton England 13 E3 54 20N 1 26W
Northam England 18 C3 51 02N 4 14W
Northampton England 15 F2 52 14N 0 54W
Northamptonshire co.
  England 15 E2/F2 52 20N 1 00W
North Ayrshire u.a.
  Scotland 11 E2 55 30N 5 05W
North Baddesley
  England 16 B1 50 58N 1 27W
North Ballachulish
  Scotland 8 D1 56 42N 5 11W
North Berwick Scotland 11 G3 56 04N 2 44W
North Carolina state
  USA 91 L4 36 00N 80 00W
North Channel
  British Isles 10 D1/D2 55 20N 5 50W
North Dakota state
  USA 90/91 F6/G6 47 00N 102 00W
North Dorset Downs
  England 19 E2 50 40N 2 30W
North Down co. NI 10 D1 54 40N 5 40W
North Downs England 16 C2 51 13N 0 30W
North East Lincolnshire
  u.a. England 13 F2 53 30N 0 10W
Northern Ireland UK 10 B1/C1 54 40N 7 00W
NORTHERN MARIANAS
  100 F9
North Foreland England 17 E2 51 23N 1 27E
North Hykeham
  England 13 F2 53 12N 0 34W
Northiam England 17 D1 50 59N 0 36E
North Hykeham [North Kessock Scotland] 9 E2 57 30N 4 15W
North Kessock Scotland 9 E2 57 30N 4 15W
NORTH KOREA 69 N5/N6
North Lanarkshire u.a.
  Scotland 11 E2/F2 55 50N 3 55W
Northleach England 15 E1 51 51N 1 50W
North Lincolnshire u.a.
  England 13 F2 53 40N 0 40W
North Petherton
  England 19 D3 51 06N 3 01W
North Pole
  Arctic Ocean 101 90 00N
North Ronaldsay i.
  Scotland 7 B2 59 23N 2 26W
North Shields England 13 E4 55 01N 1 26W
North Somercotes
  England 13 G2 53 28N 0 08E
North Somerset u.a.
  England 19 E3 51 15N 2 50W
North Sound Rol 21 B3 53 11N 9 43W
North Sound, The
  Scotland 7 B2 59 17N 2 45W
North Tawton England 18 D2 50 48N 3 53W
North Tidworth
  England 16 B2 51 16N 1 40W
North Uist i. Scotland 8 B2 57 04N 7 15W
Northumberland co.
  England 12 D4 55 10N 2 05W
North Walsham
  England 17 E3 52 50N 1 24E
Northwest Highlands
  Scotland 8/9 D2/E3 58 00N 5 00W

Northwest Territories
  territory Canada 88 L6/N6 65 15N 115 00W
North Wheatley
  England 13 F2 53 22N 0 52W
Northwich England 12 D2 53 16N 2 32W
North Wingfield
  England 13 E2 53 09N 1 24W
North York Moors
  England 13 F3 55 22N 0 45W
North Yorkshire co.
  England 13 E3/F3 54 10N 2 10W
Norton England 13 F3 54 08N 0 48W
NORWAY 49 C2/F4
Norwich England 17 E3 52 38N 1 18E
Norwich USA 93 F2 41 32N 72 05W
Noss Head Scotland 9 F3 58 28N 3 04W
Nottingham England 15 E2 52 58N 1 10W
Nottinghamshire co.
  England 13 E2/F2 53 20N 1 00W
Nouakchott Mauritania 80 A5 18 09N 15 58W
Novara Italy 54 C6 45 27N 8 37E
Nova Scotia prov.
  Canada 89 Y2/Y3 44 30N 65 00W
Novgorod Russia 62 F8 58 30N 31 20E
Novi Sad
  Serbia & Montenegro 55 H6 45 15N 19 51E
Novosibirsk Russia 63 L8 55 04N 83 05E
Nubian Desert Sudan 81 M6 21 00N 33 00E
Nullarbor Plain
  Australia 72 E4 32 00S 128 00E
Nuneaton England 15 E2 52 32N 1 28W
Nuoro Italy 54 C4 40 20N 9 21E
Nuremberg Germany 52 E4 49 27N 11 05E
Nuuk Greenland 89 AA6 64 10N 51 40W
Nyasa, Lake
  Southern Africa 82 F5 12 00S 35 00E
Nykøbing Denmark 49 D1 54 47N 11 53E
Nyköping Sweden 49 E2 58 45N 17 03E
Nyons France 50 G3 44 22N 5 08E

O

Oadby England 15 E2 52 36N 1 04W
Oakengates England 15 D2 52 42N 2 28W
Oakham England 16 F2 52 40N 00 43W
Oakland USA 90 B4 37 50N 122 15W
Oakley England 16 B2 51 15N 1 11W
Oakley Scotland 11 F3 56 05N 3 35W
Ob' r. Russia 62 J10 65 30N 66 00E
Oban Scotland 8 D1 56 25N 5 29W
Oberhausen Germany 52 C5 51 27N 6 50E
Ob', Gulf of
  Gulf of Russia 62 K10 68 00N 74 00E
O'Briensbridge Rol 21 C2 52 45N 8 30W
Ochil Hills Scotland 11 F3 56 15N 3 30W
Odda Norway 49 C3 60 03N 6 34E
Oddsta Scotland 7 D3 60 37N 0 59W
Odense Denmark 49 D2 55 24N 10 25E
Oder r. Europe 52 G6 52 00N 15 00E
Odessa Ukraine 57 D4 46 30N 30 46E
Offaly co. Rol 20 D3 53 15N 7 35W
Offenbach am Main
  Germany 52 D5 50 06N 8 46E
Offenburg Germany 52 C4 48 29N 7 57E
Ohio state USA 91 K5 40 00N 83 00W
Ohio r. USA 91 J4 38 00N 86 00W
Oilgate Rol 21 E2 52 25N 6 32W
Ōita Japan 70 B1 33 15N 131 36E
Okehampton England 18 C2 50 44N 4 00W
Oklahoma state USA 91 G4 36 00N 98 00W
Oklahoma City USA 91 G4 35 28N 97 33W
Öland i. Sweden 49 E2 56 45N 16 50E
Olbia Italy 54 C4 40 56N 9 30E
Oldbury England 15 D2 52 30N 2 00W
Oldcastle Rol 20 D3 53 46N 7 10W
Oldenburg Germany 52 D6 53 08N 8 13E
Old Fletton England 16 C3 52 34N 0 12W
Oldham England 12 D2 53 33N 2 07W
Old Head of Kinsale c.
  Rol 21 C1 51 40N 8 30W
Oldmeldrum Scotland 9 G2 57 20N 2 20W
Olhão Portugal 51 B2 37 01N 7 50W
Ollerton England 13 E2 53 12N 1 00W
Olney England 16 C3 52 09N 0 43W
Olsztyn Poland 53 K6 53 48N 20 29E
Olten Switz. 52 C3 47 22N 7 55E
Ólympos mt. Greece 55 J4 40 05N 22 21E
Omagh NI 10 B1 54 36N 7 18W
Omagh district NI 10 B1 54 37N 7 30W
Omaha USA 91 G5 41 15N 96 00W
OMAN 65 F2/G3
Oman, Gulf of
  Iran/Oman 65 G3 24 30N 58 30E
Omdurman Sudan 81 M5 15 37N 32 29E
Omeath Rol 20 E4 54 06N 6 17W
Omsk Russia 62 K8 55 00N 73 22E
Ōmuta Japan 70 B1 33 02N 130 26E
Onezhskoye Ozero l.
  Russia 62 F9 62 00N 40 00E
Ontario prov. Canada 89 S4/U4 51 00N 91 00W
Ontario, Lake
  Canada/USA 93 E2 43 45N 78 00W
Oola Rol 21 C2 52 33N 8 16W
Oostende Belgium 48 A4 51 13N 2 55E
Opava Czech Rep. 53 H4 49 58N 17 55E
Opole Poland 53 H5 50 40N 17 56E
Oporto Portugal 51 A4 41 09N 8 37W
Oran Algeria 80 D9 35 45N 0 38W

Orange France 50 G3 44 08N 4 48E
Oranmore RoI 20 C3 53 16N 8 54W
Örebro Sweden 49 E2 59 17N 15 13E
Oregon state USA 90 B5/C5 44 00N 120 00E
Oregon City USA 90 B6 45 21N 122 36W
Orel Russia 62 F7 52 58N 36 04E
Orenburg Russia 62 H7 51 50N 55 00E
Orense Spain 51 B5 42 20N 7 52W
Orford England 17 E3 52 06N 1 31E
Orihuela Spain 51 E3 38 05N 0 56W
Orinoco r. Venezuela 96 E15 8 00N 64 00W
Oristano Italy 54 C3 39 54N 8 36E
Orkney Islands u.a.
 Scotland 7 A1/B2 59 00N 3 00W
Orlando USA 91 K2 28 33N 81 21W
Orléans France 50 E4 47 54N 1 54E
Ormskirk England 12 D2 53 35N 2 54W
Oronsay i. Scotland 10 C3 56 00N 6 15W
Orrell England 12 D2 53 33N 2 45W
Orsha Belarus 56 D5 54 30N 30 23E
Orthez France 50 D2 43 29N 0 46W
Ortigueira Spain 51 B5 43 43N 8 13W
Ortona Italy 54 F5 42 21N 14 24E
Orvieto Italy 54 E5 42 43N 12 06E
Orwell r. England 17 E3 52 00N 1 15E
Ōsaka Japan 70 C1 34 40N 135 30E
Oshawa Canada 89 V2 43 53N 78 51W
Oslo Norway 49 D2 59 56N 10 45E
Osmaniye Turkey 57 E2 37 04N 36 15E
Osnabrück Germany 52 D6 52 17N 8 03E
Ossett England 13 E2 53 41N 1 35W
Östersund Sweden 49 D3 63 10N 14 40E
Östervall Sweden 49 E3 62 20N 15 06E
Ostrava Czech Rep. 53 J4 49 50N 18 15E
Oswaldtwistle England 12 D2 53 44N 2 24W
Oswestry England 14 C2 52 52N 3 03W
Otford England 17 D2 51 19N 0 12E
Otley England 13 E2 53 54N 1 41W
Otranto Italy 55 H4 40 08N 18 30E
Ottawa Canada 89 V3 45 24N 75 38W
Otterburn England 12 D4 55 14N 2 10W
Ottery St. Mary
 England 19 D2 50 45N 3 17W
Ouagadougou Burkina 80 D4 12 20N 1 40W
Oughterard RoI 20 B3 53 26N 9 19W
Oulart RoI 21 E2 53 30N 6 23W
Oulu Finland 49 G4 65 02N 25 27E
Oundle England 15 F2 52 29N 0 29W
Ouse r. North Yorkshire
 England 13 E3 54 05N 1 15W
Ouse r. East Sussex
 England 16 D1 50 55N 0 03E
Outer Hebrides is.
 Scotland 8 B2/B3 58 00N 7 00W
Outwell England 17 D3 52 37N 0 14E
Overton England 16 B2 51 15N 1 15W
Overton Wales 14 D2 52 58N 2 56W
Oviedo Spain 51 C5 43 21N 7 18W
Owen Sound Canada 89 U2 44 3N 80 56W
Oxford England 16 B2 51 46N 1 15W
Oxfordshire co.
 England 16 B2 51 50N 1 25W
Oxted England 16 C2 51 15N 0 01W
Oysterhaven RoI 21 C1 51 41N 8 26W
Ozero Balkhash l.
 Kazakhstan 62 K6 46 00N 75 00E
Ozero Baykal l. Russia 63 N7 54 00N 109 00E
Ozieri Italy 54 C4 40 35N 9 01E

P

Pacific Ocean 100
Padang Indonesia 71 C3 1 00S 100 21E
Paddock Wood tn.
 England 17 D2 51 11N 0 23E
Paderborn Germany 52 D5 51 43N 8 44E
Padiham England 12 D2 53 49N 2 19W
Padstow England 18 C2 50 33N 4 56W
Padua Italy 54 D6 45 24N 11 53E
Paisley Scotland 11 E2 55 50N 4 26W
PAKISTAN 66 B5/C5
PALAU 100 D8 7 30N 134 30E
Palawan i. Philippines 71 F5/F6 10 00N 119 00E
Palembang Indonesia 71 C3 2 59S 104 45E
Palencia Spain 51 C3 41 01N 4 32W
Palermo Italy 54 E3 38 08N 13 23E
Palma de Mallorca
 Spain 51 G3 39 35N 2 39E
Palmer USA 88 F6 61 35N 149 10W
Palmyra Syria 64 C5 34 40N 38 10E
Pamiers France 50 E2 43 07N 1 36E
Pampas geog. reg.
 Argentina 97 E6 36 00S 63 00W
Pamplona Spain 51 E5 42 49N 1 39W
PANAMA 95 H1/J1
Panama Canal Panama 95 J1 9 00N 80 00W
Panama City Panama 95 J1 8 57N 79 30W
Pangbourne England 16 B2 51 29N 1 05W
Papa Sound Scotland 7 B2 59 20N 2 54W
Papa, Sound of Scotland 7 C3 60 37N 1 40W
Papa Stour i. Scotland 7 C3 60 20N 1 42W
Papa Westray i. Scotland 7 B3 59 22N 2 54W
PAPUA NEW GUINEA 73 H9/K9
PARAGUAY 96 F9
Paraguay r.
 Paraguay/Argentina 96 F8 26 30S 58 00W

Paramaribo Suriname 96 F15 5 52N 55 14W
Paraná r.
 Paraguay/Argentina 96 F7 27 00S 56 00W
Paris France 50 F5 48 52N 2 20E
Parkano Finland 49 F3 62 03N 23 00E
Parma Italy 54 D6 44 48N 10 19E
Parnaíba Brazil 96 J13 2 58S 41 46W
Páros Greece 55 L2 37 04N 25 06E
Parrett r. England 19 E3 51 05N 2 54W
Parthenay France 50 D4 46 39N 0 14W
Partry RoI 20 B3 53 42N 9 16W
Partry Mountains RoI 20 B3 53 39N 9 27W
Pașcani Romania 53 N3 47 14N 26 46E
Passage East RoI 21 E2 52 13N 6 59W
Passage West tn. RoI 21 C1 51 52N 8 20W
Passau Germany 52 F4 48 35N 13 28E
Patagonia geog. reg.
 Argentina 97 C2/D4 48 00S 70 00W
Pateley Bridge tn.
 England 13 E3 54 05N 1 45W
Patna Scotland 11 E2 55 20N 4 30W
Patras Greece 55 J3 38 14N 21 44E
Patrickswell RoI 21 C2 52 36N 8 42W
Patrington England 13 F2 53 41N 0 02W
Pau France 50 D2 43 18N 0 22W
Pavia Italy 54 C6 45 12N 9 09E
Pavullo nel Frignano
 Italy 54 D6 44 20N 10 49E
Peacehaven England 16 C1 50 47N 0 01E
Peč
 Serbia & Montenegro 55 J5 42 40N 20 19E
Pécs Hungary 53 J3 46 04N 18 15E
Peebles Scotland 11 F2 55 39N 3 12W
Peel Isle of Man 12 B3 54 14N 4 42W
Pelopónnisos geog. reg.
 Greece 55 J2/K2 37 00N 22 00E
Pembridge England 14 D2 52 14N 2 53W
Pembroke Wales 14 B1 51 41N 4 55W
Pembroke Dock Wales 14 B1 51 42N 4 56W
Pembrokeshire u.a.
 Wales 14 A1/B1 51 50N 5 00W
Pembury England 17 D2 51 08N 0 19E
Penarth Wales 14 C1 51 27N 3 11W
Pencoed Wales 14 C1 51 31N 3 30W
Pendine Wales 14 B1 51 34N 4 35W
Penicuik Scotland 11 F2 55 50N 3 14W
Penistone England 13 E2 53 32N 1 37W
Penkridge England 15 D2 52 44N 2 07W
Penmaenmawr Wales 14 C2 53 16N 3 54W
Pennines England 12/13 D3/E2 54 30N 2 10W
Pennsylvania state
 USA 91 L5 41 00N 78 00W
Penrhyndeudraeth
 Wales 14 B2 52 56N 4 04W
Penrith England 12 D3 54 40N 2 44W
Penryn England 18 C2 50 09N 5 06W
Pensilva England 18 C2 50 30N 4 25W
Pentland Firth Scotland 7 A1 58 45N 3 10W
Pentland Hills Scotland 11 F2 55 45N 3 30W
Pen-y-ghent sum.
 England 12 D3 54 10N 2 14W
Penygroes Wales 14 B3 53 04N 4 17W
Penzance England 18 B2 50 07N 5 33W
Périgueux France 50 E3 45 12N 0 44E
Perm' Russia 62 H8 58 01N 56 10E
Pernik Bulgaria 55 K5 42 36N 23 03E
Péronne France 50 F5 49 56N 2 57E
Perpignan France 50 F2 42 42N 2 54E
Perranporth England 18 B2 50 20N 5 09W
Perth Australia 72 C4 31 58S 115 49E
Perth Scotland 9 F1 56 42N 3 28W
Perth and Kinross u.a.
 Scotland 9 F1 56 45N 3 50W
PERU 96B11/C11
Perugia Italy 54 E5 43 07N 12 23E
Pesaro Italy 54 E5 43 54N 12 54E
Pescara Italy 54 F5 42 27N 14 13E
Peshawar Pakistan 66 C6 34 01N 71 40E
Pessac France 50 D3 44 49N 0 37W
Peterborough England 16 C2 52 35N 0 15W
Peterculter Scotland 9 G2 57 05N 2 16W
Peterhead Scotland 9 H2 57 30N 1 46W
Peterlee England 13 E3 54 46N 1 19W
Petersfield England 16 C2 51 00N 0 56W
Petrolina Brazil 96 J12 9 22S 40 30W
Petworth England 16 C1 50 59N 0 38W
Pevensey England 17 D1 50 49N 0 20E
Pewsey England 16 B2 51 21N 1 46W
Pforzheim Germany 52 D4 48 53N 8 41E
Phenix City USA 91 J3 32 28N 85 01W
Philadelphia USA 91 L4 40 00N 75 10W
PHILIPPINES, THE 71 G7/H5
Phnom Penh Cambodia 71 C6 11 35N 104 55E
Phoenix USA 90 D3 33 30N 112 03W
Piacenza Italy 54 C6 45 03N 9 41E
Pickering England 13 F3 54 14N 0 46W
Píndhos Greece 55 J3 40 00N 21 00E
Pinsk Belarus 57 C5 52 08N 26 01E
Pinwherry Scotland 10 E2 55 09N 4 50W
Piombino Italy 54 D5 42 56N 10 32E
Pýrgos Greece 55 J2 37 40N 21 27E
Pirineos mts.
 Spain/France 51 E5/F5 42 50N 0 30E
Pirmasens Germany 52 C4 49 12N 7 37E
Pisa Italy 54 D5 43 43N 10 24E
Pistoia Italy 54 D5 43 56N 10 55E
Piteă Sweden 49 F4 65 19N 21 30E

Pitești Romania 53 M2 44 51N 24 51E
Pitlochry Scotland 9 F1 56 43N 3 45W
Pitmedden Scotland 9 G2 57 19N 2 11W
Pittenweem Scotland 11 G3 56 13N 2 44W
Pittsburgh USA 91 L5 40 26N 80 00W
Planalto de Mato Grosso
 geog. reg. Brazil 96F11/G11 13 00S 56 00W
Plasencia Spain 51 B4 40 02N 6 05W
Platte r. USA 90 F5 41 00N 100 00W
Plauen Germany 52 F5 50 29N 12 08E
Pleven Bulgaria 55 L5 43 25N 24 04E
Płock Poland 53 J6 52 32N 19 40E
Ploiești Romania 53 M2 44 57N 26 01E
Plovdiv Bulgaria 55 L5 42 08N 24 45E
Plymouth England 18 C2 50 23N 4 10W
Plympton England 18 C2 50 23N 4 03W
Plymstock England 18 C2 50 21N 4 07W
Plynlimon mt. Wales 14 C2 52 28N 3 47W
Plzeň Czech Rep. 52 F4 49 45N 13 25E
Po r. Italy 54 D6 45 00N 10 00E
Pocklington England 13 F2 53 56N 0 46W
Podgorica
 Serbia & Montenegro 55 H5 42 28N 19 17E
Point-Noire tn. Congo 82 B7 4 46S 11 53E
Poitiers France 50 E4 46 35N 0 20E
POLAND 53 J6/K6
Polegate England 17 D1 50 50N 0 15E
Polesworth England 15 E2 52 44N 1 36W
Policoro Italy 55 G4 40 12N 16 40E
Pollensa Spain 51 G3 39 52N 3 01E
Polperro England 18 C2 50 19N 4 31W
Polýgyros Greece 55 K4 40 23N 23 25E
Pondicherry India 66 D2 11 59N 79 50E
Ponferrada Spain 51 B5 42 33N 6 35W
Pont r. England 12 E4 55 02N 1 55W
Ponta Grossa Brazil 96 G8 25 07S 50 09W
Pont-à-Mousson
 France 50 H5 48 55N 6 03E
Pontardawe Wales 14 C1 51 44N 3 52W
Pontardulais Wales 14 B1 51 43N 4 02W
Pontefract England 13 E2 53 42N 1 18W
Ponteland England 13 E4 55 03N 1 44W
Ponte Leccia France 50 J2 42 28N 9 12E
Ponterwyd Wales 14 C2 52 25N 3 50W
Pontevedra Spain 51 A5 42 25N 8 39W
Pontivy France 50 C5 48 04N 2 58W
Pontrilas England 14 D1 51 57N 2 53W
Pontyclun Wales 14 C1 51 33N 3 23W
Pontycymer Wales 14 C1 51 36N 3 35W
Pontypool Wales 14 C1 51 43N 3 02W
Pontypridd Wales 14 C1 51 37N 3 22W
Poole England 19 F2 50 43N 1 59W
Poole u.a. England 19 F2 50 43N 1 59W
Poole Bay b. England 19 F3 50 41N 1 52W
Poolewe Scotland 8 D2 57 45N 5 37W
Pooley Bridge tn.
 England 12 D3 54 38N 2 49W
Popacatepetl mt.
 Mexico 94 E3 19 02N 98 38W
Pordenone Italy 54 E6 45 58N 12 39E
Pori Finland 49 F3 61 28N 21 45E
Porlock England 19 D3 51 14N 3 36W
Portadown NI 10 C1 54 26N 6 27W
Portaferry NI 10 D1 54 23N 5 33W
Portalegre Portugal 51 B3 39 17N 7 25W
Portarlington RoI 21 D3 53 10N 7 11W
Port Askaig Scotland 10 C2 55 51N 6 07W
Portavogie NI 10 D1 54 28N 5 25W
Port Ellen Scotland 10 C2 55 39N 6 12W
Port Erin Isle of Man 12 B3 54 05N 4 45W
Port-Eynon Wales 14 B1 51 34N 4 12W
Port Gentil Gabon 82 A7 0 40S 8 50E
Port Glasgow Scotland 11 E2 55 56N 4 41W
Portglenone NI 10 C1 54 52N 6 29W
Port Harcourt Nigeria 80 F2 4 43N 7 05E
Porthcawl Wales 14 C1 51 29N 3 43W
Porthleven England 18 BB2 50 30N 5 21W
Porthmadog Wales 14 B2 52 55N 4 08W
Portimão Portugal 51 A2 37 08N 8 32W
Port Isaac England 18 C2 50 35N 4 49W
Portishead England 19 E3 51 30N 2 46W
Portknockie Scotland 9 G2 57 42N 2 52W
Portland USA 90 B6 45 32N 122 40W
Portlaoise RoI 21 D3 53 02N 7 17W
Portlaw RoI 21 D2 52 17N 7 19W
Portlethen Scotland 9 G2 57 03N 2 07W
Portmahomack Scotland 9 F2 57 49N 3 50W
Port Moresby PNG 73 J9 9 30S 147 07E
Portnaguran Scotland 8 C3 58 17N 6 13W
Portnahaven Scotland 10 C2 55 41N 6 31W
Porto Alegre Brazil 97 G7 30 03S 51 10W
Port of Ness Scotland 8 C3 58 29N 6 13W
Port-of-Spain
 Trinidad and Tobago 95 V15 10 38N 61 31W
Porto Novo Benin 80 E3 6 30N 2 47E
Porto Tórres Italy 54 C4 40 51N 8 24E
Porto-Vecchio France 50 J1 41 35N 9 16E
Pôrto Velho Brazil 96 E12 8 45S 63 54W
Portpatrick Scotland 10 D2 54 51N 5 07W
Portreath England 18 B2 50 15N 5 17W
Portree Scotland 8 C2 57 24N 6 12W
Portrush NI 10 C2 55 12N 6 40W
Portskerra Scotland 9 F3 58 33N 3 55W
Portsmouth England 16 B1 50 48N 1 05W

Portsmouth u.a.
 England 16 B1 50 48N 1 05W
Portsmouth USA 91 L4 36 50N 76 20W
Portsoy Scotland 9 G2 57 41N 2 41W
Portstewart NI 10 C2 55 11N 6 43W
Port Talbot Wales 14 C1 51 36N 3 47W
PORTUGAL 51 A3/B3
Portumna RoI 21 C3 53 06N 8 13W
Port Wemyss Scotland 10 C2 55 42N 6 29W
Port William Scotland 11 E1 54 46N 4 35W
Potenza Italy 54 F4 40 38N 15 48E
Potomac r. USA 91 L4 39 10N 77 30W
Potsdam Germany 52 F6 52 24N 13 04E
Potter's Bar England 16 C2 51 42N 0 11W
Potton England 16 C3 52 08N 0 14W
Poulton-le-Fylde
 England 12 D2 53 51N 3 00W
Powell River tn. Canada 88 L3 49 54N 124 34W
Power Head RoI 21 C1 51 47N 8 10W
Powfoot Scotland 11 F1 54 59N 3 20W
Powys u.a. Wales 14 C2 52 10N 3 30W
Poznań Poland 53 H6 52 25N 16 53E
Prague Czech Rep. 52 G5 50 06N 14 26E
Prato Italy 54 D5 43 53N 11 06E
Prawle Point England 18 D2 50 12N 3 44W
Preesall England 12 D2 53 55N 2 57W
Prešov Slovakia 53 K4 49 00N 21 10E
Prestatyn Wales 14 C3 53 20N 3 24W
Presteigne Wales 14 C2 52 17N 3 00W
Preston England 12 D2 53 46N 2 42W
Prestonpans Scotland 11 G2 55 57N 3 00W
Prestwich England 12 D2 53 32N 2 17W
Prestwick Scotland 11 E2 55 30N 4 37W
Pretoria RSA 82 D3 25 45S 28 12E
Příbram Czech Rep. 52 G4 49 42N 14 01E
Prince Albert Canada 89 P4 53 13N 105 45W
Prince Edward Island
 prov. Canada 89 Y3 46 30N 63 00W
Prince Rupert Canada 88 J4 54 09N 130 20W
Princes Risborough
 England 16 C2 51 44N 0 51W
Princetown England 18 C2 50 33N 3 59W
Pripyats' r. Belarus 56 B5/C5 52 30N 27 00E
Priština
 Serbia & Montenegro 55 J5 42 39N 21 20E
Privas France 50 G3 44 44N 4 36E
Prokop'yevsk Russia 63 L7 53 55N 86 45E
Providence USA 91 M5 41 50N 71 28W
Provins France 50 F5 48 34N 3 18E
Prudhoe England 13 E3 54 58N 1 51W
Prudhoe Bay tn. USA 88 F8 70 05N 148 20W
Pruszków Poland 53 K6 52 10N 20 47E
Prut r. Romania 53 P3 47 00N 28 00E
Pskov Russia 62 E8 57 48N 28 26E
Puddletown England 19 E2 50 45N 2 21W
Pudsey England 13 E2 53 48N 1 40W
Puebla Mexico 94 E3 19 03N 98 10W
Pueblo USA 90 F4 38 17N 104 38W
Puertollano Spain 51 C3 38 41N 4 07W
PUERTO RICO 95 L3
Pulborough England 16 C1 50 58N 0 30W
Pumsaint Wales 14 C2 52 03N 3 58W
Pune India 66 C3 18 34N 73 58E
Punta Arenas Chile 97 C3 53 10S 70 56W
Purfleet England 17 D2 51 29N 0 14E
Puri India 67 F3 19 49N 85 54E
Puulavesi l. Finland 49 G3 61 50N 26 40E
Pwllheli Wales 14 B2 52 53N 4 25W
Pyle Wales 14 C1 51 32N 3 42W
Pyongyang N. Korea 69 N5 39 00N 125 47E
Pyrénées mts.
 France/Spain 50 E2 42 50N 0 30E
Pýrgos Greece 55 L1 35 00N 25 10E

Q

QATAR 65 F4
Qingdao China 69 M5 36 04N 120 22E
Qiqihar China 69 M7 47 23N 124 00E
Quantock Hills England 19 D3 51 10N 3 15W
Québec prov. Canada 89 V4/X4 52 00N 75 00W
Québec Canada 89 W3 46 50N 71 15W
Queenborough England 17 D2 51 26N 0 45E
Queen Charlotte Islands
 Canada 88 J4 53 00N 132 30W
Queen Elizabeth Islands
 Canada 89 N9/S9 77 30N 105 00W
Queensbury England 12 E2 53 46N 1 50W
Queenstown Australia 73 J2 42 07S 145 33E
Querétaro Mexico 94 D3 20 38N 100 23W
Quetta Pakistan 66 B6 30 15N 67 00E
Quezon City Philippines 71 G6 14 39N 121 02E
Quiberon France 50 C4 47 29N 3 07W
Quigley's Point RoI 20 D5 55 10N 7 08W
Quimper France 50 B4 48 00N 4 06W
Quito Ecuador 96 B13 0 14S 78 30W
Quorn England 15 E2 52 45N 1 10W

R

Raahe Finland 49 F3 64 42N 24 30E
Raasay i. Scotland 8 C2 57 25N 6 05W
Rabat-Salé Morocco 80 C8 34 02N 6 51W
Radcliffe England 12 D2 53 34N 2 20W
Radcliffe on Trent
 England 15 E3 52 57N 1 03W
Radlett England 16 C2 51 41N 0 19W

Radom Poland 53 K5 51 26N 21 10E
Radstadt Austria 52 F3 47 23N 13 28E
Radstock England 19 E3 51 18N 2 28W
Raglan Wales 14 D1 51 47N 2 51W
Ragusa Italy 54 F2 36 56N 14 44E
Rainford England 12 D2 53 30N 2 48W
Rainier, Mount USA 90 B6 46 25N 121 45W
Rainworth England 13 E2 53 08N 1 08W
Raipur India 66 E4 21 16N 81 42E
Rame Head England 18 C2 50 19N 4 13W
Ramore Head NI 10 C2 55 13N 6 39W
Ramsbottom England 12 D2 53 39N 2 19W
Ramsey England 16 C3 52 27N 0 07W
Ramsey Isle of Man 12 B3 54 19N 4 23W
Ramsey Island Wales 14 A1 51 53N 5 20W
Ramsgate England 17 E2 51 20N 1 25E
Randalstown NI 10 C1 54 45N 6 19W
Rangpur Bangladesh 67 F5 25 45N 89 21E
Rannoch Moor Scotland 9 E1 56 35N 4 50W
Rannoch Station
  Scotland 9 E1 5642N 4 34W
Rapallo Italy 54 C6 44 21N 9 13E
Raphoe RoI 20 D4 54 52N 7 36W
Rastatt Germany 52 D4 48 51N 8 13E
Rathangan RoI 20 E3 53 12N 6 59W
Rathcoole RoI 20 E3 53 17N 6 28W
Rathcormack RoI 21 C2 52 05N 8 17W
Rathdowney RoI 21 D2 52 51N 7 35W
Rathdrum RoI 21 E2 52 56N 6 13W
Rathfriland NI 10 C1 54 14N 6 10W
Rathkeale RoI 21 C2 52 32N 8 56W
Rathlackan RoI 20 B4 54 18N 9 15W
Rathlin Sound NI 10 C2 55 20N 6 25W
Rath Luirc RoI 21 C2 52 21N 8 41W
Rathmelton RoI 20 D5 55 02N 7 38W
Rathmore RoI 21 B2 52 05N 9 13W
Rathnew RoI 21 E2 52 58N 6 05W
Rathvilly RoI 21 E2 52 53N 6 41W
Ratoath RoI 20 E3 53 31N 6 27W
Raton USA 90 F4 36 45N 104 27W
Rattray Scotland 9 F1 56 36N 3 20W
Rattray Head Scotland 9 H2 57 38N 1 45W
Rauma Finland 49 F3 61 09N 21 30E
Raunds England 15 F2 52 21N 0 33W
Ravenglass England 12 C3 54 21N 3 24W
Ravenna Italy 54 E6 44 25N 12 12E
Ravensburg Germany 52 D3 47 47N 9 37E
Ravenshead England 13 E2 53 40N 1 10W
Rawalpindi Pakistan 66 C6 33 40N 73 08E
Rawmarsh England 13 E2 53 27N 1 21W
Rawtenstall England 12 D2 53 42N 2 18W
Rayleigh England 17 D2 51 36N 0 36E
Reading England 16 C2 51 28N 0 59W
Reading u.a. England 16 B1/C1 50 25N 1 00W
Reay Forest Scotland 9 E3 58 30N 4 55W
Recife Brazil 96 L12 8 06S 34 53W
Recklinghausen
  Germany 52 C5 51 37N 7 11E
Red Bay NI 10 C2 55 04N 6 01W
Redbourn England 16 C2 51 48N 0 24W
Redbridge England 16 D2 51 34N 0 05E
Redcar England 13 E3 54 37N 1 04W
Redcar and Cleveland u.a.
  England 13 E3/F3 54 30N 1 00W
Redditch England 15 E2 52 19N 1 56W
Redhill tn. England 16 C2 51 14N 0 11W
Redon France 50 C4 47 39N 2 05W
Redruth England 18 B2 50 13N 5 14W
Red Sea Middle East 64 C4/C2 27 00N 35 00E
Reepham England 17 E3 52 46N 1 07E
Regensburg Germany 52 F4 49 01N 12 07E
Reggio di Calabria Italy 54 F3 38 06N 15 39E
Regina Canada 89 Q4 50 30N 104 38W
Reigate England 16 C2 51 14N 0 13W
Reims France 50 G5 49 15N 4 02E
Reinosa Spain 51 C3 43 01N 4 09W
Rendsburg Germany 52 D7 54 19N 9 39E
Renfrew Canada 89 V3 45 28N 76 44W
Renfrew Scotland 11 E2 55 53N 4 24W
Renfrewshire u.a.
  Scotland 11 E2 55 50N 4 40W
Rennes France 50 D5 48 06N 1 40W
Reno USA 90 C4 39 32N 119 49W
REPUBLIC OF IRELAND
  20/21
REPUBLIC OF SOUTH AFRICA
  82 D1/D2
Requena Spain 51 E3 39 29N 1 08W
Resolute Canada 89 S8 74 40N 95 00W
Retford England 13 F2 53 19N 0 56W
Rethel France 50 G5 49 31N 4 22E
Reus Spain 51 F4 41 10N 1 06E
Reutlingen Germany 52 D4 48 30N 9 13E
Reykjavik Iceland 49 K6 64 09N 21 58W
Rhayader Wales 14 C2 52 18N 3 30W
Rheden Neths 48 E5 52 01N 6 02E
Rheidol r. Wales 14 C2 52 23N 3 55W
Rhein r. Germany 52 C4 50 30N 8 00E
Rheine Germany 52 C6 52 17N 7 26E
Rhode Island state USA 91 M5 41 00N 71 00W
Rhondda Wales 14 C1 51 40N 3 30W
Rhondda Cynon Taff u.a.
  Wales 14 C1 51 40N 3 30W
Rhône r. Switz./France 50 G3 45 00N 4 50E
Rhoose Wales 14 C1 51 26N 3 22W
Rhosllanerchrugog
  Wales 14 C3 53 01N 3 04W

Rhosneigr Wales 14 B3 53 14N 4 31W
Rhossili Wales 14 B1 51 34N 4 17W
Rhubodach Scotland 10 D2 55 56N 5 09W
Rhum i. Scotland 8 C2 57 00N 6 20W
Rhyl Wales 14 C2 53 19N 3 29W
Rhymney Wales 14 C1 51 46N 3 18W
Rhynie Scotland 9 G2 57 19N 2 50W
Ribble r. England 12 D2 53 45N 2 30W
Riccall England 13 E2 53 51N 1 04W
Richhill NI 10 C1 54 22N 6 33W
Richmond England 13 E3 54 24N 1 44W
Richmond upon Thames
  England 16 C2 51 28N 0 19W
Rickmansworth
  England 16 C2 51 38N 0 29W
Ried Austria 52 F4 48 13N 13 29E
Riesa Germany 52 F5 51 18N 13 18E
Rieti Italy 54 E5 42 24N 12 51E
Riga Latvia 49 F2 56 53N 24 08E
Rimini Italy 54 E6 44 03N 12 34E
Ringabella Bay RoI 21 C1 51 46N 8 13W
Ringaskiddy RoI 21 C1 51 49N 8 18W
Ringwood England 16 B1 50 51N 1 47W
Rio de Janeiro tn. Brazil 96 I8 22 53S 43 17W
Rio de la Plata est.
  Uruguay/Argentina 97 F5 35 00S 57 00W
Rio Grande tn. Brazil 97 G7 32 03S 52 08W
Río Grande r.
  Mexico/USA 90 E3/F3 30 00N 105 00W
Ripley England 13 E2 53 03N 1 24W
Ripon England 13 E3 54 08N 1 31W
Risca Wales 14 C1 51 37N 3 07W
Rishton England 12 D2 53 47N 2 24W
Riva del Garda Italy 54 D6 45 53N 10 50E
Riverton Canada 89 R4 51 00N 97 00W
Rivne Ukraine 53 M5 50 39N 26 10E
Riyadh Saudi Arabia 65 E3 24 39N 46 46E
Roanne France 50 G4 46 02N 4 05E
Robin Hood's Bay tn.
  England 13 F3 54 25N 0 33W
Rochdale England 12 D2 53 38N 2 09W
Rochefort France 50 D3 45 57N 0 58W
Rochester Northamptonshire
  England 12 D4 55 16N 2 16W
Rochester Medway
  England 17 D2 51 24N 0 30E
Rochester USA 91 L5 43 12N 77 37W
Rochford England 17 D2 51 36N 0 43E
Rochfortbridge RoI 20 D3 53 25N 7 18W
Rockhampton Australia 73 K6 23 22S 150 32E
Rocky Mountains
  Canada/USA 88 K5/P2 55 00N 125 00W
Rodel Scotland 8 C2 57 41N 7 05W
Rodez France 50 F3 44 21N 2 34E
Roding r. England 17 D2 51 45N 0 15E
Roermond Neths 48 D4 51 12N 6 00E
ROMANIA 53 L2/M2
Romans-sur-Isère
  France 50 G3 45 03N 5 03E
Rome Italy 54 E4 41 53N 12 30E
Romney Marsh England 17 D2 51 03N 0 58E
Romorantin-Lanthenay
  France 50 E4 47 22N 1 44E
Romsey England 16 B1 50 59N 1 30W
Rona i. Scotland 8 D2 57 32N 5 59W
Ronda Spain 51 C2 36 45N 5 10W
Ronse Belgium 48 B3 50 45N 3 36E
Roosendaal Neths 48 C4 51 32N 4 28E
Roosky RoI 20 D3 53 50N 7 55W
Roquetas de Mar Spain 51 D2 36 46N 2 35W
Rora Head Scotland 7 A1 58 52N 3 26W
Rosarno Italy 54 F3 38 29N 15 59E
Roscoff France 50 C5 48 43N 3 59W
Roscommon RoI 20 C3 53 38N 8 11W
Roscommon co. RoI 20 C3 53 45N 8 10W
Roscrea RoI 21 D2 52 57N 7 47W
Rosehearty Scotland 9 G2 57 42N 2 07W
Rosenheim Germany 52 F3 47 51N 12 09E
Roskilde Denmark 49 55 39N 12 07E
Rossano Italy 54 G3 39 35N 16 38E
Rossan Point RoI 20 C4 54 40N 8 50W
Ross Carbery RoI 21 B1 51 35N 9 02W
Rosscarbery Bay RoI 21 B1 51 32N 9 00W
Rosslare RoI 21 E2 52 15N 6 22W
Rosslare Harbour tn.
  RoI 21 E2 52 15N 6 22W
Rosslare Point RoI 21 E2 52 19N 6 21W
Ross-on-Wye England 15 D1 51 55N 2 35W
Rostock Germany 52 F7 54 06N 12 09E
Rostov-na-Donu
  Russia 62 F6 47 15N 39 45E
Rostrevor NI 10 C1 54 06N 6 12W
Rothbury England 11 H2 55 19N 1 55W
Rother r. England 16 C1 51 00N 0 50W
Rother r. England 17 D2 51 00N 0 17E
Rotherham England 13 E2 53 26N 1 20W
Rothes Scotland 9 F2 57 31N 3 13W
Rothesay Scotland 10 D2 55 51N 5 03W
Rothwell West Yorkshire
  England 13 E2 53 45N 1 29W
Rothwell Northamptonshire
  England 15 F2 52 25N 0 48W
Rotterdam Neths 48 C4 51 54N 4 28E
Rottingdean England 16 C1 50 48N 0 04W
Roubaix France 50 F6 50 42N 3 10E
Rouen France 50 E5 49 26N 1 05E
Roundwood RoI 21 E3 53 04N 6 13W

Rousay i. Scotland 7 A2 59 10N 3 00W
Rovigo Italy 54 D6 45 04N 11 47E
Rowlands Gill England 13 E3 54 54N 1 45W
Royal Leamington Spa
  England 15 E2 52 18N 1 31W
Royal Tunbridge Wells
  England 17 D2 51 08N 0 16E
Royan France 50 D3 45 38N 1 02W
Royston South Yorkshire
  England 13 E2 53 37N 1 27W
Royston Hertfordshire
  England 16 C3 52 03N 0 01W
Royton England 12 D2 53 34N 2 08W
Ruabon Wales 14 C2 52 59N 3 02W
Ruddington England 15 E2 52 54N 1 09W
Rufford England 12 D2 53 39N 2 49W
Rugby England 15 E2 52 23N 1 15W
Rugeley England 15 E2 52 46N 1 55W
Ruhr r. Germany 52 D5 51 00N 7 00E
Rumney Wales 14 C1 51 30N 3 10W
Runcorn England 12 D2 53 20N 2 44W
Ruse Bulgaria 55 M5 43 50N 25 59E
Rush RoI 20 E3 53 32N 6 06W
Rushden England 15 F2 52 17N 0 36W
RUSSIAN FEDERATION
  62/63
Ruthin Wales 14 C3 53 07N 3 18W
Rutland u.a. England 15 F2 5241N 00 39W
Rutland Water England 15 F2 52 40N 0 37W
RWANDA 83 A3/B3
Ryazan' Russia 62 F7 54 37N 39 43E
Rybinsk Russia 62 F8 58 03N 38 50E
Rybnik Poland 53 J5 50 07N 18 30E
Rye Finland 16 B1 50 44N 1 10W
Rye r. England 13 E3 54 15N 1 10W
Rye England 17 D1 50 57N 0 44E
Ryton England 13 E3 54 59N 1 57W
Ryukyu Islands Japan 69 N3 27 30N 127 30E

S
Saalfeld Germany 52 E5 50 39N 11 22E
Saarbrücken Germany 52 C4 49 15N 6 58E
Sabadell Spain 51 G4 41 33N 2 07E
Sacramento USA 90 B4 38 32N 121 30W
Sacriston England 13 E3 54 50N 1 38W
Saffron Walden
  England 17 D3 52 01N 0 15E
Saga Japan 70 B1 33 16N 130 18E
Sagunto Spain 51 E3 39 40N 0 17W
Sahagún Spain 51 C3 42 23N 5 02W
St. Abbs Scotland 11 G2 55 54N 2 08W
St. Abb's Head Scotland 11 G2 55 55N 2 09W
St. Agnes England 18 B2 50 18N 5 13W
St. Albans England 16 C2 51 46N 0 21W
St Alban's or St Aldheim's Head
  England 19 E2 50 34N 2 04W
St. Andrews Scotland 9 G1 56 20N 2 48W
St Anne Channel Islands 19 E2 49 43N 2 12W
St. Asaph Wales 14 C3 53 15N 3 26W
St. Austell England 18 C2 50 20N 4 48W
St. Bees England 12 C3 54 29N 3 35W
St. Blazey England 18 C2 50 22N 4 43W
St. Bride's Bay Wales 14 A1 51 50N 5 15W
St-Brieuc France 50 C5 48 31N 2 45W
St. Catharines Canada 89 V2 43 10N 79 15W
St-Chamond France 50 G3 45 29N 4 32E
St. Clears Wales 14 B1 51 50N 4 30W
St. Columb Major
  England 18 C2 50 26N 4 56W
St. David's Wales 14 A1 51 54N 5 16W
St. David's Head Wales 14 A1 51 55N 5 19W
St.-Dié France 50 H5 48 17N 6 57E
St.-Dizier France 50 G5 48 38N 4 58E
Saintes France 50 D3 45 44N 0 38W
St.-Étienne France 50 G3 45 26N 4 23E
Saintfield NI 10 D1 54 28N 5 50W
St. Finnan's Bay RoI 21 A1 51 50N 10 23W
St. Gallen Switz. 52 D3 47 25N 9 23E
St.-Gaudens France 50 E2 43 07N 0 44E
St. George's Grenada 94 R11 12 04N 61 44W
St. George's Channel
  British Isles 21 E2 52 00N 6 00W
St.-German en-Laye
  France 50 F5 48 54N 2 04E
St-Girons France 50 E2 42 59N 1 08E
St. Helens England 12 D2 53 28N 2 44W
St. Helier
  Channel Islands 19 E1 49 12N 2 07W
St. Ives England 16 C3 52 20N 0 05W
St. Ives England 18 B2 50 12N 5 29W
St. Jean-de-Luz France 50 D2 43 23N 1 39W
Saint John Canada 89 X3 45 16N 66 03W
St. John's Canada AA3 47 34N 52 41W
St. John's Point NI 10 D1 54 15N 5 35W
St Johnstown RoI 20 D4 54 56N 7 28W
St John's Town of Dalry
  Scotland 11 E2 55 07N 4 10W
St. Just England 18 B2 50 07N 5 41W
St. Keverne England 18 B2 50 03N 5 06W
St. Kilda i. Scotland 8 A2 57 49N 8 34W
ST. KITTS AND NEVIS 94 P9
St. Lawrence r.
  Canada/USA 89 X3 46 55N 55 24W
St. Leonards England 19 F2 50 50N 1 50W
St-Lô France 50 D5 49 07N 1 05W
St. Louis USA 91 H4 38 40N 90 15W

ST. LUCIA 94R11/R12
St. Malo France 50 C5 48 39N 2 00W
St. Margaret's at Cliffe
  England 17 E2 51 10N 1 23E
St. Mawes England 18 B2 50 09N 5 01W
St. Monance Scotland 11 G3 56 13N 2 46W
St. Moritz Switz. 52 D3 46 30N 9 51E
St.-Nazaire France 50 C4 47 17N 2 12W
St. Neots England 16 C3 52 14N 0 17W
St.-Omer France 50 F6 50 45N 2 15E
St. Paul USA 91 H5 45 00N 93 10W
St. Peter Port
  Channel Islands 19 E1 49 27N 3 32W
St. Petersburg Russia 62 F8 59 55N 30 25E
Saint-Pierre & Miquelon
  is. Atlantic Ocean 89 Z3 47 00N 56 20W
St. Pölten Austria 53 G4 48 13N 15 37E
St.-Quentin France 50 F5 49 51N 3 17E
St.-Tropez France 50 H2 43 16N 6 39E
ST. VINCENT AND THE GRENADINES
  94 R11
Sakhalin i. Russia 63 S7 50 00N 143 00E
Salamanca Spain 51 C4 40 58N 5 40W
Salcombe England 18 D2 50 13N 3 47W
Sale England 12 D2 53 26N 2 19W
Salen Scotland 8 D1 56 43N 5 47W
Salen Scotland 8 D1 56 31N 5 57W
Salerno Italy 54 F4 40 40N 14 46E
Salford England 12 D2 53 30N 2 16W
Salisbury England 16 B2 51 05N 1 48W
Salisbury Plain
  England 16 B2 51 10N 1 55W
Salmon USA 90 D6 45 11N 113 55W
Salo Finland 49 F3 60 23N 23 10E
Salò Italy 54 D6 45 37N 10 31E
Salon-de-Provence
  France 50 G2 43 38N 5 06E
Salt Jordan 64 N11 32 03N 35 44E
Saltash England 18 C2 50 24N 4 12W
Saltburn-by-the-Sea
  England 13 F3 54 35N 0 58W
Saltcoats Scotland 11 E2 55 38N 4 47W
Saltdal Norway 49 E4 67 06N 15 25E
Saltdean England 16 C1 50 48N 0 02W
Saltfleet England 13 G2 53 26N 0 10E
Saltillo Mexico 94 D5 25 30N 101 00W
Salt Lake City USA 90 D5 40 45N 111 55W
Salvador Brazil 96 K11 12 58S 38 29W
Salween r.
  China/Myanmar 71 B8 20 00N 103 00E
Salzburg Austria 52 F3 47 48N 13 03E
Salzgitter Germany 52 E6 52 13N 10 20E
Samara Russia 62 H7 53 10N 50 10E
SAMOA 100 J6
Samsun Turkey 57 E3 41 17N 36 22E
Sana Yemen 64 D2 15 23N 44 14E
San Antonio USA 91 G2 29 25N 98 30W
Sanda Island Scotland 10 D2 55 18N 5 35W
Sanday i. Scotland 7 B2 59 15N 2 30W
Sandbach England 12 D2 53 09N 2 22W
Sandhead Scotland 10 E1 54 48N 4 58W
Sandhurst England 16 C2 51 21N 0 48W
San Diego USA 90 C3 32 45N 117 10W
Sandown England 16 B1 50 39N 1 09W
Sandray i. Scotland 8 B1 56 53N 7 30W
Sandringham England 17 D3 52 50N 0 31E
Sandwich England 17 E2 51 17N 1 20E
Sandy England 16 C3 52 08N 0 18W
San Fernando Spain 51 B2 36 28N 6 12W
San Francisco USA 90 B4 37 45N 122 27W
San José Costa Rica 95 H1 9 59N 84 04W
San José USA 90 B4 37 20N 121 55W
San Juan Puerto Rico 95 L3 18 29N 66 08W
San Juan Bautista
  Spain 51 F3 39 05N 1 31E
SAN MARINO 54 E5 44 00N 12 00E
Sanmenxia China 69 K4 34 46N 111 17E
Sanming China 69 L3 26 16N 117 35E
Sannox Scotland 10 D2 56 41N 5 08W
Sanquhar Scotland 11 F2 55 22N 3 56W
San Remo Italy 54 B5 43 48N 7 46E
San Salvador
  El Salvador 94 G2 13 40N 89 10W
San Sebastián Spain 51 E5 43 19N 1 59W
San Severo Italy 54 F4 41 41N 15 23E
Santa Barbara USA 90 C3 33 29N 119 01W
Santa Cruz Spain 80 A7 28 28N 16 15W
Santa Fe USA 90 E4 35 41N 105 57W
Santander Spain 51 D5 43 28N 3 48W
Sant'Antioco Italy 54 C3 39 04N 8 27E
Santarém Brazil 96 G13 2 26S 54 41W
Santarém Portugal 51 A3 39 14N 8 40W
Santa Teresa Gallura
  Italy 54 C4 41 14N 9 12E
Santiago Chile 97 C6 33 30S 70 40W
Santiago de Compostela
  Spain 51 A5 42 52N 8 33W
Santo Andre Brazil 96 H9 23 39S 46 29W
Santo Domingo
  Dom. Rep. 95 L3 18 30N 69 57W
Santoña Spain 51 D5 43 27N 3 26W
São Francisco r. Brazil 96 J11 15 00S 44 00W
São Luís Brazil 96 J13 2 34S 44 16W
Saône r. France 50 G4 46 28N 4 55E
São Paulo Brazil 96 H9 23 33S 46 39W
SÃO TOMÉ AND PRINCIPE
  80 F2

Sapporo Japan 70 D3 43 05N 141 21E
Sarajevo
Bosnia-Herzegovina 55 H5 43 52N 18 26E
Saratov Russia 62 G7 51 30N 45 55E
Sardinia i. Italy 54 C3/C4 40 00N 9 00E
Sark i. Channel Islands 19 E1 49 26N 2 22W
Sarnia Canada 89 U2 42 58N 82 23W
Sarrebourg France 50 H5 48 43N 7 03E
Sarreguemines France 50 H5 49 06N 6 55E
Sartène France 50 J1 41 37N 8 58E
Saskatchewan prov.
Canada 88/89 P5/Q5 53 50N 109 00W
Saskatoon Canada 88 P4 52 10N 106 40W
Sassari Italy 54 C4 40 43N 8 34E
Sassnitz Germany 52 F7 54 32N 13 40E
Sassuolo Italy 54 D6 44 32N 10 47E
Satu Mare Romania 53 L3 47 48N 22 52E
SAUDI ARABIA 64/65 D3/F3
Sault Ste. Marie
Canada 89 U3 46 31N 84 20W
Saumur France 50 D4 47 16N 0 05W
Saundersfoot Wales 14 B1 51 43N 4 43W
Savannah USA 91 K3 32 04N 81 07W
Savona Italy 54 C6 44 18N 8 28E
Sawbridgeworth
England 17 D2 51 50N 0 09E
Sawel mt. NI 10 B1 54 49N 7 02W
Sawston England 17 D2 52 07N 0 10E
Saxilby England 13 F2 53 17N 0 40W
Saxmundham England 17 E3 52 13N 1 29E
Saxthorpe England 17 E3 52 50N 1 09E
Scafell Pike mt.
England 12 C3 54 27N 3 14W
Scalasaig Scotland 10 C3 56 04N 6 12W
Scalby England 13 F3 54 18N 0 27W
Scalloway Scotland 7 C3 60 08N 1 17W
Scalpay i. Scotland 8 C2 57 52N 6 40W
Scalpay i. Scotland 8 D2 57 15N 6 00W
Scapa Scotland 7 B1 58 58N 2 59W
Scapa Flow sd. Scotland 7 A1 58 55N 3 00W
Scarborough England 13 F3 54 17N 0 24W
Scarinish Scotland 8 C1 56 29N 6 48W
Scarp i. Scotland 8 B3 58 02N 7 08W
Scarriff RoI 21 C2 52 55N 8 37W
Scartaglin RoI 21 B2 52 10N 9 26W
Schaffhausen Switz. 52 D3 47 42N 8 38E
Schefferville Canada 89 X4 54 50N 67 00W
Schleswig Germany 52 D7 54 32N 9 34E
Schwäbisch Gmünd
Germany 52 D4 48 49N 9 48E
Schwarzwald mts.
Germany 52 D4 47 00N 8 00E
Schwaz Austria 52 E3 47 21N 11 44E
Schwechat Austria 53 H4 48 09N 16 27E
Schweinfurt Germany 52 E5 50 03N 10 16E
Schwerin Germany 52 E6 53 38N 11 25E
Schwyz Switz. 52 D3 47 02N 8 39E
Sciacca Italy 54 E2 37 31N 13 05E
Scilly, Isles of England 18 A1 49 56N 6 20W
Sconser Scotland 8 C2 57 18N 6 07W
Scotland UK 6 56 00N 4 00W
Scottish Borders u.a.
Scotland 11 F2/G2 55 30N 2 55W
Scourie Scotland 8 D3 58 20N 5 08W
Scrabster Scotland 9 F3 58 37N 3 34W
Scunthorpe England 13 F2 53 35N 0 39W
Seaford England 17 D1 50 46N 0 06E
Seaham England 13 E3 54 50N 1 20W
Seahouses England 11 H2 55 35N 1 38W
Seascale England 12 C3 54 24N 3 29W
Seaton Devon England 19 D2 50 43N 3 05W
Seaton Cumbria
England 12 C3 54 40N 3 30W
Seaton Delaval England 13 E4 55 04N 1 31W
Seattle USA 90 B6 47 35N 122 20W
Sedan France 50 G5 49 42N 4 57E
Sedbergh England 12 D3 54 20N 2 31W
Segovia Spain 51 C4 40 57N 4 07W
Seine r. France 50 E5 49 15N 1 15E
Selborne England 16 C2 51 06N 0 56W
Selby England 13 E2 53 48N 1 04W
Sélestat France 50 H5 48 16N 7 28E
Selkirk Scotland 11 G2 55 33N 2 50W
Selsey England 16 C1 50 44N 0 48W
Selsey Bill p. England 16 C1 50 43N 0 48W
Semarang Indonesia 71 E2 6 58S 110 29E
Sendai Japan 70 D3 38 16N 140 52E
SENEGAL 80 A4/B4
Senlis France 50 F5 49 12N 2 35E
Sennen England 18 B2 50 05N 5 42W
Sennybridge Wales 14 C1 51 57N 3 34W
Sens France 50 F5 48 12N 3 18E
Seoul S. Korea 69 N5 37 32N 127 00E
Sept-Îles tn. Canada 89 X4 50 10N 66 00W
SERBIA AND MONTENEGRO
55 H6/K6
Serov Russia 62 J8 59 42N 60 32E
Serra Brazil 96 J10 20 06S 40 16W
Sérres Greece 55 K4 41 03N 23 33E
Sète France 50 F2 43 25N 3 43E
Settle England 12 D3 54 04N 2 16W
Setúbal Portugal 51 A3 38 31N 8 54W
Sevastopol' Ukraine 57 D3 44 36N 33 31E
Seven Head c. RoI 21 C1 51 34N 8 42W
Severn r.
England/Wales 14 C2 52 30N 3 15W
Severodvinsk Russia 62 F9 64 35N 39 50E

Sevilla Spain 51 C2 37 24N 5 59W
Seward USA 88 F6 60 05N 149 34W
SEYCHELLES 103
Sézannes France 50 F5 48 44N 3 44E
Sfântu Gheorghe
Romania 53 M2 45 51N 25 48E
Sfax Tunisia 80 G8 34 45N 10 43E
Sgurr Mór mt. Scotland 9 D2 57 42N 5 03W
Shaftesbury England 19 E3 51 01N 2 12W
Shaldon England 18 D2 51 35N 3 30W
Shanghai China 69 M4 31 06N 121 22E
Shanklin England 16 B1 50 38N 1 10W
Shannon RoI 21 C2 52 41N 8 55W
Shannon r. RoI 21 C2/B2 52 45N 8 57W
Shap England 12 D3 54 32N 2 41W
Shapinsay i. Scotland 7 B2 59 03N 2 51W
Sheerness England 17 D2 51 27N 0 45E
Sheffield England 13 E2 53 23N 1 30W
Shefford England 16 C3 52 02N 0 20W
Shelburne Canada 89 X2 43 37N 65 20W
Shenandoah USA 91 K4 40 48N 95 22W
Shenyang China 69 M6 41 50N 123 26E
Shepetovka Ukraine 53 N5 50 12N 27 01E
Shepperton England 16 C2 51 23N 0 28W
Sheppey, Isle of
England 17 D2 51 25N 0 50E
Shepshed England 15 E2 52 47N 1 18W
Shepton Mallet
England 19 E3 51 12N 2 33W
Sherborne England 19 E2 52 57N 2 31W
Sherbrooke Canada 89 W3 45 24N 71 54W
Shercock RoI 20 E3 53 59N 6 54W
Sheringham England 17 E3 52 57N 1 12E
Sherkin Island RoI 21 B1 51 28N 9 25W
's-Hertogenbosch
Neths 48 D4 51 41N 5 19E
Shetland Islands u.a.
Scotland 7 C2/D3 60 00N 1 15W
Shieldaig Scotland 8 D2 57 31N 5 39W
Shifnal England 15 D2 52 41N 2 22W
Shijiazhuang China 69 K5 38 04N 114 28E
Shilbottle England 11 H2 55 23N 1 42W
Shildon England 13 E3 54 38N 1 39W
Shillelagh RoI 21 E2 52 45N 6 32W
Shipley England 13 E2 53 50N 1 47W
Shipston-on-Stour
England 15 E2 52 04N 1 37W
Shipton England 13 E3 54 01N 1 09W
Shiraz Iran 65 F4 29 38N 52 34E
Shirebrook England 13 E2 53 13N 1 13W
Shoeburyness England 17 D2 51 32N 0 48E
Shoreham-by-Sea
England 16 C1 50 49N 0 16W
Shotton Wales 14 C3 53 12N 3 02W
Shotts Scotland 11 F2 55 49N 3 48W
Shrewsbury England 14 D2 52 43N 2 45W
Shrewton England 16 B2 51 12N 1 55W
Shropshire co.
England 14/15 D2 52 35N 2 25W
Shumen Bulgaria 55 M5 43 17N 26 55E
Sible Hedingham
England 17 D2 51 58N 0 35E
Sicily i. Italy 54 E2/F2 37 00N 14 00E
Siderno Italy 54 G3 38 16N 16 17E
Sidi Bel Abbès Algeria 80 D9 35 15N 0 39W
Sidlaw Hills Scotland 9 F1/G1 56 30N 3 10W
Sidmouth England 19 D2 50 41N 3 15W
Siegen Germany 52 D5 50 52N 8 02E
Siena Italy 54 D5 43 19N 11 19E
SIERRA LEONE 80 B3
Sierra Madre Occidental
mts. Mexico 94 C5/D4 26 00N 107 00W
Sierra Nevada mts.
Spain 51 D2 37 00N 3 20W
Sierra Nevada mts.
USA 90 C4 37 00N 119 00W
Sighişoara Romania 53 M3 46 12N 24 48E
Sigüenza Spain 51 D4 41 04N 2 38W
Sileby England 15 E2 52 44N 1 05W
Silistra Bulgaria 55 M6 44 06N 27 17E
Silloth England 12 C3 54 52N 3 23W
Silverton England 18 D2 50 48N 3 30W
Silves Portugal 51 A2 37 11N 8 26W
Simferopol' Ukraine 57 D3 44 57N 34 05E
Simonsbath England 18 D3 51 09N 3 45W
Sinclair's Bay Scotland 9 F3 58 30N 3 07
SINGAPORE 71 C4
Sintra Portugal 51 A3 38 48N 9 22W
Sion Switz. 52 C3 46 14N 7 22E
Sion Mills NI 10 B1 54 47N 7 28W
Siracusa Italy 54 F2 37 04N 15 19E
Sisak Croatia 55 G6 45 30N 16 22E
Sisteron France 50 G3 44 16N 5 56E
Sittingbourne England 17 D2 51 21N 0 44E
Sixmilebridge RoI 21 C2 52 45N 8 46W
Sjaelland i. Denmark 49 D2 55 15N 11 30E
Skagerrak sd.
Denmark/Norway 49 C2 57 30N 8 00E
Skegness England 13 G2 53 10N 0 21E
Skellefteå Sweden 49 F3 64 45N 21 00E
Skelmanthorpe
England 13 E2 53 36N 1 40W
Skelmersdale England 12 D2 53 55N 2 48W
Skelmorlie Scotland 10 D2 55 51N 4 53W
Skelton England 13 F3 54 33N 0 59W

Skerries RoI 20 E3 53 35N 6 07W
Skibbereen RoI 21 B1 51 33N 9 15W
Skiddaw mt. England 12 C3 54 40N 3 08W
Skien Norway 49 C2 59 14N 9 37E
Skipton England 12 D2 53 58N 2 01W
Skokholm Island Wales 14 A1 51 42N 5 16W
Skomer Island Wales 14 A1 51 45N 5 18W
Skopje FYROM 55 J4 42 00N 21 28E
Skövde Sweden 49 D2 58 24N 13 52E
Skull RoI 21 B1 51 32N 9 40W
Skye i. Scotland 8 C2 57 20N 6 15W
Slaidburn England 12 D2 54 00N 2 26W
Slane RoI 20 E3 54 43N 6 33W
Slaney r. RoI 21 E2 52 24N 6 33W
Slatina Romania 53 M2 44 26N 24 22E
Slave r. Canada 88 N5 59 20N 111 10W
Slavonski Brod Croatia 55 G6 45 09N 18 02E
Sleaford England 13 F2 53 00N 0 24W
Sleat, Point of Scotland 8 C2 57 01N 6 01W
Sleat, Sound of Scotland 8 D2 57 00N 5 55W
Sledmere England 13 F3 54 04N 0 35W
Sleights England 13 F3 54 26N 0 40W
Slieve Donard mt. NI 10 D1 54 11N 5 55W
Slieve Gamph hills RoI 20 C4 54 11N 8 53W
Slieve Mish Mountains
RoI 21 B2 51 12N 10 00W
Sligo RoI 20 C4 54 17N 8 28W
Sligo co. RoI 20 C4 54 10N 8 40W
Sligo Bay b. RoI 20 C4 54 15N 8 55W
Sliven Bulgaria 55 M5 42 40N 26 19E
Slough England 16 C2 51 31N 0 36W
Slough u.a. England 16 C1 50 25N 0 40W
SLOVAKIA 53 J4/K3
SLOVENIA 54 F6
Smethwick England 15 E2 52 30N 1 58W
Smolensk Russia 62 F7 54 49N 32 04E
Smolyan Bulgaria 55 L4 41 34N 24 42E
Snaefell mt. Isle of Man 12 B3 54 16N 4 28W
Snake r. USA 90 C5 44 00N 118 00W
Sneek Neths 48 D6 53 02N 5 40E
Sneem RoI 21 B1 51 50N 9 45W
Snodland England 17 D2 51 20N 0 27E
Snowdon mt. Wales 14 B3 53 04N 4 05W
Snowy Mountains
Australia 73 J3 36 50S 147 00E
Soar r. England 15 E2 52 50N 1 15W
Soay i. Scotland 8 C2 57 08N 6 14W
Socotra i. Yemen 66 F1 12 05N 54 10E
Söderhamn Sweden 49 E3 61 19N 17 10E
Södertälje Sweden 49 E2 59 11N 17 39E
Sofia Bulgaria 55 K5 42 40N 23 18E
Soham England 17 D3 52 20N 0 20E
Soissons France 50 F5 49 23N 3 20E
Solāpur India 66 D3 17 43N 75 56E
Solent, The sd. England 16 B1 50 45N 1 25W
Soligorsk Belarus 53 N6 52 50N 27 32E
Solihull England 15 E2 52 25N 1 45W
Sollefteå Sweden 49 E3 63 09N 17 15E
Sóller Spain 51 G3 39 46N 2 42E
SOLOMON ISLANDS 73 L9/M9
Solothurn Switz. 52 C3 47 13N 7 32E
Soltau Germany 52 D6 52 59N 9 50E
Solway Firth Scotland 11 F2 54 45N 3 40W
SOMALIA 81 Q2/Q3
Somerset co. England 19 D3/E3 51 10N 3 00W
Somerton England 19 E3 51 03N 2 44W
Sompting England 16 C1 50 50N 0 21W
Sønderborg Denmark 49 C1 54 55N 9 48E
Sondrio Italy 54 C7 46 11N 9 52E
Sonning Common tn.
England 16 C2 51 31N 0 59W
Sopron Hungary 53 H3 47 46N 16 35E
Sora Italy 54 E4 41 43N 13 37E
Soria Spain 51 D4 41 46N 2 28W
Soroca Moldova 53 P4 48 08N 28 12E
Sosnowiec Poland 53 J5 50 16N 19 07E
Souillac France 50 E3 44 53N 1 29E
Southam England 15 E2 52 15N 1 23W
Southampton England 16 B1 50 55N 1 25W
Southampton u.a.
England 16 B1 50 50N 1 20W
Southampton Water sd.
England 16 B1 50 50N 1 20W
South Ayrshire u.a.
Scotland 11 E2 55 20N 4 40W
South Ballachulish
Scotland 8 D1 56 42N 5 09W
South Bank tn. England 13 E3 54 35N 1 10W
South Benfleet England 17 D2 51 33N 0 34E
Southborough England 17 D2 51 10N 0 15E
South Brent England 18 D2 50 25N 3 50W
South Carolina state
USA 91 K3 34 00N 81 00W
South Cave tn. England 13 F2 53 46N 0 35W
South Cerney England 15 E1 51 41N 1 57W
South Dakota state
USA 90 F5 45 00N 102 00W
South Dorset Downs
England 19 E2 50 40N 2 30W
South Downs England 16 C1 50 50N 0 30W
Southend u.a. England 17 D2 51 32N 0 50E
Southend Scotland 11 D1 55 20N 5 38W
Southend-on-Sea
England 17 D2 51 33N 0 43E
Southerness Point
Scotland 11 F1 54 53N 3 37W
Southern Ocean 101

South Esk r. Scotland 9 F1 56 50N 3 10W
South Foreland c.
England 17 E2 51 09N 1 23E
South Gloucestershire
u.a. England 15 D1 51 30N 2 30W
South Hayling England 16 C1 50 47N 0 59W
South Island NZ 73 N1/P2 42 30S 172 00E
South Kirkby England 13 E2 53 34N 1 20W
SOUTH KOREA 69 N5
South Lanarkshire u.a.
Scotland 11 E2/F2 55 35N 3 55W
Southminster England 17 D2 51 40N 0 50E
South Molton England 18 D3 51 01N 3 50W
South Normanton
England 13 E2 53 06N 1 20W
South Ockendon
England 17 D2 51 32N 0 18E
South Petherton
England 19 E2 50 58N 2 49W
South Pole Antarctica 101 90 00S
Southport England 12 C2 53 39N 3 01W
South Queensferry
Scotland 11 F2 55 59N 3 25W
South Shields England 13 E3 55 00N 1 25W
South Tyne r. England 12 D3 54 52N 2 30W
South Uist i. Scotland 8 B2 57 20N 7 15W
South Walls i. Scotland 7 A1 58 47N 3 11W
Southwick England 16 C1 51 01N 0 14W
Southwold England 17 E3 52 20N 1 40E
South Woodham Ferrers
England 17 D2 51 38N 0 38E
South Yorkshire co.
England 13 E2 53 30N 1 30W
Sowerby Bridge
England 13 E2 53 43N 1 54W
SPAIN 51 C3/E3
Spalding England 16 C3 52 47N 0 10W
Spárti Greece 55 K2 37 05N 22 25E
Spean Bridge tn.
Scotland 9 E1 56 53N 4 54W
Spennymoor England 13 E3 54 42N 1 35W
Sperrin Mountains NI 10 B1 54 49N 7 06W
Spey r. Scotland 9 F2 57 15N 3 45W
Spiddle RoI 20 B3 53 15N 9 18W
Spilsby England 13 G2 53 11N 0 05E
Spink RoI 21 D2 52 53N 7 12W
Spithead sd. England 16 B1 50 45N 1 10W
Spitsbergen i.
Arctic Ocean 62 D12 79 00N 15 00E
Spittal an der Drau
Austria 52 F3 46 48N 13 30E
Split Croatia 55 G5 43 31N 16 28E
Spokane USA 90 C6 47 40N 117 25W
Spoleto Italy 54 E4 42 44N 12 44E
Springfield Illinois USA 91 J4 39 49N 89 39W
Springfield Masachusetts
USA 91 M5 42 07N 72 35W
Spurn Head England 13 G2 53 36N 0 07E
SRI LANKA 66 E1
Srinagar Kashmir 66 C6 34 08N 74 50E
Stacks Mountains RoI 21 B2 52 19N 9 33W
Staffa i. Scotland 8 C1 56 30N 6 15W
Stafford England 15 D2 52 48N 2 07W
Staffordshire co.
England 15 D2/E2 52 50N 2 00W
Staines England 16 C2 51 26N 0 30W
Stainforth England 13 E2 53 36N 1 01W
Stalbridge England 19 E2 50 58N 2 23W
Stalybridge England 12 D2 53 29N 2 04W
Stamford Bridge tn.
England 13 F2 53 59N 0 55W
Standish USA 93 D2 43 59N 83 58W
Standish England 12 D2 53 35N 2 40W
Stane Scotland 11 F2 55 50N 3 47W
Stanhope England 12 D3 54 45N 2 01W
Stanley England 13 G2 53 44N 1 28W
Stanley England 13 E3 54 53N 1 42W
Stansted Mountfitchet
England 17 D2 51 54N 0 12E
Stapleford England 15 E2 52 56N 1 15W
Staplehurst England 17 D2 51 10N 0 33E
Starachowice Poland 53 K5 51 03N 21 00E
Stara Zagora Bulgaria 55 L5 42 25N 25 37E
Start Bay England 18 D2 50 16N 3 35W
Start Point England 18 D2 50 13N 3 38W
Staunton USA 91 L4 38 10N 79 05W
Stavanger Norway 49 C2 58 58N 5 45E
Staveley England 13 E2 53 16N 1 20W
Stavropol' Russia 62 G6 45 03N 41 59E
Staxton England 13 F3 54 11N 0 26W
Steeping r. England 13 G2 53 10N 0 10E
Stendal Germany 52 E6 52 36N 11 52E
Stenhousemuir
Scotland 11 F3 56 02N 3 49W
Stevenage England 16 C2 51 55N 0 14W
Stevenston Scotland 11 E2 55 39N 4 45W
Stewart Canada 88 J5 55 56N 130 01W
Stewarton Scotland 11 E2 55 41N 4 31W
Stewartstown NI 10 C1 54 35N 6 41W
Steyning England 16 C1 50 53N 0 20W
Steyr Austria 52 G3 48 04N 14 25E
Stilton England 16 C3 52 29N 0 17W
Stinchar r. Scotland 11 E2 55 06N 5 00W
Stirling Canada 88 N3 49 34N 112 30W
Stirling u.a. Scotland 11 E3 56 10N 4 15W
Stirling Scotland 11 F3 56 07N 3 57W
Stockbridge England 16 B2 51 07N 1 29W
Stockerau Austria 53 H4 48 24N 16 13E

Place	Page	Grid	Lat	Long
Stockholm Sweden	49	E2	59 20N	18 05E
Stockport England	12	D2	53 25N	2 10W
Stocksbridge England	13	E2	53 27N	1 34W
Stockton-on-Tees England	13	E3	54 34N	1 19W
Stockton-on-Tees u.a. England	13	E3	54 33N	1 24W
Stoer, Point of Scotland	8	D3	58 25N	5 25W
Stoke-on-Trent u.a. England	12	D2	53 00N	2 10W
Stokenchurch England	16	C2	51 40N	0 55W
Stoke-on-Trent England	12	D2	53 00N	2 10W
Stoke Poges England	16	C2	51 33N	0 35W
Stokesley England	13	E3	54 28N	1 11W
Stone England	15	D2	52 54N	2 10W
Stonehaven Scotland	9	G1	56 58N	2 13W
Stonehouse Scotland	11	F2	55 43N	3 59W
Stony Stratford England	16	C3	52 04N	0 52W
Størdal Norway	49	D3	63 18N	11 48E
Støren Norway	49	D3	63 03N	10 16E
Stornoway Scotland	8	C3	58 12N	6 23W
Storrington England	16	C1	50 55N	0 28W
Storr, The mt. Scotland	8	C2	57 30N	6 11W
Storuman Sweden	49	E4	65 05N	17 10E
Stotfold England	16	C3	52 01N	0 15W
Stour r. Warwickshire England	15	E2	52 05N	1 45E
Stour r. Suffolk England	17	D3	52 10N	0 30E
Stour r. Kent England	17	E2	51 10N	1 10E
Stour r. Dorset England	19	E2	50 50N	2 10W
Stourbridge tn. England	15	D2	52 27N	2 09W
Stourport-on-Severn England	15	D2	52 21N	2 16W
Stow Scotland	11	G2	55 42N	2 51W
Stowmarket England	17	E3	52 11N	1 00E
Stow-on-the-Wold England	15	E1	51 56N	1 44W
Strabane NI	10	B1	54 49N	7 27W
Strabane district NI	10	B1	54 45N	7 30W
Strachur Scotland	10	D3	56 10N	5 04W
Stradbally Rol	21	D3	53 00N	7 08W
Stradone Rol	20	D3	53 59N	7 14W
Stralsund Germany	52	F7	54 18N	13 06E
Strangford Lough NI	10	D1	54 30N	5 35W
Stranorlar Rol	20	D4	54 48N	7 46W
Stranraer Scotland	10	D2	54 55N	5 02W
Strasbourg France	50	H5	48 35N	7 45E
Stratford-upon-Avon England	15	E2	52 12N	1 41W
Strathaven Scotland	11	E2	55 41N	4 05W
Strathcarron Scotland	8	D2	57 26N	5 27W
Strathpeffer Scotland	9	E2	57 35N	4 33W
Strathy Scotland	9	F3	58 33N	3 59W
Strathy r. Scotland	9	F3	58 30N	4 00W
Strathy Point Scotland	9	F3	58 35N	4 02W
Stratton England	18	C2	50 50N	4 31W
Straubing Germany	52	F4	48 53N	12 35E
Street England	19	3	51 03N	2 45W
Stretford England	12	D2	53 27N	2 19W
Strimonas r. Greece	55	K4	41 00N	23 00E
Strokestown Rol	20	C3	53 47N	8 06W
Stroma i. Scotland	7	A1	58 40N	3 08W
Stromboli mt. Italy	54	F3	38 48N	15 15E
Stromeferry Scotland	8	D2	57 21N	5 34W
Stromness Scotland	7	A1	58 57N	3 18W
Stronsay i. Scotland	7	B2	59 07N	2 37W
Stronsay Firth Scotland	7	B2	59 00N	2 55W
Strontian Scotland	8	D1	56 41N	5 34W
Strood England	17	D2	51 24N	0 28E
Stroud England	15	D1	51 45N	2 12W
Strumble Head Wales	14	A2	52 02N	5 04W
Stryy Ukraine	53	L4	49 16N	23 51E
Stubbington England	16	B1	50 49N	12 13W
Studley England	15	E2	52 16N	1 52W
Sturminster Marshall England	19	E2	50 48N	2 04W
Sturminster Newton England	19	E2	50 55N	2 18W
Stuttgart Germany	52	D4	48 47N	9 12E
Subotica Serbia & Montenegro	55	H7	46 04N	19 41E
SUDAN	81	L4/M4		
Sudbury Canada	89	U3	46 30N	81 01W
Sudbury England	17	E2	52 02N	0 44E
Suffolk co. England	17	D3/E3	52 10N	1 00E
Suhl Germany	52	E5	50 37N	10 43E
Sulawesi i. Indonesia	71	F3/G3	2 00S	120 00E
Sumatera i. Indonesia	71	B4/C3	0 00	100 00E
Sumburgh Head Scotland	7	C2	59 51N	1 16W
Summerhill Rol	20	E3	53 29N	6 44W
Sumy Ukraine	56	D5	50 55N	34 49E
Sunderland England	13	E3	54 55N	1 23W
Sundsvall Sweden	49	E3	62 22N	17 20E
Sunningdale England	16	C2	51 24N	0 37W
Superior, Lake Canada/USA	92	C3	48 00N	88 00W
Surabaya Indonesia	71	E2	7 14S	112 45E
Surat India	66	C4	21 10N	72 54E
SURINAME	96	F14		
Surrey co. England	16	C2	51 15N	0 30W
Sutton England	16	C2	51 22N	0 12W
Sutton Coldfield England	15	E2	52 34N	1 48W
Sutton in Ashfield England	13	E2	53 08N	1 15W
Sutton on Sea England	13	G2	53 19N	0 17E
Suwalki Poland	53	L7	54 06N	22 56E
Suzhou China	69	M4	31 21N	120 40E
Svilengrad Bulgaria	55	M4	41 45N	26 14E
Swadlincote England	15	E2	52 46N	1 33W
Swaffham England	17	D3	52 39N	0 41E
Swale r. England	12	D3	54 20N	2 00W
Swanage England	19	F2	50 37N	1 58W
Swanley England	17	D2	51 24N	0 12E
Swanlinbar Rol	20	D4	54 12N	7 42W
Swanscombe England	17	D2	51 26N	0 18E
Swansea Wales	14	C1	51 38N	3 57W
Swansea Bay Wales	14	C1	51 35N	3 55W
Swansea u.a. Wales	14	B1/C1	51 35N	4 10W
SWAZILAND	82	F2		
SWEDEN	49	D2/E4		
Swiebodzin Poland	53	G6	52 15N	15 31E
Swilly r. Rol	20	D4	54 55N	7 45W
Swindon England	16	B2	51 34N	1 47W
Swindon u.a. England	16	B2	51 34N	1 47W
Swinford Rol	20	C3	53 57N	8 57W
Swinoujscie Poland	52	G6	53 55N	14 18E
Swinton England	13	E2	53 30N	1 19W
SWITZERLAND	52	C3/D3		
Swords Rol	21	E3	53 28N	6 13W
Sydney Australia	73	K4	33 55S	151 10E
Sylt i. Germany	52	D7	54 00N	8 00E
Symbister Scotland	7	D3	60 21N	1 02W
Symington Scotland	11	F2	55 37N	3 35W
Syracuse USA	91	L5	43 03N	76 10W
SYRIA	64	C6		
Syzran' Russia	62	G7	53 10N	48 29E
Szczecin Poland	52	G6	53 25N	14 32E
Szeged Hungary	53	K3	46 15N	20 09E
Szombathely Hungary	53	H3	47 14N	16 38E

T

Place	Page	Grid	Lat	Long
Tábor Czech Rep.	52	G4	49 25N	14 39E
Tabriz Iran	65	E6	38 05N	46 18E
Tacoma USA	90	B6	47 16N	122 30W
Tadcaster England	13	E2	53 53N	1 16W
Tadley England	16	B2	51 21N	1 08W
Taegu S. Korea	69	N5	35 52N	128 36E
Taejon S. Korea	69	N5	36 20N	127 26E
Tafalla Spain	51	E5	42 32N	1 41W
Taff r. Wales	14	C1	51 30N	3 10W
Taghmon Rol	21	E2	52 19N	6 39W
Taibei Taiwan	69	M3	25 05N	121 32E
Tain Scotland	9	E2	57 48N	4 04W
TAIWAN	69	M2		
Taiyuan China	69	K5	37 50N	112 30E
TAJIKISTAN	62	J4/K4		
Tajo r. Spain/Portugal	51	B3	39 00N	7 00W
Takamatsu Japan	70	B1	34 20N	134 01E
Talgarth Wales	14	C1	52 00N	3 15W
Tallaght Rol	20	E3	53 17N	6 21W
Tallahassee USA	91	K3	30 26N	84 16W
Tallinn Estonia	49	F2	59 22N	24 48E
Tallow Rol	21	C2	52 05N	8 01W
Tal-y-bont Wales	14	C2	52 29N	3 59W
Tamanrasset Algeria	80	F6	22 50N	5 28E
Tamar r. England	18	C2	50 32N	4 13W
Tambov Russia	62	G7	52 44N	41 28E
Tame r. England	15	E2	52 40N	1 45W
Tampa USA	91	K2	27 58N	82 38W
Tampere Finland	49	F3	61 32N	23 45E
Tamworth England	15	E2	52 39N	1 40W
Tandragee NI	10	C1	54 22N	6 25W
Tanganyika, Lake East Africa	83	B1	7 00S	30 00E
Tangier Morocco	80	C9	35 48N	5 45W
Tangshan China	69	L5	39 37N	118 05E
TANZANIA	83	B1/D1		
Tapachula Mexico	94	F2	14 54N	92 15W
Taransay i. Scotland	8	B2	57 55N	7 00W
Táranto Italy	55	G4	40 28N	17 15E
Tarazona Spain	51	E4	41 54N	1 44W
Tarbert Rol	21	B2	52 32N	9 23W
Tarbert Western Isles Scotland	8	C2	57 54N	6 49W
Tarbert Argyle and Bute Scotland	10	D2	55 52N	5 26W
Tarbes France	50	E2	43 14N	0 05E
Tarbet Scotland	11	E3	56 12N	4 43W
Tarbolton Scotland	11	E2	55 31N	4 29W
Târgovişte Romania	53	M2	44 56N	25 27E
Târgu Mureş Romania	53	M3	46 33N	24 34E
Tarleton England	12	D2	53 41N	2 50W
Tarporley England	12	D2	53 10N	2 40W
Tarragona Spain	51	F4	41 07N	1 15E
Tarrasa Spain	51	G4	41 34N	2 00E
Tarsus Turkey	57	D2	26 25N	34 52E
Tartu Estonia	49	G2	58 20N	26 44E
Tashkent Uzbekistan	62	J5	41 16N	69 13E
Taunton England	19	D3	51 01N	3 06W
Taunus mts. Germany	52	D5	50 00N	8 00E
Tauranga NZ	73	Q3	37 41S	176 10E
Taverham England	17	E3	52 41N	1 10E
Tavira Portugal	51	B2	37 07N	7 39W
Tavistock England	18	C2	50 33N	4 08W
Tavy r. England	18	C2	50 36N	4 04W
Taw r. England	18	C2	50 46N	3 55W
Tay r. Scotland	9	F1	56 30N	3 25W
Taynuilt Scotland	10	D1	56 25N	5 14W
Tayport Scotland	9	G1	56 27N	2 53W
T'bilisi Georgia	57	F3	41 43N	44 48E
Tczew Poland	53	J7	54 05N	18 46E
Tebay England	12	D3	54 26N	2 35W
Tees r. England	12	D3	54 40N	1 20W
Tegucigalpa Honduras	94	G2	14 05N	87 14W
Tehran Iran	65	F6	35 40N	51 26E
Teifi r. Wales	14	B2	52 03N	4 30W
Teign r. England	18	D2	50 42N	3 48W
Teignmouth England	18	D2	50 33N	3 30W
Teith r. Scotland	11	E3	56 10N	4 08W
Tejo r. Portugal	51	B3	39 30N	8 15W
Tel Aviv-Yafo Israel	64	B5	32 05N	34 46E
Telford England	15	D2	52 42N	2 28W
Teme r. England	15	D2	52 15N	2 25W
Tempio Pausania Italy	54	C4	40 54N	9 07E
Templemore Rol	21	D2	52 48N	7 50W
Templenoe Rol	21	B1	51 51N	9 41W
Tenbury Wells England	15	D2	52 19N	2 35W
Tenby Wales	14	B1	51 41N	4 43W
Tenerife i. Spain	80	A7	28 15N	16 35W
Tennessee r. USA	91	J4	35 00N	88 00W
Tennessee state USA	91	J4	35 00N	87 00W
Tenterden England	17	D2	51 05N	0 41E
Teramo Italy	54	E5	42 40N	13 43E
Teresina Brazil	96	J12	5 09S	42 46W
Termim Imerese Italy	54	E2	27 59N	13 42E
Termoli Italy	54	F4	42 00N	15 00E
Terni Italy	54	E5	42 34N	12 39E
Terracina Italy	54	E4	41 17N	13 15E
Terrasini Italy	54	E3	38 09N	15 50E
Terre Haute USA	91	J4	39 27N	87 24W
Teruel Spain	51	E4	40 21N	1 06W
Teslin Canada	88	J6	60 10N	132 42W
Test r. England	16	B2	51 05N	1 30W
Tetbury England	15	D1	51 39N	2 10W
Tetney England	13	F2	53 30N	0 01W
Tétouan Morocco	80	C9	35 34N	5 22W
Teviotdale Scotland	11	G2	55 20N	3 00W
Teviothead Scotland	11	G2	55 19N	2 56W
Tewkesbury England	15	D1	51 59N	2 09W
Texas state USA	90	G3	31 00N	100 00W
THAILAND	71	B7/C7		
Thame r. England	16	B2	51 45N	1 05W
Thame England	16	C2	51 45N	0 59W
Thames r. England	16	C2	51 32N	0 50W
Thar Desert India	66	C5	27 30N	72 00E
Thatcham England	16	B2	51 25N	1 15W
Thaxted England	17	D2	51 57N	0 20E
The Downs tn. Rol	20	D3	53 30N	7 14W
The Everglades USA	91	K2	26 00N	81 00W
The Mumbles tn. Wales	14	C1	51 35N	3 59W
The Peak mt. England	13	E2	53 24N	1 51W
Thermaïkós Kólpos g. Greece	55	K3/K4	40 00N	22 50E
The Rower tn. Rol	21	D2	52 27N	6 57W
Thessaloníki Greece	55	K4	40 38N	22 58E
Thetford England	17	D3	52 25N	0 45E
Thiers France	50	F3	45 51N	3 33E
Thimphu Bhutan	67	F5	27 32N	89 43E
Thionville France	50	H5	49 22N	6 11E
Thira i. Greece	55	L2	36 00N	25 00E
Thirsk England	13	E3	54 14N	1 20W
Thiva Greece	55	K3	38 19N	23 19E
Thomastown Rol	21	D2	52 31N	7 08W
Thompson Canada	89	R5	55 45N	97 54W
Thornaby-on-Tees England	13	E3	54 34N	1 18W
Thornbury England	15	D1	51 37N	2 32W
Thorne England	13	F2	53 37N	0 58W
Thorney England	16	C3	52 37N	0 07W
Thornhill Scotland	11	F2	55 15N	3 46W
Thornton England	12	D2	53 53N	3 00W
Thorpe-le-Soken England	17	E2	51 52N	1 10E
Thouars France	50	D4	46 59N	0 13W
Thrapston England	15	F2	52 24N	0 32W
Thuin Belgium	48	C3	50 21N	4 18E
Thun Switz.	52	C3	46 46N	7 38E
Thurcroft England	13	E2	53 24N	1 16W
Thurles Rol	21	D2	52 41N	7 49W
Thurrock u.a. England	17	D2	51 30N	0 25E
Thursby England	12	C3	54 51N	3 03W
Thurso Scotland	9	F3	58 35N	3 32W
Thurso r. Scotland	9	F3	58 20N	3 40W
Thurso Bay Scotland	9	F3	58 37N	3 34W
Tianjin China	69	L5	39 08N	117 12E
Tiberias Israel	64	N11	32 45N	35 30E
Tibesti mts. Chad	81	J6	21 00N	17 00E
Tickhill England	13	E2	53 26N	1 06W
Tighnabruaich Scotland	10	D2	55 56N	5 14W
Tigris r. Turkey/Iraq	65	E5	32 00N	46 00E
Tijuana Mexico	94	A6	32 29N	117 10W
Tilburg Neths	48	D4	51 34N	5 05E
Tilbury England	17	D2	51 28N	0 23E
Till r. England	11	G2	55 38N	2 08W
Till r. England	13	F2	53 20N	0 40W
Tillicoultry Scotland	11	F3	56 09N	2 45W
Tilt r. Scotland	9	F1	56 50N	3 45W
Timişoara Romania	53	L2	45 45N	21 15E
Timor i. Indonesia	71	G1/H2	9 00S	125 00E
Tinahely Rol	21	E2	52 48N	6 28W
Tingwall Scotland	7	A2	59 04N	3 03W
Tintagel England	18	C2	50 40N	4 45W
Tintagel Head England	18	C2	50 41N	4 46W
Tipperary Rol	21	C2	52 29N	8 10W
Tipperary co. Rol	21	D2	52 30N	8 00W
Tiptree England	17	D2	51 49N	0 45E
Tiranë Albania	55	H4	41 20N	19 49E
Tiree i. Scotland	8	C1	56 30N	6 55W
Titu Romania	53	M2	44 40N	25 32E
Tiverton England	18	D2	50 55N	3 29W
Tivoli Italy	54	E4	41 58N	12 48E
Tlemcen Algeria	80	D8	34 53N	1 21W
Tobercurry Rol	20	C4	54 03N	8 43W
Tobermore NI	10	C1	54 48N	6 42W
Tobermory Scotland	8	C1	56 37N	6 05W
Todmorden England	12	D2	53 43N	2 05W
Toe Head Rol	21	B1	51 30N	9 12W
Toe Head Scotland	8	B2	57 50N	7 07W
TOGO	80	E3		
Tokelau Islands Pacific Ocean	100	J7	9 00S	168 00W
Tokyo Japan	70	C2	35 40N	139 45E
Toledo Spain	51	C3	39 52N	4 02W
Toledo USA	91	K5	41 40N	83 35W
Tolmezzo Italy	54	E7	46 24N	13 01E
Tolosa Spain	51	D5	43 09N	2 04W
Tolsta Head Scotland	8	C3	58 20N	6 10W
Toluca Mexico	94	E3	19 20N	99 40W
Tomar Portugal	51	A3	39 36N	8 25W
Tomatin Scotland	9	F2	57 20N	3 59W
Tomelloso Spain	51	D3	39 09N	3 01W
Tomintoul Scotland	9	F2	57 14N	3 22W
Tomsk Russia	63	L8	56 30N	85 05E
Tonbridge England	17	D2	51 12N	0 16E
TONGA	100	J5		
Tongue Scotland	9	E3	58 28N	4 25W
Tønsberg Norway	49	D2	59 16N	10 25E
Tonyrefail Wales	14	C1	51 36N	3 25W
Toomyvara Rol	21	C2	52 51N	8 02W
Topsham England	18	D2	50 42N	3 27W
Tor Bay England	18	D2	50 27N	3 30W
Torbay England	18	D2	50 27N	3 30W
Tordesillas Spain	51	C4	41 30N	5 00W
Tore Scotland	9	E2	57 27N	4 21W
Torfaen u.a. Wales	14	C1	51 38N	3 04W
Tornio Finland	49	F4	65 50N	24 10E
Toronto Canada	89	V2	43 42N	79 46W
Torpoint tn. England	18	C2	50 22N	4 11W
Torre del Greco Italy	54	F4	40 46N	14 22E
Torrelavega Spain	51	C3	43 21N	4 03W
Torremolinos Spain	51	C2	36 38N	4 30W
Torrente Spain	51	E3	39 27N	0 28W
Torres Vedras Portugal	51	A3	39 05N	9 15W
Torrevieja Spain	51	E2	37 59N	0 40W
Torridge r. England	18	C2	50 56N	4 22W
Torridon Scotland	8	D2	57 33N	5 31W
Tortosa Spain	51	F4	40 49N	0 31E
Torún Poland	53	J6	53 01N	18 35E
Tory Island Rol	20	C5	55 16N	8 14W
Tory Sound Rol	20	C5	55 15N	8 05W
Totland England	16	B1	50 40N	1 32W
Totnes England	18	D2	50 25N	3 41W
Tottington England	12	D2	53 37N	2 20W
Totton England	16	B1	50 56N	1 29W
Touggourt Algeria	80	F8	33 08N	6 04E
Toul France	50	G5	48 41N	5 54E
Toulon France	50	G2	43 07N	5 55E
Toulouse France	50	E2	43 33N	1 24E
Tourcoing France	50	F6	50 44N	310E
Tours France	50	E4	47 23N	0 42E
Toward Scotland	10	E2	55 54N	4 58W
Towcester England	15	F2	52 08N	1 00W
Townsville Australia	73	J7	19 13S	146 48E
Toyama Japan	70	C2	36 42N	137 14E
Toyota Japan	70	C2	35 05N	137 09E
Tralee Rol	21	B2	52 16N	9 42W
Tralee Bay Rol	21	B2	52 20N	9 55W
Tramore Rol	21	D2	52 10N	7 10W
Tramore Bay Rol	21	D2	52 08N	7 08W
Tranent Scotland	11	G2	55 57N	2 57W
Trani Italy	55	G4	41 17N	16 25E
Trápani Italy	54	E3	38 02N	12 32E
Traun Austria	52	G4	48 14N	14 15E
Trawsfynydd Wales	14	C2	52 54N	3 55W
Tredegar Wales	14	C1	51 47N	3 16W
Tregaron Wales	14	C2	52 13N	3 55W
Tregony England	18	C2	50 16N	4 55W
Tremadog Bay Wales	14	B2	52 50N	4 15W
Trent r. England	13	F2	53 30N	0 50W
Trento Italy	54	D7	46 04N	11 08E
Tresco i. England	18	A1	49 57N	6 20W
Treviso Italy	54	E6	45 40N	12 15E
Trevose Head England	18	B2	50 33N	5 01W
Trier Germany	52	C4	49 45N	6 39E
Trieste Italy	54	E6	45 39N	13 47E
Trikala Greece	55	J3	39 33N	21 46E
Trim Rol	20	E3	53 34N	6 47W
Tring England	16	C2	51 48N	0 40W
TRINIDAD AND TOBAGO	95	M2		
Trípoli Greece	55	K2	37 31N	22 22E
Tripoli Lebanon	64	C5	34 27N	35 50E
Tripoli Libya	81	G8	32 54N	13 11E
Trois-Rivières tn. Canada	89	W3	46 21N	72 34W
Trollhätten Sweden	49	D2	58 17N	12 20E
Tromsø Norway	49	E4	69 42N	19 00E
Trondheim Norway	49	D3	63 36N	10 23E
Troon Scotland	11	E2	55 32N	4 40W
Trotternish p. Scotland	8	C2	57 00N	6 00W
Troup Head Scotland	9	G2	57 41N	2 19W
Trouville France	50	E5	49 22N	0 05E
Trowbridge England	16	A2	51 20N	2 13W

Troyes France 50 G5 48 18N 4 05E
Trujillo Spain 51 C3 39 28N 5 53W
Truro England 18 B2 50 16N 5 03W
Tuam RoI 20 C3 53 31N 8 50W
Tübingen Germany 52 D4 48 32N 9 04E
Tubruq Libya 81 K8 32 05N 23 59E
Tucson USA 90 D3 32 15N 110 57W
Tudela Spain 51 E5 42 04N 1 37W
Tudweiliog Wales 14 B2 52 55N 4 39W
Tula Russia 62 F7 54 11N 37 38E
Tulcea Romania 53 P2 45 10N 28 50E
Tulla RoI 21 C2 52 52N 8 45W
Tullamore RoI 20 D3 53 16N 7 30W
Tulle France 50 E3 45 16N 1 46E
Tullow RoI 21 E2 52 48N 6 44W
Tulsa USA 91 G4 36 07N 95 58W
Tulsk RoI 20 C3 53 47N 8 15W
Tummel r. Scotland 9 E1 56 40N 4 00W
Tummel Bridge
  Scotland 9 F1 56 43N 3 58W
Tunis Tunisia 80 G9 36 50N 10 13E
TUNISIA 80 F8/G8
Tŭrgovishte Bulgaria 55 M5 43 14N 26 37E
Turgutlu Turkey 55 M3 38 30N 27 43E
Turin Italy 54 B6 45 04N 7 40E
Turkana, Lake
  Ethiopia/Kenya 83 D6/E6 4 00N 36 00E
TURKEY 57 C2/E2
TURKMENISTAN 62 H4/J4
Turks and Caicos Islands
  W. Indies 95 K4 21 30N 72 00W
Turku Finland 49 F3 60 27N 22 15E
Turnberry Scotland 10 E2 55 20N 4 50W
Turriff Scotland 9 G2 57 32N 2 28W
Tutbury England 15 E2 52 52N 1 40W
Tuttlingen Germany 52 D4 47 59N 8 49E
TUVALU 100 H7
Túy Spain 51 A5 42 03N 8 39W
Tuz Gölü l. Turkey 57 D2 38 40N 33 35E
Tuzla
  Bosnia-Herzegovina 55 H6 44 33N 18 41E
Tver' Russia 62 F8 56 49N 35 57E
Tweed r.
  Scotland/England 11 G2 55 45N 2 10W
Tweedmouth England 11 G2 55 47N 2 00W
Twin Falls tn. USA 90 D5 42 34N 114 30W
Twyford England 16 C2 51 29N 0 53W
Twyford England 16 B2 51 01N 1 19W
Tyldesley England 12 D2 53 32N 2 29W
Tylers Green England 16 C2 51 37N 0 42W
Tyndrum Scotland 9 E1 57 27N 4 44W
Tyne r. Scotland 11 G2 55 58N 2 43W
Tyne and Wear co.
  England 13 E3 55 00N 1 10W
Tynemouth tn. England 13 E4 55 01N 1 24W
Tynset Norway 49 D3 62 17N 10 47E
Tywi r. Wales 14 B1 51 50N 4 25W
Tywyn Wales 14 B2 52 35N 4 05W

U

Uaupés Brazil 96 D13 0 07S 67 05W
Uberaba Brazil 96 H10 19 47S 47 57W
Uckfield England 17 D2 50 58N 0 05E
Uddevalla Sweden 49 D2 58 20N 11 56E
Udine Italy 54 E7 46 04N 13 14E
Uelzen Germany 52 E6 52 58N 10 34E
Ufa Russia 62 H7 54 45N 55 58E
Uffculme England 19 D2 50 54N 3 21W
UGANDA 83 B6/C6
Ugie r. 9 H2 57 31N 1 55W
Uig Scotland 8 C2 57 35N 6 22W
Uithuizen Neths 48 E6 53 24N 6 41E
UKRAINE 56 C4/D4
Ulan Bator Mongolia 69 J7 47 54N 106 52E
Ulan-Ude Russia 63 N7 51 55N 107 40E
Ullapool Scotland 8 D2 57 54N 5 10W
Ullswater l. England 12 D3 54 35N 2 55W
Ulm Germany 52 D4 48 24N 10 00E
Ulva i. Scotland 8 C1 56 30N 6 15W
Ulverston England 12 C3 54 12N 3 06W
Umeå Sweden 49 F3 63 50N 20 15E
Unapool Scotland 9 D3 58 14N 5 01W
Ungava Bay Canada 89 X5 59 00N 67 30W
Unimak Island USA 88 C4 55 00N 164 00W
UNITED ARAB EMIRATES
  65 F3
UNITED KINGDOM 6
UNITED STATES OF AMERICA
  90/91
Unst i. Scotland 7 D3 60 45N 0 55W
Upavon England 16 B2 51 18N 1 49W
Upper Lough Erne NI 10 B1 54 15N 7 30W
Upper Tean England 15 E2 52 57N 2 00W
Uppingham England 15 F2 52 35N 0 43W
Uppsala Sweden 49 E2 59 55N 17 38E
Upton West Yorkshire
  England 13 E2 53 37N 1 17W
Upton Dorset England 19 E2 50 42N 2 02W
Ural r. Asia 62 H6 48 00N 52 00E
Ural Mountains Russia 62 H7/H9 57 00N 60 00E
Ure r. England 13 E3 54 20N 1 55W
Urlingford RoI 21 D2 52 43N 7 35W
Urmston England 12 D2 53 27N 2 21W
Urr r. Scotland 11 F2 55 05N 3 57W
URUGUAY 97 F6

Uruguay r.
  Uruguay/Argentina 97 F6 32 00S 57 40W
Ürümqi China 68 E6 43 43N 87 38E
Ushaw Moor tn.
  England 13 E3 54 47N 1 39W
Usk r. Wales 14 C1 51 55N 3 40W
Ussel France 50 F3 45 32N 2 18E
Ust'-Ilimsk Russia 63 N8 58 03N 102 39E
Utah state USA 90 D4 39 0N 112 00W
Utah Lake USA 90 D5 40 10N 111 50W
Utrecht Neths 48 D5 52 05N 5 07E
Utrera Spain 51 C2 37 10N 5 47W
Uttoxeter England 15 E2 52 54N 1 52W
UZBEKISTAN 62 J5

V

Vác Hungary 53 J3 47 46N 19 08E
Valdepeñas Spain 51 D3 38 46N 3 24W
Val-d'Or Canada 89 V3 48 07N 77 47W
Valence France 50 G3 44 56N 4 54E
Valencia Spain 51 E3 39 29N 0 24W
Valencia Venezuela 96 D16 10 14N 67 59W
Valencia, Gulf of Spain 51 F3 39 30N 0 20E
Valencia Island i. RoI 21 A1 51 52N 10 20W
Valenciennes France 50 F6 50 22N 3 32E
Vale of Glamorgan, The
  u.a. Wales 14 C1 51 30N 3 30W
Valladolid Mexico 94 G4 20 40N 88 11W
Valladolid Spain 51 C4 41 39N 4 45W
Valletta Malta 54 F1 35 54N 14 32E
Valley tn. Wales 14 B3 53 17N 4 34W
Valverde del Camino
  Spain 51 B2 37 35N 6 45W
Vanadzor Armenia 57 F3 40 49N 44 30E
Vancouver Canada 88 L3 49 13N 123 06W
Vancouver USA 90 B6 45 38N 122 40W
Vänern l. Sweden 49 D2 59 00N 13 30E
Van Gölü l. Turkey 57 F2 38 33N 42 46E
Vanna i. Norway 49 E5 70 05N 19 50E
Vännäs Sweden 49 E3 63 56N 19 50E
Vannes France 50 C4 47 40N 2 44W
Vantaa Finland 49 F3 60 20N 24 50E
VANUATU 73 N7
Varanasi India 66 E5 25 20N 83 00E
Vardø Norway 49 K6 70 22N 31 06E
Varese Italy 54 C6 45 49N 8 49E
Varkhaus Finland 49 G3 62 20N 27 50E
Varna Bulgaria 55 M5 43 12N 27 57E
Värnamo Sweden 49 D2 57 11N 14 03E
Vaslui Romania 53 N3 46 37N 27 46E
Västerås Sweden 49 E2 59 36N 16 32E
Västervik Sweden 49 E2 57 45N 16 40E
Vasto Italy 54 F5 42 07N 14 43E
Vatersay i. Scotland 8 B1 56 55N 7 32W
Vatra Dornei Romania 53 M3 47 20N 25 21E
Vättern l. Sweden 49 D2 58 20N 14 20E
Växjö Sweden 49 D2 56 52N 14 50E
Vejle Denmark 49 C2 55 43N 9 33E
Velebit mts. Croatia 54 F6 44 00N 15 00E
Vélez-Málaga Spain 51 C2 36 47N 4 06W
Vélez Rubio Spain 51 D2 37 39N 2 04W
Vementry i. Scotland 7 C3 60 20N 1 28W
Vendôme France 50 E4 47 48N 1 04E
VENEZUELA 96 D15
Venice Italy 54 E6 45 26N 12 20E
Venissieux France 50 G3 45 42N 4 46E
Venlo Netherland 48 E4 51 22N 6 10E
Ventnor England 16 B1 50 36N 1 11W
Ventura USA 90 C3 34 16N 119 18W
Vera Spain 51 E2 37 15N 1 51W
Veracruz Mexico 94 E3 19 11N 96 10W
Vercelli Italy 54 CC6 45 19N 8 26E
Verdun-sur-Meuse
  France 50 G5 49 10N 5 24E
Verin Spain 51 B4 41 55N 7 26W
Vermont state USA 91 M5 44 00N 73 00W
Verona Italy 54 D6 45 26N 11 00E
Versailles France 50 F5 48 48N 2 07E
Verviers Belgium 48 D3 50 36N 5 52E
Verwood England 19 F2 50 53N 1 52W
Vesoul France 50 H4 47 38N 6 09E
Vesuvio vol. Italy 54 F4 40 49N 14 26E
Veszprém Hungary 53 H3 47 06N 17 54E
Vetlanda Sweden 49 E2 57 26N 15 05E
Vevey Switz. 52 C3 46 28N 6 51E
Viano do Castelo
  Portugal 51 A4 41 41N 8 50W
Viareggio Italy 54 D5 43 52N 10 15E
Viborg Denmark 49 C2 56 28N 9 25E
Vibo Valentia Italy 54 G3 38 40N 16 06E
Vicenza Italy 54 D6 45 33N 11 32E
Vichy France 50 F4 46 07N 3 25E
Victoria Canada 88 L3 48 26N 123 20W
Victoria, Lake
  East Africa 83 C4 2 00S 33 00E
Vienna Austria 53 H4 48 13N 16 22E
Vienne France 50 G3 45 32N 4 54E
Vientiane Laos 71 C7 17 59N 102 38E
Vierzon France 50 F4 47 14N 2 03E
VIETNAM 71 D7
Vigo Spain 51 A5 42 15N 8 44W
Vila Nova de Gaia
  Portugal 51 A4 41 08N 8 37W
Vila Real Portugal 51 B4 41 17N 7 45W
Vilhelmina Sweden 49 E3 64 38N 16 40E
Villach Austria 52 F3 46 37N 13 51E

Villalba Spain 51 B5 43 17N 7 41W
Villarrobledo Spain 51 D3 39 16N 2 36W
Villefranche-sur-Saône
  France 50 G3 46 00N 4 43E
Villena Spain 51 E3 38 39N 0 52W
Villeneuve-sur-Lot
  France 50 E3 44 25N 0 43E
Villeurbanne France 50 G3 45 46N 4 54E
Vilnius Lithuania 49 G1 54 40N 25 19E
Vinaroz Spain 51 F4 40 29N 0 28E
Vipiteno Italy 54 D7 46 54N 11 27E
Virginia RoI 20 D3 53 50N 7 04W
Virginia USA 91 H6 47 30N 92 28W
Virginia state USA 91 L4 38 00N 77 00W
Virginia Water tn.
  England 16 C2 51 24N 0 34W
Virgin Islands W. Indies 95 M3 18 00N 64 30W
Visby Sweden 49 E2 57 32N 18 15E
Viseu Portugal 51 B4 40 40N 7 55W
Viterbo Italy 54 E5 42 24N 12 06E
Vitória Brazil 96 J9 20 20S 40 18W
Vitoria Gasteiz Spain 51 D5 42 51N 2 40W
Vitry-le-François
  France 50 G5 48 44N 4 36E
Vitsyebsk Belarus 56 D6 55 10N 30 14E
Vittoria Italy 54 F2 36 58N 14 32E
Vladimir Russia 62 G8 56 08N 40 25E
Vladivostok Russia 63 R5 43 09N 131 53E
Vlissingen Neths 48 B4 51 27N 3 35E
Voitsberg Austria 52 G3 47 04N 15 09E
Volga r. Russia 62 G6 50 00N 45 00E
Volgograd Russia 62 G6 48 45N 44 30E
Volta, Lake Ghana 80 D3 7 30N 0 30W
Vóreioi Sporádes is.
  Greece 55 K3/L3 39 00N 24 00E
Vosges mts. France 50 H5 48 10N 6 50E
Voss Norway 49 C3 60 38N 6 25E
Voxnan Sweden 49 E3 61 22N 15 39E
Vukovar Croatia 55 H6 45 19N 19 01E

W

Waal r. Neths 48 D4 51 50N 5 07E
Waalwijk Neths 48 D4 51 42N 5 04E
Waddesdon England 16 C2 51 51N 0 56W
Waddington England 13 F3 53 10N 0 32W
Wadebridge England 18 C2 50 32N 4 50W
Wadhurst England 17 D2 51 04N 0 21E
Wainfleet All Saints
  England 13 G2 53 06N 0 15E
Wakefield England 13 E2 53 42N 1 29W
Wales UK 14 C2 52 40N 3 30W
Wallasey England 12 C2 53 26N 3 03W
Wallingford England 16 B2 51 37N 1 08W
Wallis and Futuna is.
  Pacific Ocean 100 J6 13 16S 176 15W
Walls Scotland 7 C3 60 14N 1 34W
Wallsend England 13 E3 55 00N 1 31W
Walney, Isle of England 12 C3 54 05N 3 10W
Walsall England 15 E2 52 35N 1 58W
Waltham Abbey
  England 16 D2 51 41N 0 00
Waltham Forest
  England 16 C2 51 36N 0 00
Waltham on the Wolds
  England 15 F2 52 49N 0 49W
Walton-le-Dale England 12 D2 53 45N 2 41W
Walton-on-the-Naze
  England 17 E2 51 51N 1 16E
Walvis Bay tn. Namibia 82 B3 22 59S 14 31E
Wanganui NZ 73 P3 39 56S 175 03E
Wanlockhead Scotland 11 F2 55 24N 3 47W
Wantage England 16 B2 51 36N 1 25W
Warboys England 16 C3 52 24N 0 06W
Ward Hill Scotland 7 A1 58 54N 3 20W
Ware England 16 C2 51 49N 0 02W
Wareham England 19 E2 50 41N 2 07W
Warley England 15 E2 52 30N 1 59W
Warlingham England 16 C2 51 19N 0 04W
Warminster England 16 A2 51 13N 2 12W
Warrenpoint tn. NI 10 C1 54 06N 6 15W
Warrington England 12 D2 53 24N 2 37W
Warsaw Poland 53 K6 52 15N 21 00E
Warsop England 13 E2 53 13N 1 10W
Warton England 12 D2 53 46N 2 54W
Warwick England 15 E2 52 17N 1 34W
Warwickshire co.
  England 15 E2 52 15N 1 40W
Washingborough
  England 13 F2 53 14N 0 28W
Washington England 13 E3 54 54N 1 31W
Washington state USA 90 B6/C6 47 00N 120 00W
Washington D.C. USA 91 L4 38 55N 77 00W
Wash, The b. England 17 D3 52 55N 0 10E
Watchet England 19 D3 51 12N 3 20W
Waterbeach England 16 D3 52 16N 0 11E
Waterford RoI 21 D2 52 15N 7 06W
Waterford co. RoI 21 D2 52 10N 7 30W
Waterford Harbour RoI 21 E2 52 10N 7 00W
Watergrasshill RoI 21 C2 52 00N 8 20W
Waterlooville England 16 B1 50 53N 1 02W
Waterville RoI 21 A1 51 50N 10 10W
Watford England 16 C2 51 39N 0 24W
Watlington England 16 B2 51 39N 1 00W
Watton England 17 D3 52 34N 0 50E

Waveney r. England 17 E3 52 30N 1 30E
Wavre Belgium 48 C3 50 43N 4 37E
Wear r. England 13 E3 54 45N 2 05W
Weaverham England 12 D2 53 16N 2 35W
Wedmore England 19 E3 51 14N 2 49W
Weedon Bec England 15 E2 52 14N 1 05W
Weiden Germany 52 F4 49 40N 12 10E
Weimar Germany 52 E5 50 59N 11 20E
Weissenfels Germany 52 E5 51 12N 11 58E
Welland r. England 16 C3 52 50N 0 10
Welland r. England 15 F2 52 30N 0 50W
Wellingborough
  England 15 F2 52 19N 0 42W
Wellington Telford and Wrekin
  England 15 D2 52 43N 2 31W
Wellington Somerset
  England 19 D2 50 59N 3 15W
Wellington NZ 73 P2 41 17S 174 46E
Wells England 19 E3 51 13N 2 39W
Wells-next-the-Sea
  England 17 D3 52 58N .0 51E
Wels Austria 52 F4 48 10N 14 02E
Welshpool Wales 14 C2 52 40N 3 09W
Welton England 13 F2 54 47N 3 00W
Welwyn Garden City
  England 16 C2 51 48N 0 13W
Wem England 15 D2 52 51N 2 44W
Wemyss Bay Scotland 10 E2 55 55N 4 53W
Wendover England 16 C2 51 46N 0 46W
Wensum r. England 17 D3 52 45N 1 10E
Wenzhou China 69 M3 28 02N 120 40E
West Berkshire u.a.
  England 16 B2 51 28N 1 00W
West Bridgford England 15 E2 52 56N 1 08W
West Bromwich
  England 15 E2 52 31N 1 59W
Westbury England 16 A2 51 16N 2 11W
West Dunbartonshire u.a.
  Scotland 11 E3 56 02N 4 39W
Westerham England 16 D2 51 16N 0 05E
Western Ghats mts. India 66 C3/D2 15 30N 74 00E
Western Isles u.a.
  Scotland 8 B2/B3 57 45N 7 30W
WESTERN SAHARA 80 B6/B7
Western Sayan mts.
  Russia 63 M7 52 30N 92 30E
West Felton England 14 E2 52 49N 2 58W
West Haddon England 15 E2 52 20N 1 04W
Westhill Scotland 9 G2 57 11N 2 16W
West Horsley England 16 C2 51 16N 0 26W
West Indies is.
  Caribbean Sea 95 K4/L4 22 00N 69 00W
West Kilbride Scotland 10 E2 55 42N 4 51W
West Kirby England 12 C2 53 22N 3 10W
West Loch Tarbert
  Western Isles Scotland 8 B2/C2 57 55N 6 52W
West Loch Tarbert
  Argyll and Bute Scotland 10 D2 55 48N 5 31W
West Lothian u.a.
  Scotland 11 F2 55 50N 3 36W
Westmeath co. RoI 20 D3 53 30N 7 30W
West Mersea England 17 D2 51 47N 0 55E
West Midlands co.
  England 15 D2 52 35N 2 00W
Weston-super-Mare
  England 19 E3 51 21N 2 59W
Westport England 20 B3 53 48N 9 32W
Westport Bay RoI 20 B3 53 49N 9 37W
Westray i. Scotland 7 A2 59 18N 3 00W
West Sussex co.
  England 16 C1 51 00N 0 25W
West Thurrock England 17 D2 51 28N 0 20E
West Virginia state
  USA 91 K4 39 00N 81 00W
Westward Ho! England 18 C3 51 02N 4 15W
West Wittering
  England 16 C1 50 47N 0 54W
West Yorkshire co.
  England 13 E2 53 50N 1 30W
Wetherby England 13 E2 53 56N 1 23W
Wetzlar Germany 52 D5 50 33N 8 30E
Wexford RoI 21 E2 52 25N 6 35W
Wexford co. RoI 21 E2 52 20N 6 27W
Wexford Bay RoI 21 E2 52 25N 6 10W
Wexford Harbour RoI 21 E2 52 20N 6 25W
Wey r. England 16 C2 51 18N 0 30W
Weybridge England 16 C2 51 22N 0 28W
Weyburn Canada 89 Q3 49 39N 103 51W
Weymouth England 19 E2 50 37N 2 25W
Whaley Bridge England 12 E2 53 20N 1 59W
Whalley England 12 D2 53 49N 2 24W
Wharfe r. England 13 E2 53 40N 2 05W
Wharfedale v. England 12 D3 54 05N 2 00W
Wheatley England 16 B2 51 45N 0 52W
Whernside sum. England 12 D3 54 14N 2 23W
Whickham England 13 E3 54 57N 1 40W
Whitburn England 13 E2 53 44N 1 21W
Whitburn Scotland 11 F2 55 52N 3 42W
Whitby England 13 F3 54 29N 0 37W
Whitchurch Shropshire
  England 15 D2 52 58N 2 41W
Whitchurch Buckinghamshire
  England 16 C2 51 53N 0 51W
Whitchurch Hampshire
  England 16 B2 51 14N 1 20W
Whitefield England 12 D2 53 34N 2 18W

Whitegate RoI 21 C1 51 50N 8 14W
Whitehaven England 12 C3 54 33N 3 35W
Whitehead NI 10 D1 54 45N 5 43W
Whitehills Scotland 9 G2 57 40N 2 35W
White Horse, Vale of
England 16 B2 51 35N 1 30W
Whiten Head Scotland 9 E3 58 34N 4 32W
Whiteparish England 16 B2 51 01N 1 39W
Whitfield England 17 E2 51 09N 1 17E
Whithorn Scotland 11 E1 54 44N 4 25W
Whitland Wales 14 B1 51 50N 4 37W
Whitley Bay tn. England 13 E4 55 03N 1 25W
Whitney, Mount USA 90 C4 36 35N 118 17W
Whitsand Bay England 18 C2 50 20N 4 25W
Whitstable England 17 E2 51 22N 1 02E
Whittington England 14 C2 52 52N 3 00W
Whittlesey England 16 C3 52 34N 0 08W
Whitton England 13 F2 53 43N 0 38W
Whitworth England 12 D2 53 40N 2 10W
Wichita USA 91 G4 37 43N 97 20W
Wick Scotland 9 F3 58 26N 3 06W
Wick r. Scotland 9 F3 58 26N 3 10W
Wickford England 17 D2 51 38N 0 31E
Wickham England 16 B1 50 54N 1 10W
Wickham Market
England 17 E3 52 09N 1 22E
Wicklow RoI 21 E2 52 59N 6 03W
Wicklow co. RoI 21 E2 52 55N 6 25W
Wicklow Mountains
RoI 21 E2/E3 53 00N 6 20W
Widnes England 12 D2 53 22N 2 44W
Wiener Neustadt
Austria 53 H3 47 49N 16 15E
Wierden Neths 48 E5 52 21N 6 35E
Wiesbaden Germany 52 D5 50 05N 8 15E
Wigan England 12 D2 53 33N 2 38W
Wigston England 15 E2 52 36N 1 05W
Wigton England 12 C3 54 49N 3 09W
Wigtown Scotland 11 E1 54 52N 4 26W
Wigtown Bay Scotland 11 E1 54 45N 4 20W
Wil Switzerland 52 D3 47 28N 9 03E
Wilberfoss England 13 F2 53 57N 0 53W
Wilhelmshaven
Germany 52 D6 53 32N 8 07E
Willington England 13 E3 54 43N 1 41W
Williton England 19 D3 51 10N 3 20W
Wilmslow England 12 D2 53 20N 2 15W
Wilton England 16 B2 51 05N 1 52W
Wiltshire co. England 16 A2/B2 51 30N 2 00W
Wimborne Minster
England 19 F2 50 48N 1 59W
Wincanton England 19 E3 51 04N 2 25W
Winchelsea England 17 D1 50 55N 0 42E
Winchester England 16 B2 51 04N 1 19W
Windermere tn England 12 D3 54 23N 2 54W
Windermere l. England 12 D3 54 20N 3 10W
Windhoek Namibia 82 C3 22 34S 17 06E
Windsor Canada 89 U2 42 18N 83 00W
Windsor England 16 C2 51 29N 0 38W
Windsor and Maidenhead
u.a. England 16 C1 50 25N 0 50W
Windward Islands
Lesser Antilles 95 M2 12 30N 62 00W
Wingate England 13 E3 54 55N 1 23W
Wingerworth England 13 E2 53 13N 1 28W
Winkleigh England 18 D2 50 51N 3 56W
Winnipeg Canada 89 R3 49 53N 97 10W
Winnipeg, Lake Canada 89 R4 52 30N 97 30W
Winnipegosis, Lake
Canada 89 Q4 52 10N 100 00W
Winschoten Neths 48 F6 53 07N 7 02E
Winscombe England 19 E3 51 28N 2 52W
Winsford England 12 D2 53 11N 2 31W
Winslow England 16 C2 51 57N 0 54W
Winterbourne England 15 D1 51 30N 2 31W
Winterthur Switz. 52 D3 47 30N 8 45E
Winterton-on-Sea
England 17 E3 52 43N 1 42E
Wirksworth England 13 E2 53 05N 1 34W
Wisbech England 17 D3 52 40N 0 10E
Wisconsin state USA 91 H6/J6 45 00N 90 00W
Wishaw Scotland 11 F2 55 47N 3 56W
Wisła r. Poland 53 J6 53 00N 19 00E
Wismar Germany 52 E6 53 54N 11 28E
Wissembourg France 50 H5 49 02N 7 57E
Witham r. England 13 F2 53 05N 0 40W
Witham England 17 D2 51 48N 0 38E
Witheridge England 18 D2 50 55N 3 42W
Withernsea England 13 G2 53 44N 0 02E
Witley England 16 C2 51 08N 0 39W
Witney England 16 B2 51 48N 1 29W
Wittenberg Germany 52 F5 51 53N 12 39E
Wittenberge Germany 52 E6 52 59N 11 45E
Wittlich Germany 52 C4 49 59N 6 54E
Wiveliscombe England 19 D3 51 03N 3 19W
Wivenhoe England 17 D2 51 52N 0 58E
Woburn Sands tn.
England 16 C3 52 01N 0 39W
Woking England 16 C2 51 20N 0 34W
Wokingham England 16 C2 51 25N 0 51W
Wokingham u.a.
England 16 C1 50 25N 0 55W
Wolfsberg Austria 52 G3 46 50N 14 50E
Wolfsburg Germany 52 E6 52 27N 10 49E
Wollaston England 15 F2 52 16N 0 41W
Wollongong Australia 73 K4 34 25S 150 52E
Wolsingham England 13 E3 54 44N 1 52W

Wolverhampton
England 15 D2 52 36N 2 08W
Wolverton England 15 C3 52 04N 0 50W
Wombourne England 15 D2 52 32N 2 11W
Wombwell England 13 E2 53 32N 1 24W
Woodbridge England 17 E3 52 06N 1 19E
Woodford Halse
England 15 E2 52 10N 1 13W
Woodhall Spa England 13 F2 53 09N 0 14W
Woodlands tn. Canada 92 A4 50 12N 97 40W
Woodstock England 16 B2 51 52N 1 21W
Wool England 19 E2 50 41N 2 14W
Woolacombe England 18 C3 51 10N 4 13W
Wooler England 11 G2 55 33N 2 01W
Wootton Bassett
England 16 B2 51 33N 1 54W
Worcester England 15 D2 52 11N 2 13W
Worcester USA 91 M5 42 17N 71 48W
Worcestershire co.
England 15 D2 52 15N 2 15W
Workington England 12 C3 54 39N 3 33W
Worksop England 13 E2 53 18N 1 07W
Worms Germany 52 D4 49 38N 8 23E
Worms Head Wales 14 B1 51 34N 4 20W
Worsbrough England 13 E2 53 33N 1 29W
Worthing England 16 C1 50 48N 0 23W
Wotton-under-Edge
England 15 D1 51 39N 2 21W
Wrangle England 13 G2 53 02N 0 07E
Wrath, Cape Scotland 9 D3/E3 58 37N 5 01W
Wrexham tn Wales 14 C3 53 03N 3 00W
Wrexham u.a. Wales 14 C3/D3 53 00N 3 00W
Writtle England 17 D2 51 44N 0 26E
Wrocław Poland 53 H5 51 05N 17 00E
Wrotham England 17 D2 51 19N 0 19E
Wroughton England 16 B2 51 31N 1 48W
Wroxham England 17 E3 52 42N 1 24E
Wuhan China 69 K4 30 35N 114 19E
Wuppertal Germany 52 C5 51 15N 7 10E
Würtzburg Germany 52 D4 49 48N 9 57E
Wuxi China 69 M4 31 35N 120 19E
Wye England 17 D2 51 11N 0 56E
Wylye England 16 B2 51 08N 2 01W
Wylye r. England 16 A2 51 08N 2 13W
Wymondham England 17 E3 52 34N 1 07E
Wyoming state USA 90 E5 43 00N 108 00W

X

Xi'an China 69 J4 34 16N 108 54E

Y

Yakutsk Russia 63 Q9 62 10N 129 50E
Yamoussoukro
Côte d'Ivoire 80 C3 6 50N 5 20W
Yangon Myanmar 71 B7 16 47N 96 10E
Yaoundé Cameroon 80 G2 3 51N 11 31E
Yarmouth England 16 B1 50 42N 1 29W
Yaroslavl' Russia 62 F8 57 34N 39 52E
Yate England 15 D1 51 32N 2 25W
Yateley England 16 C2 51 20N 0 51W
Yatsushiro Japan 70 B1 32 32N 130 35E
Yatton England 19 E3 51 24N 2 49W
Yaxley England 16 C3 52 31N 0 16W
Yeadon England 13 E2 53 52N 1 41W
Yealmpton England 18 D2 50 21N 3 59W
Yekaterinburg Russia 62 J8 56 52N 60 35E
Yell i. Scotland 7 C3 60 35N 1 10W
Yellowknife Canada 88 N6 62 30N 114 29W
Yelverton England 18 C2 50 30N 4 05W
YEMEN REPUBLIC 64/65 D2/E2
Yeovil England 19 E2 50 57N 2 39W
Yerevan Armenia 57 F3 40 10N 44 31E
Yokohama Japan 70 C2 35 27N 139 38E
York England 13 E2 53 58N 1 05W
York u.a. England 13 E2 53 56N 1 02W
York, Cape Australia 73 H8 10 42S 142 32E
Yorkshire Wolds
England 13 F3 54 00N 0 45W
York, Vale of England 13 E3 54 10N 1 20W
Youghal RoI 21 D1 51 51N 7 50W
Youghal Bay RoI 21 D1 51 55N 7 48W
Yoxford England 17 E3 52 16N 1 30E
Ystalyfera Wales 14 C1 51 47N 3 47W
Ystrad Aeron Wales 14 B2 52 10N 4 10W
Ystradgnylais Wales 14 C1 51 47N 3 45W
Ystwyth r. Wales 14 C2 52 20N 3 55W
Ytterhogdal Sweden 49 D3 62 10N 14 55E
Yucatán p. Mexico 94 G3 19 00N 89 00W
Yuci China 69 K5 37 40N 112 44E
Yukon r. Canada/USA 88 D6 63 30N 159 40W
Yukon Territory territory
Canada 88 H6/J6 64 15N 135 00W
Yumen China 68 G5 39 54N 97 43E
Yverdon Switz. 52 C3 46 47N 6 38E
Yvetot France 50 E5 49 37N 0 45E

Z

Zaanstad Neths 48 C5 52 27N 4 49E
Zadar Croatia 54 F6 44 07N 15 14E
Zafra Spain 51 B3 38 25N 6 25W
Żagań Poland 52 G5 51 37N 15 20E
Zagreb Croatia 54 F6 45 48N 15 58E
Zagros Mountains Iran 65 E5/F5 32 45N 48 50E
Zakopane Poland 53 J4 49 17N 19 54E

Zákynthos i. Greece 55 J2 37 45N 20 50E
Zambezi r.
Zambia/Zimbabwe 82 D4 16 00S 23 00E
ZAMBIA 82 D5/E5
Zamora Spain 51 C4 41 30N 5 45W
Zanzibar Tanzania 83 F1 6 10S 39 12E
Zaragoza Spain 51 E4 41 39N 0 54W
Zeebrugge Belgium 48 B4 51 20N 3 13E
Zell-am-See tn. Austria 52 F3 47 19N 12 47E
Zenica
Bosnia-Herzegovina 55 G6 44 11N 17 53E
Zermatt Switz. 52 C3 46 01N 7 45E
Zhengzhou China 69 K4 34 45N 113 38E
Zhmerynka Ukraine 53 P4 49 00N 28 02E
Zhytomyr Ukraine 53 P5 50 18N 28 40E
Zibo China 69 L5 36 51N 118 01E
Zielona Góra Poland 53 G5 51 57N 15 30E
ZIMBABWE 82 E4/F4
Zlín Czech Rep. 53 H4 49 14N 17 40E
Zug Switz. 52 D3 47 10N 8 31E
Zugspitze mt. Austria 52 E3 47 25N 11 00E
Zürich Switz. 52 D3 47 23N 8 33E
Zvolen Slovakia 53 J4 48 34N 19 08E
Zwettl Austria 52 G4 48 37N 15 11E
Zwickau Germany 52 F5 50 43N 12 30E
Zwolle Neths 48 E5 52 31N 6 06E

Acknowledgements

The publishers would like to thank the following for permission to reproduce photographs:

Corbis UK Ltd, p.15; FAO-UN, p.76;
NASA, p.76, 84, 97, 106, 113, 127;
Oxford Scientific Films, p.114, 115;
spaceimaging.com, p.87;
Science Photo Library, p.108, 113, 114;
US Geological Survey, p.126;
Visual Insights, p.131.

Cover image:
Visible Earth / Rich Irish, Landsat 7 Team, NASA GSFC;
data provided by EROS Data Center.
Globes / GEOATLAS.

The page design is by Adrian Smith.

The publishers are grateful to the following colleagues in geography education for their helpful comments and advice during the development stages of this atlas:

Pam Boardman, Graham Butt, Kathryn Clayton, Alan Cottle, Ruth Crossley, Rachel Dean, Bob Digby, Ian Douglass, Tony Field, Martyn Gill, Joel Griffiths, Matthew Gunn, Gareth Huws, Kathryn Jones, Irfon Morris Jones, David Langham, Patrick Lewis, Bob Newman, Andrew Parkinson, Liz Roodhouse, John Sadler, Toni Schiavone, Natasha Sirin, Andrea Wade, Patrick Wherity, Steve Wilkes, and Malcolm Yates.

The publishers would also like to thank the many individuals, companies, societies, and institutions who gave assistance in the gathering of data.